DAVID

With thanks for
fellowship in 2018

1 CORINTHIANS

[signature]

Christmas 2018

1 CORINTHIANS

by
John M Riddle

RITCHIE
John Ritchie Publishing

40 Beansburn, Kilmarnock, Scotland

ISBN-13: 978 1 912522 42 2

Typeset by John Ritchie Ltd., Kilmarnock
Printed by Hobbs the Printers Ltd.

Contents

1 Corinthians

Preface

This book which, again, does not purport to be a commentary in the usual sense of the word, represents the substance of Bible Class discussions on Friday evenings between September 2014 and December 2015 at Mill Lane Chapel, Cheshunt.

Since previous publications in this series were beginning to appear before 2014, it would hardly be true to say, as on past occasions, that the original notes were written without any thought of their eventual appearance in the public domain! Even so, their emergence in book form remained somewhat remote at the time, and no attempt has been made to 'edit out' anything that might prove unacceptable to some readers, or to promote views which might 'curry favour' with others. Having said that, it would be quite wrong to suppose that the brother leading the discussion was surrounded by a circle of robots, all nodding their computerised heads in agreement, without any ability or desire to query anything! Not so! But at all times, let it be said, questions are asked, and contributions are made, with warmth and to profit.

First century assemblies were often troubled places, and we must bow to acknowledge the divine wisdom which permitted problems to arise so early in the history of the church. Had God insulated infant local churches against doctrinal and moral error, and then, years later, allowed problems and difficulties to arise, who then would have been in a position to give them help and guidance? The apostles, uniquely competent men, would no longer be available. As it was, God saw to it that spiritually-qualified men were available, not only to deal with circumstances at the time, but through their epistles to help succeeding generations of believers – including ourselves – beset, as we are, with the very same problems. Paul's First Epistle to the Corinthians is as relevant to assembly life in the Twenty-First Century as it was at the time of writing.

As before, and not as mere courtesy, the Bible Class at Cheshunt remains genuinely indebted to John Ritchie Ltd for their willingness to publish its notes, something first mooted by Mr. John Grant, and to Mr. Fraser Munro and the John Ritchie 'team' for their invaluable help in formatting and editing the material submitted to them. The Bible Class also continues to be grateful to Miss Lesley Prentice for having checked and corrected the original manuscripts, something she continues to do, and to Mr. Eric Browning for his considerable help in sending copies of current studies by Email to a large number of believers in the U.K. and Overseas.

John Riddle
Cheshunt, Hertfordshire
November 2018

1 CORINTHIANS

The church planted

Read Acts 18:1-17; 1 Corinthians 3:1-23

The church at Corinth was founded as a result of Paul's visit to the city during his second 'missionary journey'. In Luke's words: "And after these things Paul departed from Athens, and came to Corinth" (Acts 18:1). He travelled from Athens, the centre of learning, to Corinth, a corrupt commercial city. "Although he was scoffed at by the 'high brows' at Athens, his witness was not entirely fruitless even if not so successful as at other places: 'certain men clave unto him, and believed: among the which was Dionysius the Areopagite, and a woman named Damaris, and others with them' (Acts 17:34). In contrast, a great work was accomplished in corrupt Corinth, chiefly among Gentiles and largely, it would seem, among the lower classes who were immersed in pagan darkness (1 Corinthians 10:20; 12:2)" (J.H. Large). See also 1 Corinthians 1 verses 26-29.

According to J. Anderson, Corinth was some eighty miles by land to the west of Athens, but only about forty-five miles by sea. It lay on the land-bridge connecting the Peloponnese with Central and Northern Greece (a map will explain this) at the junction of sea routes to the west and east, and of land routes to the north and south. (We should note the wisdom of God in directing Paul in this way. Corinth was an ideal place from which the gospel could be spread.) It had two ports, Lechaeum which pointed westwards to the Ionian Sea and the central and western Mediterranean, and Cenchrea (see Acts 18:18) which pointed eastwards to the Aegean Sea, the eastern Mediterranean, and the Black Sea.

The city visited by Paul had been refounded by Julius Caesar in 44 B.C., having been levelled to the ground by the Roman general Lucius Mummius in 146 B.C. after rebelling against Rome. Julius Caesar despatched a colony of freed men to Corinth in connection with rebuilding the city, hence the occurrence of Latin names such as Fortunatus, Crispus and Achaicus in 1 Corinthians. In 27 B.C. it became the seat of administration of the Roman province of Achaia, when it regained its old commercial prosperity. Merchants flocked there from all parts of Greece: Jews were attracted there by the facilities of commerce; wealth, art, literature and luxury revived.

It also regained something of its past reputation for licentiousness, which made it the most notorious city of the ancient world. Corinth was a vile place, so much so that the Greek language made a verb out of the city's name - 'to corinthianise' meaning 'to practice whoredom'. Just south of the isthmus (the land-bridge) stands the Acro-Corinthus, a vertical mountain rising to a height of 1,886 feet. At the summit stood a temple, dedicated to Aphrodite, with the most appalling reputation.

"Even as late as the seventeenth century, the 'Corinthian' in Shakespearean dramas was always a debauchee, making his entry on the stage in a state of drunkenness" (Supplied by J. Waldron). J.H. Large describes Corinth as "the moral cesspit of the Mediterranean into which drained all the vices of East and West". Paul gives us a dreadful summary of life at Corinth in 1 Corinthians 6 verses 9-11: "Be not deceived, neither fornicators, nor idolators, nor adulterers, nor effeminate, nor abusers of themselves with mankind, nor thieves, nor covetous, nor drunkards, nor revilers, nor extortioners, shall inherit the kingdom of God. And such were some of you..."

But both 1 & 2 Corinthians begin in the same way: "Paul … unto the **church of God** which is at Corinth" (1 Corinthians 1:1-2; 2 Corinthians 1:1). When Job asked the question: "Who can bring a clean thing out of an unclean?" he answered it himself: "Not one" (Job 14:4). But that is exactly what God did at Corinth, leading Paul to say of the assembly there: "But ye are (were) washed, but ye are (were) sanctified, but ye are (were) justified, in the name of the Lord Jesus (RV 'Christ') and by (in) the Spirit of our God" (1 Corinthians 6:11).

Luke tells us how it all started in Acts 18 verses 1-18. In this connection we must note the following: *(1)* that God prepared the way (vv.1-3); *(2)* that Paul preached the gospel (vv.4-11); *(3)* that the Jews provoked trouble (vv.12-17); *(4)* that Paul spent further time there (v.18).

1) GOD PREPARED THE WAY, vv.1-3

It began with two events. Right at 'the top of the tree', Emperor Claudius (the most important man in the world at the time) "commanded all Jews to depart from Rome" (v.2), and right at the bottom, years before, two Jewish fathers taught their little boys the craft of tent-making (v.3). As a result, Paul had somewhere to live and work when he arrived in Corinth! God was 'one step ahead!' In the words of A.C. Gooding: "God must have wanted an assembly at Corinth to do that!" He had provided for His servant before he even reached the place, reminding us that He is in complete control of history, whether it's the big events or the little events. Earlier, God had used another Roman emperor to accomplish His will. See Luke 2 verse 1. There is no such thing as coincidence as far as He is concerned.

It is generally assumed, on the basis of something written by Suetonius seventy years after the event, that Claudius expelled the Jews because they were "indulging in constant riots at the instigation of Chrestus". (We could call this 'ethnic cleansing'). If 'Chrestus' is a variant spelling of 'Christus' then F.F. Bruce may be right in saying that "Suetonius' statement, in fact, points to dissension and disorder within the Jewish community of Rome resulting from the introduction of Christianity into one or more of the synagogues of the city". The important point in all this is that God had prepared for Paul's visit to the city, otherwise he would have been a complete stranger there without means of support.

Paul and Aquila were "tentmakers" (*'skenopoios'*) which, according to F.F. Bruce, might have the more general meaning of 'leatherworkers'. According to a note supplied by J. Waldron: "The Jewish law, after the exile, held that a father who taught not his son a trade, taught him to be a thief". We should notice that, when necessary, "Paul, as a matter of policy, earned his living in this way during his missionary career (cf. Acts 20:34; 1 Corinthians 9:3-18; 2 Corinthians 11:7; 1 Thessalonians 2:9; 2 Thessalonians 3:8)" (F.F. Bruce). Foreseeing future criticism of Paul's service, God arranged, as we have already noted, for young Saul, as he then was, to learn the trade of tentmaker, which he followed on arrival at Corinth (Acts 18:3). Thus, initially, he supported himself. Latterly he was supported by the Macedonian brethren (2 Corinthians 11:8-10). Hence he could write in connection with his entitlement to local support: "But I have used none of these things" (1 Corinthians 9:15), and "When I was present with you, and wanted, I was chargeable to no man" (2 Corinthians 11:9).

The references in the New Testament to Aquila and Priscilla make a fascinating and profitable study. See Acts 18 verses 2, 18 and 26; Romans 16 verse 3; 1 Corinthians 16:19; 2 Timothy 4:19. Start with their *marriage*: you can divide the six references into two groups - Aquila and Priscilla, and Priscilla (or Prisca) and Aquila. Now that's interesting! Then look at their *movements*: they pop up all over the place! Finally, think about their *ministry.* It has been nicely said that 'their home was a shelter for Paul (here), a school for Apollos (Acts 18:26) and a sanctuary for the church (1 Corinthians 16:19)'. So far as we can judge, Aquila and Priscilla were believers before they reached Corinth. It can certainly be said of them that "the steps of a good man (or woman) are ordered by the Lord" (Psalm 37:23).

2) PAUL PREACHED THE GOSPEL, vv.4-11

Having arrived at Corinth, Paul "reasoned in the synagogue every sabbath, and persuaded the Jews and the Greeks" (v.4). We meet two familiar words here (see Acts 17:2, 4; 18:4): "reasoned" *(dialegomai),* giving rise to the English word 'dialogue' (it's the 'cut and thrust' of debate again), and "persuaded" *(peitho)* meaning "to apply persuasion, to prevail upon or win over, to persuade, bringing about a change of mind by the influence of reason or moral considerations" (W.E. Vine). The "Greeks" were God-fearing Gentiles.

There can be no doubt that when Luke tells us that Paul "reasoned in the synagogue every sabbath", he followed the pattern at Thessalonica where he "reasoned with them *out of the scriptures*" (Acts 17:2). He did not 'reason with them' about politics, or the economy! As at Thessalonica, so at Corinth. At Thessalonica, we find him "opening and alleging that Christ must needs have suffered, and risen again from the dead", and having established from the scriptures that Christ, the Messiah, must die and rise from the dead, then asserting "that this Jesus, whom I preach unto you, is Christ" (Acts 17:3). This should be compared with Acts 18 verses 4-5. Paul himself confirms that he "reasoned" at Corinth in this way: "For I delivered unto you first of all that which I also received, how that Christ died for our sins *according to the scriptures*; and that he was buried, and that he rose again the third day *according to the scriptures"* (1 Corinthians 15:1-4). See also 1 Corinthians 2 verses 1-2.

We should notice where Paul preached the gospel. In accordance with his usual practice, he preached first of all in the synagogue. The word 'synagogue' means 'bringing together'. Paul therefore had a ready audience at Corinth. He preached where people were to be found! We should also bear in mind that the existence of a synagogue at Corinth accounts for the assembly's possession of the gift of tongues, which is specifically said to be a sign to the Jews: "In the law it is written, With men of other tongues and other lips will I speak unto **this people**; and yet for all that they will not hear me, saith the Lord" (1 Corinthians 14:21).

We must draw attention to at least four things in these verses: *(a)* he preached with conviction (v.5); *(b)* he warned his hearers (vv.6-7); *(c)* he saw conversions (v.8); *(d)* he received encouragement (vv.9-11).

a) He preached with conviction, v.5

"And when Silas and Timotheus were come from Macedonia, Paul was pressed in the spirit, and testified to the Jews that Jesus was Christ" (v.5). It was after Timothy's return from Thessalonica (1 Thessalonians 3:6) that Paul evidently wrote 1 Thessalonians. Quite possibly, either Timothy or Silas, or both, brought him a gift from Macedonia. (See 2 Corinthians 11:9.) It, therefore, appears that once his mind was settled in connection with his beloved brethren at Thessalonica and his fears allayed (1 Thessalonians 3:7-9), he gave himself without distraction to the work at Corinth. There are some illuminating facts in the narrative, and one of them is that Paul was not some kind of superman who brushed aside problems and concerns. As we all know, it is far from easy to concentrate on even the Lord's work when we are distracted by fears and difficulties.

We must not forget either that fellowship is a tremendous encouragement in the Lord's work. Paul did not travel alone on his three 'missionary journeys'. He was emboldened and strengthened by fellowship. As he approached the end of his life, Paul sorely needed Timothy's fellowship: "Do thy diligence to come shortly unto me: for Demas hath forsaken me, having loved this present world, and is departed unto Thessalonica; Crescens to Galatia, Titus unto Dalmatia … Do thy diligence to come before winter" (2 Timothy 4:9-10, 21).

The words "Paul was pressed in the spirit (from *pneuma*, AV text)" are otherwise translated "constrained by the word" (from *logos*, RV text) or "pressed in respect of the word" (JND) with the footnote: "or earnestly occupied with the word". Paul was gripped and galvanised into action by the word of God. The word "pressed" (*sunecho*) is translated 'constrained' in 2 Corinthians 5 verse 14. F.F. Bruce translates this, simply, as 'Paul devoted himself to preaching', but it does seem to be rather stronger than that. It was not just a lecture. He "testified (*diamarturomai,* 'to testify or protest solemnly') to the Jews that Jesus was Christ". Compare Acts 17 verse 3. He said in effect, with deep feeling: 'Jesus is our Messiah'. We must remember that he was "an Hebrew of the Hebrews" (Phil. 3: 5) with a deep love for his people. (See Romans 9:1-3; 10:1.) Paul himself refers to his deep, Spirit-given conviction, whilst at Corinth: "And my speech and my preaching was not with enticing words of man's wisdom, but in demonstration of the Spirit and of power" (1 Corinthians 2:4). Compare 2 Corinthians 1 verse 19: "For the Son of God, Jesus Christ, who was preached among you by us, even by me and Silvanus and Timotheus, was not yea and nay, but *in him was yea*".

How earnest are *we* in the Lord's service, particularly in our concern for the salvation of our fellow men and women? Paul said: "Woe is unto me, if I preach not the gospel!" (1 Corinthians 9:16). He certainly didn't 'play to the gallery' in the synagogue at Corinth, or anywhere else for that matter, and, in consequence, he had good reason to write: "We preach Christ crucified, unto the Jews a stumblingblock..." (1 Corinthians 1:23). This follows:

b) He warned his hearers, vv.6-7

"And when they opposed themselves (we would say 'set themselves in opposition') and blasphemed ('as they opposed and spoke injuriously', JND), he shook his raiment, and said unto them, Your blood be on your own heads; I am clean: from henceforth I will go unto the Gentiles" (v.6). Compare Acts 20 verses 26-27. He had discharged *his* duty by preaching the gospel to them. The responsibility now lay with *them.* To find out what Paul meant by saying: "I am clean", read Ezekiel 3 verses 17-21; 33 verses 1-9, particularly Chapter 3 verse 19: "If thou warn the wicked, and he turn not from his wickedness, nor from his wicked way, he shall die in his iniquity; but thou hast delivered thy soul". See also Ezekiel 33 verse 9. Compare Acts 20 verse 26. The words: "Your blood be on your own heads" recall the cry of the Lord's accusers: "His blood be on us, and on our children" (Matthew 27:25). (Compare this with Acts 2 verse 39: "for the *promise* is unto you, and to your children": what grace!).

In shaking his raiment (compare Luke 9:5; Acts 13:51), dramatically "shaking out his cloak so that not a speck of dust from the synagogue might adhere to it", Paul signified that he would have nothing in common with those who rejected "The One whom he proclaimed as Messiah and Lord" (F.F. Bruce).

This suffices to remind us that **we** have a debt to discharge in telling others about the Lord Jesus. Paul wrote: "I am debtor both to the Greeks, and to the Barbarians; both to the wise, and to the unwise. So, as much as in me is, I am ready to preach the gospel to you that are at Rome also" (Romans 1:14-15).

If one door closed, then another door opened, and it was the house next door! "And he departed thence, and entered into a certain man's house, named Justus, one that worshipped God (*sebomai,* meaning 'to revere', 'to be filled with awe'), whose house joined hard to the synagogue" (v.7). This took no small courage in view of the opposition from 'the people next door!' According to the RV his name was 'Titus Justus'. This does not necessarily mean that Paul took up residence in the house of Justus, but rather that Justus made his house available for Paul's use in preaching the gospel. Justus was a God-fearing Gentile (he has a Roman name) who was evidently amongst those who had been 'persuaded' by Paul's arguments (v.4). Some commentators suggest that Titus Justus (a Roman *nomen* and *cognomen*) was none other than Gaius (which, it is argued, could be his *praenomen*). See 1 Corinthians 1 verse 14 and Romans 16 verse 23. Whatever his full name, the important thing to notice is that his house was used in the Lord's service, just like the home of Aquila and Priscilla (v.3).

c) He saw conversions, v.8

"And Crispus, the chief ruler of the synagogue, believed on the Lord with all his house; and many of the Corinthians hearing believed, and were baptized" (v.8). In Paul's own words: "So we preach, and so ye believed" (1 Corinthians 15:11). We must notice the order of events:

i) They heard. Well, what did they hear? We have to look no further than 1 Corinthians 15 verses 3-4: "For I delivered unto you first of all (that is, 'first of all' in relation to importance) that which I also received, how that Christ died for our sins according to the scriptures; and that he was buried, and that he rose again the third day according to the scriptures; and that he was seen ..."

ii) They believed. The word (*pisteuo*) means "to place confidence in, to trust" and therefore "reliance upon, not mere credence" (W.E. Vine). Believing in the Lord Jesus is defined as 'receiving' Him. See John 1 verse 12.

iii) They were baptised. Crispus and Gaius were baptised by Paul (1 Corinthians 1:14). As J. Anderson points out, apart from the rather special case in Chapter 19 verse 5, this is the last mention of baptism following conversion in the book of Acts. "From now on we can take for granted the baptism of new converts."

As usual, antagonism proved no hindrance to the progress of the gospel, reminding us of events in Egypt: "But the more they afflicted them, the more they multiplied and grew" (Exodus 1:12).

d) He received encouragement, vv.9-11

"Then spake the Lord to Paul in the night by a vision, Be not afraid, but speak, and hold not thy peace: for I am with thee, and no man shall set on thee to hurt thee: for I have much people in this city" (vv.9-10). Some years later, Paul said, "Having therefore obtained help of God, I continue unto this day, witnessing both to small and great" (Acts 26:22). In serving God, we can be certain of His presence and help. Read Hebrews 13 verses 5-6. Opposition and difficulty were accompanied by a special sense of the Lord's presence. Compare the way in which He saw His disciples "toiling in rowing" and went to them with the words: "Be of good cheer: it is I; be not afraid" (Mark 6:48-50). Paul was about to be brought before the Roman "judgment seat" (the *bema*) at Corinth, but **before** this the Lord, who knew exactly what was going to happen, assures him of His presence and help. We should notice the following:

i) He ministers His peace. "Be not afraid, but speak, and hold not thy peace" (v.9). Do remember that he said: "I was with you in weakness, and in fear, and in much trembling" (1 Corinthians 2:3). Opposition did not mean that Paul was unmoved and unafraid.

ii) He pledges His presence. "I am with thee" (v.10). As we have noticed, it would seem that the arrival of Silas and Timothy helped to put fresh heart in Paul, but this was even better!

iii) He promises His protection. "No man shall set on thee to hurt thee" (v.10). J.H. Large has the following to say about this: "Paul's gracious Master, who had experienced all the same trials, understood His over-wrought servant and sympathising with his natural apprehensions, assured him that at Corinth, at least, he would have some respite from ill usage". He had already encountered opposition (v.6) and would do so again (vv.12-17), but he was not to leave the city.

iv) He speaks about His people. "I have much people in this city" - rather like the assurance given to Elijah (1 Kings 19:18) - but in this case it is "much people" in prospect. Paul was the channel through which the gospel would reach them. As Alfred Barnes observes: "God has a purpose in regard to the salvation of sinners" and "that purpose is so fixed in the mind of God that *He* can say that those in relation to whom it is formed are *His.* There is no chance; no haphazard; no doubt in regard to His gathering them to Himself".

Paul *was* encouraged by this: "he continued there a year and six months, teaching the word of God among them" (v.11).

3) THE JEWS PROVOKED TROUBLE, vv.12-17

True to His promise, "no man shall set on thee to hurt thee", Paul was preserved from harm when the Jews seized the opportunity to accuse him before Gallio, the Roman "deputy" or proconsul. "And when Gallio was the deputy of Achaia, the Jews made insurrection with one accord against Paul ('the Jews with one consent rose against Paul', JND), and brought him to the judgment seat, saying, This fellow persuadeth men to worship God contrary to the law" (vv.12-13). As our contributor Justin Waldron observes, the believers at Corinth would have had no difficulty in understanding Paul's reference to the "judgment seat (*bema*) of Christ" (2 Corinthians 5:10) since they would have been familiar with Gallio's "judgment seat" (*bema*).

According to F.F. Bruce: "The charge which was preferred against Paul before Gallio was that of propagating a religion, and on that basis forming a society not countenanced by Roman law ... Paul's accusers maintained that the gospel he preached had nothing to do with their ancestral faith: it was no true form of Judaism, and therefore should not share in the protection extended to Judaism by Roman law".

But it didn't get them anywhere! When Paul was "about to open his mouth, Gallio said unto the Jews, If it were a matter of wrong or wicked lewdness ('criminality', JND, or 'villany', RV), O ye Jews, reason would that I should bear with you; but if it be a question of words and names, and of your law, look ye to it; for I will be no judge of such matters. And he drave them from the judgment seat" (vv.14-16). Gallio "quickly decided that the dispute was internal to the Jewish community, that it concerned conflicting interpretations of Jewish religious law. Paul was obviously as much a Jew as his accusers were. What Paul was propagating, Gallio reckoned, was simply a variety of Judaism which did not happen to commend itself to the leaders of the local Jewish community … they must settle it themselves. So he bade them begone from his tribunal" (F.F. Bruce).

What then followed illustrates how quickly Gentiles seized the opportunity to vent their hatred of the Jews. "Then all the Greeks took Sosthenes, the chief ruler of the synagogue, and beat him before the judgment seat. And Gallio cared for none of these things" (v.17). Sosthenes, the new "chief ruler of the synagogue", got a thrashing in an anti-Jewish demonstration, and Gallio 'couldn't have cared less' about it. His predecessor, Crispus, obviously didn't last long in the synagogue after he became a Christian (v.8), which isn't surprising! It is tempting to think that Sosthenes also became a believer and that Paul refers to him in 1 Corinthians 1 verse 1, but we have no means of knowing if this was the case.

After remaining in Corinth for "a good while", Paul returned to Syria (Antioch) via Ephesus (vv.18-22). He was next in Corinth in Acts 20 verses 2-3, by which time 1 & 2 Corinthians had been written. There was no time for an intervening visit, as some infer from 2 Corinthians 13 verse 1. However, we must now notice that:

4) PAUL SPENT FURTHER TIME AT CORINTH, v.18

We know that he was in Corinth for eighteen months before the "Jews made insurrection with one accord" against him, and that this time was spent in "teaching the word of God" (v.11). We now learn that his visit was extended further, in Luke's words, for "a good while" or "yet many days" (RV). F.F. Bruce suggests that this refers to the winter following Gallio's decision (vv.14-16), which was probably made "in the summer or early fall of A.D.51". It would be most surprising if Paul did not continue "teaching the word of God" during this additional period, and we are indebted to him for giving us further information, particularly in 1 Corinthians 3, in connection with the way in which the assembly there was founded.

But, before this, we should notice that when Paul ultimately left Corinth, Luke tells us that he "took his leave of *the brethren*". Having "testified to the Jews" and gone "unto the Gentiles", he "took his leave of the brethren!"

(vv.5, 6, 18). Compare Acts 16 verse 40 where, before leaving Philippi, Paul and Silas "entered into the house of Lydia and when they had seen **the brethren**, they comforted them and departed". All this reminds us that the human race is divided into three sections: "the Jews…the Gentiles… the church of God" (1 Corinthians 10:32), and that in "the church of God" (referring to the *local* assembly) there are no ethnic distinctions: Christ has "broken down the middle wall of partition…to make in himself of twain one new man, so making peace" (Ephesians 2:14-15).

We should also notice, that Paul evidently left the newly-established assembly at Corinth in good health: "I thank my God always on your behalf, for the grace of God which is given you by Jesus Christ; that in everything ye are enriched by him, in all utterance, and in all knowledge; even as the testimony of Christ was confirmed in you; so that ye come behind in no gift; waiting for the coming of our Lord Jesus Christ" (1 Corinthians 1:4-7). As we have noticed, this was not accomplished overnight: it involved time (vv.11, 18). Compare the time spent at Antioch: "a whole year they (Barnabas and Saul) assembled themselves with the church, and taught much people" (Acts 11:26). Newly-planted assemblies - and well-established assemblies for that matter - need Bible teaching at length. At Corinth, this involved the following:

i) It involved fellowship with others. "I have planted, Apollos watered; but God gave the increase" (1 Corinthians 3:6). Planting and building an assembly involves different servants of God. In saying that "Apollos watered", Paul does not mean that he 'watered the work with his prayers' (a frequently-heard expression). The way in which he "watered" is defined elsewhere: "And when he (Apollos) was disposed to pass into Achaia, the brethren wrote, exhorting the disciples to receive him: who, when he was come, helped them much which had believed through grace…" (Acts 18:27-28).

ii) It involved fellowship with God. In no way did Paul claim ownership of the assembly at Corinth.

- He recognised that the assembly belonged to God: "Ye are **God's husbandry** (cultivated field)", suggesting developing life and fruitfulness: "Ye are **God's building** (a temple)" (1 Corinthians 3:9). David defines the purpose of a temple as follows: "In his temple doth every one speak of his glory" (Psalm 29:9).

- He recognised, in view of the above, that Apollos and himself were simply servants, claiming nothing for themselves and recognising that all ability and authority came from God: "Who then is Paul, and who is Apollos, but ministers by whom ye believed, even as the Lord gave to every man?" (1 Corinthians 3:5).

- He recognised that since "the Lord gave to every man", there could be no suggestion of rivalry between servants: "he that planteth and he that watereth are one … for we are labourers together with God (God's fellow-labourers)".

iii) It involved laying a foundation. "According to the grace of God which is given unto me, as a wise masterbuilder, I have laid the foundation" (1 Corinthians 3:10). The word "masterbuilder" (*architekton*) refers to "a principal artificer" rather than to an architect. To quote W.E. Vine, "The examples from the papyri and from inscriptions, as illustrated by Moulton and Milligan, show that the word had a wider application than our 'architect', and confirm the rendering 'masterbuilder' in this passage, which is of course, borne out by the context". Paul, as a builder, worked to a plan, beginning with the foundation. The "foundation" truth in assembly-building is doctrine concerning the Lord Jesus: "For other foundation can no man lay than that is laid, which is Jesus Christ (1 Corinthians 3:11). The "wise masterbuilder" laid this foundation at Corinth. All 'assembly teaching' takes its character from "the foundation". Following on from this:

iv) It involved local builders. "But let every man take heed how he buildeth thereupon … Now if any man build upon this foundation gold, silver, precious stones, wood, hay stubble; every man's work shall be made manifest: for the day shall declare it, because it shall be revealed by fire; and the fire shall try every man's work of what sort it is" (1 Corinthians 3:10, 12, 13). The 'builders" here are the assembly teachers. This is confirmed by the Lord's reference to the religious leadership in saying "The stone which *the builders* rejected is become the head of the corner" (Mark 12:10). The very people who taught the nation, the "builders", had lamentably failed. It would be equally tragic if assembly teachers failed in their ministry to give pre-eminence in their teaching to the Lord Jesus.

An assembly cannot be properly established, and an assembly cannot be expected to flourish, unless "in all things", Christ has "the pre-eminence" (Colossians 1:18).

1 CORINTHIANS

The epistle outlined

Read the whole Epistle

The very existence of the church at Corinth was a testimony to the grace and power of God. "The church of God which is at Corinth" (1 Corinthians 1:2; 2 Corinthians 1:1) is an amazing statement. As we have already considered, Job asked the question: "Who can bring a clean thing out of an unclean?" To which he answered: "Not one" (Job 14:4). But his answer should be amended. God did exactly that at Corinth! He had "much people in this city" (Acts 18:10). We should also remember that the Lord Jesus "came to Nazareth, where he had been brought up" (Luke 4:16), a place of some ill-repute, leading Nathanael to exclaim: "Can there any good thing come out of Nazareth?", to which Philip replied "Come and see" (John 1:46). Philip took Nathanael to see a man who "knew no sin", who "did no sin", and "in him is no sin" (2 Corinthians 5:21; 1 Peter 2:22; 1 John 3:5). A "clean" man came out of an "unclean" place.

1 Corinthians deals primarily with local church problems. It has been suggested that many of these arose from the character of the city. In fact, the assembly at Corinth has been called 'the church in vanity fair', and it does seem that the environment was beginning to influence the church there. It could be said that the city of Corinth was influencing the assembly politically, philosophically, legally, and morally:

- ***Politically***. According to James Hastings (*Dictionary of the Bible*): "The Greeks were famous for factions; their cities could never combine together for long", and "factions" were certainly present in the assembly: "Every one of you saith, I am of Paul; and I of Apollos; and I of Cephas; and I of Christ" (1 Corinthians 1:12).

- Philosophically. Corinth was a Greek city, and inhabitants of Greek cities loved to philosophise. They certainly did this at Athens (Acts 17:18), and it appears that they did the same at Corinth. Paul, therefore, emphasises that when he preached he did not use "wisdom of words" (1 Corinthians 1:17), or to put it another way: "not with enticing words of man's wisdom" (1 Corinthians 2:4). See also Chapter 2 verse 13.

- Legally. Leaving aside serious questions of crime and fraud, the Greeks were accustomed to taking smaller matters to arbitration, and believers at Corinth were evidently settling disputes among themselves in this way. See Chapter 6 verses 1-8.

- Morally. Corinth was renowned for its licentiousness. It was a byword for sensuality. The city was given, principally, to the worship of Epathrodite, and "it is said that a thousand devadasis (temple virgins or prostitutes) were kept at the temple of Aphrodite for the service of strangers. Fornication was considered as an act of consecration to the goddess rather than an act of desecration of the body" (J.M. Davies). Paul saw the dangers of idolatry and warned the believers at Corinth against the associated immorality. See, for example, Chapter 6 verses 9-20. He deals with the question of idolatry from a different point of view in Chapter 10 verses 23-33.

It has been suggested that the problems at Corinth arose from the influence of the world, the flesh, and the devil. See Addendum.

While 1 Corinthians may be divided in different ways, it can be said that the book has two major sections: the first emphasising problems arising from individual members in the assembly (Chapter 1:10 - 11:16), and the second emphasising problems arising in corporate assembly life (Chapter 11:17 - 16:18). This division is suggested with reference to the expression "ye come together" (1 Corinthians 11:17, 20; Chapter 14:23, 26 etc). It should be pointed out that the expression "when ye are gathered together" does occur in the first of these two sections (1 Corinthians 5:4), but this is in connection with an individual. However, it is certainly worth pointing out that assemblies do comprise individual believers, and, therefore, the assembly will not rise above the spiritual level of its members. In this connection, we should notice the occurrence of the phrase "among you". See Chapter 1 verses 10-11; Chapter 5 verse 1; Chapter 6 verse 7; Chapter 11 verses 18-19 and Chapter 15 verse 12.

The teaching of the epistle may be set out in the following way. After the introduction (Chapter 1 verses 1-9), the body of the epistle can be divided, with acknowledgements to J. Sidlow Baxter, into two major sections: *(1) Reproof* (Chapters 1-6); *(2) Replies* (Chapters 7-16). In the first, Paul deals with things he had *heard* about the assembly at Corinth. See Chapter 1 verse 11 and Chapter 5 verse 1. In the second, he deals with things about which he had been *asked* by the assembly at Corinth. See Chapter 7 verse 1: "Now concerning the things whereof ye wrote unto me" and the expressions "now concerning" or "now as touching" (1 Corinthians 7: 25; 8:1; 12:1 and 16:1). The order is significant. He deals with things about which he had *not* been asked first!

1) REPROOF, Chapters 1-6

As noted above, Paul deals first of all with the things he had heard about the assembly at Corinth. In this connection, he addresses two reports which had reached him. He deals with the first report (1 Corinthians 1:11) in Chapters 1-4, and the second (1 Corinthians 5:1) in Chapters 5-6. The first deals with discord amongst assembly members: the second addresses the need for discipline in the assembly.

a) The first report, Chapters 1-4

The first report brought news of *discord amongst assembly members*. This had been related to him by "the house of Chloe" (1 Corinthians 1:11). They had told Paul that various factions existed in the assembly and that these were saying, "I am of Paul; and I of Apollos; and I of Cephas; and I of Christ" (1 Corinthians 1:12). They were glorying in men. The situation is summed up in Chapter 3 verse 21 "Therefore let no man glory in men". To do so is "carnal" (1 Corinthians 3:1-4). Chapters 1-4 deal with the situation:

- In Chapter 1, Paul emphasises that their salvation and calling were divine, not human. That is, they had no reason to glory in men in the matter: "For ye see your calling, brethren, how that not many wise men after the flesh, not many mighty, not many noble, are called … that no flesh should glory in his presence" (1 Corinthians 1:26-29). Rather: "He that glorieth, let him glory in the Lord" (1 Corinthians 1:31).

- In Chapter 2, Paul emphasises that the preaching under which they were saved, and the teaching imparted once they were saved, did not reflect

human wisdom. Both preaching and teaching found their source in divine wisdom, and were imparted in divine power. There was, therefore, no reason to glory in men in the matter.

- In Chapter 3, Paul emphasises that those who had been responsible for the establishment and development of the assembly at Corinth were simply servants (1 Corinthians 3:5). They were directed and empowered by God whose work it was (1 Corinthians 3:7). Again, therefore, there was no reason to glory in men in the matter. Hence: "Therefore let no man glory in men" (1 Corinthians 3:21).

- In Chapter 4, Paul emphasises that the final and only assessment of service must be left to the Lord Himself (1 Corinthians 4:5). The Corinthian believers could not assess service, and rank servants of God according to their assessment. In any case, all ability was God-given, and therefore no credit was due to men. Hence, "what hast thou that thou didst not receive? now if thou didst receive it, why dost thou glory as if thou hadst not received it?" (1 Corinthians 4:7).

b) The second report, Chapters 5-6

This was a general report, and raised the necessity for **discipline in the assembly.** "It is reported commonly that there is fornication among you…" (1 Corinthians 5:1). The connection with Chapters 1-4 is clear. The believers at Corinth were very pleased with themselves, but Paul now says in effect: 'Take another look at yourselves'. We should notice the following:

- In Chapter 5, Paul emphasises the necessity for assembly discipline. "Put away from among yourselves that wicked person" (v.13). In this connection we should notice that although they were prepared to judge Paul (1 Corinthians 4:3), they were not prepared to judge evil amongst themselves!

- In Chapter 6, Paul emphasises the necessity for self-discipline. In verses 1-8, it is self-discipline as far as the believer and his **brother** is concerned. In verses 9-20, it is self-discipline as far as the believer and his **body** is concerned. In connection with the first, notice that although they were "puffed up for one against another" (1 Corinthians 4:6), and thought themselves "wise in Christ" (1 Corinthians 4:10), Paul was obliged to say: "Is it so, that there is not a wise man among you?" (1 Corinthians 6:5).

It has been suggested that some had over-reacted to Paul's teaching in connection with the believer and his body (vv.9-20), and that this led to his teaching in Chapter 7, but this does seem unlikely. However, this brings us to:

2) REPLIES, Chapters 7-16

As noted above, in this section Paul deals with questions he had been asked by the assembly at Corinth. So: "Now concerning the things whereof ye wrote unto me…" (1 Corinthians 7:1). See also the expressions "now concerning" or "now as touching" (1 Corinthians 7:25; 8:1; 12:1 and 16:1) and "Mine answer to them that do examine me is this…" (1 Corinthians 9:3).

In this section, Paul deals first of all with matters of *personal* conduct (Chapters 7-9), and then with matters of *assembly* conduct (Chapters 11-16).

a) Personal Conduct, Chapters 7-10

In this section, he deals with differences that had arisen in connection with Christian liberty. Note the use of the word "liberty" in Chapters 7 verse 39; 8: 9 and 10: 29.

- *In Chapter 7*, Paul deals with *marriage*. Amongst other things, He deals with the position of "the unmarried and widows" (vv.8, 32), with the position of the "married" in differing circumstances (vv.10-16), and with remarriage (v.39).

- *In Chapter 8*, Paul deals with *eating food offered to idols*. "As concerning therefore the eating of those things that are offered in sacrifice unto idols, we know that an idol is nothing in the world, and that there is none other God but one … Howbeit there is not in every man that knowledge …" (vv.4, 7), and therefore "take heed lest by any means this liberty of yours become a stumblingblock to them that are weak" (v.9).

- *In Chapter 9,* Paul deals with *entitlement to support*. "Have we not power to lead about a sister, a wife, as well as other apostles, and as the brethren of the Lord, and Cephas? Or I only and Barnabas, have not we power to forbear working … Even so hath the Lord ordained that they which preach the gospel should live of the gospel" (vv.5-7, 14).

The principal point in these chapters is that 'liberty is not licence'. In Paul's own words, "All things are lawful unto me, but all things are not expedient" (1 Corinthians 6:12; 10:23). Although there was liberty for all to marry, for all to eat meats, and for full-time workers to receive support, Paul did not exercise these liberties himself. In Chapter 7, he did not do so to secure greater freedom in service (vv.7-8, 32); in Chapter 8, he did not do so to secure the welfare of a weaker brother (v.13); in Chapter 9, he did not do so to secure his position against criticism (v.15).

But this isn't the end of the matter. The subject of "liberty" is extended into Chapter 10 where Paul points out that the privileges we enjoy must not lull us into a false sense of security that we are immune from divine displeasure. Just look at what happened to Israel! Paul illustrates from the Old Testament (see vv.1-11) how a believer could become "a castaway" (1 Corinthians 9:27), and concludes: "Wherefore let him that thinketh he standeth take heed lest he fall … Wherefore, my dearly beloved, flee from idolatry" (vv.12, 14). This isn't all. The "liberty" that believers have to eat "those things that are offered in sacrifice unto idols" (1 Corinthians 8:4) is reintroduced from two new angles (vv.16-33). In the first case, partaking in food offered to idols brings the participants into contact with demon power (vv.16-22), and in the second, it could play havoc with another brother's conscience (vv.23-33).

To sum up: in our personal conduct, we are to "do all to the glory of God" and "give none offence, neither to the Jews, nor to the Gentiles, nor to the church of God" (vv.31-32). Paul did exactly that (v.33).

b) Assembly Conduct, Chapters 11-16

This section can be summarised as follows: *(i)* disorder in assembly gatherings (Chapters 11-14); *(ii)* doctrinal error in the assembly (Chapter 15); *(iii)* distribution by the assembly (Chapter 16: 1-4).

i) Disorder in assembly gatherings, Chapters 11-14

It may come as a surprise to discover that early churches, as early as the apostolic era, were beset by various problems, and that a number of New Testament letters were written to address them. Some of these were internal problems, and we think of 1 & 2 Corinthians particularly here. Paul deals with the rather delicate problem of a fractured relationship in Philippians. Some were external problems, and in this case we think particularly of 1 &

2 Thessalonians, and the severe persecution which faced those believers. It could be argued that the gravest problem of all is addressed in the Epistle to the Galatians where Paul deals with an attack on the great doctrine of justification by faith. In addressing the problems at Corinth, Paul deals with the following:

- *In Chapter 11 verses 2-16,* Paul deals with disorders in relation to the headship of Christ. "I would have you know, that the head of every man is Christ; and the head of the woman is the man; and the head of Christ is God. Every man praying or prophesying, having his head covered, dishonoureth his head. But every woman that prayeth or prophesieth with her head uncovered dishonoureth her head ..." (vv.3-5).

- *In Chapter 11 verses 17-34*, Paul deals with disorders in relation to the Lord's supper. "When ye come together therefore into one place, this is not to eat the Lord's supper. For in eating every one taketh before other his supper: and one is hungry, and another is drunken ..." (vv.20-21).

- *In Chapters 12-14*, Paul deals with disorders in relation to the gifts of the Spirit. In this connection we should notice that, in general, *Chapter 12* deals with the way in which gifts have been *provided* ("the manifestation of the Spirit is given to every man to profit withal", v.7); *Chapter 13* deals with the atmosphere by which they must be *permeated* (love is indispensable, v.2); *Chapter 14* deals with the principles on which they must be *practised* ("Let all things be done unto edifying ... Let all things be done decently and in order", vv.26, 40).

ii) Doctrinal error in the assembly, Chapter 15

The Chapter, which deals with the doctrine of resurrection, may be simply divided into two major sections, each dealing with a question. In the first case, *the fact of resurrection* was denied (vv.1-34): "How say some among you that there is no resurrection of the dead?" (v.12). In the second case, *the form of resurrection* was questioned (vv.35-58): "But some man will say, How are the dead raised up? And with what body do they come?" (v.35).

Alternatively, the first major section (vv.1-34) could be rightly entitled '*The resurrection of the Saviour*', and the second (vv.35-58) '*The resurrection of the saints*'.

It has been suggested that the doctrine of the Sadducees had infected the assembly at Corinth. "How say *some* among you …" See Matthew 22 verse 23: "The same day came unto him the Sadducees, which say that there is no resurrection"; Acts 23 verse 8: "For the Sadducees say that there is no resurrection, neither angel, nor spirit".

iii) Distribution by the assembly, Chapter 16: 1-4

"Now concerning the collection for the saints, as I have given order to the churches of Galatia, even so do ye" (v.1); "And when I come, whomsoever ye shall approve by your letters, them will I send to bring your liberality unto Jerusalem" (v.3).

The Epistle concludes with references to Paul's current circumstances, to some of his fellow-labourers, and with greetings. See Chapter 16 verses 5-24.

Addendum

It has been suggested that the problems at Corinth fall into three categories: problems arising from *(1)* the influence of the world; *(2)* the influence of the flesh; *(3)* the influence of Satan.

1) The influence of the world

It is suggested that this is particularly observable in Chapters 1 to 4. The influence of the world is seen *(a)* in selected leaders (1 Cor. 1: 10-16); *(b)* in worldly wisdom (1 Corinthians 1:17 - 4:21).

As to the former: "Every one of you saith, I am of Paul; and I of Apollos; and I of Cephas; and I of Christ" (1 Corinthians 1:12). This is answered in the following verse (1 Corinthians 1:13). The assembly is not a place where democracy is exercised, but where theocracy is exercised.

As to the latter: the world claims to speak with authority. Notice reference to "the wisdom of this world" (1 Corinthians 1:20; 2:6; 3:19). Paul deals very thoroughly with worldly wisdom in Chapter 1 verses 18-25. He answers it with two words - "Christ crucified" (1 Corinthians 1:23). We should note that this does not refer to the gospel. The words, "Christ died" apply in this case. The words: "Christ crucified" are the condemnation of worldly wisdom. Worldly wisdom put Him outside, and since we died with Him, we do not employ worldly wisdom in His service and in the assembly.

2) The influence of the flesh

It is suggested that this is particularly observable in Chapters 5-7. These chapters deal with moral relationships. Paul deals with the report that "there is fornication among you" (1 Corinthians 5:1); with involvement with the temple prostitutes (1 Corinthians 6:16); with husband/wife relationships etc. (1 Corinthians 7:1-40). Or, in a succinct summary supplied by Justin Waldron, the influence of the flesh is seen in immorality (1 Corinthians 5); in the defilement of the body (1 Corinthians 6); in marriage relationships (1 Corinthians 7).

3) The influence of Satan

It is suggested that this is particularly observable in Chapters 8, 10 and 12. These chapters all deal with the dangers of idolatry with its demonic control. This is highlighted in Chapter 10: "the things which the Gentiles sacrifice, they sacrifice to devils (demons), and not to God: and I would not that ye should have fellowship with devils (demons). Ye cannot drink the cup of the Lord, and the cup of devils (demons): ye cannot be partakers of the Lord's table, and of the table of devils (demons)" (vv.20-21).

In Chapter 12, Paul demonstrates that there are two types of spiritual manifestations: those attributable to the Holy Spirit, and those attributable to satanic power. It was, therefore, a matter of great importance that the saints at Corinth should be in a position to discern between divine spiritual manifestations, and others of a totally different source. Hence the need for the gift of "discerning of spirits" (v.10). The importance abides to the present day, but at Corinth there was added necessity to fully clarify the matter. Tongues were used - excessively so - as Chapter 14 makes clear - and in an atmosphere where so many were evidently participating, it would be easy for all to claim the direction of the Holy Spirit, when in point of fact, their contributions did not derive from Him at all.

In order to provide clear guidance in the matter, Paul compares the way in which the Corinthians had been spiritually influenced in the past, with the way in which they were now spiritually directed. In the past, prior to their conversion, the believers at Corinth had been given to idolatry. Paul uses significant language when describing their spiritual condition at this time: "Ye know that ye were Gentiles *carried away* unto these dumb idols, even as ye were *led*". The words, "carried away … as ye were led", refer back to Chapter 10. "What say I then? that the idol is anything, or that which is sacrificed to idols is anything? But I say, that the things which the Gentiles sacrifice, they sacrifice to devils, and not to God: and I would not that ye should have fellowship with devils" (vv.19-20).

1 CORINTHIANS

"Unto the church of God which is at Corinth"

Read Chapter 1:1-9

As we noticed in outlining the Epistle, Paul deals in Chapters 1-6 with things that he had heard, and in Chapters 7-16 with things that he had been asked. The order is significant. He deals firstly with things about which he had ***not*** been asked! So far as Chapters 1-6 are concerned, Paul addresses two reports which had reached him. See 1 Corinthians 1 verse 11 and 5 verse 1. Chapters 1-4 deal with the first report, and Chapters 5-6 with the second report.

But before this, the introduction. This occupies verses 1-9, which may be divided as follows: *(1)* the writer (v.1); *(2)* the readers (v.2); *(3)* the greeting (v.3); *(4)* the thanksgiving (vv.4-9).

1) THE WRITER, v.1

"Paul, called to be an apostle of Jesus Christ through the will of God, and Sosthenes our brother", or "Paul, a called apostle of Jesus Christ, by God's will, and Sosthenes the brother" (JND).

Paul describes himself as 'a called apostle' as opposed to "false apostles, deceitful workers, transforming themselves into the apostles of Christ" (2 Corinthians 11:13). This emphasises both his authority and his humility:

- His authority. This was divinely-given. He was "an apostle of Jesus Christ through the will of God". He emphasises this particularly in writing to the Galatians: "Paul, an apostle, (not of men), neither by man, but by Jesus Christ, and God the Father, who raised him from the dead…" (Galatians 1:1). The plural here ("neither of men") and the singular ("neither by man") are significant. In the first case, he emphasises that his apostleship was not by human appointment, and he is evidently referring to the apostles acting together as in the case of Matthias (Acts 1:15-26). In the second, he emphasises that it was not by human mediation, and is evidently referring here to one prominent man, such as Peter. His apostleship was not human in origin, and no human channel was used in bestowing it upon him. Amongst other things, this means that we must recognise that his teaching is nothing less than "the commandments of the Lord" (1 Corinthians 14:37).

But there is more: Paul was "an apostle of Jesus Christ **through the will of God** ". The will of God for Paul was certainly not a divine after-thought. Just listen to this: "But when it pleased God, who separated me from my mother's womb (so his service was determined before his birth), and called me by his grace, to reveal his Son in me, that I might preach him among the heathen…" (Galatians 1:15-16). Paul was clearly thinking of the commissioning of Jeremiah when he wrote this. See Jeremiah 1 verses 4-5. Jeremiah was a prophet and Paul was an apostle, but this does not mean that God only predetermines the service of prominent people. Each one of us are 'key personnel' in His service. Very clearly, both Jeremiah and Paul had no doubts about their calling, and neither should we, even though our work for God may seem so lowly and unpretentious. We too have been called (see v.9)

- His humility. Paul did not boast about his authority. He was deeply conscious that with others, he was simply a servant and completely dependent on God: "Who then is Paul, and who is Apollos, but ministers, by whom ye believed, even as the Lord gave to every man?" (1 Corinthians 3:5), or, putting Apollos first, "Who then is **Apollos**, and who is Paul? Ministering servants, through whom ye have believed, as the Lord has given to each" (JND). The RV goes further: "**What** then is Apollos? And **what** is Paul? Ministers through whom ye believed: and each as the Lord gave to him". It is not **who** we are, but **what** we are that is important! Paul makes the point that no believer, and no assembly, has any right to self-congratulation: "What hast thou that thou didst not receive? Now if thou didst receive it, why dost thou glory, as if thou hadst not received it?" (1 Corinthians 4:7).

A deep sense of our calling will keep us walking humbly with God (Micah 6:8). It certainly won't make us aloof. Paul is happy to be associated with Sosthenes, a lesser-known brother! The description of Sosthenes - literally, "the brother" (JND) - could well be intended to distinguish him from

"Sosthenes, the chief ruler of the synagogue" (Acts 18:17). It would be nice to think that they were one and the same, but this cannot be proved.

Paul's calling was particular in nature: he was "an apostle" (the word "called" is an adjective), whereas the following verse speaks about a calling common to all believers: "called … saints", where the word "called" is also an adjective.

2) THE READERS, v.2

"Unto the church *of* God which is *at* Corinth, to them that are sanctified in Christ Jesus, called to be saints, with all that in every place call upon the name of Jesus Christ our Lord ('call on the name of our Lord Jesus Christ', JND), both theirs and ours". We should notice: *(a)* whose they were: "*the church of God*"; *(b)* where they were: "*at Corinth*"; *(c)* what they were: "*sanctified in Christ Jesus*".

a) Whose they were

"*The church of God*." The word translated "church" (*ekklesia*) has two simple parts: *ek* meaning 'out of', and *klesis* meaning 'a calling'. We, therefore, learn, immediately, that in the New Testament, the word "church" cannot refer to the building in which people meet, but to the people themselves. In fact, *ekklesia* is more accurately rendered 'assembly' or 'congregation'. It is also worth pointing out that the word 'assembly' is not a denominational title (we sometimes hear people say: 'churches and assemblies'), but a good Bible word. In simple terms, it describes people who have been gathered or called out *from* something, and gathered or called *to* something. As its usage in Acts 19 makes clear, the word was used generally in New Testament times. In this particular case, it was used to describe people who had been called out of their homes and from their workshops to attend a meeting in the theatre (Acts 19:32, 41). How then is the word *ekklesia* used in the New Testament to describe Christians?

We can answer this by citing 1 Corinthians 1 verse 2: "the church of God which is at Corinth … them that are sanctified in Christ Jesus". Corinth was a vile place (see 1 Corinthians 6:9-11), but there was a body of people in the city who were totally different. The words "the church of God which is at Corinth" describe men and women who had severed their association with the immorality and depravity of Corinth, and who had been brought into fellowship with God. In short, the church is a body of people *called out of*

the world with its sin and immorality, with its pleasures and pursuits, and with its politics and religion, and **called into sacred fellowship with God** through His Son, the Lord Jesus Christ. They now belonged to God. They were "God's husbandry … God's building" (1 Corinthians 3:9). They were "the temple of God" (1 Corinthians 3:16). Even though there were disorders amongst the believers at Corinth, they were still "the church of God". It might be helpful to add that the expression "church of God" or "churches of God" generally (some say 'always') refers to a local church or local churches.

b) Where they were

The words, "**the church of God which is at Corinth**" are remarkable. The expression, "the church of God", indicates a sacred place: the words "at Corinth" indicate a profane place. As we noted in outlining the Epistle, Job asked the question: "Who can bring a clean thing out of an unclean?" To which he answered, "Not one" (Job 14:4). But God did exactly that at Corinth! He had "much people in this city" (Acts 18:10). Paul describes the change in the believers at Corinth as follows: "Be not deceived: neither fornicators, nor idolaters, nor adulterers, nor effeminate, nor abusers of themselves with mankind, nor thieves, nor covetous, nor drunkards, nor revilers, nor extortioners, shall inherit the kingdom of God. And such were some of you: but ye are washed, but ye are sanctified, but ye are justified in the name of the Lord Jesus, and by the Spirit of our God" (1 Corinthians 6:9-11). This is in itself a splendid definition of "the church of God which is at Corinth". In summary, we have a holy people in a wicked environment, but although remaining in that environment, they were "called out" from it. It was "the church **of** God which is **at** Corinth". The assembly was located at Corinth, but it belonged to God.

c) What they were

The character of the local church is defined: "to them that are **sanctified in Christ Jesus … called saints**". It is worth noticing that it is "sanctified in Christ Jesus", that is, in the Lord Jesus in His risen and ascended glory. There is a difference of emphasis in the names "Jesus Christ" and "Christ Jesus". The former emphasises that He was here on earth but is now glorified in heaven: the latter emphasises that He is now glorified in heaven having been here on earth.

In the words of J. Hunter (*What the Bible Teaches - 1 Corinthians*): "'sanctified in Christ Jesus' means they are set apart to God by virtue of their faith-union with Christ. This is a divine act, the act of God. It is their standing before Him. We are then told that they are 'called saints' ('saints by divine calling', JND margin). They have not attained to be saints: this is the name God has bestowed upon them. In this sense every believer is a saint from the moment of conversion". With this in mind, we should notice, as above, that Paul does not say "called *to be* saints" (AV). Notice the italicised words. The word "saints" does not refer to a human attainment, but to a divine accomplishment. The fact that the "saints" at Corinth were not acting in a 'saintly' way did not in any way alter their position before God.

We should add that the expression "church of God" (singular) emphasises their collective responsibility, and that the word "saints" (plural) emphasises their individual responsibility. In passing, the very words "sanctified in Christ Jesus … called saints" must have been, perhaps 'should have been', a rebuke to their toleration of immorality. See Chapter 5 verses 1-13. It should also be said that in other passages, reference is made to practical and progressive sanctification. See, for example, 1 Thessalonians 4 verses 3-4. Our practice must correspond with our position.

As J. Hunter observes, the added words, 'with all that in every place call upon the name of Jesus Christ our Lord', "widens its teaching right down to the present time". It emphasises the calling of every believer, and we must not miss its application to every assembly. No local church can suit themselves when it comes to doctrine and practice. Hence we read: "as I teach everywhere in every church" (1 Corinthians 4:17); "and so ordain I in all the churches" (1 Corinthians 7:17); "we have no such custom, neither the churches of God" (1 Corinthians 11:16); "as in all the churches of the saints" (1 Corinthians 14:33). It is a contradiction in terms to use the expression "church of God", and not to recognise and obey the Word of God. The expression "call upon" the name of our Lord Jesus Christ implies submission to His authority: it is "**Lord** Jesus Christ". We should note the five references to "Lord" in verses 1-9. See verses 2, 3, 7, 8, 9. The words, "both theirs and ours" emphasise that "all … in every place" submit to the same authority. Had this been practised at Corinth, nobody would have said, "I am of Paul … Apollos … Cephas … Christ" (1 Corinthians 1:12).

3) THE GREETING, v.3

"Grace be unto you, and peace, from God our Father, and from the Lord

Jesus Christ". Note the order: "grace … peace". There could be no "peace" without "grace". The word "grace" (*charis*) was the Greek greeting, whereas "peace" (*shalom*) was the Hebrew greeting. It has been nicely said that "grace" is what the Lord Jesus brought (see Titus 2:11) and "peace" is what He left (John 14:27).

4) THE THANKSGIVING, vv.4-9

Paul's thanksgiving entirely concerns God's provision for them. He does not mention any spiritual qualities in them as he does, for example, in giving thanks at the commencement of the Colossian, Philippian and Thessalonian epistles. None the less there is thanksgiving here, even though disorders were present in the assembly. Galatians commences without any giving of thanks at all, for the simple reason that there was serious doctrinal error present in the assemblies in Galatia, and thanksgiving was not in order in those circumstances.

Although assembly disorders existed at Corinth, Paul did not lose sight of all that grace had accomplished: "I thank my God always on your behalf for the grace of God which is given (aorist tense: simply 'given', JND) by Jesus Christ ('in Christ Jesus', JND)" (v.4). We should notice the expressions "my God" (compare Philippians 4:19) and "always" (Phil. 1: 4). Other things call for attention. Paul's reference to the "grace of God" here reminds us that it is not limited to salvation alone. The apostle continues by explaining in verses 5-7 what the "grace of God" had provided. The same word (*charis*) is translated "benefit" in 2 Corinthians 1 verse 15. Now that really is a good definition of "grace"! Every 'benefit' we receive, whether in salvation or otherwise, is "*in* Christ Jesus" (JND). All God's blessings are in Him. Moreover, they are "in **Christ** Jesus' (JND). That is, as already noted, in the glorified Christ at God's right hand. See Ephesians 4 verses 7-8.

This divine provision covers past, present, and future: *(a)* what has been accomplished (vv.5-6); *(b)* what was being accomplished (v.7); *(c)* what will be accomplished (vv.8-9).

a) What has been accomplished, vv.5-6

"I thank my God always … that in every thing ye are enriched by him, in all utterance, and in all knowledge; even as the testimony of Christ was confirmed in you." So "the grace of God" here had enriched the believers at Corinth: "in everything ye have been enriched". We should carefully note that "all utterance" and "all knowledge" do not mean 'all spirituality' as this very epistle makes clear. The gifts of the Spirit *to* us are not the same as the work of the Spirit *in* us. The grace of God:

- ***Meets all our needs***. Here, this is expressed corporately (the needs of the assembly) although, of course, it is equally true individually: "in **every thing** ye are enriched by him".

- ***Makes us wealthy***: "in every thing ye are **enriched** by him". We have a rich God. Paul refers elsewhere to "the riches of his grace" (Ephesians 1:7) and "the riches of his mercy" (Ephesians 2:4). His wealth has become ours at infinite cost: "For ye know the grace of our Lord Jesus Christ, that, though he was rich, yet for your sakes he became poor, that ye though his poverty might be rich" (2 Corinthians 8:9).

The assembly at Corinth had been enriched by him "in all utterance, and in all knowledge". "In all utterance (*logos*)", that is, they had been enriched outwardly. The word *logos* is used elsewhere in this way: see, for example 1 Corinthians 2 verse 13; 12 verse 8. "In all knowledge", that is, inwardly. Or, to put it differently, they had been enriched in ability to **communicate** ("in all utterance") the mind of God, and in their grasp of the **content** of God's Word and God's will ("in all knowledge"). This has particular reference to the ministry of the prophets: see Chapter 14 verses 29-30. God, in Christ, had made adequate provision for the needs of His people, and for their spiritual enrichment.

The existence of these gifts in the assembly at Corinth was confirmation (or validation) that they had received the gospel message: "Even as the testimony of Christ (that is, the gospel - the testimony borne to Christ) was confirmed in you". The word "confirmed" (*bebaioo*), meaning 'to make firm, establish, make secure' (W.E. Vine), translates a term in Greek commercial law which denotes a guarantee of title. The bestowal of divinely-given gifts on the assembly at Corinth was evidence of their salvation. This is confirmed by the words which follow, "so that ye come behind in no gift…", which brings us to:

b) What was being accomplished, v.7

"So that ye come behind in no gift, waiting for the coming of our Lord Jesus Christ", or "waiting for the revelation of our Lord Jesus Christ" (RV). The word "coming" (*apokalupsis*) means 'unveiling' or 'uncovering'. The word "gift" (*charisma)* means 'a gift of grace'. All gifts are 'charismatic!' They are all 'gifts of grace'. The word "waiting" (*apekdechomai*) means 'to await or expect eagerly' (W.E.Vine). It occurs again, for example, in Philippians 3 verse 20, "we look (*apekdechomai)* for the Saviour". How eagerly are *we* awaiting His coming?

While it is often said that "the revelation of our Lord Jesus Christ" (RV) refers particularly to His public manifestation in glory on earth, it could simply refer here to that wonderful day when "we shall see him as he is" (1 John 3:2), which will take place *before* His public manifestation! We must also bear in mind that "waiting for the revelation ('coming', AV) of our Lord Jesus Christ" is far more than a technical reference to the order of future events: it is light from the future for present living. See, for example 1 John 3 verse 3 and 2 Peter 3 verse 11.

c) What will be accomplished, vv.8-9

"Who shall also confirm you unto the end, that ye may be blameless in the day of our Lord Jesus Christ. God is faithful, by whom ye were called unto the fellowship of his Son Jesus Christ our Lord."

In saying, "Who shall also confirm you unto the end", Paul assures them that the Lord Jesus will continue to provide for them until He comes again. He will continue to attest the reality of their salvation by providing the gifts necessary for the assembly to function. More than that, those gifts are provided to ensure the spiritual preservation of His people so that they will be "blameless (*anankletos,* meaning 'unreproveable', or 'unimpeachable', 'cannot be called into account') in the day of our Lord Jesus Christ". So the gifts He imparts, including those of "utterance … knowledge", are bestowed with the spiritual welfare of His people in view.

"The day of our Lord Jesus Christ" must be carefully distinguished from "the day of the Lord". The latter refers to judgment and administration on earth: the former refers to assessment and reward at the judgment seat of Christ in heaven. In this connection, we should notice the following: "Every man's work shall be made manifest: for *the day* shall declare it" (1 Corinthians 3:13); "Therefore judge nothing before the time, until the Lord come, who both will bring to light the hidden things of darkness, and will make manifest the counsels of the hearts: and then shall every man have praise of God" (1 Corinthians 4:5); "he which hath begun a good work in you, will perform it until the **day of Jesus Christ**" (Philippians 1:6)); "that ye may be sincere and without offence till the **day of Christ**" (Philippians 1:10); "holding forth the word of life; that I may rejoice in the **day of Christ**, that I have not run in vain" (Philippians 2:16)). It is also called "that day" (2 Timothy 1:12; 4: 8).

Having said, "who shall also confirm you unto the end" (v.8), Paul makes it clear that "this is not a vain boast. It is a sure confidence grounded on the fact that 'God is faithful'" (Leon Morris). God, who has called us "unto the fellowship of his Son", will not let us down! He will not withdraw His fellowship. We can rest on God's **faithfulness**, and we can rest in Christ's **fellowship.** The word translated "fellowship" (*koinonia*) first occurs in the New Testament as "partners" (Luke 5:10). Within that fellowship, He supplies the needs of His people, here in particular, their assembly needs.

As Leon Morris points out, "Paul goes back to beginnings. This faithful God had called the Corinthian Christians 'unto the fellowship of his Son Jesus Christ our Lord'. The opening words of this Epistle reminded us that Paul's position as an apostle was due to the divine call. Now we see that there is a call to every believer".

In saying, "called unto ('into', JND) the fellowship of his Son Jesus Christ our Lord", Paul states some important things about our fellowship with the Lord Jesus:

- It is with "**his Son**", with God's Son. This emphasises the **dignity** of our fellowship. Compare Galatians 4 verse 6: "And because ye are sons, God hath sent forth the Spirit of his Son into your hearts…"

- It is with "**Jesus**". This emphasises the **sympathy** in our fellowship. He is "Jesus the Son of God" (Hebrews 4:14). As "Jesus", the perfect man, He is able to act as our "great high priest".

- It is with "**Christ** ". This emphasises the **glory** of our fellowship. "God hath made that same Jesus … both Lord and Christ" (Acts 2:36).

- It is with the "**Lord** ". This emphasises the authority in our fellowship. Not our authority, but His authority. It is "the fellowship of his Son Jesus Christ **our** Lord". Had the believers at Corinth fully recognised this, they would not have said, as already noted, "I am of Paul … Apollos … Cephas … Christ" (1 Corinthians 1:12).

1 CORINTHIANS

"There are contentions among you"

Read Chapter 1:10-17

As we have already noticed, the epistle is addressed to "the church of God which is at Corinth, to them that are sanctified in Christ Jesus, called (to be) saints" (v.2). Paul's description of the church in this way emphasises at least two most important facts:

- The assembly there was a sacred place in a profane place. It was **not** 'the church of God which is **of** Corinth', but "the church **of** God which is **at** Corinth". Bearing in mind the character of Corinth, the assembly there has been called 'the church in vanity fair'.

- The assembly there comprised men and women "sanctified in Christ Jesus, called (to be) saints" and "enriched by him, in all utterance, and in all knowledge … waiting for the coming of our Lord Jesus Christ … called unto the fellowship of his Son Jesus Christ our Lord" (vv.5-9).

Sadly, however, the believers at Corinth had failed to ensure that their practices corresponded to their position. Christians are sanctified, set apart for God, at the moment of their conversion. At that happy moment they "are sanctified in Christ Jesus". They become "called … saints" (the word "called" is an adjective). This status is bestowed upon them. But, they are to practice what God has made them.

Alas, these believers were not behaving in a 'saintly' manner, and this becomes clear as we read through the epistle. As we have noted, Chapters 1-6 deal with things Paul had heard **about** the assembly at Corinth and Chapters 7-16 deal with things about which he had been **asked** by the assembly at Corinth. Confining ourselves now to the first section of the epistle

(Chapters 1-6), Paul deals with two reports which had reached him (see 1 Corinthians 1:11; 5:1). Chapters 1-4 deal with first report and Chapters 5-6 with the second. We must say again that the order is significant. He deals first with things about which he had *not* been asked! These were:

- The cliques among them, Chapters 1-4. The section commences as follows: "It hath been declared unto me of you, my brethren ... that there are contentions among you. Now this I say, that every one of you saith, I am of Paul; and I of Apollos; and I of Cephas; and I of Christ" (1 Corinthians 1:11-12). The assembly had come to resemble a 'tug-of-war' competition.

- The immorality among them, Chapters 5-6. This section commences as follows: "It is reported commonly that there is fornication among you, and such fornication as is not so much as named among the Gentiles, that one should have his father's wife" (1 Corinthians 5: 1).

Paul addresses the first report by pointing out that they had no valid reason whatsoever for grouping themselves under their self-appointed champions, with all the resultant boasting and rivalry. Just listen to the "I" of pride! "I am of Paul ... Apollos ... Cephas ... Christ." Paul therefore emphasises that they had no justification at all for this, and does so in four different ways:

- In Chapter 1, he emphasises that their salvation and calling were divine, not human. That is, they had no reason to glory in men in the matter: "For ye see your calling, brethren, how that not many wise men after the flesh, not many mighty, not many noble, are called ... that no flesh should glory in his presence" (1 Corinthians 1:26-29). Rather, "He that glorieth, let him glory in the Lord" (1 Corinthians 1:31). Chapter 1 emphasises that it was not man's wisdom that operated in the way they had been saved, or in the type of people who were saved.

- In Chapter 2, he emphasises that the preaching under which they were saved and the teaching imparted once they were saved did not reflect human wisdom. Both preaching and teaching found their source in divine wisdom, and were imparted in divine power. There was, therefore, no reason to glory in men in the matter.

- In Chapter 3, he emphasises that those who had been responsible for the establishment and development of the assembly at Corinth were simply servants (1 Corinthians 3:5), executing their Master's interests with

His wisdom and at His direction. They were directed and empowered by God whose work it was (1 Corinthians 3:7). Again, therefore, there was no reason to glory in men in the matter. Hence, "Therefore let no man glory in men" (1 Corinthians 3:21). It should be noted that Paul refers here to what was *observable.*

- In Chapter 4, he emphasises that the final and only assessment of service must be left to the Lord Himself (1 Corinthians 4:5). The men in whose wisdom they were boasting were responsible alone to the Master, whose **stewards** they were. The Corinthian believers could not assess service, and rank servants of God according to their assessment. It should be noted that Paul refers here to what was *not observable*: "the Lord … will bring to light the hidden things of darkness, and will make manifest the counsels of the heart". He alone knew the motives of His servants.

In any case, all ability was God-given, and therefore no credit was due to men. Hence: "What hast thou that thou didst not receive? now if thou didst receive it, why dost thou glory as if thou hadst not received it?" (1 Corinthians 4:7).

To sum up, they had no reason whatsoever to "glory in men" (1 Corinthians 3:21). Rather, "he that glorieth, let him glory in the Lord" (1 Corinthians 1:31).

With this in mind, we can now address the current passage (1 Corinthians 1:10-17), which may be divided as follows: *(1)* the avoidance of divisions (v.10); *(2)* the presence of divisions (vv.11-12); *(3)* the implications of divisions (v.13); *(4)* the safeguard against divisions (vv.14-17).

1) THE AVOIDANCE OF DIVISIONS, v.10

"Now I beseech you, brethren, by the name of our Lord Jesus Christ, that ye all speak the same thing, and that there be no divisions among you; but that ye be perfectly joined together in the same mind, and in the same judgment." How sad! Having spoken of "the *fellowship* … of Jesus Christ our Lord" (v.9), Paul now speaks about "*divisions*". We must notice *(a)* how Paul approaches the problem; *(b)* how he addresses the problem.

a) Approaching the problem

"Now I beseech you, brethren, by the name of our Lord Jesus Christ …"

Every word counts:

- In saying: "**Now** I beseech you, brethren …", Paul refers to what he had just said about them: "sanctified in Christ Jesus, called (to be) saints … called unto ('into', JND) the fellowship of his Son Jesus Christ our Lord". Paul urges them to act in conformity with their calling. They were to face up to their responsibilities.

- In saying: "Now I **beseech** you, brethren …", Paul stresses the urgency of the matter. The word "beseech" (*parakaleo*) is stronger than 'ask' (*aiteo*). It is rendered elsewhere 'intreated' (Luke 15:28) and 'intreating' (Acts 9: 38, RV: 'desiring', AV). The centurion (Matthew 8:5), the leper (Mark 1:40), and Jairus (Mark 5:23) all used the same word. There was urgency in each case. Assembly disunity is a matter of urgency.

- In saying: "Now I beseech you, **brethren**…", Paul stresses, not only the tenderness of his appeal, but his relationship with **all** the believers at Corinth, not just those who said "I am of Paul!" See also verse 11 (where he says "my brethren") and 1 Corinthians 1 verse 26; Chapter 2 verse 1 and Chapter 3 verse 1. Believers can refer to each other as "brethren" because of their relationship with the Lord Jesus, who is 'not ashamed to call them brethren' (Hebrews 2:11).

- In saying: "Now I beseech you, brethren, by the name of **our** Lord Jesus Christ", Paul emphasises that "this one name stands over against all party names" (Leon Morris). See also verses 2 (JND), 7 and 8. Note Paul's exact words in this connection: "Jesus Christ **our** Lord" (v.9). The very fact that we acknowledge His Lordship should effectively preserve us from a party spirit. It should be a bulwark against sectarianism.

b) Addressing the problem

"That ye all speak the same thing, and that there be no divisions among you; but that ye be perfectly joined together in the same mind and in the same judgment."

Paul uses the word translated "divisions" ('*schisma*', meaning a cleft or rent) later in the epistle when he describes the way in which God has "tempered" (mixed or blended) the (human) body together, having given more abundant honour to that part which lacked: "that there should be no **schism** in the

43

body" (1 Cor. 12:24-25). Paul is not, therefore, appealing for **uniformity** in utterance or thought, but for **unity** as in the diversity yet unity of the body.

Paul's appeal in this way does not imply that they were to be regimented in word and thought to the extent that they all used exactly the same phraseology! He was deeply concerned, rather, that they should not divide into different 'schools of thought' ("I am of Paul; and I of Apollos ...") with all the divisiveness that this brings. He is "appealing for doctrinal unity, the abandonment of the personality cult" (J. Hunter). This is very relevant to assembly life. How often believers group themselves around prominent teachers, instead of saying: "What saith the scripture?" (Rom. 4: 3) in which we listen to the Lord's voice. The Lord's people should speak with a united voice on all matters of doctrine and practice. There should be no: "every one of you saith ..." (v.12).

In saying: "that ye be **perfectly joined together** in the same mind and in the same judgment", Paul actually uses one word (from the verb *katartizo*) rendered 'perfected' (RV). It is used in the Scriptures for mending nets (Matthew 4:21; Mark 1:19): it is translated "restore" in Galatians 6:1. The word does not always have the sense of repairing damage, but may well do so here. In a marginal note, J.N. Darby explains its meaning as follows: a position "where all the members have each its own place, or make a whole: or, if broken, are restored to one complete and perfect whole". Paul later refers to himself and Apollos as examples of being 'perfectly joined together': "Now he that planteth and he that watereth are one ..." (1 Corinthians 3:8). That is, there was no rivalry between them. They were one in purpose and desire. The Corinthians were to recognise the necessity for this, and so deal with the divisive situation.

It might be helpful to point out that Paul uses a different word (*dichostasia*) in Romans 16 verse 17 ("Mark them which cause **divisions** among you). There, the word means 'a standing apart'. It is rendered "seditions" in Galatians 5 verse 20.

2) THE PRESENCE OF DIVISIONS, vv.11-12

"For it hath been declared unto me of you, my brethren, by them which are of the house of Chloe, that there are contentions among you. Now this I say, that every one of you saith, I am of Paul; and I of Apollos; and I of Cephas; and I of Christ."

The words, "Now this I say" ('Now this I mean', RV), can be otherwise read as "I am now qualifying what I mean in saying that 'there are contentions among you'. I mean that 'every one of you saith, I am of Paul; and I of Apollos; and I of Cephas; and I of Christ'".

Paul reveals the names of his informants. There is no question of tale-bearing or gossip. There is all the difference in the world between tittle-tattle, and the disclosure of information to a person who is spiritually competent to deal with problems that have arisen. Some people spread rumours, and others tell the truth from the wrong motive, but not so here. We know nothing further about "the house of Chloe". Presumably Chloe was known to the believers at Corinth. Perhaps she, with her household, was a member of the assembly there.

It is worth pointing out that what begins as "contentions" ('*eris*', v.11: rendered "variance", Galatians 5:20), meaning 'strife, quarrel, especially rivalry, contention, wrangling' (W.E. Vine), leads to "divisions" ('*schisma*', v.10) meaning 'a cleft' or 'rent' (see Matthew 9:16), which in turn leads to "heresies" or sects (1 Corinthians 11:19), which W.E. Vine calls "a division matured and established". 'Tall oaks from little acorns grow', and it is so important to deal with problems in their infancy.

We are only given the 'bare bones' of the situation: "Every one of you saith, I am of Paul; and I of Apollos; and I of Cephas; and I of Christ". But we need nothing further: as already noted, it was the big "I" of pride. Each faction felt superior to the other, and Paul therefore points out (vv.13-17) that:

- It was folly to say "I am" of any man, since their blessings did not derive from man, and did not become theirs through any man's power.

- It was folly for any one to say "I am of Christ", since every believer (see, for example, v.30) derives their blessings from Him.

Since we are not given the underlying reasons for which people were saying "I am of Paul; and I of Apollos; and I of Cephas; and I of Christ", we can only conjecture, something we really ought not to do! However, it **might** be something like this:

- *"I am of Paul."* This could refer to those who were present at the inception of the assembly. 'I have been here from the start.' Or to those who had a particular liking for logical argument.

- "I am of Apollos." This could refer to those who were impressed with eloquence. See Acts 18: 24. They liked an impressive preacher! In the words of Leon Morris, 'Probably Apollos was more elaborate and rhetorical than Paul". ('Paul is rather stodgy, you know!)

- "I am of Cephas." This could refer to Jewish element at Corinth. Or perhaps to those who were unimpressed by the eloquence of Apollos and preferred to listen to simpler people, to "unlearned and unlettered men". Or perhaps to people who might have said: 'We like to go back to the original twelve, you know!' Or, 'Peter (Cephas) is an older man, isn't he?' By the way, we don't know whether Peter ever went to Corinth!

- "I am of Christ." This could also refer to the Jewish party, which might have gloried in the nationality of the Messiah. It all sounded very spiritual, as if they were a cut above their brethren. But it was divisive none-the-less. It was, perhaps, the attitude which said: 'You follow men - but we follow Christ!' It was sectarian all the same!

But enough of this speculation. What follows is of much more importance. We come therefore to:

3) THE IMPLICATIONS OF DIVISIONS, v.13

"Is Christ divided? Was Paul crucified for you? or were ye baptized in the name of Paul?"

The way in which the believers at Corinth were saying: "I am of Paul; and I of Apollos; and I of Cephas; and I of Christ" was a total misrepresentation. It was a total misrepresentation of the Lord Jesus: "Is Christ divided?", and it was a total misrepresentation of Paul: "was Paul crucified for you? or were ye baptized in the name of Paul?" In all, Paul asks three incisive questions.

The first question: "Is Christ divided?" is addressed to the last faction, and the questions: "Was Paul crucified for you? Or were ye baptized in the name of Paul?" are addressed to the first named of the three other factions. It is worth noting that Paul puts the interests of Christ first.

a) It misrepresented the Lord Jesus

As we have noted, Paul had spoken of "Jesus Christ *our* Lord" (v.2) and "*our* Lord Jesus Christ" (vv.7, 8), but those who said: "I am of Christ" were evidently under the impression that they had a special relationship with Him. Paul counters this with the question: "Is Christ divided?" Leon Morris is most helpful here in suggesting, bearing in mind that the verb is likely to be passive, that this means: 'Has Christ been apportioned?' (that is, to one of conflicting groups) … or 'Has Christ been divided up?' He cites Moffatt here: 'Has Christ been parcelled out?' Leon Morris concludes: "Paul is envisaging an utter impossibility. Christ is one, and the church, which is His body must be one". This is well-supported by the fact that Paul uses the definite article: "Is *the* Christ divided?" (JND). The expression 'the Christ' refers to what has been called 'the mystical Christ', that is Christ united to the church, His body. See 1 Corinthians 12 verse 12: "For as the (human) body is one, and hath many members, and all the members of that one body, being many, are one body; so also is Christ ('so also is *the* Christ, JND)". As J. Hunter so rightly points out: "The presence of such divisions in the assembly at Corinth was a denial of the unity of the whole body".

b) It misrepresented the work of Paul

"Was Paul crucified for you? Or were ye baptized in the name of Paul?" or "Have you been baptized unto the name of Paul?" (JND). Here are the second and third of the three questions.

The second question: "Was Paul crucified for you?" also refers "to something unthinkable … None other than Christ could accomplish the crucial work of redemption" (Leon Morris). As J. Hunter says in confirmation: "How could they elevate a servant to the detriment of Christ? How could they forget the centrality of the Cross where Christ accomplished the crucial work of redemption and laid the basis for such unity?"

The third question: "Were ye baptized in ('*eis*', 'into' or 'unto') the name of Paul?" reminded them of the significance of their baptism. "They had been baptized into Christ, not unto any man. Their allegiance accordingly was to Christ alone" (Leon Morris). To say: "I am of Paul" was utterly false. Paul does not say how wrong it was to follow men, but how wrong it was to follow *him*!

4) THE SAFEGUARD AGAINST DIVISIONS, vv.14-17

"I thank God that I baptized none of you but Crispus and Gaius; lest any should say that I baptized in my own name. And I baptized also the household of Stephanas; besides, I know not whether I baptized any other. For Christ sent me not to baptize, but to preach the gospel: not with wisdom of words, lest the cross of Christ should be made of none effect."

These verses need little comment. Paul makes the point that the fact that he baptized so few at Corinth emphasised that he made no attempt to bind converts to him personally. In his own words: "I baptized none of you but Crispus (Acts 18:8) and Gaius (Romans 16:23; thought to be 'Justus', Acts 18:7) lest any should say that I baptized in my own name". Very clearly, he did not keep a list of those he baptized: "I baptized also the household of Stephanas (see 1 Corinthians 16:15, 17); besides, I know not whether I baptized any other". Had he kept a list, it might have been construed that he had particular affinity with them, leading them to say: "I am of Paul". For this he thanked God, which suggests that this was providentially overruled.

J. Hunter makes the valid comment that "Paul did not do everything himself, but was happy to let others do what they could. Again, it was not because baptism was unimportant to him, but its validity was not impaired if performed by one other than an apostle". Once again we must note the providential overruling of God in all this. Paul might not have visualised the party spirit which arose at Corinth, but the Lord did, and put Paul in a position beforehand to deal with the matter.

Paul evidently regarded preaching as his primary work. He was "separated unto the gospel of God" (Romans 1:1) and "separated from his mother's womb" to preach Christ "among the heathen" (Galatians 1:15-16). But God also appointed the way in which he was to preach: "not with wisdom of words, lest the cross of Christ should be made of none effect". Leon Morris is splendid here: "Some at least of the Corinthians were setting too high a value on human wisdom and human eloquence in line with the typical Greek admiration of rhetoric and philosophical studies. In the face of this Paul insists the preaching with *wisdom of words* was no part of his commission. That kind of preaching would draw men to the preacher. It would nullify the cross of Christ. The faithful preaching of the cross results in men ceasing to put their trust in any human device, and relying rather on God's work in Christ. A reliance on rhetoric would cause men to trust in men, the very antithesis of what the preaching of the cross is meant to effect".

In summary, Paul made no attempt to 'hog the limelight', either by both preaching and baptizing (doing everything), or by employing "excellency of speech or of wisdom" (1 Corinthians 2:1). He 'walked humbly with God' (Micah 6:8). Men like that are not responsible for divisions! It is an effective safeguard against them.

1 CORINTHIANS

"We preach Christ crucified"

Read Chapter 1:18-31

As we have already noted, in the former part of the epistle Paul addresses two dangers which had arisen at Corinth:

- The cliques among them, Chapters 1-4. "It hath been declared unto me of you, my brethren … that there are contentions among you. Now this I say, that every one of you saith, I am of Paul; and I of Apollos; and I of Cephas; and I of Christ" (1 Corinthians 1:11-12).

- The immorality among them, Chapters 5-6. "It is reported commonly that there is fornication among you, and such fornication as is not so much as named among the Gentiles, that one should have his father's wife" (1 Corinthians 5:1).

In dealing with the first of these, Paul highlights the sad spiritual results: "There is among you envying and strife, and divisions" (1 Corinthians 3:3-4), and goes on to say: "Therefore let no man glory in men …" (1 Corinthians 3:21). Paul's object in Chapters 1-4 is to demonstrate that the believers at Corinth had no reason to "glory in men" and every reason to "glory in the Lord" (1 Corinthians 1:31). Only then could they "all speak the same thing" and be "perfectly joined together in the same mind and in the same judgment" (1 Corinthians 1:10). He undertakes this in four ways:

- He reminds them that the way in which they had been saved, and the type of people who are saved, gave no reason to glory in men (1 Corinthians 1:18-31).

- He reminds them that the way in which he preached at Corinth, and

the manner in which he taught them after they were saved, gave no reason to glory in men (1 Corinthians 2:1-16).

- He reminds them that the manner in which the assembly at Corinth had been planted left no reason to glory in men (1 Corinthians 3:1-11).

- He reminds them that the assessment of God's servants must be left to the judgment seat of Christ (1 Corinthians 4:1-6): "Therefore judge nothing before the time, until the Lord come" (v.5). Having said: "Let a man so account of us, as of the ministers ('servants') of Christ" (v.1), Paul continues: "that ye may learn in us not to think of men above that which is written" (v.6). By 'glorying in men' ("I am of Paul ... of Apollos ... of Cephas ...") and in some cases going further by saying: "I am of Christ", the believers at Corinth were proudly saying that they had the ability to assess servants of God, something only the Lord Himself could accomplish.

Bearing in mind then that Paul sets out to demonstrate that the believers at Corinth had no reason to "glory in men" (1 Corinthians 3:21), and every reason to "glory in the Lord" (1 Corinthians 1:31), he now reminds them of the preaching under which they were saved (vv.18-25) and the kind of people who are saved (vv.26-31). Most certainly, neither gave ground for any at Corinth to say: "I am of Paul". What wisdom in both cases! In the first case, Paul refers to "us which are *saved*" (v.18), and in the second, "unto them which are *called*" (v.24), and in this connection he refers to their divine "calling" (v.26) and divine choice ("chosen", vv.27-28).

1) THE WISDOM OF GOD IN THEIR SALVATION, vv.18-25

It should be noted that in speaking about the death of Christ, Paul emphasises His crucifixion. He refers to the "cross of Christ" (v.17); to "the preaching of the cross" (v.18); to "Christ crucified" (v.23). Men "crucified the Lord of glory" (1 Corinthians 2:8). He was "taken, and by wicked hands ... crucified and slain" (Acts 2:23). The 'death of Christ' is the basis of our relationship with God, and "the cross of Christ" is the basis of our relationship with the world: "God forbid that I should glory, save in the cross of our Lord Jesus Christ, by whom the world is crucified unto me, and I unto the world" (Galatians 6:14). Paul is, therefore, explaining that "the cross of Christ", which condemns worldly wisdom (salvation comes – just think of it – through a Man who was crucified!), should turn believers away from all forms of human glory, including glorying in men ("I am of Paul ... of Apollos ... of Cephas").

These verses (vv.18-25) refer *(a)* to mankind generally (vv.18-21); *(b)* to Jew and Gentile particularly (vv.22-25). In the first case, where Paul speaks *generally*, he refers to "the world" (vv.20, 21) which is divided into two classes: "them that perish … us which are saved". In the second case, where Paul speaks *particularly*, he refers to three divisions: "the Jews … the Greeks … them that are called, both Jews and Greeks".

a) Mankind generally, verses 18-21

We should notice the following: *(i)* the preaching of the Cross divides men (v.18); *(ii)* the preaching of the Cross was determined beforehand (v.19); *(iii)* the preaching of the Cross destroys human wisdom (v.20); *(iv)* the preaching of the Cross delivers salvation (v.21).

i) The preaching of the Cross divides men, verse 18. "For the preaching of the cross is to them that perish foolishness (meaning 'stupid … silly … worthless', W.E. Vine), but unto us which are saved it is the power of God." Men say that "the preaching of the cross is foolishness", but God says that anything but the preaching of the Cross is foolishness! (vv.20-21). The "preaching of the cross" divides humanity. Paul makes the point again in verses 23-24 where he emphasises that "the preaching of the cross" was a "stumblingblock" and "foolishness" to Jew and Gentile respectively, but "the power of God, and the wisdom of God" to "them which are called, both Jews and Greeks".

The words: "the preaching of the cross" are, literally: "the word (*'logos'*) of the cross" (JND) or: "the word which [speaks] of the cross" (JND margin). W.E. Vine and others point out that "it is not the act of preaching, but the substance of the testimony, all that God had made known concerning the subject". The tenses employed: "them that perish … us which are saved" indicate 'work in progress', so that Paul refers here to those who are perishing ('the perishing', W.E. Vine) and those who are being saved. He emphasises the ultimate destination of both sections of humanity.

It is worth noticing that instead of saying: "unto us which are saved it is the *wisdom* of God", which would have been the natural antithesis to "foolishness", Paul says: "unto us which are saved it is the *power* (*'dunamis'*) of God", which J. Hunter delightfully describes as: "the mighty saving dynamic of the message". As Leon Morris observes: "It is not simply good advice to men, telling them what they should do. Nor is it a message about

God's power. It *is* God's power". Compare Romans 1 verse 16: "For I am not ashamed of the gospel of Christ: for it is the power (*'dunamis'*) of God unto salvation …"

ii) The preaching of the Cross was determined beforehand, verse 19.
"For it is written, I will destroy (*'appolumai',* not extinguishing, but ruining) the wisdom of the wise, and will bring to nothing (*'atheteo'*, set aside) the understanding of the prudent." As Leon Morris observes: "The principle Paul is expounding is nothing new". The apostle refers here to Isaiah 29 verse 14: "Therefore, behold, I will proceed to do a marvellous work among this people, even a marvellous work and a wonder: for the wisdom of their wise men shall perish, and the understanding of their prudent men shall be hid". The passage refers to God's use of Sennacherib in bringing judgment on Jerusalem. Judah sought help, not from the Lord, but from Egypt (Isaiah 30:1-2). But the wisdom of men in this way would fail when God stretched out His hand and "both he that helpeth shall fail, and he that is holpen shall fall down, and they shall all fall together" (Isaiah 31:3). Only then, when the folly of human wisdom was exposed, would God intervene to save His people (Isaiah 31:4-5). Man's wisdom cannot accomplish salvation: that can only be accomplished by the power of God through the preaching of the Cross.

iii) The preaching of the Cross destroys human wisdom, verse 20.
"Where is the wise? where is the scribe? Where is the disputer of this world? Hath not God made foolish the wisdom of this world?" God had announced that He would "destroy the wisdom of the wise, and … bring to nothing the understanding of the prudent" (v.19), and He had duly fulfilled His promise. He is "God, that cannot lie" (Titus 1:2). He fulfilled His promise through "the foolishness of preaching".

The first occurrence in the verse of the word "world" ("the disputer of this world" or 'age'), refers to a period of time (*'aion'*), in this case to the present period of time marked by darkness. See Ephesians 6 verse 12. The second occurrence of "world" ("the wisdom of this world") denotes human affairs (*'kosmos'*). It occurs again in verse 21 ("the world by wisdom knew not God"). It does seem that in referring to "the wise … the scribe … the disputer", Paul is speaking generally about "those who are learned and acute as the world counts wisdom" (Leon Morris). According to J. Hunter: "'Wise' refers to one versed in philosophical ideas; 'scribe' to one who is versed in literature; 'disputer' to one versed in intellectual discussions".

iv) ***The preaching of the Cross delivers salvation, verse 21.*** "For after that in the wisdom of God the world by wisdom knew not God, it pleased God by the foolishness of preaching to save them that believe." It was never God's purpose to save men by their own wisdom, but to save them through the gospel: "the foolishness of ***the*** preaching (*kerugma,* a proclamation by a herald)" (JND). Once again, W.E. Vine explains that Paul refers here to "the substance of what is preached as distinct from the act of preaching". In passing, we should notice that the words: "the world by wisdom knew not God" explain that Paul is not speaking here about human wisdom in general, but about human wisdom in seeking and knowing God.

Most certainly: "the world by wisdom knew not God". In fact, the reverse is true: "professing themselves to be wise, they became fools" (Romans 1:22). Romans 1 refers to God's revelation of Himself in creation (vv.19-20), and continues by telling us what men have made of it (vv.21-22). The "Athenians and strangers which were there, spent their time in nothing else, but either to tell, or to hear some new thing …", but Paul still found "an altar with this inscription, TO THE UNKNOWN GOD" (Acts 17:21, 23). Men are "ever learning, and never able to come to a knowledge of the truth" (2 Timothy 3:7).

But why does Paul say: "after that in the wisdom of God, the world by wisdom knew not God"? If otherwise, it would have given men reason to congratulate themselves on their achievement, but in any case, how could sinful man ever know God? How glad we are that God has "devised means that his banished be not expelled from him" (2 Samuel 14:14). Human wisdom can never discern God, causing Zophar to say: "Canst thou by searching find out God? Canst thou find out the Almighty unto perfection?" (Job 11:7). Again, if God could be known by human wisdom, then only the wise would ever know Him. The knowledge of God would be limited to them alone. This brings us to:

b) Jew and Gentle particularly, verses 22-25

These verses repeat and expand what has been said in the preceding verses. If in verse 18 the preaching of the Cross brings about the watershed of all men, then in verses 22-24 it brings about the watershed for Jew and Gentile. If in verse 21 it is "them that believe" then in verse 22 we have the Jews requiring a sign before they will believe and the Greeks requiring a logical proposition before they will believe.

It could be said that the mind-set of Jew and Greek here - "For the Jews require a sign, and the Greeks seek after wisdom" (v.22) - explains why Paul states that "the preaching of the cross is to them that perish foolishness" (v.18). He refers to "the Jews" and "the Greeks" three times in these verses. His teaching may be summarised as follows: *(i)* their common demand (v.22); *(ii)* their common refusal (v.23); *(iii)* their common salvation (v.24).

i) Their common demand, verse 22. Both wanted confirmation: "for the Jews require a sign, and the Greeks seek after wisdom": a confirming sign in one case and confirming logic in the other other.

- "The Jews require a sign." (Compare Psalm 74:9). Leon Morris explains this well: "They thought of God as manifesting Himself in history in signs and mighty wonders. In the light of this they demanded a sign from the Lord Jesus." Hence we read: "Master, we would see a sign from thee" (Matthew 12:38); "And the Pharisees came forth, and began to question with him, seeking of him a sign from heaven, tempting him" (Mark 8:11); "What sign sheweth thou then that we may see, and believe thee? What dost thou work?" (John 6:30). To them, a crucified Messiah was a contradiction in terms.

- "The Greeks seek after wisdom." That is, rational evidence. The Greeks were proud of their wisdom and of their celebrated thinkers and philosophers. To them a crucified Saviour was totally illogical. It defied their wisdom.

ii) Their common refusal, verse 23. "But we preach Christ crucified, unto the Jews a stumblingblock, and unto the Greeks ('nations', JND) foolishness."

- "Unto the Jews a stumblingblock." The word "stumblingblock ('*skandalon*') means 'an occasion of offence'. To the Jews a crucified Messiah ("we preach **Christ** crucified") was a total impossibility. The Jews anticipated a victorious Messiah and a visible kingdom established in power. The Cross was the antithesis of all this and was completely unacceptable. A Messiah like this could never achieve their ideals. "To present to them one crucified as a malefactor as their Messiah was the greatest possible insult" (Charles Hodge). Paul uses the word '*skandalon*' again in Galatians 5 verse 11 ("the offence of the cross"), and Peter follows suit in 1 Peter 2 verse 8 ("a stone of stumbling"). But, notwithstanding Jewish reaction in this way, Paul says: "But we preach Christ crucified ..."

- "Unto the Greeks foolishness." To the Greeks ('Gentiles', RV), salvation

through a crucified man was totally illogical. It was foolishness. But, notwithstanding Gentile reaction in this way, Paul says: "But we preach Christ crucified …"

The unfavourable response to his preaching did not bring him to a grinding halt. He continued preaching. He was, in his own words "instant in season, out of season" (2 Timothy 4:2). At Corinth, he "testified to the Jews that Jesus was Christ" (Acts 18:5) and "continued there a year and six months teaching the word of God among them" (Acts 18:11), even though the Jews "opposed and spoke injuriously" (Acts 18: 6, JND).

In the circumstances, we might ask: 'Why preach at all?' The answer follows: both Jews and Greeks had been saved! This brings us to:

iii) Their common salvation, verse 24 "But unto them which are called, both Jew and Greek, Christ the power of God, and the wisdom of God." In passing, we should notice that men and women at Corinth were divided into three groups: "the Jews … the Gentiles … the church of God" (1 Corinthians 10:32).

The words: "them which are called" refer to what is often called: 'the effectual calling' of God. While at Corinth Paul was told: "Be not afraid, but speak, and hold not thy peace … for I have much people in this city" (Acts 18:9-10). The people in question were not yet saved. The Jews "required a sign". They sought an exhibition of divine power before they would believe, not knowing that "Christ crucified" is "the power of God". The "Greeks seek after wisdom, not knowing that "Christ crucified" is "the wisdom" of God", but not "the wisdom of this world, nor of the princes of this world" (1 Corinthians 2:6). He is the complete reverse of human opinion. As Leon Morris observes: "The sign-seeking Jews were blind to the greatest sign of all when it was before them. The wisdom-loving Greeks could not discern the most profound wisdom of all when they were confronted with it". What seemed to them as utterly foolish and utterly weak - after all, could there be anything so foolish and so weak as salvation though a crucified man - was stronger than anything man could ever produce or provide. Just think of it: the "preaching of the cross" has resulted in the formation of "the church of God which is at Corinth"!

Having listened to Paul's teaching on the wisdom in their salvation (vv.18-25), we now come to:

2) THE WISDOM OF GOD IN THEIR CALLING, verses 26-31

The purpose of this section is to demonstrate yet again how wrong the saints at Corinth were to "glory in men". Their salvation exhibited divine wisdom, and so did their calling.

These verses may be divided as follows: *(a)* their own insignificance, leading to a conclusion (vv.26-29); *(b)* their enrichment in Christ, leading to a conclusion (vv.30-31).

a) Their own insignificance, verses 26-29

"For ye see your calling, brethren, how that not many wise men after the flesh, not many mighty, not many noble, are called" (v.26). The word "calling" here refers, not so much to election, but to God's deliberate choice in calling, in the main, common-place men and women, so demonstrating that human wisdom and glory are not advantageous when it comes to salvation and spiritual life. He has chosen people who, having no human attainments, know themselves to be nothing. It has been suggested that the membership of New Testament churches was largely made up of converted slaves. Paul asks the believers at Corinth to take a good look at themselves. There was nothing in them that called for special treatment. They could not sit in their assembly meetings congratulating themselves on the fact that it was their wisdom and elevated status in life that made them the subjects of divine choice!

We should notice that the words: "not many wise men after the flesh, not many mighty, not many noble, are called", imply - none the less - that there were *some.* The Countess of Huntingdon, a member of the English aristocracy (and a thorough evangelical) is said to have remarked that she was glad that Paul did not say: 'not *any* noble, are called!' The overall point is clear: God does not take account of natural attainments and human refinement in blessing men and women. "But God hath chosen the foolish things of the world, to confound the wise; and God hath chosen the weak things of the world, to confound the things which are mighty; and base things of the world, and things which are despised, hath God chosen, yea, and things which are not, to bring to nought things that are" (vv.26-28). We should notice the 'pairing' in these verses:

i) "Not many wise men after the flesh" (v.26), but "the foolish things of the world to confound the wise" (v.27). The neuter is used here ("things"),

emphasising not so much the individuals themselves, but their qualities. While the words: "of the world" (v.27) could mean: 'in the world's estimate', it may well be that Paul is referring to those who really are the *foolish* and the *weak* of this world" (Leon Morris). The word "confound" means to put to shame. Hence, when they (the Jewish leadership) "perceived that they (Peter and John) were unlearned and ignorant men", they marvelled" (Acts 4:13). As Leon Morris observes: this did not "come about because the only people who would interest themselves in Christianity were the depressed classes. It came about because God chose to work His marvels through people who were, from the human point of view, the most unpromising".

ii) "Not many mighty" (v.26) but *"the weak things of the world to confound the things which are mighty"* (v.27). "Mighty" is "a general term for principal people" (Leon Morris). It has been nicely said that "Under the control of God, ordinary instruments become extraordinary".

iii) "Not many noble" (v.26) but *"the base things of the world, and things which are despised, hath God chosen"* (v 28). The word "noble" applies to family and denotes noble rank. The word "base" means ignoble - of low birth. The word "despised" means to regard as nothing: to treat with contempt. See, for example, the proud Pharisee's prayer: "even as this publican" (Luke 18:11). Paul then adds to the above:

iv) "And things which are not, to bring to nought things that are", v.28. The words: "things which are not" mean: 'nonentities', and: "bring to nought" mean: 'to render inoperative'. If "things which are despised" refers to things which 'are treated of no account', then "things which are not" is even stronger. "God's activity in men is creative. He takes that which is nothing at all and makes of it what He pleases" (Leon Morris).

Why does Paul say all this? The answer lies in his conclusion: "that no flesh should glory in his presence". And the believers at Corinth were doing just that: "I am of Paul ... Apollos ... Cephas ... Christ."

b) Our enrichment in Christ, verses 30-31

"But of him are ye in Christ Jesus, who of God is made unto us wisdom, and righteousness, and sanctification, and redemption" or: "But of him are ye in Christ Jesus who has been made to us wisdom from God, and righteousness, and holiness, and redemption" (JND). Our new life derives from God, and it is made good to us in Christ. It certainly does not come from men, or through men.

According to Leon Morris, the Greek text seems to suggest that "righteousness … sanctification … redemption" are subordinate to "wisdom" and an explanation of it. If so, then we might say that God's wisdom has been expressed in three ways: as to the past, in our *justification* (righteousness before God); as to the present, in our *sanctification*; as to the future, in the completion of God's purpose for us in final *redemption.*

However, for the purpose of this study, we will take "wisdom, and righteousness, and sanctification, and redemption" in their AV setting, and listen to Harry Bell, late of Jarrow-on-Tyne, who likened these verses to a tour of Corinth.

i) When he was taken to the *university* of Corinth, Paul said: *'Christ is made unto us wisdom'.* What sort of wisdom? Not human wisdom: "I will destroy the wisdom of the wise" (v.19); "for after that in the wisdom of God, the world by wisdom knew not God, it pleased God by the foolishness of preaching (not the act of preaching, but the content of the preaching) to save them that believe" (v.21); "Christ crucified … the power of God and the wisdom of God" (vv.23-24).

ii) When he was taken to the *courts* at Corinth, Paul said: *'Christ is made unto us righteousness'.* Paul addresses this great subject elsewhere in his New Testament correspondence. For example: "Now we know, that what things soever the law saith, it saith to them who are under the law; that every mouth may be stopped, and all the world may become guilty before God. Therefore by the deeds of the law there shall no flesh be justified in his sight: for by the law is the knowledge of sin. But now the righteousness of God without the law is manifested, being witnessed by the law and the prophets; even the righteousness of God, which is by faith of Jesus Christ, unto all and upon all them that believe" (Romans 3:19-22); "For he hath made him to be sin for us, who knew no sin, that we might be made (become) the righteousness of God in him" (2 Corinthians 5:21).

iii) When he was taken to the *temple* at Corinth, Paul said: *'Christ is made unto us sanctification'.* The temple at Corinth was a vile place, but the assembly at Corinth is described as a holy temple: "the temple of God is *holy* (separated to God), which temple ye are" (1 Corinthians 3:17). As we have noticed, the epistle is addressed to: "the church of God which is at Corinth, to them that are **sanctified** in Christ Jesus, called (to be) saints" (1 Corinthians 1:2). Paul told the believers at Ephesus that "Christ also loved the church, and gave himself for it; that he might **sanctify** and cleanse it with the washing of water by the word" (Ephesians 5:25-26).

iv) When he was taken to the **slave-market** at Corinth, Paul said: **'Christ is made unto us redemption'.** The word "redemption" (*'apolutrosis'*) means to release on payment of a ransom. The Lord Jesus, "by his own blood ... entered in once into the holy place, having obtained eternal **redemption** (*'lutrosis'*) for us" (Hebrews 9:12); He "gave himself for us that he might **redeem** (*'lutroo'*) us from all iniquity" (Titus 2: 14); we are "not **redeemed** (*'lutroo'*) with corruptible things as silver and gold ... but with the precious blood of Christ" (1 Peter 1:18).

If, after verses 26-28, Paul concluded: "that no flesh should glory in his presence", verse 29, now, after verse 30, he concludes: "That, according as it is written, He that glorieth, let him glory in the Lord" v.31. Certainly, "let no man glory in men" (3:21). Not in Paul ... Apollos ... Cephas. We are indebted to **the Lord** for everything. This was God's settled purpose, and Paul takes his supporting text from the prophecy of Jeremiah. Here is the complete passage: "Thus saith the LORD, Let not the wise man glory in his wisdom, neither let the mighty man glory in his might, let not the rich man glory in his riches: but let him that glorieth glory in this, that he understandeth and knoweth me, that I am the LORD which exercise lovingkindness, judgment and righteousness in the earth: for in these things I delight, saith the LORD" (Jeremiah 9:23-24).

1 CORINTHIANS

"Not with excellency of speech or of wisdom"

Read Chapter 2:1-5

In our previous studies we have noted, more than once, that in the former part of the epistle (Chapters 1-6) Paul addresses two dangers which had arisen at Corinth.

The first danger lay with **the cliques among them, Chapters 1-4**. "It hath been declared unto me of you, my brethren … that there are contentions among you. Now this I say, that every one of you saith, I am of Paul; and I of Apollos; and I of Cephas; and I of Christ" (1 Corinthians 1:11-12).

The second danger lay with **the immorality among them, Chapters 5-6.** "It is reported commonly that there is fornication among you, and such fornication as is not so much as named among the Gentiles, that one should have his father's wife" (1 Corinthians 5:1). This is followed by a warning against involvement with the temple prostitutes (1 Corinthians 6:13-20).

In dealing with the first of these, Paul highlights the sad spiritual results: "There is among you envying and strife, and divisions" (1 Corinthians 3:3-4), and goes on to say: "Therefore let no man glory in men …" (1 Corinthians 3:21). Paul's object in Chapters 1-4 is to demonstrate that the believers at Corinth had no reason to "glory in men", and every reason to "glory in the Lord" (1 Corinthians 1:31). Only then could they "all speak the same thing", and be "perfectly joined together in the same mind and in the same judgment" (1 Corinthians 1:10). He deals with this in four ways:

1) He reminds them of the way in which they had been saved, Chapter 1:18-31

The way which they had been saved, together with the type of people who are saved, gave no reason to glory in men. In this connection, we noted the following:

When referring to the **way** in which people are saved, Paul writes: "Where is the wise? where is the scribe? where is the disputer of this world? hath not God made foolish the wisdom of this world? For after that in the wisdom of God, the world by wisdom knew not God, it pleased God by the foolishness of preaching to save them that believe. For the Jews require a sign, and the Greeks seek after wisdom: but we preach Christ crucified, unto the Jews a stumblingblock, and unto the Greeks foolishness; but unto them which are called, both Jews and Greeks, Christ the power of God, and the wisdom of God. Because the foolishness of God is wiser than men; and the weakness of God is stronger than men" (1 Corinthians 1:20-25).

When referring to the **type** of people, generally speaking, who are saved, Paul observes: "For ye see your calling, brethren, how that not many wise men after the flesh, not many mighty, not many noble, are called: but God hath chosen the foolish things of the world, to confound the wise ... that no flesh should glory in his presence. But of him are ye in Christ Jesus, who of God is made unto us wisdom, and righteousness, and sanctification, and redemption: that, according as it is written, He that glorieth, let him glory in the Lord" (1 Corinthians 1:26-31).

We should notice that in these verses Paul discusses what the Corinthian believers were **not** by nature - so there was no reason for them to glory in themselves (vv.26-29), and what they **were** by grace - so there was every reason for them to glory in the Lord (vv.30-31).

2) He reminds them of the way in which he had preached, Chapter 2:1-16

The way in which he had proclaimed the gospel at Corinth, and the way in which he taught them after they were saved, gave no reason to glory in men. The manner of Paul's preaching and the content of his preaching left no room for human glory, either on Paul's part or on the part of the Corinthians themselves.

3) He reminds them of the way in which the assembly had been established, Chapter 3:1-11

The way in which the assembly had been planted at Corinth left no reason to glory in men. The men responsible for establishing the assembly were simply servants. They were directed by God. The assembly at Corinth was "God's husbandry" and "God's building" (v.9). How could they then say: "I am of Paul … I am of Apollos" (v.4)?

4) He reminds them of the time when God's servants will be assessed, Chapter 4:1-6

This will be at the judgment seat of Christ, and all assessment must be left until then. "Therefore judge nothing before the time, until the Lord come" (v.5). Having said: "Let a man so account of us as of the ministers ('servants') of Christ" (v.1), Paul continues: "that ye may learn in us not to think of men above that which is written" (v.6). By 'glorying in men' ("I am of Paul … of Apollos … of Cephas …"), the believers at Corinth were proudly saying that they had the ability to assess servants of God, something only the Lord Himself could rightly undertake.

Having noticed, in **Chapter 1**, how the believers at Corinth had been saved (human wisdom could never have visualised salvation through a Man on a cross), and invited them to take a good look at themselves (human wisdom would not have selected people like them), Paul now, in **Chapter 2**, goes further, and emphasises that the manner of his preaching and the content of his teaching left no reason for them to glory in him. In both cases, he did nothing and said nothing to foster their admiration. His ministry was devoid of worldly wisdom, but it was permeated by divine wisdom. His ministry was devoid of impressive oratory, but it was stamped by divine power. Whether preaching the gospel or teaching the converts, Paul's ministry was in the power and wisdom of the Holy Spirit (vv.4, 10, 11, 12, 13, 14).

The Chapter clearly falls into two sections: *(1)* how Paul preached the gospel (vv.1-5); *(2)* how Paul taught the saints (vv.6-16).

In the first case, Paul says: "For I determined not to know anything *among you*, save Jesus Christ, and him crucified" (v.2). These verses emphasise the wisdom Paul did *not* use: "I came *not* with excellency of speech or of wisdom" (v.1); "my speech and my preaching was *not* with enticing words of man's wisdom" (v.4); "that your faith should *not* stand in the wisdom of men" (v.5).

In the second case, he says: "Howbeit we speak wisdom *among them* that are perfect" (v.6). These verses emphasise the wisdom that Paul **did** use: "Howbeit we speak wisdom among them that are perfect" (v.6); "but we speak the wisdom of God in a mystery (v.7); "Which things also we speak, not in the words which man's wisdom teacheth, but which the Holy Ghost teacheth" (v.13).

1) HOW PAUL PREACHED THE GOSPEL, verses 1-5

We should notice five things here: *(a)* the method of Paul's preaching at Corinth (v.1); *(b)* the message Paul preached at Corinth (v.2); *(c)* the manner in which Paul preached at Corinth (v.3); *(d)* the might (or power) of Paul's preaching at Corinth (v.4); *(e)* the motive (or purpose) of Paul's preaching at Corinth (v.5). Paul refers in these verses to his declaration (v.1), his determination (v.2), and to the demonstration (v.4).

a) The method of Paul's preaching at Corinth, v.1

"And I, brethren, when I came to you, came not with excellency of speech or of wisdom, declaring unto you the testimony of God."

The word translated "excellency" (a noun, '*huperoche*'), is rendered "authority" in 1 Timothy 2 verse 2 ("all that are in *authority*"). It occurs as a verb in Philippians 3 verse 8 ("the *excellency* of the knowledge of Christ Jesus my Lord"), and means, literally: "the act of overhanging ... or the thing which overhangs, hence, superiority, pre-eminence" (W.E. Vine). The word "speech" ('*logos*') refers to the **conveying** of the message, and the word "wisdom" to the **content** of the message.

We learn from this that Paul did not resort to impressive speech or impressive argument in his preaching. He made no deliberate appeal to human wisdom in this way. Here is a weighty piece from Ian Steele (*Assembly Testimony*, March/April 2011): "The late Jack Hunter said in his analysis of this passage, 'Let us learn the lesson that we can never make Christ or the gospel popular to men'. We must therefore be extremely cautious not to be governed by what unbelievers think, neither in our preaching nor assembly practice! There is a tendency that says, 'Give them what they want and they will listen to what we have to say'. Make it more attractive and appealing and talk to them in their own terms and they will understand! This is human logic and not Divine instruction". Ian Steele continues: "Let us be clear that they did not understand the preaching even of the Lord Jesus, as John 8 would illustrate. The Lord asked the Jews, 'Why do ye not understand my speech? even because ye cannot hear my word' (v.43). This had nothing to do with the message or the words He used. It was because of a basic inability in them and indeed in all unbelievers, 'ye **cannot** hear'. In verse 47, He further amplifies this fact, 'He that is of God heareth God's words; ye therefore hear them not because ye are not of God'. Our preaching then is not to be determined by the **understanding** of the unbeliever. Neither is it to be governed by the **acceptance** of the unbeliever. Again in John chapter 8 it is evident that the preaching of the Lord Jesus was not acceptable to them for they took up stones to stone Him (v.59)".

The words: "declaring (proclaiming) unto you the testimony of God" reminds us that in preaching the gospel we are "bearing witness to given facts ... Preaching the gospel is not delivering edifying discourses, beautifully put together. It is bearing witness to what God has done in Christ for man's salvation" (Leon Morris). We must never forget that the gospel is "the gospel of God" (Romans 1:1). It is equally "the gospel of Christ" (Romans 1:16). It is "the gospel of the glory of the blessed God" (1 Timothy 1:11, RV), and "the gospel of the glory of Christ" (2 Corinthians 4:4, RV).

Paul has already used the word *'marturion'* in saying: "even as the *testimony* of Christ was confirmed in you" (1 Corinthians 1:6). It was "the witness sourced and characterised in God Himself. Note well these two principles - sourced from God, and characterised by God. It is from Him we receive our words, matter and message and what we say must bear witness to and be in character with His holy and divine attributes and Presence!" (Ian Steele).

In some manuscripts the word *'musterion'* is used instead of *'marturion'*, and this reading is adopted by the Revised Version: "proclaiming to you the **mystery** of God". W.E. Vine, who espouses this view, states that "it denotes the mystery of the gospel as embodied in and proclaiming and revealing Christ". He suggests that this is "agreeable with the teaching in verses 7-16, particularly verse 7". Speaking generally, the word "mystery" refers to something outside natural apprehension and made known by divine revelation. Hence it is the antithesis of human wisdom. If this is the case here, then the 'mystery of God' may refer, bearing in mind the context, to the death of Christ - Christ crucified. See Chapter 1 verses 22-24. His death cannot be understood by human wisdom: its truth is divinely-revealed.

b) The message Paul preached at Corinth, verse 2

"For I determined not to know anything among you, save Jesus Christ, and him crucified."

Paul did not proclaim Christ as a teacher and example, or as a perfect man, but *"crucified"*. That is, Paul deliberately refused to broaden his preaching in order to accommodate his audiences: "But we preach Christ crucified, unto the Jews a stumblingblock, and unto the Greeks foolishness ..." (1 Corinthians 1:23).

In saying: "For I determined (resolved) not to know ...", Paul makes clear that he had weighed the issues and made his decision: he would not divert attention from "Jesus Christ and him crucified". He would not court popularity by making the gospel attractive to men. "Jesus Christ and him crucified" is offensive to the *Jewish* mind (their Messiah crucified - away with the thought!) and illogical to the *Greek* mind (a Saviour on a cross? - not sensible!). Paul did not cater for the wishes or aspirations of his audience. It should be said that he "determined not to know anything among you, save Jesus Christ, and him crucified", for the simple reason that there was no other way in which men and women could be saved!

The lesson for us is clear: however unpopular, we must continue to preach God's Word, and only God's Word: nothing more and nothing less. In Paul's words elsewhere: "Preach the word; be instant ('constantly ready') in season, out of season ..." (2 Timothy 4:2). As far as unsaved people are concerned, there is hardly ever a 'convenient time' to proclaim the Gospel!

c) The manner in which Paul preached at Corinth, verse 3

"And I was with you in weakness, and in fear, and in much trembling." Paul could well be referring here to discouragement *en route* to Corinth. "At Philippi he had had a promising beginning smashed by opposition from fanatical Jews. The same thing had happened at Thessalonica and Berea. In Athens he had little success" (Leon Morris). However, it seems more likely that he is referring to his experiences at Corinth itself. See Acts 18 verses 6-10: "And when they opposed themselves, and blasphemed ... Then spake the Lord to Paul in the night by a vision, Be not afraid, but speak, and hold not thy peace: for I am with thee, and no man shall set on thee to hurt thee ..." However, it is worth noting John Heading's suggestion that Paul "was in fear and trembling lest his inborn natural ability should tend to displace the spiritual power of God working through him". This finds support in the following verse: "And my speech and my preaching was not with enticing words of man's wisdom, but in demonstration of the Spirit and of power" (v.4).

Human weakness does not spell disaster for the servant of God. We must listen to Paul again: "For this thing (the 'thorn in the flesh') I besought the Lord thrice, that it might depart from me. And he said unto me, My grace is sufficient for thee: for *my strength is made perfect in weakness.* Most gladly therefore will I rather glory in my infirmities, that the power of Christ may rest upon me. Therefore I take pleasure in infirmities, in reproaches, in necessities, in persecutions, in distresses for Christ's sake: for *when I am weak, then am I strong*" (2 Corinthians 12:8-10). Our weakness serves only to make us rely more completely on the Lord. Service for God ought always to be undertaken with a deep sense of our own limitations and frailty. As William MacDonald observes: Paul himself "was an example of how God uses weak things to confound the mighty".

Perhaps Paul is emphasising this fact for the benefit of the faction at Corinth which said: "I am of Paul". They had no reason to glory in him. He was not a kind of superman, but subject to the weaknesses and fears of men generally. He did not visit Corinth brimming over with self-confidence. There were, however, at least some alleged believers in Corinth who were not at all impressed with him: "For his letters, say they, are weighty and powerful; but his bodily presence is weak, and his speech contemptible" (2 Corinthians 10:10). Perhaps they said that because he did not come "with excellency of speech or wisdom" (1 Corinthians 2:1), or "with enticing words of man's wisdom" (1 Corinthians 2:4).

d) The power of Paul's preaching at Corinth, verse 4

"And my speech (*'logos'*, word) and my preaching (*'kerugma'*) was not with enticing words (*'peithos'*, 'persuasive words'*) of man's wisdom, but in demonstration of the Spirit and of power (*'dunamis').*" The words: "speech" (or 'word') and "preaching" refer respectively to: the **conveying** of the message and the **content** of the message. The word "preaching" (*'kerugma'*) denotes: "a proclamation by a herald … a message, a preaching (the substance of what is preached as distinct from the act of preaching)" (W.E. Vine).

Paul's reference to 'persuasive words' emphasises that he did not rely on his own skill in argument or persuasion, or, in the words of W.E. Vine, on "the attempted methods of proof by rhetorical arts and philosophical arguments". There are two types of persuasion: one is human, as here: the other is divine as, for example, in Acts 13 verse 43 (Paul and Barnabas "persuaded (*'peitho'*) them to continue in the grace of God"); Acts 19 verse 8 (Paul "spake boldly for the space of three months, disputing and persuading (*'peitho'*) the things concerning the kingdom of God"). "Paul is certainly not rejecting preaching, even persuasive preaching (his sermon before Agrippa in Acts 26 is a remarkable example of persuasive preaching): rather he is rejecting any reliance on the preacher's ability to persuade with human wisdom" (supplied by Justin Waldron).

The word "demonstration" means 'a showing forth', in this case 'a showing forth of the Spirit and of power'. Paul's preaching was "in demonstration of the Spirit and of power", not in the sense that Paul was a powerful preacher, but in the *results* of his preaching. While it could certainly be said that Paul preached out of conviction wrought within him by the Spirit of God, and that the power of his preaching was that of the Holy Spirit, the particular emphasis here is on the *proof* that his ministry was in the power of the Holy Spirit. For this we have only to read Luke's record of Paul's visit to Corinth: "Crispus, the chief ruler of the synagogue, believed on the Lord with all his house; and many of the Corinthians hearing believed, and were baptized" (Acts 18:8). W.E. Vine points out that the word rendered "demonstration" (*'apodeixis'*), only found here in the New Testament, "literally signifies 'a showing forth': it has the force of a proof". Leon Morris makes the point that "it is possible for arguments to be logically irrefutable, yet totally unconvincing", but "Paul's preaching carried conviction because of the power of the Holy Spirit". It has been nicely said that "Paul knew that it is the preacher's job to preach, and that it is the Holy Spirit's job to demonstrate" (supplied by Justin Waldron).

In this connection, we should notice that the article ("the") is absent in the Greek text, which reads, literally: 'in demonstration of Spirit and of power', leading W.E. Vine to point out that this stresses: "the character of the power (i.e., the Holy Spirit's power in operation)".

All this reminds us that "If any man speak, let him speak as the oracles of God; if any man minister, let him do it as of the ability which God giveth: that God in all things may be glorified through Jesus Christ, to whom be praise and dominion for ever and ever. Amen" (1 Peter 4:11). The gospel preacher will not attempt to persuade his hearers by human reasoning, but wait upon

God to apply the word by the Spirit to heart and conscience. Hence we read: "For our gospel came not unto you in word only, but also in power, and in the Holy Ghost" (1 Thessalonians 1:5).

e) The purpose of Paul's preaching at Corinth, verse 5

"That your faith should not stand in the wisdom of men, but in the power of God." As J. Hunter so rightly points out: "If the preaching had been marked by clever arguments and secular wisdom and powerful eloquence, then the 'converts' would have been at the mercy of a more clever man with a superior show of logic and oratory, and thus would have had no settled peace. But Paul, in his simple, direct approach in the power of the Spirit, had grounded their faith in the power of God which guaranteed permanence, and rendered them independent of human wisdom".

The word "in" ("*in* the power of God") indicates where faith has its roots. While the "wisdom of men" can be overthrown by a better argument, the "power of God", that is, what has been wrought by the Spirit of God, cannot be overthrown.

In conclusion, we should notice the involvement of the Godhead in Paul's gospel preaching:

- The source of Paul's preaching - "the testimony of **God** " (v.1).

- The content of Paul's preaching - "**Jesus Christ** " (v.2).

- The power of Paul's preaching - "**the Spirit** " (v.4)

Having noticed the way in which Paul preached the gospel (vv.1-5), we must next consider how Paul taught the saints (vv.6-16).

1 CORINTHIANS

"We speak the wisdom of God in a mystery"

Read Chapter 2:6-16

We could write over Chapters 1-4 the words: "that ye might learn in us not to think of men above that which is written" (1 Corinthians 4:6). To prove that no one at Corinth had any reason to say: "I am of Paul … Apollos … Cephas", Paul points out in Chapter 1 that the way in which they had been saved and, generally speaking, the type of people who were saved, did not give any ground for 'glorying in men'. To say: "I am of Paul" was utterly wrong. They had not been saved through his wisdom. In Chapter 2, Paul goes further and points out that the preaching under which they were saved, and the teaching given after they were saved, did not give any grounds for 'glorying in men' either. To give Paul credit for his preaching and teaching was, again, utterly wrong. Neither flowed from his wisdom.

In outlining Chapter 2, we suggested that the passage clearly falls into two parts: *(1)* how Paul preached the gospel (vv.1-5); *(2)* how Paul taught the saints (vv.6-16).

1) HOW PAUL PREACHED THE GOSPEL, verses 1-5

In this connection, we noticed the following: *(a)* the method of Paul's preaching at Corinth (v.1); *(b)* the message Paul preached at Corinth (v.2); *(c)* the manner in which Paul preached at Corinth (v.3); *(d)* the might (or power) of Paul's preaching at Corinth (v.4); *(e)* the motive (or purpose) of Paul's preaching at Corinth (v.5). This brings us to:

2) HOW PAUL TAUGHT THE SAINTS, verses 6-16

As Leon Morris observes: "Up to this point Paul has been insisting that the gospel owes nothing to human wisdom … But he does not mean that

Christianity is contemptible, and now proceeds to show something of its profundity and dignity. It embodies *the wisdom of God.* In the light of this all petty human wisdom fades away". Before we address the details of the passage, we must take time to notice the occurrences of: "**not** ... **but**" in the chapter. As J.M. Davies (*The Epistles to the Corinthians*) observes: "The apostle follows a common practice of teaching by contrasts": *(i)* "And my speech and my preaching was **not** with enticing words of man's wisdom, **but** in demonstration of the Spirit and of power" (v.4); *(ii)* "That your faith should **not** stand in the wisdom of men, **but** in the power of God" (v.5); (*iii*) "Howbeit we speak wisdom among them that are perfect: yet **not** the wisdom of this world ... **but** we speak the wisdom of God in a mystery" (vv.6-7); *(iv)* "Eye hath **not** seen, nor ear heard, neither have entered into the heart of man, the things which God hath prepared for them that love him. **But** God hath revealed them unto us by his Spirit" (vv.9-10); *(v)* "Now we have received **not** the spirit of the world, **but** the Spirit which is of God" (v.12); *(vi)* "Which things also we speak, **not** in words which man's wisdom teacheth, **but** which the Holy Ghost teacheth" (v.13); *(vii)* "But the natural man receiveth **not** the things of the Spirit of God: for they are foolishness unto him: neither can he know them, because they are spiritually discerned. **But** he that is spiritual judgeth all things, yet he himself is judged of no man" (vv.14-15).

Having said that his preaching was "in demonstration of the Spirit and of power: that your faith should not stand in the wisdom of men, but in the power of God" (vv.4-5), Paul now turns to the wisdom that he *did* use: "Howbeit we speak wisdom among them that are perfect: yet not the wisdom of this world, nor of the princes (*archon*, a ruler) of this world, that come to nought" (v.6). He emphasises that the wisdom he employed **was not his own**. They had therefore no reason to glory in him.

This section of the chapter may be divided as follows: *(a)* the use of divine wisdom (vv.6-8); *(b)* the revelation of divine wisdom (vv.9-11); *(c)* the purpose of divine wisdom (v.12); *(d)* the imparting of divine wisdom (v.13); *(e)* the recipients of divine wisdom (vv.14-16).

a) The use of divine wisdom, verses 6-8

"Howbeit we speak wisdom among them that are perfect: yet **not** the wisdom of this world, nor of the princes of this world that come to nought: **but** we speak the wisdom of God in a mystery, even the hidden wisdom, which

God ordained before the world unto our glory: which none of the princes of this world knew: for had they known it, they would not have crucified the Lord of glory."

The use of the word "howbeit" indicates that the emphasis of the Chapter is changing. In verses 1-5, Paul has been emphasising that he did not employ *human* wisdom in his preaching, but that is not to say that he never used wisdom at all. In his own words: "We speak wisdom among them that are perfect", the difference being that it was *divine* wisdom. It should be said, of course, that whether Paul was preaching the gospel or teaching the saints, he *always* used divine wisdom. In the first case, apart from "them which are called, both Jews and Greeks", the gospel message was a "stumblingblock" to the former and "foolishness" to the latter. In the second case, Paul refers to saved men and women who had the capacity to understand and enjoy the treasures of divine wisdom.

We should notice some further contrasts:

i) Paul contrasts two kinds of wisdom, verse 6. He contrasts "the wisdom of this world ('*aion*', meaning 'age')" (see also 1 Corinthians 1:20) and "of the princes ('*archon*', meaning 'rulers') of this world" (v.6) with "the wisdom of God" (v.7). Paul contrasts the wisdom of earthly rulers ("the princes of this world", v.6), with the wisdom of the Supreme Ruler ("God", v.7).

The "princes (rulers) of this world" are mentioned because they, above all people, ought to have exhibited more wisdom than anyone else. Some commentators, "both ancient and modern" (Leon Morris) suggest that "the princes of this world" are demons, but this can hardly be the case in view of what is said about them in verse 8. Demons certainly knew the identity of the Lord Jesus (see, for example, Mark 1:24, 34).

ii) Paul contrasts two kinds of people, verse 6. He contrasts "them that are perfect" with "the princes of this world". The word "perfect" ('*teleios*') means 'full grown' or 'mature'. Perhaps there is a touch of irony here: the believers at Corinth were behaving in a most immature way (see 1 Corinthians 3:1-4). Some hold that Paul is referring here to saved men and women ("them that are perfect") as opposed to unbelievers, but this hardly seems likely. Leon Morris must be right in saying that Paul "simply recognises the facts". Not all Christians have full understanding. He refers to "babes" among them (1 Corinthians 3:1). "The wisdom of which he speaks is appreciated by those who are mature in the faith. To them he can impart 'all the counsel of God' (Acts 20:27) … When men first believe they do not all at once grasp the full implications of the faith. At first all are 'babes'. But the way to advance is open to everyone. There is no spiritual truth that is not available for even the humblest believer to appropriate" (Leon Morris). By contrast "the princes of this world" have no conception of divine wisdom.

iii) Paul contrasts two destinations, verses 6-7. He contrasts the "princes of this world" which "come to nought (will be rendered inactive)" (v.6), with believers who are heading for "glory" (v.7). We cannot overlook the fact that in His incomparable wisdom, God had in mind "our glory", as we shall see next, "before the world"! The word rendered "ordained" ('*proorizo*') "denotes to mark out beforehand, to determine before" (W.E. Vine). Staggering, isn't it?!

iv) Paul contrasts two ages, verses 6-7. He contrasts "***this world*** ('aion', meaning 'age')" with its wisdom and princes, with God's sovereignty "***before the world***" ('before the ages' '*aion*')." Even more staggering!

v) Paul contrasts two conditions, verse 7. He is either contrasting the clarity of his preaching with the inability of man to understand it (it is "hidden" from him), or stating the fact that he is teaching what had been previously unrevealed. "But we speak the wisdom of God in a mystery, even the hidden wisdom …"

- As to the former, Leon Morris observes that "the word 'mystery' signifies a secret which man is wholly unable to penetrate. But it is a secret which God has now revealed … Paul describes the secret as the hidden wisdom emphasising the fact that men outside Christ are still in the dark about it. It is revealed to believers, but it is not a matter of common knowledge among the sons of men. It remains hidden from unbelievers", reminding us of the Lord's words: "Thou hast hidden these things from the wise and prudent, and hast revealed them unto babes" (Matthew 11:25-26).

- As to the latter, J.M. Davies makes the pertinent observation that Paul "states very clearly that the gospel had been the subject of promise and prophecy (Romans 1:1-2; Galatians 3:8). But the truth regarding the church, the union of Jew and Gentile in one body with the exalted Christ as its head, was a hidden mystery revealed only in New Testament times". This explanation does seem to be supported by what follows: "the hidden wisdom, which God ordained before the world unto our glory." Charles

Hodge (*1 & 2 Corinthians*) is most helpful here: "Having in verse 6 stated what this wisdom is not, he here states what it is. It is, first, the wisdom of God; secondly, it is mysterious or hidden; thirdly, it is a system of truth which God from eternity had determined to reveal for the salvation of His people. In other words, it is the revelation of the counsels of eternity in reference to the redemption of man".

vi) Paul contrasts two dignities, verse 8. "But we speak the wisdom of God in a mystery … which none of the princes of this world knew: for had they known it, they would not have crucified the Lord of glory." On the one hand we have: "the princes of this world" and on the other: "the Lord of glory".

- "The princes of this world." Paul's statement here about the ignorance of the "princes of this world" agrees with words of the Lord Jesus Himself: "Father, forgive them; for they know not what they do" (Luke 23:34). Notice what the Jews said in John 10 verse 33, but the 'dying thief' evidently knew who He was (Luke 23:42). "The act and the attitude of 'the princes of this world' exhibit a complete, not to say wilful, ignorance of the nature, character and grandeur of the Lord and of the purpose which He came to accomplish" (W.E. Vine). We should add that it was in the wisdom of God that they did not know it. "In the wisdom of God, the world by wisdom knew not God" (1 Corinthians 1:21). The Lord Jesus is "the Prince (*'archegos'*, author) of life" (Acts 3:15).

- "The Lord of glory." We cannot fail to note the contrast: they "crucified the Lord of glory": crucifixion, with all its degradation and shame; "the Lord of glory", said to be "the loftiest title Paul ever applies to Christ". Paul certainly assigned to Christ "the highest place of all" (Leon Morris). Compare Acts 7 verse 2, "The God of glory"; Psalm 24 verses 7-10, "the King of glory". The words: "They … crucified the Lord of glory" are reduced to two words by Matthew: "And sitting down they watched *him there*" (Matthew 27:36).

b) The revelation of divine wisdom, verses 9-11

"But as it is written, Eye hath not seen, nor ear heard, neither have entered into the heart of man, the things which God hath prepared for them that love him. But God hath revealed them unto us by his Spirit: for the Spirit searcheth all things, yea, the deep things of God. For what man knoweth the things of a man, save the spirit of man which is in him? Even so the things of God knoweth no man, but the Spirit of God."

We should notice here *(i)* what has been revealed (v.9), and *(ii)* how it has been revealed (vv.10-11).

*i) **What has been revealed, verse 9.*** "But as it is written, Eye hath not seen, nor ear heard, neither have entered into the heart of man, the things which God hath prepared for them that love him."

The 'flow' of the passage becomes clear when we read verses 7-9 as follows: "But we speak the wisdom of God in a mystery … which none of the princes of this world knew … But as it is written, Eye hath not seen, nor ear heard, neither have entered into the heart of man, the things which God hath prepared for them that love him. But God hath revealed them unto us by his Spirit". Since God's eternal purpose for His people is "a mystery", it is 'hidden wisdom', it cannot be understood by natural faculties ("Eye hath **not** seen, nor ear heard …"), but only as it is revealed by God ("**But** God hath revealed them unto us by his Spirit"). It is through Him that we acquire this heavenly and divine wisdom.

Verse 9 cites Isaiah 64 verse 4: "For since the beginning of the world men have not heard, nor perceived by the ear, neither hath the eye seen, O God, beside thee, what he hath prepared for him that waiteth for him". The words "beside thee" emphasise that this was divinely sealed and not made known to men, which is not at all surprising when we read on: "Behold, thou art wroth; for we have sinned … But we are all as an unclean thing, and all our righteousnesses are as filthy rags …." (Isaiah 64:5-6). Ezekiel was told: "Son of man, behold with thine eyes, and hear with thine ears, and set thine heart upon all that I shall shew thee …" (Ezekiel 40:4). What Ezekiel was to see and hear was previously unrevealed, but was now to be made known to him by the Lord.

We are told that "in the last days perilous times shall come" and "men shall be lovers of their own selves … ever learning and never able to come to the knowledge of the truth" (2 Timothy 3:1-7). But here Paul refers to those that love God. Through grace, we have responded to His love for us, and, wonder of wonders, He responds to our love for Him: "Eye hath not seen, nor ear heard, neither have entered into the heart of man, the things which God hath prepared for **them that love him**". Compare Romans 8 verse 28.

*ii) **How it has been revealed, verses 10-11.*** "But God hath revealed them unto us by his Spirit: for the Spirit searcheth all things, yea, the deep things of

God. For what man knoweth the things of a man, save the spirit of man which is in him? Even so the things of God knoweth no man, but the Spirit of God."

We must complete the often uncompleted quotation: "But God hath **revealed** them unto us (initially to the apostles and prophets, and through them to the Lord's people generally) by his Spirit". That is, we **do** know "the things which God hath prepared for them that love him". We could not have known them, however, apart from the ministry of the Holy Spirit. The words "unto us" are important. These things have been made known, not to "learned philosophers" but to "humble Christians" (Leon Morris). Not that this should give us any sense of superiority: it is not because of our skill or wisdom that we know these things, but solely due to the fact that God has revealed them to us by the Holy Spirit.

The ability of the Holy Spirit to reveal divine truth to us is explained as follows: "for the Spirit searcheth all things, yea, the deep things of God. For what man knoweth the things of a man, save the spirit of man which is in him? Even so the things of God knoweth no man, but the Spirit of God" (vv.10-11). Amongst other things, this emphasises His personality and His deity. The word "searcheth" does not mean searching in the sense of acquiring information not previously known to Him, but searching in the sense of scanning the counsels and purposes of God. In the words of Leon Morris: "It is a way of saying that He penetrates into *all things*". It stresses His complete knowledge and understanding. "In particular Paul specifies *the deep things of God. Deep* is often used of the mighty deeps of the sea, and thus comes to signify 'unfathomable'. It points to the impossibility of any creature knowing the innermost recesses of the divine counsel, 'the depths of God'. But they are known to the Spirit, and it is the Spirit who has revealed the truths of which Paul speaks" (Leon Morris).

The words: "For what man knoweth (*oida:* to see or perceive, to have fulness of knowledge) the things of a man, save the spirit of man which is in him? Even so the things of God knoweth (*oida*) no man, but the Spirit of God" (v.11), mean that just as it is impossible to know what is in a person's mind by external observation, since only the person concerned knows that, so it is impossible to know what is in the mind of God by external observation. Only the Spirit of God knows this. Hence Paul is teaching that it must be divine revelation. Put another way, as no one knows the thoughts of a man but the man himself, so no one knows the thoughts of God but God himself. Therefore no one but a divine Person is competent to reveal them.

c) The purpose of divine wisdom, verse 12

"Now we have received, **not** the spirit of the world, **but** the spirit ('Spirit', JND) which is of God; that we might know ('*oida*') the things that are freely given ('*charizomai*', to bestow graciously) to us of God." There was no reluctance on God's part in preparing "for them that love him". Everything is "freely given to us of God".

We are privileged to be in the good of the only means of knowing the mind of God! "That we might know the things that are freely given us of God." We are told that this is in the aorist tense: the things that have been once and for all given to us.

The verse emphasises what has been said in verses 9-11. We could put it like this: 'I have been telling you that divine things can only be known as they are revealed to us by the Holy Spirit. Now this is the very Holy Spirit that we have actually received. If it was the spirit of the world, then we could never know these things, but since it is the Spirit which is of God, we can know them'.

d) The imparting of divine wisdom, verse 13

"Which things also we speak, **not** in the words which man's wisdom teacheth, **but** which the Holy Ghost teacheth; comparing spiritual things with spiritual." While we must agree with Leon Morris in saying: "What the Christian receives, he passes on", Paul evidently refers here to the transmission of God's Word as revealed to His spokesmen.

Thus far Paul has spoken of reception of divine wisdom, now he speaks about its communication to others. If in verse 10 we have 'revelation' by the Holy Spirit, and in verse 12 'illumination' by the Holy Spirit, then in verse 13 we have 'inspiration' by the Holy Spirit (J.M. Davies). Paul received 'divine wisdom' through the Holy Spirit, and he imparted it by the Holy Spirit.

The words: "comparing spiritual things with spiritual" are not easily explained, but since the word "comparing" ('*sunkrino*') means 'to join fitly, to combine' (W.E. Vine), leading to the translation: "communicating spiritual [things] by spiritual [means]" (JND). According to Leon Morris, this depends on the gender of the second occurrence of 'spiritual' ('*pneumatikos*') being neuter. If it is masculine, then the meaning is conveyed by the RV footnote (supported by W.E. Vine) 'interpreting spiritual things to spiritual men'.

If Paul is referring here to his preaching in general, then we have to decide which of the two suggestions is more appropriate, but if Paul is referring to the inspiration of Scripture, then there is no doubt about the meaning. He is speaking about the verbal inspiration of Scripture, that is, that the "men used by God to write the Holy Scriptures did not use words of their own choosing, but put down the words as directed by God … The Holy Ghost supplies the language as well as the substance of revelation" (J. Hunter). It follows, of course, that divine truth must always be conveyed in a spiritual manner, not by means which appeal to men, nor by human ingenuity and wisdom.

e) The recipients of divine wisdom, verses 14-16

"The natural man (the unrenewed man: man under the influence of his fallen nature) receiveth **not** ('*dechomai'*, referring to a ready and favourable reception) the things of the Spirit of God: for they are foolishness unto him: neither can he know them, because they are spiritually discerned ('*anakrino'*). **But** he that is spiritual judgeth ('*anakrino'*) all things, yet he himself is judged ('*anakrino'*) of no man. For who hath known the mind of the Lord, that he may instruct him? But we have the mind of Christ."

It is a case of the natural man versus the spiritual man. As pointed out above the words "discerned … judgeth … judged" all translate the same word ('*anakrino'*). Because they are in possession of the Spirit of God and are taught by Him, the children of God (not just leaders and teachers) have the faculty of discerning and understanding spiritual things. The unsaved do not have this faculty. "The man whose equipment is only of this world, the man who has not received the Holy Spirit of God, has not the ability to make an estimate of things spiritual" (Leon Morris). They are "spiritually discerned", not 'rationally discerned'. The "natural man" might be an educated man, or a man with theological training, but he is still not fitted to receive and understand "the things of the Spirit of God".

The words: "But he that is spiritual judgeth all things, yet he himself is judged of no man" mean that while the spiritual man (the man indwelt by the Spirit of God) has the ability to make a right judgment about "all things", the "secular, as well as the sacred" (Leon Morris), the unregenerate man ("the natural man", v.14), who cannot understand divine things ("they are foolishness unto them", v.14), cannot understand the people who do understand divine things! Christians are a riddle to non-Christians. They cannot understand why we enjoy spiritual things. So we must not expect to be understood!

The closing words of the chapter: "For who hath known the mind of the Lord, that he may instruct him?", citing Isaiah 40 verse 13 ("Who hath directed the Spirit of the LORD, or being his counsellor hath taught him?"), emphasise what has already been said, namely, "the things of God knoweth no man". But the added words, "but by the Spirit of God" (v.11), indicate that believers do know "the mind of the Lord". Through the indwelling Holy Spirit, who "searcheth all things, yea, the deep things of God" (v.10) believers "have the mind of Christ". (The fact that "the mind of the Lord" in Paul's reference to the Old Testament, is the "mind of Christ" in the New Testament, emphasises the deity of the Lord Jesus). As Leon Morris points out, Paul does not mean by this "that the Christian is able to understand all the thoughts of Christ" but that the "spiritual man … does not see things from the viewpoint of the worldly. He sees them from the viewpoint of Christ".

1 CORINTHIANS

"Ye are God's husbandry, ye are God's building"

Read Chapter 3:1-11

As we have noted in several of our previous studies, Chapters 1-6 of the epistle are devoted to two dangers which had arisen at Corinth.

The first danger lay with **the cliques among them, Chapters 1-4**. "It hath been declared unto me of you, my brethren … that there are contentions among you. Now this I say, that every one of you saith, I am of Paul; and I of Apollos; and I of Cephas; and I of Christ" (1 Corinthians 1:11-12).

The second danger lay with **the immorality among them, Chapters 5-6.** "It is reported commonly that there is fornication among you, and such fornication as is not so much as named among the Gentiles, that one should have his father's wife" (1 Corinthians 5:1). This is followed by a warning against involvement with the temple prostitutes (1 Corinthians 6:13-20).

In dealing with the first of these, Paul highlights the sad spiritual results: "There is among you envying and strife, and divisions" (1 Corinthians 3:3-4), and goes on to say: "Therefore let no man glory in men …" (1 Corinthians 3:21). Paul's object in Chapters 1-4 is to demonstrate that the believers at Corinth had no reason to "glory in men", and every reason to "glory in the Lord" (1 Corinthians 1:31). Only then could they "all speak the same thing", and be "perfectly joined together in the same mind and in the same judgment" (1 Cor. 1: 10). He deals with this in four ways:

- He reminds them of the way in which they had been saved, Chapter 1: 18-31. The way in which they had been saved (1 Corinthians 1:18-25), together with the type of people, generally speaking, who are saved (1 Corinthians 1:26-31), gave no reason to "glory in men". Having emphasised that their salvation and calling were divine, Paul concludes, firstly: "That no flesh should glory in his (God's) presence" and, secondly: "That, according as it is written, He that glorieth, let him glory in the Lord" (1 Corinthians 1:29, 31).

- He reminds them of the way in which he had preached, Chapter 2: 1-16. The way in which he had proclaimed the gospel at Corinth (1 Corinthians 2:1-5), and the way in which he taught them after they were saved (1 Corinthians 2:6-16), gave no reason to glory in men. The manner of Paul's preaching and the content of his preaching left no room for human glory, either on Paul's part or on the part of the Corinthians themselves.

- He reminds them of the way in which the assembly had been established, Chapter 3: 1-11. The way in which the assembly had been planted at Corinth left no reason to glory in men. The men responsible for establishing the assembly were simply servants. They were directed by God. The assembly at Corinth was "God's husbandry" and "God's building" (v.9). How could they then say "I am of Paul … I am of Apollos"? (v.4).

- He reminds them of the time when God's servants will be assessed, Chapter 4:1-6.
This will be at the judgment seat of Christ, and all assessment must be left until then. "Therefore judge nothing before the time, until the Lord come" (v.5). Having said: "Let a man so account of us as of the ministers ('servants') of Christ" (v.1), Paul continues: "that ye may learn in us not to think of men above that which is written" (v.6). By 'glorying in men' ("I am of Paul … of Apollos … of Cephas …"), the believers at Corinth were proudly saying that they had the ability to assess servants of God, something only the Lord Himself could rightly undertake.

We have already dealt with Paul's teaching in Chapters 1-2, which brings us to the way in which the assembly had been established at Corinth. As before, this emphasises the wisdom of God rather than the wisdom of men.

Chapter 3 may be divided as follows: *(1)* the carnality of the Corinthians (vv.1-4); *(2)* the humility of the preachers (vv.5-11); *(3)* the quality of the work (vv.12-15); *(4)* the sanctity of the building (vv.16-17); *(5)* the futility of the wise (vv.18-20); *(6)* the immensity of the resources (vv.21-23).

In our current study, we will deal with the first two of these:

1) THE CARNALITY OF THE CORINTHIANS, verses 1-4

The word "carnal" occurs four times in this section, but there is an important difference in the underlying word: "And I, brethren, could not speak unto you as unto spiritual, but as unto **carnal ('sarkinos')** …For ye are yet **carnal ('sarkikos')**: for whereas there is among you envying, and strife, and divisions, are ye not **carnal ('sarkikos')**, and walk as men? For while one saith, I am of Paul; and another, I am of Apollos; are ye not **carnal ('sarkikos')**?" (vv.1, 3, 4). The Greek word *'sarkinos'* signifies: "partaking of the nature of the flesh", whereas *'sarkikos'* signifies: "under the control of the fleshly nature instead of being governed by the Spirit of God" (W.E. Vine).

Paul refers here to the situation described in Chapter 1: "It hath been declared unto me of you, my brethren, by them which are of the house of Chloe, that there are contentions among you. Now this I say, that every one of you saith, I am of Paul; and I of Apollos; and I of Cephas; and I of Christ" (vv.11-12). In our current passage (1 Corinthians 3:1-4), Paul describes the results of the situation, and reminds them of its cause. In this connection we must take the opportunity to notice Paul's three 'men': *(a)* the natural man; *(b)* the spiritual man; *(c)* and the carnal man (1 Corinthians 2: 4-15; 3:1).

a) The natural man

"But the **natural man** receiveth not the things of the Spirit of God: for they are foolishness unto him: neither can he know them, because they are spiritually discerned" (1 Corinthians 2:14). The "natural man" (the 'soulish' man) is the unrenewed man: man under the influence of his fallen nature: man in Adam. He might be an educated man, or a man with theological training, but he is still not fitted to receive and understand "the things of the Spirit of God". The underlying word (*'psuchikos'*) occurs elsewhere as follows: "**sensual**, having not the Spirit" (Jude v.19). He is an unregenerate man, and therefore unable to rise above the level of human understanding and desires. He lives only on that plain.

b) The spiritual man

Paul describes the spiritual man as: "**He that is spiritual** (*'pneumatikos'*)" (1 Corinthians 2:15). In the words of G.B. Fyfe: 'the pneumatic man!' He is the exact opposite of the "natural man". Because he is enlightened by God and indwelt by the Holy Spirit, he can appreciate spiritual realities. The association between "spiritual ('*pneumatikos*')" and the Holy Spirit ('*pneuma*') is clear. The "spiritual" man lives on a higher plain than the "natural man". In the words of W.E. Vine: "The spiritual man is one who walks by the Spirit both in the sense of Galatians 5:16 ('Walk in the Spirit, and ye shall not fulfil the lust of the flesh') and Galatians 5:25 ('If we live in the Spirit, let us also walk in the Spirit'), and who himself manifests the fruit of the Spirit in his own ways". We have a good example of a spiritual man in Psalm 1.

c) The carnal man

The carnal man is a person who, though in the good of the Spirit's presence and indwelling, is actuated by the desires of the natural man. In other words, a 'carnal man' is a 'spiritual man' behaving like a 'natural man' (A. Leckie). Hence: "for whereas there is among you envying, and strife, and divisions, are ye not **carnal** *('sarkikos')*, and **walk as men?**" (1 Corinthians 3:3).

We must now re-read verses 1-4, and make at least two observations in connection the 'carnal man' above:

i) To be carnal hinders spiritual growth. It was impossible for Paul to feed them with "meat" in the circumstances. In Paul's own words: "And I brethren, could not speak unto you as unto spiritual, but as unto carnal, even as unto babes in Christ. I have fed you with milk ('I have given you milk to drink', JND), and not with meat: for hitherto ye were not able to bear it, neither yet now are ye able" (vv.1-2). What follows is taken from the Mill Lane Bible Studies notes on Hebrews 5 verses 11-14 dating back to the mid-1980s:

"But what's the difference between 'milk' and 'meat'? Both are good wholesome foods - but are we talking about different doctrines - different subjects - when we talk about 'milk' and 'meat'? The difference between the two is not one of doctrine, but of the measure in which that doctrine is taught and understood. For example, we are all well aware of the fact that 'Christ died for our sins'. This is part of the spiritual ABC. We all start there - we **must** all start there. But the subsequent months and years of Bible reading have revealed more and more of the infinite dimensions of His great work at Calvary. Its implications for Himself, for God, for us, for the Jews, for the material world, for Satan … You see, we begin with milk - and progress to meat. It is the same wonderful truth - but its content and meaning grow in our hearts and minds. Baptism affords another example. The deeper implications of baptism become more and more apparent as we progress in spiritual understanding. We all began with the 'milk' and were baptised because it was the Lord's will. No better reason than that either: We **must** all begin there. But surely we know a great deal more about it now, don't we? You see, we're moving from 'milk' to 'meat'. The same truth, but understood at new levels".

A nutritionist at the time did some work on the difference between the two, and came up with the answer that that they are basically the same, but with this difference, that 'meat' is more '**energy-dense**' than 'milk'. That looks like a very helpful definition! How necessary it is to "grow in grace, and in the knowledge of our Lord and Saviour Jesus Christ" (2 Peter 3:18).

We, therefore, learn that "envyings and strife" ('jealousy and strife', RV) prevent spiritual nourishment, and so impede spiritual maturity. The saints feed on the trouble, and not on the Word of God.

ii)To be carnal means conformity to the world. It means that God's people "walk as men". So "envyings and strife ('*eris*', 'contentions', 1 Corinthians 1:11)" remove the distinction between believers and the world. What marks the world also marks God's people.

As noted above, the words: "Are ye not carnal and walk as men?" are explained: "For whilst one saith, I am of Paul: and another I am of Apollos, are ye not carnal?" (v.4). What does the world do? It glories in men, and follows men. It names its champions. At the present time in U.K. politics: 'I am of May … I am of Corbyn … I am of Sturgeon'. This recalls Mark 9 verses 33-35, where the disciples had "disputed among themselves who should be the greatest" (that was carnality) only to learn: "If any man desire to be first, the same shall be last of all, and the servant of all". But it happens in other ways: some Christians say in effect: 'I am of Calvin … I am of Arminius' or: 'I am of Darby … I am of Kelly'. And there we had better leave it!

Hence in verses 5-9, Paul discusses himself and Apollos. Since they were glorying in them, they ought to know a little more about them! They ought also to know a little more about their service! All of which brings us to:

2) THE HUMILITY OF THE PREACHERS, verses 5-11

The Corinthians gloried in men (v.4), but Paul and Apollos gloried in the Lord. In describing themselves as "ministers" (servants), Paul emphasises that their service was "even as **the Lord** gave to every man" (v.5). In describing their work, Paul emphasises that "**God** gave the increase" (vv.6-7), and that it was "according to the **grace of God** which is given unto me" (v.10) that he had "laid the foundation". Paul refers here **(a)** to the servants (v.5); **(b)** to their service (vv.6-11).

a) The servants, v.5

"Who then is Paul, and who is Apollos, but ministers by whom ye believed, even as the Lord gave to every man". We should note the following:

i) They were just "ministers", that is, servants. "Who then is Paul, and who is Apollos, but ministers (*'diakonoi'*) by whom ye believed", or "What then is Apollos? and what is Paul? Ministers through whom ye believed" (RV: JND concurs). It was not a question of **who** they were, but **what** they were: they were servants. Wigram's *Word Study Concordance* has a little note against '*diakonos*': '*diako*, to run errands'. How about that! Notice that Paul puts Apollos first (RV/JND). This must have shocked the party at Corinth who said, "I am of Paul"!

ii) "Even as the **Lord** gave to every man (to each man)". So the glory belongs to the Lord, not to Apollos and Paul. Compare 1 Corinthians 4 verse 7 ("What hast thou that thou didst not receive? Now if thou didst receive it, why dost thou glory, as if thou hadst not received it?"); Romans 12 verse 3 ("For I say, through the grace of God given unto me, to every man that is among you, not to think of himself more highly than he ought to think; but to think soberly, according as God hath dealt to every man the measure of faith").

b) Their service, vv.6-11

Paul describes their service in two ways: *(i)* labouring in the field (vv.6-8); *(ii)* laying the foundation (vv.10-11). The 'transition verse' (v.9) links the two aspects of service: "For we are labourers with God: ye are God's **husbandry**, ye are God's **building**". These verses clearly refer to service in connection with the local church.

i) Labouring in the field, vv.6-8. This emphasises the **co-operation** between the servants. There was no rivalry between Apollos and Paul, even if there was in the assembly!

- Paul. "I have planted" (v.6). Acts 18 verses 1-18 now becomes compulsory reading. Luke provides the historical background and we should notice that having "reasoned in the synagogue every sabbath, and persuaded the Jews and the Greeks", followed by Jewish opposition, Paul "continued there a year and six months, teaching the word of God among them" (vv.4, 11). 1 Corinthians 15 verses 1-3 tells us more.

- Apollos. "Apollos watered" (v.6). Acts 18 verses 27-28 also becomes compulsory reading: "And when he (Apollos) was disposed to pass into Achaia, the brethren wrote, exhorting the disciples to receive him: who, when he was come, helped them much which had believed through grace; for he mightily convinced the Jews, and that publicly, shewing by the scriptures that Jesus was Christ". The word "watered" refers, not to 'watering with our prayers' (good as that is), but to the way in which Apollos helped in developing and encouraging the assembly at Corinth. But this is not all:

- God. "But **God** gave the increase" (v.6). Amongst other things, this emphasises that the **servants have no power to secure blessing**. That is God's work. He does the "real work" (Leon Morris), and therefore the glory for successful service belongs to Him alone: the servant is quite powerless in himself. In Paul's own words, "So then neither is he that planteth any thing, neither he that watereth; but God that giveth the increase" (v.6). W.E. Vine has the following to say here: "The preacher ever needs to realize his own insignificance, and his entire dependence on God for fruit to his ministry". Paul must therefore have recognised that the fruit of his labour at Corinth was divinely given: "many of the Corinthians hearing, believed, and were baptized" (Acts 18:8).

It also emphasises that the **servants should not be regarded as rivals,** and they certainly should not regard each other as rivals. See v.4. Again, in Paul's own words, "Now he that planteth and he that watereth are one (literally 'one thing')" (v.8): "one in aim, interest and operation" (W.E. Vine). This is stressed in v.9: "we are labourers together with God" or "God's fellow-workmen" (JND), or "fellow-workers with one another in God's service" (Leon Morris). There is no hint of rivalry in 1 Corinthians 16: 12! As W.E. Vine observes, "God has called us into fellow-service, which demands both the realization of our unity and the need of attributing everything to Him in the service we render to Him".

We should also notice that while the servants are "one" *now*, their *future* reward will be individual: "*every man* shall receive *his own* reward (or 'wage') according to *his own* labour (toil)" (v.8). This should be carefully noted. While God gives "the increase", the servants receive the reward! But what exactly will God reward? The reward is not based on the blessing seen on the labour, but on *the labour itself*. The bestowal of blessing, or otherwise, is God's prerogative. The fact that some servants of God labour faithfully for years and perhaps never see outpoured blessing on their labour does not mean that their reward will be nil. It will be a case of: "Well done, thou good and *faithful* servant" (Matthew 25:21). How well are *we* labouring? Compare Ezekiel 2 verse 5.

Finally on the subject, and this brings us to the 'transition verse', servants of God *must regard themselves in that way, not as masters and lords.* (Elders must regard themselves in the same way, 1 Peter 5:3)). Paul declines any sectarian headship: "Ye are *God's* husbandry ('*georgian*': 'tillage' or 'cultivated field'), ye are *God's* building" (v.9). (We should be filled with holy awe when we gather; just think of it, we are "*God's* husbandry… *God's* building"!).

As already noted, Paul (v.9) now changes the figure in describing the local assembly from "God's *husbandry*", which involved planting and watering (vv.6-8), to "God's *building*", involving a foundation and a superstructure (vv.10-11). We come therefore to:

ii) Laying the foundation, vv.10-11. This emphasises the *care* of the servant. We shall see that the building is in fact a temple (vv.16-17). It is the dwelling place of God, and therefore special care is required. Here are the verses: "According to the grace of God which is given unto me, as a wise masterbuilder, I have laid the foundation, and another buildeth thereupon. But let every man take heed how he buildeth thereon. For other foundation can not man lay than that is laid, which is Jesus Christ". We should notice:

- The workman. Attention is drawn to his humility. Paul takes no credit for the work. It was "according to the *grace of God* which is given unto me" (v.10), which agrees with his earlier statement, "Who then is Paul. And who is Apollos, but ministers by whom ye believed, even as *the Lord gave* to every man" (v.5). Paul describes himself as "a wise master-builder ('*architekton*')". While our English word 'architect' certainly comes from the Greek word here, it actually means an *artificer* (a 'principal artificer') rather than an architect. Paul was given skill (according to W.E. Vine, the word

"wise" has that meaning) to labour at Corinth with reference to the plan of the divine Architect.

- The work. "I have laid the foundation" (v.10). As we have seen, this refers to his visit to Corinth described in Acts 18 verses 1-18. This passage enables us to see exactly how the foundation was laid: "He reasoned in the synagogue **every sabbath**, and persuaded the Jews, and the Greeks" (v.4); "He continued there **a year and six months**, teaching the word of God among them" (v.11); "And Paul, having tarried after this **yet many days**, took his leave of the brethren, and sailed thence for Syria" (v.18). It took a **long time** to lay that foundation! We should also notice that while at Corinth Paul was "pressed in spirit ('constrained by the word', RV)" (v.5). That is, he was in earnest. So he did not labour **casually**. Neither was he deterred by opposition (vv.12-18).

Having said, "I have laid the foundation", Paul continues: "another buildeth thereon. But let every man take heed how he buildeth thereupon" (v.10) or "But let each man take heed how he buildeth thereon" (RV). It has been pointed out that this does not mean 'every person' since Paul evidently has in mind teaching in the assembly. Compare Acts 4 verse 11: "This is the stone which was set at nought of you builders". The "builders" here were the "rulers…elders…scribes" at Jerusalem. Since Paul refers to the way in which the work was to be done ("let every man take heed **how** he buildeth thereupon") we can conclude that he is again warning against envy, rivalry, and a party spirit.

- The foundation. "For other foundation can no man lay than that is laid, which is Jesus Christ" (v.11). It does seem that the words, "But let every man take heed how he buildeth thereupon" are a parenthesis, and the main thrust of the passage lies in reading as follows: "According to the grace of God which is given unto me, as a wise masterbuilder, I have laid the foundation, and another ('*allos*', 'another of the same kind') buildeth thereupon…For other foundation can no man lay than that is laid, which is Jesus Christ". If this is the case, then the words, "But let every man take heed how he buildeth thereupon", are developed in vv.12-15.

Paul laid this foundation at Corinth, among other things, by testifying "to the Jews that Jesus was Christ" (Acts 18: 5). See, again, 1 Corinthians 15 verses 3-5: "For I delivered unto you first of all that which I also received, how that Christ died for our sins according to the Scriptures: and that he was buried, and that he rose again the third day according to the Scriptures. And that he was seen of Cephas, then of the twelve". Compare 1 Corinthians 1 verses 21-24.

As W.E. Vine points out: "The one foundation for each church is 'Jesus Christ', the Person, the historical Christ, the One who 'came forth from the Father', became man, was despised and rejected, and by His expiatory death and His burial, resurrection and ascension, is the Saviour of men". Each local church should be built on Him, and this necessitates understanding who He is, and what He has accomplished. Nothing else will do: "For *other foundation* can no man lay than ('besides', JND) that is laid, which is Jesus Christ". Compare Ephesians 2 verse 20. As Leon Morris observes: "This is still worthy of emphasis in a day when so many build their 'Christianity' without Christ, on a foundation of good works, or humanism, or science".

Having described the work *he* had done, Paul next describes the work *they* should be doing.

1 CORINTHIANS

"Every man's work shall be made manifest"

Read Chapter 3:12-23

In our previous study, we suggested that this Chapter may be divided as follows: *(1)* the carnality of the Corinthians (vv.1-4); *(2)* the humility of the preachers (vv.5-11); *(3)* the quality of the work (vv.12-15); *(4)* the sanctity of the building (vv.16-17); *(5)* the futility of the wise (vv.18-20); *(6)* the immensity of the resources (vv.21-23).

1) THE CARNALITY OF THE CORINTHIANS, vv.1-4

The Corinthians were acting "as men", that is, as 'natural men'. As already noted, the carnal man is a person who, though in the good of the Spirit's presence and indwelling, is actuated by the desires of the natural man. In other words, a 'carnal man' is a 'spiritual man' behaving like a 'natural man' (A. Leckie). The believers at Corinth gloried in their party politics, causing Paul to say: "For ye are yet carnal: for whereas there is among you envying, and strife, and divisions, are ye not carnal, and walk *as men*? For whilst one saith, I am of Paul: and another I am of Apollos, are ye not carnal?" They emulated the world, where people glory in men and follow men.

2) THE HUMILITY OF THE PREACHERS, vv.5-11

Paul and Apollos acted as 'spiritual men'. They claimed to be nothing but servants, ascribing all honour to God and to Christ. They only served "as *the Lord* gave to every man", and it was "*God* that giveth increase". Paul made it clear that it was only "according to the *grace of God* given unto me" that he was able to lay "the foundation" at Corinth. In this connection, we noticed that the assembly there was "*God's husbandry*" and "*God's building*". In the first case this involved labouring in the field (vv.6-8), and in the second, laying the foundation (vv.10-11).

The balance of the chapter discusses the character of assembly building. It is to be spiritual: not carnal. It is to have the qualities of "gold, silver, precious stones ('costly stones', RV), not "wood, hay stubble". This brings us to:

3) THE QUALITY OF THE WORK, vv.12-15

Paul discusses three things here: *(a)* the materials for the work (v.12); *(b)* the assessment of the work (v.13); *(c)* the reward for the work (vv.14-15).

a) The materials for the work, v.12

But first of all, who are the builders? The answer becomes clear as we ask and answer a second question - what is the foundation? Paul has made it clear that "other foundation can no man lay than that is laid, which is Jesus Christ" (v.11). But in what sense is He the foundation? We must let Paul answer the question: "I delivered unto you first of all that which I also received, how that Christ died for our sins according to the scriptures; and that he was buried, and that he rose again the third day according to the scriptures: and that he was seen ..." (1 Corinthians 15:3-5). The "foundation" comprised the doctrine concerning Christ, which we might call "the things concerning himself" (Luke 24:27). Paul, as "a wise masterbuilder", laid a firm doctrinal foundation at Corinth. Peter describes this foundation as: "a chief corner stone, elect, precious: and he that believeth on *him* shall not be confounded" (1 Peter 2:6.)

Bearing this in mind, we can conclude that 'builders' here are those who build on that doctrinal foundation, that is, the teachers in the assembly. This is the third of four references to the 'builders'. (The fourth reference is in verse 14.)

- We have noticed *where* the teachers are to build: "I have laid the foundation, and another buildeth thereon" (v.10). They build in the local church.

- We have noticed *how* they are to build: "But let every man take heed how he buildeth thereupon" (v. 10). In building there is to be no envy, rivalry, or party spirit.

- Now we must notice *what* they are to build: "Now if any man build upon this foundation gold, silver, precious stones, wood, hay, stubble ..." (v.12). After all, "the fire shall try every man's work of what *sort* it is". This raises two further questions -

i) Do the materials refer to particular doctrines? It does not seem necessary to press the details, but if we wish to do so, then *"gold"* might well remind us of the glory and Godhead of Christ. Its extensive use in the tabernacle and in the temple could support this suggestion. *"Silver"* might well remind us of the redemptive work of Christ. See, for example, Exodus 30: 11-16; 38: 25-28. *"Precious stones"* might well remind us of "the excellencies of the character of Christ" (W.E. Vine). While the word "precious" (*'timios'*) is elsewhere rendered 'costly' (RV/JND), there can be no doubt that *'timios'* does mean "precious stones", in the accepted sense, in such passages as Revelation 17:4; 18:12, 16; 21:19.

However, Charles Hodge suggests that "precious stones" here "mean stones valuable for building, such as granite and marble". Hodge continues: "Gold and silver were extensively employed in adorning ancient temples, and are therefore appropriately used as symbols of pure doctrine. Wood, hay, and stubble are the perishable materials out of which ordinary houses were made, but not temples. Wood for the doors and posts; hay, dried grass mixed with mud, for the walls; and straw for the roof". It is a case of short-term materials versus long-term materials. We, therefore, ask:

ii) Do the materials refer to doctrine generally? This is more likely as J.M. Davies (*The Epistles to the Corinthians*) observes: "The following differences may be noted in connection with the two kinds of materials. There is a vast difference in their *cost.* The first three are very expensive, while the others are cheap. There is also a difference in their *character.* Man cannot manufacture the first three, whereas the others are the product of nature. They represent what man can produce. Then again there is a great difference in their *construction.* Building with stones is slow and tedious, whereas a wooden structure with small bales of grass for walls and straw for a roof can be erected in a very short time. The vital difference is in their *combustibility.* Fire cannot affect the one, whereas it will quickly reduce the other to a handful of ashes. The materials cannot be taken to represent persons, saved or unsaved, as persons will not be subject to the fire. As the foundation is the doctrine concerning the person and redemptive work of Christ, so by analogy, the materials represent ministry, that which is intended to edify, to build up the assembly. That which corresponds to the first three is costly, sacrificial and time-absorbing in its preparation, whereas that which corresponds to the second group is not costly and fails to build that which is permanent and abiding". Notice some further comparisons:

- As to durability. "Gold, silver, precious stones." They will last. Not so "wood, hay, stubble". Games, entertainment, over-emphasised music are not durable. Bible study, prayer, fellowship are most durable.

- As to availability. "Gold, silver, precious stones" have to be mined or quarried. "Wood, hay, stubble" grow on the surface. One requires great effort to provide. The other is comparatively superficial.

- As to quality. "Gold, silver, precious stones" are marked by quality, not by quantity. The quality has value: the quantity has not.

Assembly building is not a matter of vying for personal position, or impressing others with the excellence of our personal qualities and superior wisdom, or attempting to surpass others. It is a matter of ministering in a way which will make the assembly the place where Christ's glory is seen. There is nothing so edifying to the saints, and so vital to building assembly character. "Wood, hay, stubble" represent the wisdom of men as outlined in earlier passages. This is the difference between spiritual building and carnal building.

b) The assessment of the work, v.13

"Every man's work shall be made manifest." For the day shall declare it, because it shall be revealed by fire, and the fire shall try every man's work of what sort it is." (It has been said that a recent fire at Corinth had destroyed the shacks of the poor, leaving the grand buildings intact.) We should notice the following:

- "Every man's work shall be made manifest". It is individual, not collective. See also verses 14 and 15: "If *any* man's work". The divine assessment will be personal. Compare 2 Corinthians 5 verse 10: "For we must all appear before the judgment seat of Christ, that *every one* may receive the things done in his body". Compare Romans 14 verse 12: "So then *every one of us* shall give account (not, 'an account') of *himself* to God". It will evidently be a private interview with the Lord. Compare the Lord Jesus and Peter (1 Corinthians 15:5): no details are given!

*- "Every man's work shall be made *manifest*." That is 'open to sight', 'visible' (*phaneros*). Compare 1 Corinthians 4 verse 5: "Therefore judge nothing before the time, until the Lord come, who both will bring to light the hidden

things of darkness, and will make **manifest** (*phaneroo*) the counsels of the heart".

- "For **the day** shall declare it." This is "the day of our Lord Jesus Christ". Here is the full quotation: "waiting for the coming of our Lord Jesus Christ: who shall confirm you unto the end, that ye may be blameless in **the day** of our Lord Jesus Christ". See other New Testament references to this day: for example, 1 Corinthians 5 verse 5; 2 Corinthians 1 verse 14; Philippians 1 verses 6 and 10; Philippians 2 verse 16 and 2 Timothy 4 verse 8. We must carefully differentiate between this "day", and the "day of the Lord" and "the day of God".

- "For the day shall **declare** it." "Declare" (*'deloo'*) means 'to make plain'. That is, "declare it" to the servant. The Lord, of course, already knows. "That 'day' will make clear what is obscure in the night, the present period" (J.M. Davies).

- "Because it shall be revealed by **fire**", or "because it is revealed in fire" (RV). "Fire" here refers to the holy character of God. See Hebrews 12 verse 18. All service will be tested by the character of God.

- "And the fire shall try every man's work of what **sort** it is." Not of what amount it is. Some servants of God served Him, so far as we can judge, for comparatively short periods. See, for example, John the Baptist and Joseph of Arimathaea. But this does not mean that all we are required to do is a good job for five minutes, and then nothing more!

c) The reward for the work, vv.14-15

"If any man's work **abide** which he hath built thereupon, he shall receive a reward. If any man's work shall be **burnt**, he shall suffer loss: but he himself shall be saved: yet so as by fire." It should be noted that this does **not** refer to the loss of salvation, but to the loss of reward. We should notice:

- "If any man's work **abide** which he hath built thereupon, he shall receive a reward." The nature of the reward is not stated. Revelation 3 verse 21 and Revelation 22 verse 5 will help.

- "If any man's work shall be **burnt**, he shall suffer loss…" The word "loss" here (*'zemioo'*) has the idea of a fine. According to W.E. Vine: "In Greek contracts a workman who put in bad work was fined; he was mulcted of his expected wage". W.E. Vine adds: "Let us see that it may not be so with us".

The expression, "so as by fire", means 'with difficulty'. In the words of Charles Hodge: "He will just escape with his life, as a man is rescued from a burning building". He continues: "Paul does not say, the man is to be saved by being purified by fire, but simply 'with difficulty', as the expression 'so as by fire' familiarly means". The deliverance of Lot illustrates the point here! The necessity for good workmanship lies in -

4) THE SANCTITY OF THE BUILDING, vv.16-17

We should notice the following: *(a)* dwelling in the temple (v.16); *(b)* defilement in the temple (vv.17).

a) Dwelling in the temple, v.16

Bearing in mind that assembly building is in view here, Paul emphasises the sacred character of the assembly. This underlines the importance of correct building, and emphasises why such work attracts such a searching test. Paul says: "Ye are the temple of God" or "Ye are *a* temple of God" (RV). The word "*temple*" occurs three times in verses 16-17. The local church, or local assembly, has the character of a holy temple, of which David said: "and in his temple doth everyone speak of his glory" (Psalm 29:9), or: "and in his temple every whit of it uttereth glory" (AV margin), or: "and in his temple every thing saith, Glory" (RV).

The interrogative form here: "Know ye not that ye are a temple of God?" stresses the fact that they should have borne this in mind. Notice other occasions in the epistle where the interrogative form is used: Chapters 5 verse 6; 6 verses 2, 3, 9, 15, 16, 19; 9 verses 13, 24. See also Romans 6 verses 3 and 16; Chapter 7 verse 1. These were things that God's people ought to have remembered.

We should notice that the word "temple" here ('*naos*') refers to the inner part of the temple or sanctuary: the place of worship. It corresponds to the inner part of the tabernacle where God dwelt. So the assembly is the dwelling place of God. It is regarded as the '*naos*': a most sacred place where God dwells by the Holy Spirit.

b) Defilement in the temple, v.17

"If any man **defile** the temple of God, him shall God **destroy**; for the temple of God is holy, which temple ye are." The words "defile" and "destroy" translate the same Greek word (*'phtheiro'*), meaning 'to corrupt or mar'. The assembly can be corrupted by evil doctrine and evil practice. This very epistle illustrates both. But what then of the words: "him will God **destroy**", bearing in mind its meaning 'to corrupt' or 'to mar'?

Whilst verses 13-15 have emphasised the acceptance or rejection of "man's work" at the judgment seat of Christ, verse 17 deals with the judgment of the believer personally. The context demands that Paul is referring to a believer here. The verse cannot, therefore, teach loss of salvation. The Lord Jesus stated: "I give unto them eternal life; and they shall never perish" (John 10:28). The fact that the word "destroy" means to 'destroy by corruption', or 'to mar', means that it cannot refer to the judgment seat of Christ, where the believer's work will be reviewed.

The verse must, therefore, refer to the government of God in the life of the believer. The words, addressed to believers, in Galatians 6 verses 7-8 are relevant: "Be not deceived; God is not mocked: for whatsoever a man soweth, that shall he also reap. For he that soweth to his flesh shall of the flesh reap corruption; but he that soweth to the Spirit shall of the Spirit reap life everlasting". The saints at Corinth had already witnessed the principle in their own assembly, though evidently without appreciating the significance of what had happened: see Chapter 11 verses 29-30.

Since, as already noted, the words "defile" and "destroy" translate the same original word (*'phtheiro'*), the verse, therefore, teaches us that if we corrupt or mar the assembly in any way, we must inevitably come under the government of God here and now on earth. By their behaviour, the saints at Corinth were defiling "the temple of God", and, therefore, stood in danger of chastening. Men were exalted at Corinth, and God would not permit those responsible for this to continue without intervention. We must guard against the introduction of anything that will mar the testimony of the assembly. To do so will entail consequences in our lives now, together with loss of reward at the judgment seat of Christ.

To corrupt or mar the local assembly is perilous. In the immediate context of the passage, the possibility of defiling the temple of God refers particularly to the party spirit which existed in the assembly at Corinth. Hence the teaching in verses 18-23, where Paul again censures the human wisdom which promoted that party spirit. This brings us to:

5) THE FUTILITY OF THE WISE, vv.18-20

The words "**wise**" and "**wisdom**" occur **five** times in these verses. "Let no man deceive himself. If any man among you seemeth to be wise in this world, let him become a fool, that he may be wise. For the wisdom of this world is foolishness with God. For it is written, He taketh the wise in their own craftiness. And again, The Lord knoweth the thoughts of the wise, that they are vain." We should notice the following:

- "If any man thinketh himself to be **wise in this world**", or "If any man thinketh that he is wise among you in this world (*'aion'*)" (RV). That is by introducing worldly wisdom into the assembly, particularly in extolling men, and in following them. As we have noted, unregenerate men boast in their parties and their leaders and, sadly, God's people at Corinth were doing the same. See verses 3-4. They were "puffed up for one against another" (Chapter 4:6, 18, 19; 5:2).

- "Let him become a **fool**, that he may be **wise**." As W.E. Vine observes: "To be wise as a follower of Christ, is to be a fool in the eyes of the world". Humility is not an impressive commodity so far as the world is concerned, but it reflects divine wisdom.

- "For the **wisdom** of this world is **foolishness** with God." J.M. Davies notes that this is "almost an echo of the words of Proverbs 3 verse 7, 'Be not wise in thine own eyes', and of Isaiah 5 verse 21, 'Woe to them that are wise in their own eyes'". As Leon Morris helpfully points out: "Their wisdom is nothing but *foolishness* in spiritual matters", something that Paul has already made clear. See Chapter 1 verses 18-25. Leon Morris continues: "Is this Paul's private opinion? Not at all. He quotes Scripture to drive home his point". This follows:

- "For it is written, He taketh the wise in their own **craftiness.** And again, The Lord knoweth the thoughts of the wise, that they are **vain** ('without result... fruitless...empty')" vv.19-20." The quotations are from Job 5 verse 13 and Psalm 94 verse 11 respectively. The **first quotation** is illustrated, as already noted, in Chapter 1 verses 18-25. "Paul does not minimise the capacity of the worldly wise in their own field. But he stoutly denies that their craftiness ('*panourgia*', literally 'all working') is of any avail against the might and wisdom of God" (Leon Morris). The **second quotation** emphasises that "the wise are unable to effect anything lasting. All their vaunted wisdom is concerned with things that pass away" (Leon Morris).

6) THE IMMENSITY OF THE RESOURCES, vv.21-23

"Therefore let no man glory in men. For all things are yours; whether Paul, or Apollos, or Cephas, or the world, or life, or death, or things present, or things to come; all are yours; and ye are Christ's; and Christ is God's." We must notice the following:

- "Therefore let no man **glory in men**" (v.21). This is exactly what they were doing at Corinth, see again 1: 12; 3: 5. To do this reflects worldly wisdom (vv.18-20). The men in whom they were glorying were but servants (v.5).

- "**For all things are yours ... all are yours**" (vv.21-22). That is, all things are arranged for your blessing, not "all things are yours" in the sense that we possess them. First of all, the benefit resident in Paul, Apollos, and Cephas, and the value of their service, belonged to **all** the saints. So the ministry of Paul did not belong only to those who said: "I am of Paul", but to every believer in the assembly, including those who said: "I am of Apollos ... Cephas".

But more than that, not only men, as Paul, Apollos, and Cephas, but literally, "**all things** are yours". They are also arranged for our blessing: they are all for our real welfare: all for our benefit: "the world, or life, or death, or things present, or things to come, all are yours". "The **world**" and all it contains; "**life**" with all its opportunities; "**death**" with its entrance into the presence of Christ (what a benefit indeed!); "**things present**", referring to all that we enjoy now; "**things to come**", all that lies ahead in eternity: all belongs to us: all is arranged for our benefit.

- "**And ye are Christ's**" (v.23). That is, for His pleasure. That is, all of the saints at Corinth belonged, not to Paul, Apollos or Cephas, but to **Christ.** What a marvellous incentive for unity in the assembly! None had a greater share in Him than anyone else. This is the final and complete answer to the situation described in Chapter 1 verse 12. It deals with those who said: "and I of Christ". In summary, **all** share in the benefits brought by the servants of God, and **all** belong to Christ.

- "***And Christ is God's***" (v.23). That is, for His pleasure. This does not infer the inferiority of the Lord Jesus, but relative position. John Heading has a nice piece here: "Rather it would refer to the Son, as the burnt offering alive again from the dead, received back by the Father into heavenly glory - the infinite possession of the Father, His well-beloved Son".

1 CORINTHIANS

"What hast thou that thou didst not receive?"

Read Chapter 4:1-21

In this chapter Paul presents his final reason why the believers at Corinth should not "glory in men" (1 Corinthians 3:21) or, to put it differently, why they should not be saying: "I am of Paul … I am of Apollos" (1 Corinthians 3:4). (See also 1 Corinthians 1:12.) For the last time in these studies, we should recall that:

- In Chapter 1, he reminds them of the way in which they had been saved (verses 18-31). The way in which they had been saved (verses 18-25), together with the type of people, generally speaking, who are saved (verses 26-31), gave no reason to "glory in men". Having emphasised that their salvation and calling were divine, Paul concludes, firstly: "That no flesh should glory in his (God's) presence" and, secondly: "That, according as it is written, He that glorieth, let him glory in the Lord" (verses 29, 31).

- In Chapter 2, he reminds them of the way in which he had preached (verses 1-16). The way in which he had proclaimed the gospel at Corinth (verses 1-5), and the way in which he taught them after they were saved (verses 6-16), gave no reason to glory in men. The manner of Paul's preaching and the content of his preaching left no room for human glory, either on Paul's part or on the part of the Corinthians themselves.

- In Chapter 3, he reminds them of the way in which the assembly had been established (verses 1-11). The way in which the assembly had been planted at Corinth left no reason to glory in men. The men responsible for establishing the assembly were simply servants. They were directed by God. The assembly at Corinth was "God's husbandry" and "God's building" (v. 9). Now:

- In Chapter 4, he reminds them of the time when God's servants will be assessed (verses 1-6). This will be at the judgment seat of Christ, and all assessment must be left until then: "Therefore judge nothing before the time, until the Lord come" (v. 5).

This Chapter may be divided as follows: *(1)* the assessment Paul desired (vv.1-5); *(2)* the application Paul made (vv.6-7); *(3)* the adversity Paul suffered (vv.8-13); *(4)* the affection Paul displayed (vv.14-17); *(5)* the authority Paul possessed (vv.18-21).

1) THE ASSESSMENT PAUL DESIRED, vv.1-5

In these verses Paul asserts that the believers at Corinth had no right to assess servants of God, and pass sentence upon them. Paul and Apollos (v. 6) were "ministers of *Christ*", and "stewards of the mysteries of *God*". They were accountable only to Him. Only the Lord could assess the service of His "ministers" and "stewards". We must notice: *(a)* the description of their service (vv.1-2); *(b)* the examination of his service (vv.3-5).

a) The description of their service, vv.1-2

"Let a man so account of us, as of the ministers of Christ, and stewards of the mysteries of God. Moreover it is required in stewards, that a man be found faithful." They were *(i)* men under authority; *(ii)* men bearing responsibility, and as such they should be, *(iii)* men marked by fidelity.

i) Men under authority. Paul and Apollos should be regarded as "the ministers of Christ". The word "ministers" ('*huperetes*', not '*diakonos*') signifies an "under rower" in a vessel, hence a "subordinate acting under another's direction" (W.E. Vine). The same word is used in Luke 4 verse 20 ("he closed the book, and he gave it again to the minister" or "the *attendant*", RV); Acts 13 verse 5 ("they had also John to their minister" or "as their *attendant*" (RV); Acts 26 verse 16 ("arise and stand upon thy feet: for to this end have I appeared unto thee, to appoint thee a *minister* and a witness...", RV). It has been pointed out that 'under rowers' must all row in harmony if the vessel is to make headway!

ii) Men bearing responsibility. They were also "stewards of the mysteries of God". The word "mysteries" refers to spiritual truths "outside the range of unassisted natural apprehension" but "made known in a manner and at a time appointed by God ... to those only who are illumined by His Spirit" (W.E. Vine). It is often pointed out that in common parlance a 'mystery' implies knowledge withheld, but in Scripture it refers to truth revealed. See 1 Corinthians 2 verse 7. Ephesians 3 verses 1-6 and Colossians 1 verses 24-27 now become compulsory reading.

A steward (*'oikonomos'*) denotes, primarily, "the manager of a household or estate" (W.E. Vine). He acted for his master. Amongst other things, an elder is a steward: "a bishop must be blameless as the **steward** of God" (Titus 1:7), and believers generally are described in the same way. They are to be "good **stewards** of the manifold grace of God" (1 Peter 4:10). As J.M. Davies observes: "This is suggestive of a position of responsibility, comparable to that of the Levites, who were to keep 'the charge of the tabernacle of testimony' (Numbers 1:53)". As noted above, this demands that 'stewards' should be:

iii) Men marked by fidelity. "Moreover, it is required in stewards, that a man be found faithful." Paul emphasises this elsewhere: "as we were allowed of God ('as we have been approved of God', RV) to be put in trust with the gospel, even so we speak; not as pleasing men, but God, which trieth our hearts" (1 Thessalonians 2:4). The Lord Jesus emphasised the need for faithfulness in His 'parable of the pounds', where each servant was given one pound each, suggesting equality of opportunity (Luke 19:12-27), and in His parable of the talents, where the servants were given differing amounts (five - two - one: "every man according to his several ability") emphasising diversity of ability (Matthew 25:14-30).

One day the Lord will say to us: "Give an account of thy stewardship (*'oikonomia'*)" (Luke 16:2). Joseph was a faithful steward (Genesis 39:4). Stewardship implies accountability, and this follows. Having noted the pre-requisite in stewards, Paul now deals with the assessment of that stewardship. This brings us to:

b) The examination of his service, vv.3-5

Paul deals with this in three ways: *(i)* the examination of his stewardship by others (v.3a); *(ii)* the examination of his stewardship by himself (vv.3b-4a); *(iii)* the examination of his stewardship by the Lord (vv.4b-5).

i) The examination of his stewardship by others, v.3a. "But with me it

is a very small thing that I should be judged of you, or of man's judgment." The words: "man's judgment" are literally: 'man's day' ('*hemera*'), and we, therefore, learn that Paul was not concerned about the light men could throw upon his service. The term: 'man's day' (JND; RV margin) only occurs here. "It denotes the period during which world government has been put into man's hands" (J.M. Davies). Just as the day throws light on things in darkness, so Paul awaited another day - the day of the Lord's coming when He "will bring to light the hidden things of darkness". Paul has already referred to this day: see Chapter 1 verse 8 ("the day of our Lord Jesus Christ"); and Chapter 3 verse 13 ("the day shall declare it").

We should remember that Paul does not refer here to moral or doctrinal deficiency (in which cases judgment **does** have to be passed), but to the assessment of service.

ii) The examination of his stewardship by himself, vv.3b-4a. "Yea, I judge not mine own self. For I know nothing by myself; yet am I not hereby justified." Paul did not assess his own service. The fact that he knew nothing against himself (RV) - that is, he was not conscious of any charges against himself - did not necessarily mean that his service was beyond reproach.

We are, therefore, reminded, firstly, that we are not competent to assess and evaluate even our own service and, secondly, that we must not think that we are always beyond reproach. None the less, happy is the man who can say: "For I know nothing against myself". See Acts 23 verse 1: "I have lived in all good conscience before God until this day"; Acts 24 verse 16: "Herein do I exercise myself, to have always a conscience void of offence towards God, and toward men"; 2 Corinthians 1 verse 12: "For our rejoicing is this, the testimony of our conscience, that in simplicity and godly sincerity, not with fleshly wisdom, but by the grace of God, we have had our conversation in the world".

iii) The examination of his stewardship by the Lord, vv.4b-5. The only true assessment is by the Lord Himself. At this point we should ask, and answer, some questions:

- Who will make the assessment? "He that judgeth me is **the Lord**." Compare 2 Timothy 4 verse 8: "Henceforth there is laid up for me a crown of righteousness, which the Lord, the **righteous** judge, shall give me at that day".

- When will He make the assessment? "Judge nothing before the time, until the **Lord come**."

- How will He make the assessment? He will "bring to light the hidden things of darkness, and make manifest the counsels of the hearts". It will be a **perfect** judgment, since it does not depend alone on visible and audible evidence. Compare Isaiah 11 verse 3: "He shall not judge after the sight of his eyes, neither reprove after the hearing of his ears".

- What will the result be of the assessment? "Then shall every man have praise of **God**." Not men's praise - but God's praise.

2) THE APPLICATION PAUL MADE, vv.6-7

Paul now applies to the Corinthians what he has said about himself and Apollos, the "us" of verse 1: "And these things, brethren, I have in a figure transferred to myself and to Apollos **for your sakes**; that ye might learn in us not to think of men above that which is written, that no one of you be puffed up for one against another" or: "Now these things, brethren, I have transferred, in their **application,** to myself and Apollos, for your sakes ..." (JND). Paul had done this that they might be "guarded against putting the servants of God on a pedestal higher than what is accorded to them in the Scriptures" (J.M. Davies). We must notice *(a)* The statement he makes (v.6); *(b)* The questions he asks (v.7).

a) The statement he makes, v.6

The Corinthians were doing what Paul said could not be done: they were assessing others, and they were assessing themselves. The apostle was unable to correctly assess and evaluate his own service - he must leave that to the Lord Himself. He was but a steward accountable to his master. The Corinthians were, however, making such assessments. They were doing for themselves what the Lord alone could do.

i) They were assessing Paul and Apollos. They were probably saying, 'my particular cause is better than yours!' Hence: "I am of Paul; and I of Apollos; and I of Cephas ..." (1 Corinthians 1:12).

ii) They were assessing themselves. Something even Paul did *not* do. "The rallying calls, 'I am of Paul ... Apollos ... Cephas' not only implied that they gloried in men (1 Corinthians 3:21), but that they gloried in their own party position. They were 'puffed up for one against another'. Pride and arrogance created huge problems in the Corinthian church, see 1 Corinthians 4:18-19; 5:2; 8:1; 13:4, and they still cause huge problems amongst God's people today. We need to remember James 4 verse 6; 1 Peter 5 verses 5-6" (supplied by J. Waldron).

The words, "above that which is written", could refer to Chapter 1 verse 31: "according as it is written: He that glorieth, let him glory in the Lord", or to Chapter 3 verses 19-20: "For the wisdom of this world is foolishness with God: for it is written, He taketh the wise in their own craftiness. And again, The Lord knoweth the thoughts of the wise, that they are vain". See also Chapter 1 verse 19: "For it is written, I will destroy the wisdom of the wise, and will bring to nothing the understanding of the prudent".

b) The questions he asks, v.7

Paul now presses the application with three rhetorical questions: "For who maketh thee to differ from another? And what hast thou that thou didst not receive? Now if thou didst receive it, why dost thou glory, as if thou hadst not received it?"

i) "Who makest thee to differ?" W.E. Vine points out that the verb '*diakrino*', rendered "maketh … to differ" signifies 'to make a distinction'. Compare Acts 15 verse 9: "and put no **difference** between us and them, purifying their hearts by faith". See Jude 22: "And of some have compassion, making a **difference**". It refers, in the present case, to "the superiority of judgment claimed by church members" to whom Paul says in effect: "Who gives you the superior discriminating power to exalt one person and disown another? The implication being that such a claim arises simply from self-conceit" (W.E. Vine). There was no reason for the Corinthians to take any other attitude than that taken by Paul and Apollos, who regarded themselves simply as servants.

The Corinthians had no right to make **distinctions** in relation to the service of men. Paul's question can be put like this: 'Who gave you the right to differentiate between the servants of God, to say that one is better than another?' The second rhetorical question follows:

ii) "And what hast thou that thou didst not receive?" They were "puffed up", and should have remembered, in any case, that any virtue which they did possess was a divine bestowal: it did not emanate from them. See Chapter 3 verse 5: "even as the **Lord** gave to every man".

iii) "Why dost thou glory, as if thou hadst not received it?" They should, therefore, have remembered that they had no cause whatsoever to glory in themselves.

3) THE ADVERSITY PAUL SUFFERED, vv.8-13

In these verses, Paul gives further emphasis to the sharp contrast between the Corinthians and Apollos and himself in verse 6: "that ye might learn in us not to think of men above that which is written, that no one of you be puffed up for one against another". Paul had described himself and Apollos as "ministers" and "stewards", but the Corinthians were "puffed up". Paul had said: "judge nothing before the time, until the Lord come" (v. 5) but the Corinthians were acting as if He **had** come, and they were already living in the coming kingdom. They had all their hearts could wish for. "Now (already) ye are full, now (already) ye are rich, ye have reigned as kings without us: and I would to God ye did reign, that we also might reign with you." In the words of J. Hunter (*What the Bible Teaches – 1 Corinthians*): "How wonderful, says Paul, if it were true, then we too would be reigning. He then goes on to delineate the true position of believers at the present time". We may therefore divide the section as follows: *(a)* conduct as if Christ were reigning (v.8); *(b)* the stigma of sharing Christ's rejection (vv.9-13).

a) Conduct as if Christ were reigning, v8

"Now (already) ye are full, now (already) ye are rich, ye have reigned as kings without us: and I would to God ye did reign, that we also might reign with you." They were acting as though they had already been before the judgment seat of Christ, and as approved people themselves, they were competent to pass judgment on others. The word "full" (*'korennumi'*), meaning "satiated or engorged", and "rich" suggests that they had a strong sense of having arrived in their Christian lives. They believed that they had it all! (Compare the Lord's words to the assembly at Laodicea: see Revelation 3: 17). This is in sharp contrast to the Lord's teaching that "Blessed are they that do hunger and thirst after righteousness" (Matthew 5: 6).

Paul emphasises two things in this connection: *(i)* the incongruity of the situation: "reigning as kings *without us*"; *(ii)* the desirability of the situation: "I would to God that ye did reign, that we also might reign with you". Paul wished that it really was the case: "for then we would reign with you". Why does he say this? He reminds them of his present circumstances in verses 9-13. It certainly wasn't the time for reigning! This brings us to:

b) The stigma of sharing Christ's rejection, vv.9-13

The Corinthians were sitting back, quite vindicated in their own judgment. They were *reigning.* Their attitude reflected their pride. The apostles were suffering reproach. They were *suffering.* Their attitude reflected their humility. Paul now describes their sufferings and tells us *(i)* how they were regarded (vv.9-10); *(ii)* how they were impoverished (vv.11-12a); *(iii)* how they reacted (vv.12b-13a); *(iv)* how they were treated (vv.13b).

i) How they were regarded, vv.9-10. "For I think that God hath set forth (*'apodeiknumi'*, not *'protithemi'*, meaning 'purposed', as in Romans 3: 25) us the apostles last, as it were doomed to death: for we are made a spectacle unto the world, and to angels, and to men" (v. 9). According to W.E. Vine, the words *"set forth"* are used here "in the technical sense of exhibiting gladiators in an arena, as a kind of *grand finale*, to provide the most thrilling entertainment for the spectators". This explains the word *"last"* ("God hath set forth us the apostles last"). The gladiators came on at the end of the show, as W.E. Vine says the *'grand finale'*. The words "*doomed to death"* or (RV) "men doomed to death" (the single adjective *'epithanatios'*), only occur here in the New Testament. The words "*a spectacle*" (*'theatron'*) hardly need comment. Paul moves from the contests in the theatre, to the theatre itself, with the universe, both angels and men, looking on (RV margin).

The purpose of Paul's teaching here is stated in verse 16: "Be ye followers (*'mimetes'*, 'imitators') of me". That is, similar in resemblance. In what way? The Corinthians were to be prepared to *suffer before reigning.* They were not to assume a reign on the basis of their own assessment. This was the only way in which they could legitimately say: "I am of Paul". As the situation stood, Paul was in the arena, and they were in the royal box.

He describes the way in which the apostles were regarded in more detail: "We are fools for Christ's sake, but ye are wise (not *'sophos'*, as in Chapter 3: 10, but *'phronimos'*, meaning 'prudent' or 'sensible') in Christ; we are weak, but ye are strong; ye are honourable, but we are despised (dishonoured)" (v.

10). Although Paul uses similar language in Chapter 1 verses 27 and 28, the context there is rather different. In our current passage, Paul is in the arena ("fools ... weak ... despised") and the Corinthians are in the gallery ("wise ... strong ... honourable"). The words are heavy with irony. Paul describes himself and his fellow-apostles as **fools** by the world's standards, because of their loyalty to Christ, whereas the Corinthians regarded themselves, in view of their union with Christ, as wise and discerning. Paul describes himself and his fellow-apostles as **weak** in the eyes of the world, whereas they regarded themselves as influential and powerful. Just listen to them again: "*I* am ... *I* am ... *I* am ..." They were **honourable**", that is, they regarded themselves as honourable, but the apostles were **without honour** (the word 'despised' means 'without honour') among men. They were treated with contempt. The word ('*atimos*') was used of those deprived of citizenship (Leon Morris). The people who said "I am of Paul ... Apollos ... Cephas" are reminded that the very 'names' they followed were 'lower than the low' so far as the world was concerned.

ii) How they were impoverished, vv.11-12a. "Even unto this present hour we both hunger, and thirst, and are naked, and are buffeted, and have no certain dwellingplace; and labour, working with our own hands." They certainly shared the Lord's rejection. He was hungry (Luke 4:2), thirsty (John 4:7), buffeted (Matthew 26:67; Mark 14:65: it means 'to strike with a clenched fist'), homeless ("no certain dwelling place": see Luke 9:58, "the Son of man hath not where to lay his head"), and worked with His hands ("Is not this the carpenter's son?" - Matthew 13:55).

iii) How they reacted, vv.12b-13a. "Being reviled ('abused', RV), we **bless**; being persecuted, we **suffer it**: being defamed we **intreat**". Once again, Paul and his colleagues walked in the steps of the Lord. He was reviled (1 Peter 2:23; compare Matthew 5:44); He was persecuted (John 15:20); He was defamed ('*dusphemeo*', meaning 'to speak injuriously', similar to '*blasphemeo*'). But He reacted without violence or intemperance.

iv) How they were treated, vv13b. "We are made as the filth of the world, and are the offscouring of all things unto this day." The word *"filth"* ('*perikatharma*') denotes "offscouring ... that which is thrown away in cleansing" (W.E. Vine). The apostles were regarded as the scum of humanity. According to W.E. Vine, the Greeks used the term to describe "victims sacrificed to make expiation" and "criminals kept at the public expense, to be thrown into the sea, or otherwise killed, at the outbreak of a pestilence, etc". The word **"offscouring"** (*'peripsema'*) meaning, 'what is wiped off', was used "especially of condemned criminals of the lowest classes, who were sacrificed as expiatory offerings … because of their degraded life" (Lightfoot, quoted by W.E. Vine).

What condemnation of the proud, arrogant, conceited, self-sufficient Corinthians! But it all flowed from Paul's desire for their blessing. This follows:

4) THE AFFECTION PAUL DISPLAYED, vv.14-17

In these verses the apostle refers to *(a)* "my beloved sons" (vv.14-16) and *(b)* "my beloved son" (v. 17).

a) "My beloved sons", vv.14-16

Paul speaks here of the motive from which his ministry flowed. He loved them as a father. The admonition (warning) was engendered by a father's love: "I write not these things to shame you, but as my beloved sons (*'teknon'*, children), I warn you. For though ye have ten thousand instructors in Christ (*'paidagogoi'*, 'a guide, or guardian or trainer of boys', W.E. Vine), yet have ye not many fathers: for in Christ Jesus I have begotten you through the gospel. Wherefore, I beseech you, be ye followers of me". "Tenderness now follows sternness" (W.E. Vine). Compare 2 Corinthians 2 verse 4: "For out of much affliction and anguish of heart I wrote unto you with many tears; not that ye should be grieved, but that ye might know the love which I have more abundantly unto you".

The words "I warn you" point to the possibility of discipline. See verses 18-21. He would come, either "with a rod, *or* in love, and in the spirit of meekness". "The Corinthians were fond of imitating the culture of Athens, so he exhorts them to follow or imitate him as their spiritual father. The fact that he could do so is an example to all true servants" (J.M. Davies). As noted above, this was entirely different from saying: "I am of Paul!"

b) "My beloved son", v.17

"For this cause have I sent unto you Timotheus, who is my beloved son, and faithful in the Lord, who shall bring you into remembrance of my ways which be in Christ, as I teach every where in every church." Compare Chapter 7:17; 11:16; 14:33, 34. If the Corinthians were his beloved children, then

Timothy was his "beloved and faithful *child* in the Lord" (RV). The saints at Corinth were "beloved children" (RV), and Timothy was his "beloved *and faithful* child". Timothy's ministry was to remind them of the manner of the man who brought them the gospel and taught them the truth. As W.E. Vine observes: "It would be Timothy's part accordingly to bring this home to them, and to disabuse their minds of any idea that Paul was the leader of a party". But what if this failed? This follows:

5) THE AUTHORITY PAUL POSSESSED, vv.18-21

He would come with apostolic authority to deal with the matter. Some were evidently saying that he would not come! "Now some are puffed up, as though I would not come unto you. But I will come to you shortly, if the Lord will (see also Romans 1:10; James 4:15); and will know, not the speech of them which are puffed up, but the power. For the kingdom of God is not in word, but in power. What will ye? shall I come unto you with a rod, or in love, and in the spirit of meekness?" "The spirit of meekness" is essential for any believer involved in spiritual restoration. See Galatians 6 verse 1.

"The kingdom of God" is the sphere of His rule and authority: its power is inward and manifest in the life, not in mere empty talk. For the present: "The kingdom of God cometh not with observation" (Luke 17:20): it is not yet manifested as it *will be* when God sets His "king upon His holy hill of Zion" (Psalm 2:6).

As J.M. Davies rightly observes, Paul "hoped that they would react in a spiritual way to his ministry and to his envoy, so that he could visit them with joy". Compare 2 Corinthians 1:23 - 2:1-4.

1 CORINTHIANS

"Purge out therefore the old leaven"

Read Chapter 5:1-13

In outlining the epistle, we noted that Paul deals first of all with the things he had heard about the assembly at Corinth. In this connection, he addresses two reports which had reached him. The first report, related to him by "the house of Chloe" (1 Corinthians 1:11), concerned **discord amongst assembly members**, and Paul deals with this in Chapters 1-4. The second report, evidently in general circulation (1 Corinthians 5:1), necessitated **discipline in the assembly**, and Paul deals with this in Chapters 5-6. We should note that in Chapters 7-10, Paul answers questions put to him, but it is significant that he deals first of all, in Chapters 1-6, with matters they had **not** raised. Paul's priorities evidently differed from the priorities of the Corinthians!

As noted above, the second of these two reports - "It is reported commonly that there is fornication among you…" (1 Corinthians 5:1) - necessitated the exercise of **discipline in the assembly.** The connection with Chapters 1-4 is clear. The believers at Corinth were very pleased with themselves (see 1 Corinthians 4:8), but Paul now says in effect: "Take another look at yourselves". We should notice the following:

- In Chapter 5, Paul emphasises the necessity for **assembly discipline**. "Put away from among yourselves that wicked person" (v.13). In this connection we should notice that although they were prepared to judge Paul (1 Corinthians 4:3), they were not prepared to judge evil amongst themselves!

- In Chapter 6, Paul emphasises the necessity for **self-discipline**. In verses 1-8, it is self-discipline in connection with the believer and his **brother.** In verses 9-20, it is self-discipline in connection with the believer and his **body.** With regard to the first, we should notice that although they were "puffed up for one against another" (1 Corinthians 4:6), and thought themselves "wise in Christ" (1 Corinthians 4:10), Paul was obliged to say: "Is it so, that there is not a wise man among you?" (1 Corinthians 6:5).

As noted above, in Chapter 5 Paul deals with the question of assembly discipline, and the passage may be divided as follows: *(1)* when is assembly discipline required? (v.1); *(2)* what does assembly discipline involve? (vv.2-5); *(3)* why is assembly discipline necessary? (vv.6-8); *(4)* who does assembly discipline concern? (vv.9-13).

But before we begin, here is an excellent piece supplied by our contributor Justin Waldron, introduced by the question: "Why should a church practise church discipline?" with the answer: "There are a number of crucial reasons". Here they are: *(i) to maintain the demands of God's holiness*: see 1 Peter 1 verse 16, Psalm 93 verse 5; *(ii) to restore the sinning believer*, see 1 Corinthians 5 verse 5; *(iii) to deter the church from sin*: see 1 Timothy 5 verse 20; *(iv) to maintain a credible testimony to the world*: see Acts 5 verses 11-14. Now to our suggested fourfold chapter division:

1) WHEN IS ASSEMBLY DISCIPLINE REQUIRED? v.1

In this connection, attention is drawn to various New Testament references to the subject.

i) In matters of practical conduct. See 2 Thessalonians 3 verses 6-15: "Now we command you, brethren, in the name of our Lord Jesus Christ, that ye withdraw yourselves from every brother that walketh disorderly ... if any man obey not our word by this epistle, note that man, and have no company with him, that he may be ashamed. Yet count him not as an enemy, but admonish him as a brother". The required procedure in this case, is not excommunication, but the avoidance of fellowship, in order to make the parties concerned aware of their unbecoming conduct. The question has to be asked, 'avoidance of fellowship in what way?' It can hardly mean participation with the brother in question at the Lord's supper but 'keeping our distance' at other times when the Lord's people are gathered together. The words "company with him" must therefore refer to fellowship at times and in places other than on the occasion of assembly gatherings. We could describe such times as 'social occasions'. An example is found in Acts 2 verse 46: "breaking bread from house to house…"

ii) In matters of dividing God's people. See Titus 3 verses 10-11: "A man that is an heretic (from a word meaning, an opinion - leading to error), after the first and second admonition reject ('have done with'); knowing that he that is such is subverted, and sinneth, being condemned of himself". This is the man who is "quarrelsome and stirs up factions through erroneous opinions, a man who is determined to go his own way and so forms parties and factions" (D.E. Hiebert). While excellent men think otherwise, it is nonetheless difficult to visualise any form of discipline here other than withdrawal of fellowship. For a believer in this category to remain in assembly fellowship would *(i)* negate the proclamation at the Lord's supper that "we being many are one bread", when this is manifestly not true in this case, and *(ii)* continue to expose assembly members to the error in question. People with such ideas tend to be persistent in propagating them.

iii) In matters of doctrinal error. Not so much a mistaken interpretation, or a slip of the tongue, but deliberate propagation of error. See 1 Timothy 1 verse 20: "Hymeneaus and Alexander; whom I have delivered unto Satan, that they may learn ('may be taught by discipline', JND) not to blaspheme". The discipline is remedial rather than judicial. In context (v.19), the 'blasphemy' here appears to be "ridiculing the simple presentation of gospel truth. In doing this they reviled the Author of truth" (J. Allen, *What the Bible Teaches - 1 Timothy*).

iv) In matters of moral behaviour. As here, in 1 Corinthians 5 verses 1 and 11. Not only immorality, but covetousness, idolatry, railing, drunkenness and extortion.

The Chapter commences by citing a case of immoral behaviour which involved an incestuous relationship: "It is reported commonly ('it is actually reported', RV) that there is fornication among you, and such fornication as is not so much named among the Gentiles, that one should have his father's wife (his stepmother)" (v.1). We should notice the opening words: "It is reported..." While in Chapter 1 verse 11, the information was disclosed by "the house of Chloe", here the information was in the public domain. It was commonly known: "It is actually reported" (RV). The absence of further reference to the woman concerned indicates that she was not in fellowship.

Verse 11 specifies a number of reasons for the exercise of assembly discipline. "I have written unto you not to keep company, if any man that is called a brother be a fornicator, or covetous, or an idolater, or a railer, or a drunkard, or an extortioner; with such an one no not to eat".

a) "A fornicator." When the word (*'porneia'*) stands alone, it denotes immorality of all kinds. When it stands with 'adultery' (*'moichao'*), it has a more specific meaning, that is, pre-marital unchastity. See, for example, Hebrews 13 verse 4: "Marriage is honourable in all, and the bed undefiled: but whoremongers ('fornicators', JND) and adulterers God will judge". We should now read Ephesians 5 verse 3.

b) "Covetous." The word (*'pleonektes'*) denotes a desire to have more: greedy of gain. It, therefore, covers, for example, all forms of gambling, together with sharp practice in business.

c) "An idolater." This denotes any false system of worship, together with sorcery and spiritism.

d) "A railer." This refers to reviling or abuse. Not *'blasphemia'* but *'loidoria'*. The word covers vilification, defamation of character, false accusation.

e) "A drunkard." This speaks for itself. According to W.E. Vine, the root word (*'methu'*) means 'mulled wine'.

f) "An extortioner." The word (*'harpax'*) covers pillage, plunder, robbery. It, therefore, includes the misappropriation of property or funds, and fraud.

2) WHAT DOES ASSEMBLY DISCIPLINE INVOLVE? vv.2-5

It involves the need *(a)* for a proper attitude Godward (v.2); *(b)* for proper action manward (vv.3-5)

a) It involves the need for a proper attitude Godward, v.2

Paul was obliged to say about the assembly: "And ye are puffed up". The expression "puffed up" (*'phusioo'*) comes from *'phusa'* meaning 'bellows'. He continues: "and have not rather mourned that he that hath done this deed might be taken away from among you". There was no concern *before God* over the sinful life of the assembly member in question. The word "mourned" (*pentheo)* also occurs, for example, in James 4 verse 9 and 2 Corinthians 12 verse 21.

The suggestion that the assembly was "puffed up" in the sense that it gloried in its toleration and open-mindedness hardly seems tenable. The phrase "puffed up" evidently refers to the subject of the previous section, see Chapter 4 verses 6, 18-19, in which case the solemn lesson emerges that we can become so engrossed in establishing our own party position that we fail to see pressing danger elsewhere. At Corinth, the saints were so involved in proclaiming their superiority over each other that God's interests had lapsed. Daniel exhibited a far more commendable attitude: "And whiles I was speaking, and praying, and confessing my sin and the sin of my people Israel …" (Daniel 9:20).

The words: "ye … have not rather mourned, that he that hath done this deed might be *taken away* from you" infer divinely-exercised discipline. Compare verse 13: "Therefore *put away* from among yourselves that wicked person". This implies that even if the Corinthians did not know how to act in the circumstances, they should, appreciating that evil was practised in their midst, have waited upon God to act in the matter. The judgment on Ananias and Sapphira is a case in point (Acts 5:1-11). This constitutes an important lesson for elders today. In times of perplexity, they must wait on God to either reveal His will, or to act directly.

Paul then proceeds to show them how they should have acted, and having done so, then urges: "Put away from yourselves that wicked person" (v.13). By the time Paul reached the end of the chapter, the assembly knew exactly what it should do. This brings us to the second requirement:

b) It involves the need for proper action manward, vv.3-5

We should notice: *(i)* the parties involved (vv.3-4); *(ii)* the punishment involved (v.5a); *(iii)* the purpose involved (v.5b).

i) The parties involved, vv.3-4

There are three parties involved in assembly discipline: "In the name of our Lord Jesus Christ, when ye are gathered together, and my spirit, with the power of our Lord Jesus Christ" (v.4).

- The Lord Jesus Christ. His authority is emphasised. The title, "the Lord Jesus Christ", occurs twice in verse 4. According to J.N. Darby, some manuscripts omit "Christ". However, following the A.V., it is "in the *name* of the Lord Jesus Christ", and "with the **power** (*'dunamis',* referring to His might) of our Lord Jesus Christ".

The passage helps us to understand Matthew 18 verses 15-20, and in particular the words: "Whatsoever ye shall bind on earth shall be (Amplified Version: 'shall have been') bound in heaven: and whatsoever ye shall loose on earth shall be (*ditto*) loosed in heaven". It is not a case of heaven ratifying assembly discipline, or forgiveness, but rather that the assembly implements heaven's judgment in the matter. Quite obviously, therefore, the assembly must be aware of heaven's will in the circumstances, and that can only be discerned from the Scriptures.

- *The gathered assembly.* "When ye are gathered together" or "Ye being gathered together" (RV). Matthew 18 verse 20, oft-quoted with a wider application, must be understood in this context. So, the **whole assembly** excludes from fellowship, just as the **whole assembly** receives into fellowship. This needs to be fully understood. Undoubtedly the elders will take a lead; that is their function. But they should not act in a clandestine, secretive way. They must carry the whole assembly with them. As Wm. MacDonald so rightly observes: "This calls for a public announcement in the church that the brother is no longer in fellowship. This announcement should be made in genuine sorrow and humiliation, and should be followed by continual prayer for the spiritual restoration of the wanderer". Believers in fellowship but not present when discipline is announced should be informed.

- *The apostolic authority of Paul.* "And my spirit." See verse 3: "For I verily, as absent in body, but present in spirit, have judged already, as though I were present, concerning him that hath done this deed". Compare 2 Corinthians 2 verse 10: "To whom ye forgive anything, I forgive also ..." Paul was bodily absent, but present in spirit. That is, they had his apostolic authority to act in this way. Compare Colossians 2 verse 5: "For though I be absent in the flesh, yet am I with you in spirit, joying and beholding your order, and the steadfastness of your faith in Christ". What a difference to 1 Corinthians 5 verse 4!

ii) The punishment involved, v.5a

That is exactly what Paul calls it in 2 Corinthians 2 verse 6: "this punishment (*'epitimia'*), which was inflicted of many". In this case; "to deliver such an one to Satan for the destruction of the flesh, that the spirit may be saved in the day of the Lord Jesus".

The words: "to deliver such an one to Satan" is another way of saying, but with a different emphasis: "put away from among yourselves that wicked person" (v.13), that is, excommunication from fellowship. What this involves is stated in verse 11, but we will pre-empt this by noting now that the man was to be counted as unsaved: "with such an one no not to eat" or, the Lord's words: "Let him be unto thee as an heathen man and a publican" (Matt. 18: 17).

The assembly is the place of the Lord's presence and blessing. The place where God dwells. The place of spiritual benefit through fellowship and communion. It is not, or it should not be, the sphere of Satan's activity. **The world** is the sphere of Satan's power. He is the "god of this world". John tells us that "the whole world lieth in wickedness" (1 John 5: 19) or "in the wicked [one]" (JND). He is "the spirit that now worketh in the children of disobedience" (Eph. 2: 2). The guilty party is, therefore, deprived of the benefits inherent in assembly fellowship, and exposed to Satan's malign attention. He is fully exposed to this. As already noted, Paul refers to Hymenaeus and Alexander "whom I have delivered unto Satan, that they may learn not to blaspheme" (1 Timothy 1:20). The words: "to deliver such an one to Satan" may be understood with reference to the Lord's words to Peter: "Simon, Simon, behold, Satan hath desired to have you that he might sift (winnow) you as wheat ..." (Luke 22:31). Exclusion from fellowship exposes those involved to Satan's taunts and accusations, all of which create desire for deliverance and restoration.

iii) The purpose involved, v.5b

This is stated as follows: "To deliver such an one unto Satan for the destruction of the flesh, that the spirit may be saved in the day of the Lord Jesus". The two expressions stand in contrast: on one hand, "the destruction of the flesh": on the other, the salvation of "the spirit".

- "The destruction of the flesh." This evidently refers to the old sinful nature. The purpose of assembly discipline - negatively - is to destroy its activity. Excommunication serves to emphasise the immense loss of the person(s) concerned, and to create desire for restoration. This leads to recognition of the nature of the sin involved, and consequent repentance.

The Greek word *('olethros')* rendered "destruction" does not mean loss of being, but loss of well-being. See, for example, "sudden destruction" (1 Thessalonians 5:3); "everlasting destruction" (2 Thessalonians 1:9). The purpose is to bring the person concerned to repentance. It is not here physical death, but 'mortifying the deeds of the body' (Romans 8:13). Compare Colossians 3 verse 5: "Mortify therefore your members which are upon the earth; fornication, uncleanness, inordinate affection ..." However, consideration should be given to the alternative suggestion that physical consequences are involved. See 1 Corinthians 11 verse 30; Acts 5 verses 1-10.

- "That the spirit may be saved in the day of the Lord Jesus." This refers to the new spiritual life. The purpose of assembly discipline - positively - is to promote its health. It has in view the guilty party's ultimate benefit and welfare. This is the sense of the words "that the spirit may be saved", and what follows indicates exactly what this means: "that the spirit may be saved *in the day of the Lord Jesus*". That is, at the judgment seat of Christ. Compare, for example Chapter 1 verse 8 and Chapter 3 verse 13. So discipline has the judgment seat of Christ in mind. The word "saved" is not used here in the sense of eternal salvation, but in the context of reward. The purpose of assembly discipline is ensure that in spite of the serious lapse, there will be something that will stand the test at the judgment seat of Christ.

3) WHY IS ASSEMBLY DISCIPLINE NECESSARY? vv.6-8

It has been suggested that in saying: "Your glorying is not good" (v.6), Paul refers to their boasting in the fact that whatever others might be doing, they were not involved in immoral living. However, it seems more likely that Paul refers here to their party spirit, their glorying in men (1 Corinthians 3:21), that is: "I am of Paul ... Apollos ... Cephas ..." This so dominated them that the immorality in their midst was well down their list of priorities. It might have seemed comparatively unimportant to them but, says Paul: "Know ye not that a little leaven leaveneth the whole lump?" That is, the whole company could be affected in at least two ways:

i) The immorality could spread. The toleration of the licentious behaviour of one person could encourage others to follow suit, since there seemed to be no penalty attaching to such behaviour.

ii) The entire testimony could be brought into disrepute. This had in fact already happened: "It is commonly reported that there is fornication among, and such fornication as is not so much as named among the Gentiles, that one should have his father's wife" (v.1).

In saying: "Know ye not that a little leaven leaveneth the whole lump?", Paul refers to the feasts of passover and unleavened bread, and the fact that "they baked unleavened cakes of the dough which they brought forth out of Egypt for it was not leavened" (Exodus 12:39.) The fact that the two 'feasts' are never divided in Scripture (see Mark 14:12; Luke 22:7) emphasises that redeemed people were to be a holy people, something that the church at Corinth needed to remember: "Christ our passover is sacrificed for us; therefore let us keep the feast, not with old leaven, neither with the leaven of malice ('*kakia*' meaning 'badness') and wickedness ('*poneria*' meaning 'wickedness'); but with the unleavened bread of sincerity ('*eilikrinia*', literally, 'tested by the sunlight') and truth ('*aletheia*', 'the reality lying at the basis of an appearance')" (vv.7-8). In saying: "therefore let us keep the feast", Paul does not refer to the Lord's Supper, but the equivalent of the feast of unleavened bread. Literally: 'let us keep festival' or, as it has been said: 'Let your whole life be a sacred festival'. Peter puts it like this: "pass the time of your sojourning here in fear: forasmuch as ye know that ye were not redeemed with corruptible things, as silver and gold ... but with the precious blood of Christ, as of a lamb without blemish and without spot" (1 Peter 1:17-19). See also Titus 2 verse 14: "our great God and Saviour Jesus Christ; who gave himself for us that he might redeem us from all lawlessness, and purify to himself a peculiar people, zealous for good works" (JND).

We should notice that they were to be 'unleavened' **practically**: "purge out therefore the old leaven, that ye may be a new lump", and that they were already 'unleavened' **positionally**: "even as ye are unleavened". They were to make their practice correspond with their position.

The principle in this section is clear: evil will spread if tolerated. Compare Galatians 5 verse 9, where the same statement is made in connection with false teaching.

4) WHO DOES ASSEMBLY DISCIPLINE CONCERN? vv.9-13

"I wrote unto you in an epistle ('my epistle', RV), not to company ('*sunanamignumi*', 'to mix up with') with fornicators" (v.9) or "I have written to you in the epistle" (JND). It does seem, therefore, that Paul may be referring to 1 Corinthians itself, which he was actually writing at the time, perhaps referring to verse 5. J. Heading (*First Epistle to the Corinthians*) cites H.P.V. Nunn who suggests that this is a case of the 'epistolary aorist', that is, the writer puts himself in the place of the readers, and describes as past an action present to himself, but which will be past to his readers once they receive his letter. (Oh for words "easy to be understood!").

We might, however, conclude that Paul is referring to another letter entirely! It is not illogical to suggest that the words: ... "I wrote unto you in an epistle, not to company with fornicators" (v.9) are logically followed by: "But *now* I have written unto you not to keep company, if any man that is called a brother be a fornicator…" (v.11) or, RV: "but *now* I write unto you…" (v.11).

The contrast between verse 10 and verse 11 needs little, if any, comment. Paul makes it clear in verse 10 that our very presence in the world obliges us to rub shoulders with sinful men and women "of this world". The only alternative is to "go out of the world". But he makes it equally clear in verse 11 that we are to disassociate ourselves from "any man that is called a brother" who is guilty of the sins enumerated. (We have already discussed these.) With such a person, the assembly was "not to keep company" and "not to eat". The latter has been sadly misapplied by some today. But the teaching is clear: there is to be no social contact. This raises some delicate questions. For example, what about other family members in such circumstances? It is not particularly easy when visiting a home to differentiate between family members. In those circumstances: "not to keep company" and: "not to eat" are not always easily observed. Then there is the question of repentance and recovery, which surely places a duty on elders to at least keep in contact with persons out of fellowship in order to monitor their spiritual progress.

The words: "what have I to do to judge them also which are *without*?" (v.12a) correspond with: "the fornicators *of this world*, or … the covetous, or extortioners, or with idolaters" (v.10), whereas the words: "do not ye judge them that are *within*" (v.12b) correspond with v.11: "if any man that is called *a brother* be a fornicator, or covetous, or an idolater, or a railer, or a drunkard, or an extortioner". It was the responsibility of the Corinthians to act in connection with their own members. It is God's prerogative to deal with the world.

The conclusion is given in verse 13: "Therefore put away from among yourselves that wicked person". Paul quotes Deuteronomy 17 verse 7 here: "So thou shalt put the evil away from among you".

Postscript

The Second Epistle makes clear that the assembly acted on the guidance given in 1 Corinthians 5: "Ye sorrowed after a godly sort .... in all things ye have approved yourselves to be clear in this matter" (2 Corinthians 7:11).

It also makes clear that the action taken by the assembly, as a result of apostolic guidance, was effective so far as the man himself was concerned: "Sufficient unto such a man is this punishment which was inflicted of many. So that contrariwise ye ought to forgive him, and comfort him lest perhaps such an one should be swallowed up with overmuch *sorrow* ..." (2 Corinthians 2:6-7). The assembly had been slow to put the man away from fellowship: now it was slow in restoring him to fellowship. Hence we read: "Wherefore I beseech you that ye would confirm your love toward him ... lest Satan should get an advantage of us: for we are not ignorant of his devices" (2 Corinthians 2:8-11).

Amongst other things, this emphasises that time is needed for guilty parties to display the reality of their repentance, rather than professing repentance 'on the spot' while in fellowship, thus obviating, some might wrongly say, the necessity for excommunication in the first place.

The Lord's words to the "woman taken in adultery": "Neither do I condemn thee; go, and sin no more" (John 8:11), were uttered in rather different circumstances to those described in 1 Corinthians 5. The woman was not in fellowship with a local assembly! The Lord's pronouncement was based on the fulfilment of the law, written "on the ground" with the Saviour's finger. There was no condemnation for the woman, because *He* would bear the condemnation of the broken law! A.W. Pink has an excellent piece here. See his *Exposition of the Gospel of John.*

1 CORINTHIANS

"Brother goeth to law with brother"

Read Chapter 6:1-8

In 1 Corinthians Chapters 5 & 6 Paul deals with moral disorders in the assembly, but from differing vantage points.

- In Chapter 5, the emphasis is on *collective responsibility.* That is, how the *assembly* is to regard fornication. The "whole lump" is in view. Because the entire assembly is affected, the entire assembly is to act.

- In Chapter 6, the emphasis is on *individual responsibility*. That is, how the *believer* is to regard fornication. His own body is in view.

But before dealing with immorality in this way, Paul extends his teaching on the necessity for the assembly to "judge them that are within" (1 Corinthians 5:12) by censuring the way in which individuals at Corinth were attempting to settle personal disputes. Rather than dealing with these in the assembly, they were resorting to "them that are without" by going "to law one with another" (1 Corinthians 6:7). With this in mind, we can say:

- In Chapter 5, we have the need for the *assembly* to act *responsibly* in connection with sin in the assembly.

- In Chapter 6, we have the need for the *individual believer* to act *responsibly* in connection with sins against themselves. They were, in fact, acting *irresponsibly*.

If in Chapter 5, the assembly does not sit in judgment on the world (vv.12-13), then in Chapter 6, the world is not to be given the opportunity to sit in judgment on the assembly (vv.5-6).

The chapter may be broadly divided as follows: *(1)* the believer and his brethren (vv.1-8); *(2)* the believer and his body (vv.9-20). We should carefully note the occurrences of: "Know ye not" in the chapter (vv.2 RV, 3, 9, 15, 16, 19).

1) THE BELIEVER AND HIS BRETHREN, vv.1-8

In Chapter 5, immorality and other matters (v.11) were to be judged with the Lord's authority (v.4), whereas in Chapter 6 matters were *not* to be resolved by man's authority (v.1). Believers at Corinth were evidently seeking legal help in settling disputes amongst themselves, necessitating Paul to say: "Dare any of you, having a matter against another, *go to law* before the unjust, and not before the saints? ... brother *goeth to law* with brother, and that before the unbelievers. Now therefore there is utterly a fault among you, because ye *go to law* one with another" (vv.1, 6, 7).

In dealing with the situation, Paul points out that their conduct was *(a)* inconsistent with future responsibility (vv.1-3); *(b)* ignored ability in the assembly (vv.4-6); *(c)* indicated pursuit of personal interests (vv.7-8).

a) Their conduct was inconsistent with future responsibility, vv.1-3

Without any preamble, Paul addresses the situation at Corinth with the question: "Dare any of you, having a matter against another, go to law before the unjust, and not before the saints?" (v.1). The word "dare" (*'tolmao'*) is used here in the sense of: 'How could you bring yourselves to do such a thing?' According to Charles Hodge the rabbis taught that "It is a statute which binds all Israelites, that if one Israelite has a cause against another, it must not be prosecuted before the Gentiles", to which Leon Morris adds: "The Corinthians did not reach even the Jewish standard". Very clearly, these lawsuits were bringing the testimony of God's people into disrepute, reminding us that there are more important things in life than our personal interests. God's interests should overrule our personal interests. Hence the necessity for unity amongst the Lord's people: "stand fast in one spirit, with one mind striving together for the faith of the gospel ..." (Philippians 1:27-28). While, in context, Paul refers to the believer's conduct in society, his injunction is equally applicable to conduct amongst believers: "Dearly beloved, avenge not yourselves, but rather give place unto wrath: for it is written, Vengeance is mine; I will repay, saith the Lord" (Romans 12:19).

It should be emphasised that Paul does not refer here to criminal cases, but rather to petty differences. We are indebted to Justin Waldron for supplying the following written by Keith Krell: "The ancient Greek courthouse was not a private room with a small gallery such as we have today. The courtroom was in the public square or the marketplace. In Athens (and Corinth was undoubtedly similar), a legal dispute was brought before a court known as The Forty. The Forty picked a public arbitrator, who had to be a citizen in his 60th year, to hear the case. If it still wasn't settled, it went to a jury court". This consisted of 201 citizens or 401 citizens, depending on the amount of money involved. Keith Krell continues: "When someone hauled a brother or sister into court there, they weren't just settling a dispute, they were holding the church up to public scrutiny and ridicule. Paul is concerned about the selfish arrogance of God's people".

Having told us about the problem (one of them) at Corinth, Paul now takes a hard look at the implications of their conduct: These verses tell us about two classes of people (v.1); two dimensions of judgment (v.2); two periods of judgment (v.3).

i) Two classes of people, v.1. The *"unjust"* ('*adikos*', unrighteous) and the *"saints"*. The former are not "unjust" in the sense that they pervert judgment. Paul is not disparaging human tribunals. Believers are to respect "the powers that be" (Romans 13:1-5). They are "unjust" (or 'unrighteous') in the sense that they are unconverted people. It does seem significant that Paul does *not* say: 'Dare any of you … go to law before the unjust (unrighteous), and not before the righteous?', *but:* "Dare any of you go to law before the unjust, and not before the *saints*?" The Lord's people are more than "righteous" - they are sanctified people, set apart for God, saints. This gives an added dimension to their righteousness!

ii) Two dimensions in judgment, v.2. "Do ye not know that the saints shall judge *the world* ('*kosmos*')? And if the world ('*kosmos*') shall be judged of you, are ye unworthy to judge the *smallest matters*?" (v.2). It is perhaps rather startling to discover that we are currently fitting ourselves for future responsibility. The parable of the pounds (Luke 19:11-27) now becomes compulsory reading. Here is an extract: "Lord, thy pound hath gained ten pounds. And he said unto him, Well, thou good servant: because thou hast been faithful in very little, have authority over ten cities". Rather sobering, isn't it! In view of our current 'track record', we really ought to ask ourselves what kind of "entrance" we can expect "into the everlasting kingdom of our

Lord and Saviour Jesus Christ" (2 Peter 1:11). Compare 2 Thessalonians 1 verses 4-5.

We must notice the contrast between coming responsibility and current conduct on the part of the believers.

- **Coming responsibility.** "Do ye not know that the saints shall judge **the world**?" This evidently refers to believers of the current dispensation, and involves, not so much judicial responsibility, but **administration and government**. The expression "the world" (*'kosmos'*) refers to human affairs. The Lord's twelve disciples will have particular responsibility in relation to Israel: "Verily I say unto you, That ye which have followed me, in the regeneration when the Son of man shall sit in the throne of his glory, ye also shall sit on twelve thrones, judging the twelve tribes of Israel" (Matthew 19:28). (It is worth noting that Israel itself will evidently have judicial responsibilities in the future: see Psalm 149:5-9.)

In this connection it is well-worth pointing out, in the Lord's own words, that "the Father judgeth no man but hath committed **all** judgment unto the Son" (John 5:22). Believers will appear before "the judgment seat of **Christ**" (2 Corinthians 5:10), the 'living nations' will appear before "the **Son of man** ... **the King**" (Matthew 25:31, 34, 40), and the wicked dead will appear in space before "a great white throne" whose Occupant has only to look and "the earth and the heaven" will flee away (Revelation 20:11). It will be His prerogative, and His alone, to execute judgment. Hence we read: "no **man in heaven, nor in earth**, was able to open the book, neither to look thereon ..." (Revelation 5:1-4). Only the "Lion of the tribe of Judah" was qualified "to open the book, and to loose the seven seals thereof" (Revelation 5:5-7).

- **Current responsibility.** "Are ye unworthy to judge the smallest matters?" The judgment of the world in the future - a weighty matter surely - is set against "the smallest matters" now! The Lord's people at Corinth were exposing themselves to the judgment of the very world which they themselves were ultimately to govern and administer!

iii) Two periods of judgment, v.3. "Know ye not that we shall judge angels? How much more things that pertain to this life?"

- **Future judgment**. "Know ye not that we **shall judge angels**?" This statement (or question) is unique in Scripture. The angels, who now "minister for them who shall be heirs of salvation" (Hebrews 1:14), will be subject to the authority and direction of the same people in administering the world. We should now read Hebrews 2 verses 5-7 (and beyond): "For unto the angels hath he *not* put in subjection the world to come, whereof we speak. But one in a certain place testified, saying, What is *man*, that thou art mindful of him? Or the son of man, that thou visitest him? Thou madest him a little lower than the angels; thou crownest *him* with glory and honour, and didst set him over the works of thy hands..." The millennial earth will see the fulfilment of God's purpose for mankind. It will, of course, be fulfilled in the perfect Man. His name is "Jesus" (Hebrews 2:9). When the world sees His "glory and honour", men and women will also see angels executing the commands of His executives. Hence the question, "Know ye not that we *shall judge* (administer) *angels*?"

To sum up, the Lord's people today will have governmental responsibilities over terrestrial beings: "Do ye not know that the saints shall judge the world?" (v.2), and over celestial beings: "Know ye not that we shall judge angels?" (v.3).

- Current judgment. "How much more things that pertain to *this life* (*'biotikos'*)?" - referring to the things pertaining to the affairs of this world. The immense responsibilities of believers in the future should give them every incentive to settle disputes now. Our knowledge of future events should influence current conduct.

b) Their conduct ignored the ability in the assembly, vv.4-6

"If ye then have judgments of things pertaining to this life, set them to judge who are least esteemed in the church." However, the verb is not necessarily an imperative, and the words may be taken as a statement ('you set them to judge ...') or a question "do ye set them to judge who are of no account in the church?" (RV). This does seem preferable. The wording: "set them to judge who are least esteemed in the church" (AV) hardly seems tenable. Men who judge in the assembly must surely be men of highest esteem, otherwise their judgment would not likely be acknowledged and heeded. W.E. Vine, following the RV, puts it clearly: "Do ye set them to judge who are of no account in the church?" – that is to say: 'Do you go outside the assembly to obtain the verdict from those who preside over Gentile courts, and who, being of the world, have no place in the assembly'. He adds: "That is the significance of the phrase rendered in the RV, 'are of no account'. The word is used here not in a contemptuous sense".

What follows needs no explanation: "I speak to your shame. Is it so ('has it come to this'), that there is not a wise man among you? no, not one that shall be able to judge between his brethren?" (v.5). The believers at Corinth were minimising spiritual intelligence in the assembly, something that should be recognised, valued, accepted, and used. Sadly, worldly expedients often replace spiritual wisdom.

The gravity of the situation is emphasised further: "But brother goeth to law with brother, and that before the unbelievers". (v.6). This emphasises that to "go to law" is a breach of brotherly relationships: "*brother* goeth to law with *brother*". Unregenerate men were being treated to the sight of a breakdown of brotherly love between believers. Compare the oft-quoted words: "And there was a strife between the herdmen of Abram's cattle, and the herdmen of Lot's cattle: and the Canaanite and the Perizzite dwelled then in the land. And Abram said unto Lot, Let there be no strife, I pray thee, between me and thee, and between my herdmen and thy herdmen; *for we be brethren*" (Genesis 13:7-8).

c) Their conduct indicated the pursuit of personal interests, vv.7-8

"Now therefore there is utterly a fault ('*hettema*', denoting a loss) among you, because ye go to law one with another, Why do ye not rather take wrong? Why do ye not rather suffer yourselves to be defrauded ('*apostereo*', 'to rob, despoil')? Nay, ye do wrong, and defraud, and that your brethren."

The result of all this was spiritual loss ('*hettema*') for the assembly at Corinth. W.E. Vine makes this clear: "The reference is to the spiritual loss sustained by the church at Corinth because of their discord and their litigious ways in appealing to the world's judges". Rather than pursuing their own interests and imperilling the entire testimony, Paul counsels them to "take wrong" and "suffer yourselves to be defrauded". As noted above, the word "defrauded" means to despise or rob: probably in character, rather than in kind. So two courses are open to the saints:

- *To bring the matter to the attention of the assembly*, particularly to the attention of men competent to judge in the assembly. See verses 4-5.

- *To take no action at all.* To "take wrong ... suffer yourselves to be defrauded". See verse 7. "That is to say, why not suffer injustice and put up with the injury, rather than suffer spiritual damage … Not only did those who were thus acting refuse to endure wrong, they were inflicting it upon their fellow-believers" (W.E. Vine). In resorting to the law, the injured party only compounds the situation. He wrongs and defrauds the very party that has wronged and defrauded him. There is an important lesson here: to 'give as good as you get' is **not** a spiritual principle. Paul's injunction can certainly be applied here: "Be not overcome of evil, but overcome evil with good" (Romans 12:21).

1 CORINTHIANS

"Glorify God in your body"

Read Chapter 6:9-20

As noted in our previous study, this Chapter may be broadly divided as follows: *(1)* the believer and his brethren (vv.1-8); *(2)* the believer and his body (vv.9-20). Once again, we should carefully note the occurrences of the phrase: "Know ye not?" in this Chapter (vv.2 RV, 3, 9, 15, 16, 19). It implies that the matter to which he refers at the time was either a well-known fact, or should have been a well-known fact.

1) THE BELIEVER AND HIS BRETHREN, vv.1-8

In Chapter 5, immorality and other matters (v.11) were to be judged with the Lord's authority (v.4), whereas in Chapter 6 matters were ***not*** to be resolved by man's authority (v.1). Believers at Corinth were evidently seeking legal help in settling disputes amongst themselves, necessitating Paul to say: "Dare any of you, having a matter against another, ***go to law*** before the unjust, and not before the saints? ... brother ***goeth to law*** with brother, and that before the unbelievers. Now therefore there is utterly a fault among you, because ye ***go to law*** one with another" (vv.1, 6, 7).

In dealing with the situation, Paul points out that their conduct was *(a)* inconsistent with future responsibility (vv.1-3); *(b)* ignored ability in the assembly (vv.4-6); *(c)* indicated pursuit of personal interests (vv.7-8). This brings us to:

2) THE BELIEVER AND HIS BODY, vv.9-20

This section of the chapter reintroduces the subject dealt with in Chapter 5. We must bear in mind the background of the saints at Corinth: "Ye were

Gentiles carried away unto these dumb idols, even as ye were led" (Chapter 12:2). As idol worshippers, their bodies were involved, *(i)* in eating food offered to idols; *(ii)* in involvement with the temple prostitutes. Once they were ensnared in all the vice and sin associated with idolatry at Corinth (see vv.9-10). Now they had a completely new life (see v.11). What now was to be their attitude to the attachments of idolatry? The answer is given in verses 12-20: *(i)* in relation to food offered to idols ("meats"), see verses 12-14; *(ii)* in relation to fornication, verses 15-20.

This part of the chapter (vv.9-20) may be divided thus: *(a)* believers and their conversion (vv.9-11); *(b)* believers and their food (vv.12-13a), referring to the lawful use of the body; *(c)* believers and immorality (vv.13b-20), referring to the unlawful use of the body.

a) Believers and their conversion, vv.9-11

i) What they were, vv.9-10. "Know ye not that the unrighteous shall not inherit the kingdom of God? Be not deceived (ten things follow): neither fornicators, nor idolators, nor adulterers, nor effeminate ('those that make women of themselves', JND), nor abusers of themselves with mankind ('nor abusers of themselves with men', RV), nor thieves (*'kleptes'*, from *'klepto'* to steal: hence our English word 'kleptomaniac'), nor covetous, nor drunkards, nor revilers ('abusive persons', JND), nor extortioners (pillagers, plunderers, robbers) shall inherit the kingdom of God." (This reminds us of the ten lepers, Luke 17:12). Compare Mark 7 verses 21-22. We should note that fornication heads the list. It does so in view of the immorality at Corinth. Note that "fornicators" and "adulterers" are distinguished. Paul's list is an accurate description of society today. It is not a case of 'current trends in society'. They are, alas, more than 'trends'. Without expanding further, it should be said that the word "effeminate" may well refer to unutterably vile practices.

No such people will "inherit the kingdom of God". This is stressed at the beginning and ending of the list. Compare Galatians 5 verse 21. Note the contrast in 2 Peter 1 verses 1-11. The phrase "kingdom of God" signifies the rule of God. It has a present application, but refers here to the future when, as already noted, "the saints shall judge the world?" (v.2). The word "inherit" means: 'to receive as one's own'. See Hebrews 12 verse 28.

ii) What they had become, v.11. "And such *were* (that is, they no longer practised sin) some of you: but ye are washed, but ye are sanctified, but ye are justified in the name of the Lord Jesus, and by the Spirit of our God." So this section of the chapter commences with: "Know ye not that the unrighteous ('*adikos*') shall not inherit the kingdom of God?" (v.9), and concludes with: "but ye are washed, but ye are sanctified, but ye are justified ('*dikaioo*')".

The words: "but ye are washed" are in the Greek 'middle voice', giving the literal rendering: 'ye washed yourselves'. That is, on faith in Christ. Compare Acts 22 verse 16. The words: "but ye are sanctified" ('ye *were* sanctified', RV) refer, not to an attainment, but to a state. See 1 Corinthians 1 verse 2; Hebrews 10 verse 10; 13: 12 and Jude verse 1 (AV). The words: "but ye are justified" ('ye *were* justified', RV) complete the three features of the new life. It has been nicely said that we are 'washed from the defilement of sin', 'sanctified from the habit of sin', and 'justified from the guilt of sin'.

But why are they stated in this order? Paul is speaking here about moral behaviour, rather than about a doctrinal position. So "washed" rests upon "sanctified" and "sanctified" rests upon "justified". A moral cleansing took place at conversion. That moral cleansing was in accord with their new position – "sanctified". They were set apart as belonging to God. That new position could only exist because of their righteous position before God – "justified". Justified people are people reckoned or declared as righteous. The passage, therefore, teaches us that just as the unrighteous are characterised by unholy ways, the righteous are characterised by holy ways.

We have been "washed ... sanctified ... justified in the name of the Lord Jesus, and by the Spirit of our God" (v.11). We should notice reference here to the Godhead: "in the name of the **Lord Jesus**, and by the **Spirit** of our **God**". The wonderful change in the life of the Corinthian believers took place:

- *"In the name of the Lord Jesus."* That is, the **authority and basis** on which this has taken place. Compare Acts 3 verse 16; 4 verse 10.

- *"By the Spirit of our God."* That is, the **power** that operated in all that took place. This phrase is only found here in the New Testament.

Paul now turns to the believer's attitude to idolatrous associations. Can we do as we please now that we are saved? We cannot and we must not.

b) Believers and their food, vv12-13a

Paul refers here to the lawful use of the body. "All things are lawful unto me, but all things are not expedient: all things are lawful to me, but I will not be brought under the power of any. Meats for the belly, and the belly for meats: but God shall destroy both it and them." We should notice three things here:

i) The legality of eating food (meats) offered to idols is not in question. Food in itself does not defile a person. See Matthew 15 verse 11. But the effect of this on other people is a different matter. "All things are lawful unto me, but all things are not expedient (*'sumphero'*, meaning profitable, helpful, advisable)" (v.12a). That is, bearing in mind 1 Corinthians 10 verses 28-29, "expedient" in terms of its benefit for others.

ii) Again, it is not a question of the legality of a thing here, but the place that it occupies in the lives of God's people: "All things are lawful to me, but I will not be brought under the power of any" (v.12b) or, as it has been said: "All things are in my power, but I shall not be overpowered by anything". There must be no loss of self-control.

iii) In any case, there was no moral significance in these things: both terminate with the termination of our present state on earth. "Meats for the belly, and the belly for meats: but God shall destroy (*'katargeo'*, to render inactive) both it and them" (v.13a). In the words of W.E. Vine, "food and digestion are matters that belong to our present transient state, and cease their operations at its termination". There are no eternal consequences.

c) Believers and immorality, vv13b-20

If there is no moral significance in eating meats offered to idols, there is certainly moral significance here. Moral laxity is another matter entirely. The importance of the subject is stressed by the three occurrences of: "Know ye not?" (vv.15, 16, 19). The overall lesson should be carefully noted: *(i)* the believer's natural appetites are temporary, and will cease" (v.13a): there is **no** moral effect here; *(ii)* the believer's body has an eternal future, and will be raised (v.14): this qualifies v.13b, "the Lord for the body": there **is** a moral effect here.

"Now the body is not for fornication, but for the Lord; and the Lord for the body. And God hath both raised (*'egeiro'*) up the Lord, and will also raise us up (*'exegeiro'*) by his own power" (vv.13b-14). We should notice two important things here:

- **"The body is ... for the Lord", v.13.** That is, for His use. **This is our part.** What **we** must do with the body. We must heed the injunction: "Present your bodies a living sacrifice, holy, acceptable unto God ..." (Romans 12:1).

- **"The Lord for the body", v.13**. This is **His** part. It is now a question of what He will do with the body. He "will also raise up us by his own power" (v.14). As Wm. MacDonald so nicely observes: "His interest in our body does not end at the time of death. He is going to raise the body of every believer to fashion it like the glorious body of the Lord Jesus".

But there is more: "Know ye not that your bodies are members of Christ? Shall I then take ('take away', RV) the members of Christ, and make them the members of a harlot? God forbid! What! Know ye not that he which is joined (*'kollao'*, 'to join fast together, to glue, cement') to an harlot is one body? For two, saith he, shall be one flesh. But he that is joined '(*kollao'*) unto the Lord is one spirit" (vv.15-17).

Our bodies are said to be: "members of Christ", that is, united to Him. Our spiritual union with Christ is manifested through our bodies. The body is the instrument through which the Lord acts. The whole man is united to Christ: hence Paul's prayer: "I pray God your whole spirit and soul and **body** be preserved blameless unto the coming of our Lord Jesus Christ" (1 Thessalonians 5:23). By being "joined to an harlot" the person concerned robs the Lord of the channel through which He delights to manifest Himself. It has been said that having asked: "Shall I then take the members of Christ, and make them the members of an harlot?" (v.15), Paul finds his own question so repugnant that he quickly answers in very strong language: "God forbid!" or "Far be the thought" (JND). This has been rendered 'May it not happen!'

The expressions: "one body ... one flesh ... one spirit" (vv.16-17) call for explanation. The first two are not synonymous.

- **"One body", v.16.** Paul refers to "one body" by asking, with seeming incredulity: "What? know ye not that he which is joined to an harlot is one body?" He indicates that the union with a harlot is purely physical and for those brief moments two bodies have been physically united and therefore are seen as "one body". This is in contrast with the high and lofty ideal of "one flesh" which is seen in marriage alone. So:

- "One flesh", v.16. "What? know ye not that he which is joined to an harlot is one body? For two, saith he, shall be one flesh." In this connection, Paul cites Genesis 2 verse 24: "Therefore shall a man leave his father and his mother, and shall cleave unto his wife: and they shall be one flesh". It is the union in "one flesh" that sanctions the most intimate relationship of marriage. Paul cannot quote anything from Genesis 2 about "one body" since that expression does not occur. Nor can he say that union with a harlot is "one flesh" since that expression is used for the permanent marriage bond. In this way, he differentiates between the two. Just in case we should think that the word "for" (v.16) explains "one body", we should note that it is simply part of the quotation from Genesis 2 verse 24. This is made clear by the punctuation of verse 16 in the Newberry Bible: "'For two", saith he, "shall be one flesh'".

What then is the difference between the expressions "one body" and "one flesh"? The former is solely a brief physical union. The latter is the union of a man and a woman in marriage, which union is formed by God and is severed only by death or the Lord's return for His people. Thus we read: "What therefore God hath joined together, let not man put asunder" (Matthew 19:6).

- "One spirit." This is the unbreakable union between the Lord and His people. The verse begins with "but" which serves to emphasise our eternal security. If the union between the husband and wife was a spiritual union then even death could not sever it. However, because it is "one flesh" it can be severed by death, and only death or His coming. But we, His people, are eternally joined to the Lord in the union of "one spirit". See John 14 verse 20 and 17 verses 21-23.

The chapter concludes by stressing the dishonourable (v.18) and honourable uses of the believer's body (vv.19-20).

i) The dishonourable use of the body, v.18: "Flee fornication. Every sin that man doeth is without the body; but he that committeth fornication sinneth against his own body." The words: "Flee fornication" mean what they say. The believer is not even to dally with the idea. He must not "temporize with it, but flee the very thought" (Leon Morris). Joseph is a perfect example of this injunction. See Genesis 39 verses 7-13. The words: "he that committeth fornication sinneth against his own body" are very well explained by: "Know ye not that your bodies are the members of Christ? Shall I then take the members of Christ, and make them the members of an harlot?" (v.15). Compare 1 Thessalonians 4 verses 4-5.

ii) The honourable use of the body, vv.19-20. "What! know ye not that your body is the temple (*'naos'*, meaning a sanctuary or shrine) of the Holy Ghost which is in you, which ye have of God, and ye are not your own? For ye are bought (*'agorazo'*, to buy out of the slave-market) with a price: therefore glorify God in your body." (The words, "and in your spirit, which are God's", are omitted by JND and in the RV). It has been nicely said that we have been 'bought and paid for".

The body is a temple of the Holy Spirit (v.19), just as the local church is a temple of the Holy Spirit (1 Corinthians 3:16). A temple is a place of worship, where God's honour dwells. See Psalm 29 verse 9. Believers have been "anointed" and "sealed" with the Holy Spirit (2 Corinthians 1:22), and He is "the earnest of our inheritance" (Ephesians 1:14). The believer's body is under new ownership. The price has been paid (v.19), and our bodies are therefore to be instruments for God's glory (v.20). This was Paul's desire: see Philippians 1 verse 20.

Scholars point out that the word "therefore" (*'de'*) does not exactly express the reason, but rather a peremptory command which may be conveyed by something like: 'I urge you' (W.E. Vine). Leon Morris puts it like this: "*De* is sometimes added to an imperative to give it a note of greater urgency … Paul does not want the command to glorify God to be taken as something that does not matter. There is an urgency about it. Let there be no delay in obeying".

1 CORINTHIANS

"Let every man have his own wife"

Read Chapter 7:1-16

With this chapter we reach a new section of the epistle in which Paul deals with various questions which had been put to him by the assembly at Corinth: "Now concerning the things whereof ye wrote unto me" (1 Corinthians 7:1); "Now concerning virgins" (Chapter 7: 25); "Now as touching things offered unto idols" (Chapter 8:1); "Mine answer to them that do examine me is this …" (Chapter 9:3); "Now concerning spiritual gifts" (Chapter 12:1); "Now concerning the collection for the saints" (Chapter 16:1).

As we have noticed, it is rather significant that in the epistle Paul deals first, not with matters about which he had been asked, but with matters about which he had *not* been asked: "It hath been declared unto me of you, my brethren, by them which are of the house of Chloe, that there are contentions among you" (1 Corinthians 1:11); "It is reported commonly (actually reported) that there is fornication among you" (1 Corinthians 5:1). Perhaps we should ask the question: 'What are *our* priorities?'

Chapters 7-9 develop matters of personal liberty in relation to marriage (Chapter 7), eating food offered to idols (Chapter 8), and entitlement to financial support (Chapter 9). We should notice that these chapters elaborate a common theme, namely that although there was liberty for all to marry, for all to eat food offered to idols, and for full-time workers to receive support, Paul himself did not exercise that liberty. In Chapter 7, he did not do so to secure greater freedom in service; in Chapter 8, he did not do so to secure the welfare of the weaker brother; in Chapter 9, he did not do so to secure his position against criticism.

1 Corinthians 7 deals particularly, though not exclusively, with marriage. The

chapter may be divided as follows: *(1)* safeguards in marriage (vv.1-9); *(2)* strains in marriage (vv.10-16); *(3)* status in life (vv17-24); *(4)* service and marriage (vv.25-35); *(5)* staying unmarried (vv.36-40).

1) SAFEGUARDS IN MARRIAGE, vv.1-9

In Chapter 6, Paul deals with the *improper* use of the body: "Every sin that a man doeth is without the body; but he that committeth fornication sinneth against his own body" (1 Corinthians 6:18). In Chapter 7, Paul deals with the *proper* use of the body. We must remember that "the body is not for fornication, but for the Lord" (Chapter 6:13).

This section of the chapter deals with two major matters: *(a)* the advantage of celibacy (v.1); *(b)* the avoidance of sin (vv.2-9).

a) The advantage of celibacy, v.1

"Now concerning the things whereof ye wrote unto me: It is good for a man (*'anthropos'*, surprisingly) not to touch a woman." It must be understood that Paul is not advocating or even recommending celibacy here: he is simply noting its advantage in the context of Christian service. With this in mind, it should be pointed out that the word "good" (*'kalos'*) indicates what is expedient or advantageous. The word "touch" (*'haptomai'*, the usual word for touch) is a euphemism for sexual relations. See Proverbs 6 verse 29: "Can one go on hot coals, and his feet be not burned? So he that goeth in to his neighbour's wife; whosoever toucheth her shall not be innocent". Having said this, we must endeavour to ascertain what, overall, is meant here. The verse has been interpreted in two ways:

- That Paul is quoting a line from the Corinthian's letter to him. John Heading sees it in this way: "They could not discern the proper course for a Christian in a scene of abounding evil around, so they confused complete abstention (from sexual relations) with a form of spirituality". If this form of asceticism was advocated at Corinth, then Paul proceeds to point out the moral danger involved in such abstention: "Nevertheless (or 'But', JND) to avoid fornication, let every man have his own wife ..." (v.2).

- That Paul is making a statement: Bearing in mind God's purpose in creation, it seems rather strange, at first glance, that Paul should say: "It is good for a man not to touch a woman". After all, God had said: "It is not

good that the man should be alone; I will make him an help meet for him … Therefore shall a man leave his father and his mother, and shall cleave unto his wife: and they shall be one flesh" (Genesis 2:18, 24). In consequence: "Marriage is honourable in all, and the bed undefiled" (Hebrews 13:4), and Paul himself warns against those who teach otherwise: "Now the Spirit speaketh expressly that in the latter times some shall depart from the faith, giving heed to seducing spirits, and doctrines of devils; speaking lies in hypocrisy; having their conscience seared with a hot iron; forbidding to marry …" (1 Timothy 4:1-3). As J.M. Davies (*The Epistles to the Corinthians*) observes: "The marriage union is symbolical of the union of 'Christ and the church' (Ephesians 5:31-32)".

However, the difficulty disappears when we read the entire passage. (How often this happens. If you encounter a 'difficult' verse or passage in Scripture, don't 'stew over it', read on, and you will often find the answer a few verses, or a few chapters, later). Read it like this: "It is *good* for a man not to touch a woman … I say therefore to the unmarried and widows, It is *good* for them if they abide even as I" (vv.1, 8). But why should it be "*good* for a man not to touch a woman?", and why should it be "*good* for them to abide even as I?" The answer lies further on in the chapter: "He that is unmarried careth for the things that belong to the Lord, how he may please the Lord: but he that is married careth for the things that are of the world, how he may please his wife …" (vv.32-34).

Paul is not, therefore, recommending celibacy as a general rule, but dealing with marriage as it affects service. But this involved moral danger, and Paul was not unmindful of "the stresses of living the Christian life at Corinth, with its constant pressure from the low standards of pagan sexual morality" (Leon Morris). Paul faces the reality of the situation in saying: "It is good for a man not to touch a woman. **Nevertheless** ('but', JND), to avoid fornication, let every man have his own wife …" Compare verses 8-9: "It is good for them if they abide even as I. **But** if they cannot contain, let them marry".

b) The avoidance of sin, vv.2-9

"Nevertheless to avoid fornication, let every man have his own wife (no polygamy), and let every woman have her own husband (no polyandry)" (v.2). It hardly needs to be said that this is not the only reason for marriage! Paul is evidently referring here to God's purpose in marriage (see, again, Genesis 2: 24), that is, one man and one woman exclusive to each other.

This is the norm in human relationships, but this does not mean that there could be no exceptions, and in such cases Paul points out that single life is not possible for all, and that there are moral dangers in attempting a way of life for which men and women might be entirely unfitted (see vv.7-9). He therefore emphasises the moral safety of marriage, and in so doing makes clear that sexual relationships are to be restricted to the marriage bond. He deals with this *(i)* with reference to those who are married (vv.3-6); *(ii)* with reference to those who are unmarried (vv.7-9).

i) With reference to those who are married, vv.3-6

Marriage is a safeguard against immorality. We should notice the couplets: "a man ... a woman" (v.1); "man ... wife"; "woman ... husband" (v.2); "husband ... wife"; "wife ... husband" (v.3); "wife ... husband"; "husband ... wife" (v.4). Attention is drawn to:

- *The obligations of marriage, v.3.* "Let the husband render unto the wife due benevolence ('her due', JND): and likewise also the wife to the husband." The word "render" ('*apodidomi*') means: 'to discharge an obligation'. Paul refers here to the obligations of the married state, that is, to conjugal rights. Observe that marriage is not an occasion for self-gratification. Compare Ephesians 5 verse 29: "So ought men to love their wives as their own bodies. He that loveth his wife loveth himself. For no man ever yet hated his own flesh; but nourisheth and cherisheth it, even as the Lord the church".

- *Ownership in marriage, v.4.* "The wife hath not power ('*exousiazo*') of her own body, but the husband: and likewise also the husband hath not power of his own body, but the wife." The words, "hath not power", refer to authority. There is no separate ownership in marriage: husband and wife are "one flesh" (Genesis 2:24). J. Hunter (*What the Bible Teaches* – 1 *Corinthians*) is worth quoting *in extenso* here: "The apostle now states the principle that governs the practice of conjugal rights. He says that the wife has surrendered the right to rule over her own body to the husband; she has given her body to him. Likewise the husband has surrendered the right to rule over his body; he has given his body to her. It is most remarkable to notice this matter of reciprocal responsibility. Both husband and wife have transferred this authority or right over their bodies equally to the other. This obligation is mutual. In wedlock, separate ownership of the body ceases. In this respect the equality of the sexes is stressed; each has an exclusive claim to the other".

- *Abstinence in marriage, vv.5-6.* "Defraud ye not one the other, except it be with consent for a time, that ye may give yourselves to fasting and prayer (JND omits 'fasting': see his footnote); and come together again, that Satan tempt you not for your incontinency." The words: "defraud not" mean: 'to refuse or deprive of what the other has a right to'. Abstention is permitted under certain conditions and for certain reasons. We may call this 'lawful abstention'. It is by mutual consent; it is temporary; it is to permit prayer.

A warning is given at the end of the verse: "And come together again, that Satan tempt you not for your incontinency". J. Hunter comments helpfully: "The couple must come together again, or Satan would take advantage of any lack of self-control in one or other of the parties concerned. Any action taken, even for a spiritual purpose, if it continues beyond the limits of natural endurance, could lead to spiritual shipwreck. If husband or wife insisted on abstinence for a prolonged period without due consideration to the needs of the other, this could lead to a breakdown in self-control, and probably to adultery. Satan would be quick to take advantage of such weakness".

E.G. Parmenter (*An Explanation of a Neglected Chapter*, published in *Assembly Testimony*) puts it nicely: "As 'heirs together of the grace of life' (1 Peter 3:7), the object of each is not self-gratification, but in selflessness having a mutual care for each other, the duty to each will be fulfilled, bearing in mind that neither the wife nor the husband have control of their own bodies. The woman who marries gives up the full right to her own body, and so the man. In view of this, the apostle exhorts the married couple in verse 5 not to defraud, i.e. refuse or deprive each other in the matter of their marital rights; unless it be for a limited time, by mutual agreement, in order to give themselves with greater concentration to prayerful exercise before God, then they must come together again".

The words: "But I speak this (referring to v.5) by permission, and not by commandment" (v.6) are elsewhere rendered: "But this I say as consenting [to], not as commanding [it]" (JND). That is, Paul is not commanding that they should abstain from conjugal rights in order to concentrate on prayer, but he is permitting it. Others look at this slightly differently, suggesting that while Paul has no command from the Lord here, he gives spiritual guidance: and that this is no less inspired. In saying: "I speak this by permission, and not of commandment", Paul is saying, in effect, that there is no "thou shalt … thou shalt not" in the circumstances.

ii) With reference to those who are unmarried, vv.7-9

Again, marriage is a safeguard against immorality. Paul spells out two alternatives in these circumstances:

- "If they abide even as I", vv.7-8. "For I would that all men were even as I myself. But every man hath his proper gift of God, one after this manner, and another after that" or: "Now I wish all men to be even as myself ..." (JND). Paul now states his own position. It does seem from this that Paul was not married. Some feel that he was a widower: others feel that his wife left him when he was converted, and cite his 'profit and loss account': "But what things were gain to me, those I counted loss for Christ. Yea doubtless, and I count all things but loss for the excellency of the knowledge of Christ Jesus my Lord: for whom I have suffered the loss of **all** things ..." (Philippians 3:7-8).

Having stated his own position, Paul now makes clear that there is no superior position in either the unmarried or the married state. God appoints the sphere: "every man hath his proper gift of God (note that the word "gift" here translates 'charisma'), one after this manner, and another after that". Whether a Christian marries or remains single, responsibility in the matter is to God alone.   Compare Matthew 19 verse 11, where, having spoken about divorce, the disciples observe: "If the case of the man be so with his wife, it is not good to marry. But he (the Lord Jesus) said unto them, All men cannot receive this saying, save they to whom it is given. For there are some eunuchs, which were so born from their mother's womb: and there are some eunuchs, which were made eunuchs of men: and there be eunuchs for the kingdom of heaven's sake. He that is able to receive it, let him receive it".

Bearing in mind his own position, Paul continues: "I say therefore to the unmarried and widows, It is good for them if they abide even as I" (v.8). Notice that there is no suggestion here of a command. "It is clear from the story of his life that he would have found it most difficult to combine marriage with his intensive and widespread missionary work" (J. Hunter).

- "If they cannot contain", v.9. "But if they cannot contain, let them marry: for it is better to marry than to burn." The words: "But if they cannot contain" mean: 'But if they have no continency' or: 'if they lack the power of self-control'. Paul obviously possessed this. The words: "it is better to marry than to burn" mean that it is better to marry than to be "inflamed with passion" (J. Hunter). He continues: "it describes the turbulent emotional struggle within". The words "to burn" are in the present tense, and indicate a "recurring condition". "To burn" is to be "consumed with inward desire, even if one does not yield to it. It could, of course, result in criminal satisfaction, or in secret devastation of the inner spiritual life".

We should notice that Paul returns to this in verses 36-37, but does so there with particular reference to service.

2) STRAINS ON MARRIAGE, vv.10-16

This paragraph divides into two sections: *(a)* vv.10-11, where Paul evidently refers to married couples who are believers: "Let not the wife depart from her husband: let not the husband put away his wife". This could not be addressed to **unbelievers!** Compare 1 Corinthians 5 verse 12. (It is only in verses 12-13 that we encounter a different relationship: "a wife … and husband that believeth not".) In this section (vv.10-11), he says, "I command, yet not I **but the Lord**". This brings us to *(b)* vv.12-16, where Paul refers to a marriage where one partner is an unbeliever. In this section, he says: "Speak I, **not the Lord**". In the first case he says: "unto the married" (v.10), and in the second he says: "to the rest" (v.12). We must therefore notice:

a) Strain on the marriage of two believers, vv.10-11

Two positions are described: *(i)* wife and husband living together (vv.10-11); *(ii)* wife and husband not living together (v.11).

*i) **Wife and husband living together, vv.10-11.*** "And unto the married I command, yet not I, but the Lord, Let not the wife depart from her husband … and let not the husband put away his wife." (The intervening words: "But and if she depart, let her remain unmarried, or be reconciled to her husband" are a parenthesis.) In saying: "yet not I, but the Lord", Paul refers to the Lord's own teaching: "Whosoever shall put away his wife, except it be for fornication, and shall marry another, committeth adultery: and whoso marrieth her which is put away doth commit adultery" (Matthew 19:3-9); "And if a woman shall put away her husband and be married to another, she (as the innocent party) committeth adultery" (Mark 10:10-12). See also Matthew 5 verse 32. The words: "I command, yet not I, but the Lord" confirm that his command is in perfect accord with what the Lord taught when He was here. We should notice the two injunctions:

- "Let not the wife depart". The position of **the wife.** E.G. Parmenter understands this as follows: "The wife is not to be unfaithful under any circumstances to her marriage covenant, neither is she to depart from her husband under any pretence".

- "Let not the husband put away his wife". The position of **the husband.** The word "depart" and the words "put away" translate different Greek words. The former: "depart" ('*chorizo*': vv.10, 11, 15) evidently refers to separation: the latter: "put away" ('*aphiemi*': vv.11, 12 & 13) evidently refers to divorce ('*apoluo*'). Do notice that "the LORD, the God of Israel, saith that he hateth putting away" (Malachi 2:16).

ii) Wife and husband not living together, v.11. "But and if she depart, let her remain unmarried, or be reconciled to her husband: and let not the husband put away his wife" or: "But if also she **shall have been** separated, let her remain unmarried, or be reconciled to her husband" (JND). That is, if the separation had taken place **prior to receipt of the epistle:** but there was no question of a separation **now that Paul had written on the subject** with apostolic authority. We should note, for the second time, that the words: "But and if she depart, let her remain unmarried (that is, no remarriage must take place), or be reconciled to her husband" (so he is still her husband), are a parenthesis: for the main thrust of the passage read: "Let not the wife depart from her husband … and let not the husband put away his wife".

In summary, Paul states, **firstly**, that a wife must not separate from her husband, but, **secondly**, if she has already left him, then she must remain unmarried, and if possible, be reconciled to him. No second marriage is contemplated. That is, while the first husband is alive. As noted above, these verses suggest a Christian marriage under strain.

b) Strain on the marriage of a believer and an unbeliever, vv.12-16

We have here a case of a divided home. These verses evidently refer to a believing partner who had been saved after marriage. In Eric Parmenter's words, "When the call of God came in the gospel through Paul the preacher, one party responded to the call and was saved, but the other party would have nothing to do with the gospel, and continued in idolatry". What now is the position of the believing husband or wife? There are two cases:

i) Where an unbelieving partner is willing to remain, vv.12-14

Firstly, a believing man with an unbelieving wife (v.12) and, **secondly**, a believing woman with an unbelieving husband (v.13).

- A believing man with an unbelieving wife, v.12. "But to the rest speak I, not the Lord: If any **brother** hath a wife that believeth not, and she be pleased to dwell with him, let him not put her away." We notice that conversion does not cancel the marriage. "If any brother hath a **wife** that believeth not ..." She is still his wife. "If she be pleased to dwell with him", then "let him not put **her away**", that is, divorce her.

We should notice that Paul says here: "But to the rest speak I, **not the Lord**". He is not disclaiming inspiration, but stating that, unlike the cases in verses 10-11, he cannot cite the Lord's personal teaching on the subject.

- A believing woman with an unbelieving husband, v.13. "And the woman which hath an husband that believeth not, and if he be pleased to dwell with her, let her not **leave him**." As noted above, the word "leave" translates 'aphiemi', elsewhere rendered "put away", that is, divorce him.

The reasons follow: "For the unbelieving husband is sanctified ('hagiazo') by the wife, and the unbelieving wife is sanctified ('hagiazo') by the husband: else were your children unclean; but now are they holy ('hagios')" (v.14). Compare 1 Timothy 4 verses 4-5: "For every creature of God is good, and nothing to be refused, if it be received with thanksgiving: for it is **sanctified** by the word of God and prayer". See also 2 Peter 1 verse 18, referring to "the **holy** mount". Just as the character of food, and of the mountain, does not alter, so the **spiritual status** of the unbelieving partner does not alter either. The unbelieving partner is sanctified in the sense that they are regarded by God as the legitimate partner of the saved wife or husband, and therefore the relationship is a proper one. If otherwise, then the children would have been born out of divinely-approved marriage. The word 'hagiazo' ("sanctified"), used in connection with the unbelieving husband or wife, is in the perfect tense, indicating a past act with continuing effects. The past act was the marriage of the man and woman concerned, when "the husband set apart his wife from all other women to be to him what no other woman could lawfully be" and vice versa. "Hence the ordinance of marriage sanctified each to the other" (John Miller, Notes on the Epistles).

Amongst other things, this proves that marriage is not a Christian institution: it is connected with creation. "Genesis 2 proves unequivocally that marriage is a divine institution, inviolate, unalterable and fixed by God. It is not a temporary contract, but a permanent and exclusive union of one man and one woman until dissolved by death. It was ordained by God for mankind before the descriptive words 'believers' and 'unbelievers' were in force, and throughout Scripture, its permanency is binding upon all who enter upon it ... Nowhere does Scripture differentiate between the marriages of believers and unbelievers: God recognises both" (E.G. Parmenter). Since the continuity of marriage and family life does not involve a sinful relationship there is no reason for divorce or separation.

ii) Where an unbelieving partner is not willing to remain, vv.15-16

"But if the unbelieving depart, let him depart. A brother or sister is not under bondage in such cases: but God has called us to peace" (v.15). The crucial question is "not under bondage" to do what? Some teach that it means "not under bondage" to remain in a single position, and therefore free to marry. But do the words: "not under bondage in such cases" mean that wilful desertion breaks the marriage bond, and that the deserted party is free to marry? This is never taught in Scripture.

We must look for another explanation. Here are two helpful comments. Firstly: "The opening statement indicates that if the unbelieving partner is determined to leave, then the Christian must accept the position. There is no way he or she can restrain the spouse. In such a situation the Christian brother or sister is not bound or enslaved to a mechanical retention of a relationship which the other has abandoned. He or she is not bound to endeavour to effect a return if the partner's mind is fully made up to leave" (J. Hunter). Secondly: "This has been construed to mean that the deserted partner is free to remarry: that the former marriage tie has been automatically severed by the act of desertion. If that were true, Paul would be guilty of contradicting what he had said earlier. See verse 11. The apostle's meaning is, that the believing wife is not to have recourse to litigation in order to compel her husband to return, neither in her anxiety should she use every effort to get him back" (E.G. Parmenter).

The words, "but God hath called us to peace" (v.15), must be understood in their context. They refer to a 'mixed marriage'. While the believing partner is not duty bound, come what may, to maintain the relationship, none the less, they are reminded that "God hath called us to peace". They should therefore do all possible to preserve the marriage. The reason follows:

"For what knowest thou, O wife, whether thou shalt save thy husband? or how knowest thou, O man, whether thou shalt save thy wife?" (v.16). Paul is expanding his previous statement: "but God hath called us to peace". In seeking to preserve the marriage, there is opportunity for the conversion of the unsaved partner. Compare 1 Peter 3 verses 1-2: "Likewise, ye wives, be in subjection to your own husbands; that, if any obey not the word, they also may without the word (that is, without preaching at him) be won by the conversation of the wives; while they behold your chaste conversation coupled with fear".

1 CORINTHIANS

"The time is short"

Read Chapter 7:17-40

As we have already noticed, 1 Corinthians 7 deals particularly, though not exclusively, with marriage. The chapter may be divided as follows: *(1)* safeguards in marriage (vv.1-9); *(2)* strains in marriage (vv.10-16); *(3)* status in life (vv17-24); *(4)* service and marriage (vv.25-35); *(5)* staying unmarried (vv.36-40). It is worth pointing out that in this chapter, Paul gives general guidance rather than commands.

1) SAFEGUARDS IN MARRIAGE, vv.1-9

This section of the chapter deals with two major matters: *(a)* the advantage of celibacy (v.1); *(b)* the avoidance of sin (vv.2-9). In connection with the former, we noted that rather than commanding or even recommending celibacy, Paul is stressing its advantages in connection with Christian service. This becomes clear as we read the chapter. See, particularly, vv.7-9; vv.32-34. But celibacy brings moral danger, and this is emphasised in verses 2-9. The section begins: "Nevertheless to avoid fornication, let every man have his own wife, and let every woman have her own husband" (v.2). Paul deals with this *(i)* with reference to those who are married (vv.3-6) and *(ii)* with reference to those who are unmarried (vv.7-9).

2) STRAINS IN MARRIAGE, vv.10-16

Without further elaboration here, we noted that Paul deals: *(i)* with strains on the marriage of two believers (vv.10-11); *(ii)* with strains on the marriage when only one partner is a believer (vv.12-16). This brings us to:

3) STATUS IN LIFE, vv.17-24

We could have called this section of the Chapter: 'Continuing in the state of marriage', but this would only be applicable to verse 17. At this point, Paul takes the opportunity to extend the principle of maintaining status in marriage to other aspects of life (vv.18-24).

The opening verse of the section is pivotal: it looks back and it looks forward: "But as God hath distributed to every man, as the Lord hath called every one, so let him walk. And so ordain I in all the churches".

- It looks back. The words: "as God hath distributed to every man" refer back to Paul's earlier statement in connection with marriage: "For I would that all men were even as myself. But every man hath his proper gift of God, one after this manner, and another after that" (vv.7-8). Having stated his own position ("I would that all men were even as myself"), Paul continues by saying that there is no superior position in either the unmarried or the married state. God appoints the sphere: "every man hath his proper gift of God, one after this manner, and another after that". It is important to maintain the personal status appointed by God.

- It looks forward. J. Hunter (*What the Bible Teaches - 1 Corinthians*) puts it admirably: "The principle that was set forth in relation to marriage, namely, if possible, remain in the circumstances in which the grace of God met and saved you, is now extended to a wider sphere".

We should notice Paul's reference to the consistency of his teaching: "And so ordain I in all the churches" (v.17). This reminds us that no local church can suit themselves when it comes to doctrine and practice. (Compare 1 Corinthians 1:2; 4:17; 11:16; 14:33.) It is a contradiction in terms to use the expression "church of God" (1 Corinthians 1:2), and not to recognise and obey the Word of God. The words: "so ordain I" ('*diatasso*', meaning 'appoint') emphasise Paul's apostolic authority. See 1 Corinthians 14 verse 37.

As noted above, Paul takes the opportunity to apply the principle of maintaining status in marriage to other spheres in life. In this connection, we should notice that he makes the point three times in the passage: "But as God hath distributed to every man, as the Lord hath called every one, **so let him walk** ... Let every man **abide in the same calling** wherein he was called ... Brethren, let every man, wherein he is called, **therein abide** with God" (vv.17, 20. 24). A case, surely, of "a threefold cord" not being "quickly broken!" (Ecclesiastes 4:12). Paul refers to two particular matters: *(a)* circumcision versus uncircumcision (vv.18-19); *(b)* bond-service versus freedom (vv.20-23).

a) Circumcision versus uncircumcision, vv.18-19

This is *a religious distinction*. "Is any man called being circumcised? let him not become uncircumcised. Is any called in uncircumcision? let him not be circumcised. Circumcision is nothing, and uncircumcision is nothing, but the keeping of the commandments of God." W.E. Vine deals with this most helpfully. Having said that "the principle of the undesirability of a change in matters related to married life is now extended to the subject of circumcision and conditions of slavery", and that "this leads to a statement of what is really the important thing in a Christian life", he continues: "Those who were converted as Jews were not to efface the external sign of their connection with God's ancient people. Those who were converted as Gentiles were not to take any step to enter the Jewish community. The matter is dealt with in Galatians 5 verse 6, where the Apostle shews that in Christ Jesus neither circumcision nor uncircumcision is capable of producing spiritual results, but that which does so is faith working through love … *To keep God's commandments is everything for the believer* … it is this which determines the character of the believer's walk here and its issues hereafter". Leon Morris agrees: "Paul calls on men to take no notice of these distinctions (circumcision/uncircumcision). They do not matter … The thing is indifferent. A man ought not to change his state … *No matter of ritual can be set alongside the keeping of the commandments*".

So far as circumcision versus uncircumcision is concerned, a higher principle is involved: "*keeping the commandments of God*". Lesser issues, in this case no issue at all, can so easily make us forget all-important things. Doing the will of God must be paramount.

b) Bond-service versus freedom, vv.20-23

This is *a social distinction.* "Let every man abide in the same calling wherein he was called. Art thou called being a servant? care not for it: but if thou mayest be free, use it rather. For he that is called in the Lord, being a servant, is the Lord's freeman: likewise also he that is called, being free, is Christ's servant. Ye are bought with a price; be not ye servants of men."

We may look at the salient points as follows:

i) The calling. As Leon Morris points out: "The principle of verse 17 is now stated another way … Here it (the calling) means the call taken in conjunction with all the external circumstances. Men should serve God in that place in life in which it pleases Him to call them. *Abide* is present imperative, with the thought of continuance". W.E. Vine agrees: "The calling is not here a matter of vocation, but of the circumstances in which the calling took place". In this case, the "calling" refers to bond-service. The person concerned is a slave.

ii) The concern. "Art thou called being a servant? care not for it" (v.21). This looks back to the time when God first spoke to the man. The meaning is: 'Were you called being a servant?', and the words: "care not for it", mean: 'do not worry unduly that you are a slave' or 'do not become burdened and anxious about it'. As Leon Morris observes: "Conversion is not the signal for a man to leave his occupation (unless it is one plainly incompatible with Christianity) and seek some other".

iii) The change. "If thou mayest be made free, use it rather" (v.21), which simply means: "If however the opportunity of becoming *free* occurs, Paul suggests that he *use* it" (Leon Morris). Scholars point out that the words: "use it rather" can be understood to mean either: 'use your bondservice', in other words, 'don't change', or: 'use the opportunity to be set free'. The latter seems preferable! "If you can be made free, then make use of your new status" (Leon Morris).

iv) The consideration. "He that is called in the Lord, being a servant, is the Lord's freeman: likewise also he that is called, being free, is Christ's servant" (v.22). Very clearly, spiritual status overrides social status.

- In the first case, where "the calling marks the time of conversion, and the phrase 'in the Lord' means that the one who is called is brought under His authority and into subjection to His will", the slave "who was brought by grace into subjection to Christ as his Master, was spiritually His freedman" (W.E. Vine). W.E. Vine continues by pointing out that "Under the Romans, a freed slave still stood in relation to his master, who was thereafter called his patron, but with the Christian slave, Christ was not his Patron but his Owner and Master. One who remained as a slave could not have his spiritual freedom destroyed thereby. Whatever happened to him, he could rest in the assurance that everything was controlled for him by the will of God".

- In the second case, the freed slave was not in a position to do exactly what he liked. As W.E. Vine so rightly points out, this would "only be prejudicial to his best interests. It should be his delight to be in devoted bond-service to Christ. Such was the case with Paul, who rejoiced in so describing himself (see Romans 1:1; Philippians 1:1; Titus 1:1)".

Perhaps it is worth saying again that whatever our social status may be, our spiritual status is infinitely more important. A believer is the "Lord's freeman" and "Christ's servant". In the first place, we are subject to a new authority giving us liberty, not to please ourselves, but to please the Lord. In the second place, putting it the other way round, we have resigned the liberty to please ourselves that we might do the will of Christ. Or, in the words of J. Hunter: "The one who was a slave socially, when converted, became free spiritually; the other who was free socially became a slave spiritually".

In summary, so far as bondservice versus freedom is concerned, there is a higher freedom for the bondservant, and a higher service for the freeman. But Paul does not say: 'Once a slave, always a slave': freedom, if granted, was to be used for God's glory.

v) The cost. "Ye are bought with a price; be not ye the servants of men" (v.23). Compare 1 Corinthians 6 verse 20: "Ye are bought with a price: therefore glorify God in your body …" However, in the present context, Paul is emphasising that our spiritual status, as slaves set free from spiritual bondage, rests upon the infinite price paid by the Lord Jesus at Calvary. In view of this, as W.E. Vine points out, we are to be at Christ's disposal and not to place ourselves "under ecclesiastical domination" or become slaves "to the judgment and will of a fellow creature". However, the injunction: "be not ye the servants of men" may well mean that bond-servants were to recognise that they must do everything "heartily, as to the Lord, and not unto men" (see Colossians 3:22-24). We should note that the words: "be not ye the servants of men" does not contradict such passages as Ephesians 6 verses 5-8; Colossians 3 verses 22-25; Titus 2 verses 9-10, where Paul is speaking about the way in which converted slaves should do their work.

Paul states his conclusion: "Brethren, let every man, wherein he is called, therein abide with God" (v.24). We must notice his words: "therein abide *with God*". We should also notice that he says: "Brethren". Whether slaves or freemen, Paul says: "Brethren!" Whatever the circumstances, bondmen or freemen, we are in them "with God". In the words of Jack Hunter: "This fellowship with God transforms every situation and enables us to be content with our lot – near to God, beside God, remaining with Him, peaceful and content, safe and happy. What a word is this in days of discontent and dissatisfaction".

4) SERVICE AND MARRIAGE, vv.25-35

His opening words at this point, "Now concerning virgins" (compare 1 Corinthians 7:1; 8:1; 12:1; 16:1) indicate that this was another matter about which the assembly at Corinth had sought his advice. We must remember, as we approach these verses, that Paul is dealing with the single and married states as they affect service. The principal point here is that unmarried people are better able to serve the Lord. So far as **men** are concerned, it is summed up in verses 32-33: "He that is unmarried careth for the things that belong to the Lord, how he may please the Lord. But he that is married careth for the things that are of the world, how he may please his wife". A similar summary follows (v.34) in connection with **sisters**: "Now concerning virgins I have no commandment of the Lord: yet I give my judgment (advice or counsel), as one that hath obtained mercy of the Lord to be faithful" (v.25). Bearing in mind that "mercy" is the expression of pity to those in need, Paul is expressing his gratitude to God for enabling him to discharge his responsibility as an apostle. In this particular case, Paul had no direct revelation from the Lord and could not refer to His teaching while here on earth. But, as W.E. Vine observes: "This does not imply that what he was now writing was not part of the God-breathed Scriptures. The record of his statements is equally inspired with any other part of Scripture".

These verses (vv.25-35) may be summarised as follows: *(a)* the preferability of single life in relation to service (vv.26-28); *(b)* the priority of the Lord's interests in all spheres (vv.29-31); *(c)* the advantages of single life in relation to service (vv.32-35). In view of the demands of service, to remain single was preferable (vv.26-28). That is not to say that it is wrong to marry (v.28). In view of the demands of service, even married people should recognise the priority of the Lord's claims (v.29). This is extended to other areas in life (vv.30-31). In view of the demands of service, Paul contrasts the advantages of the single state with the disadvantages of the married state (vv.32-35). He deals with unmarried/married men in verses 32-33, and unmarried/married women in verse 34.

a) The preferability of single life in relation to service, vv.26-28

These verses evidently expand Paul's opening words: "Now concerning virgins ..." According to J.N. Darby, the word "virgins" can refer either to male or female: see his footnote which appears to be based on the meaning of the word "such" (v.28). The passage does seem to confirm this view. John Heading is quite clear about this: "The word 'virgins' is to be understood as 'unmarried people' – certainly not to sisters only!". With this in mind we must notice what Paul says about unmarried brothers and sisters:

- In relation to a brother: "I suppose ('I think', JND) therefore that this is good for the present distress, I say, that it is good for a man so to be" or (JND) "I think then that this is good on account of the present necessity, that [it is] good for a man to remain so as he is" (v.26). The following verses (vv.27-28a) explain what Paul means by saying: "it is good for a man to remain so as he is". But what about "the present distress" or "present necessity" (JND)? This could refer, as some commentators suggest, to particular circumstances, not known to us, through which the believers at Corinth were passing at the time. On the other hand, it could refer to the problems and difficulties which have beset the Lord's people down through the ages. Alternatively, the "present necessity" could well refer to the need to serve the Lord without distraction.

As indicated above, Paul now explains what he means in saying: "it is good for a man to remain so as he is" (v.26 JND). "Art thou bound to a wife? seek not to be loosed. Art thou loosed from a wife? seek not a wife. But and if thou marry, thou hast not sinned; and if a virgin marry, she hath not sinned. Nevertheless such shall have trouble in the flesh: but I spare you" or "and I would spare you" (RV). That is, "spare you", by my advice, from the cares and responsibilities attached to marriage.

J. Hunter comments helpfully here: "Those 'bound' to a wife were not to seek a divorce; 'loosed' or 'free' from a wife in the next clause does not refer to one whose marriage has been dissolved' (NEB), or who has separated from his wife. 'Loosed' stands in contrast to being 'bound', and thus means unmarried. Such are not to seek a wife. The NIV is plain and correct: 'Are you married? Do not seek a divorce. Are you unmarried? Do not look for a wife'". Any other interpretation must, surely, contradict Paul's teaching in verse 39: "The wife is bound by the law as long as her husband liveth; but if her husband be dead, she is at liberty to be married

153

to whom she will; only in the Lord". The reverse must also be true: 'as long as his wife liveth …'

- *In relation to a sister*. Having said: "it is good for a man so to be" but "if thou marry, thou hast not sinned", Paul adds: "If a virgin marry, she hath not sinned ..." Paul believed in the equality of the sexes in the matter!

b) The priority of the Lord's interests in all spheres, vv.29-31

As noted above, in view of the demands of service, even married people should recognise the priority of the Lord's claims (v.29). This is extended to other areas in life (vv.30-31). We should notice that Paul does not say: 'time is short' (it is always short!), but "***the*** time is short ('shortened', RV: 'straitened', JND)". The Lord is coming back! In view of this, the Lord's people are to prioritise His interests: "But this I say, brethren, the time is short: it remaineth, that both they that have wives be as though they had none. And they that weep, as though they wept not; and they that rejoice, as though they rejoiced not; and they that buy, as though they possessed not. And they that use this world, as not abusing it: for the fashion of this world passeth away".

- *As touching marriage*: "they that have wives be as though they had none". This does not mean, for one moment, that a man should neglect his wife, but that the Lord's claims must be paramount. Luke 14 verse 26 should be read in this connection. Paul looks here at marriage in the light of eternity.

- *As touching sorrow*: "they that weep, as though they wept not". Paul refers here to the tragedies and bereavements of life. It is possible to allow our sorrows and disappointments to "so occupy our thoughts that we have no time for the service of the Lord … Weeping may come in to lodge at eventide but joy comes in the morning" (T. Ernest Wilson).

- *As touching joy*: "and they that rejoice, as though they rejoiced not". We must listen again to T. Ernest Wilson: "The Christian life is a life of joy but the pleasures and joys of this life are transient. Preoccupation with even our blessings can blind us to the fact that 'Men die in darkness at our side, without a hope to cheer the gloom'".

- *As touching commerce*: "and they that buy, as though they possessed not". As T. Ernest Wilson points out: "Scripture exhorts us not to be slothful in business, but it is possible to be so occupied with it that we have no time for the things of the Lord". Jack Hunter writes similarly: "Nothing we purchase, no matter how costly, must be of such importance to us that it becomes our complete preoccupation".

- **As touching the world**: "and they that use this world, as not abusing it: for the fashion of this world passeth away". The word "abuse" (*'katachraomai'*) means 'to use overmuch' (W.E. Vine). See also 1 Corinthians 9 verse 18. We are to "use this world" in the sense that our contact with it is unavoidable and legitimate, but not 'use it to the full' so that we find ourselves in an 'unequal yoke'.

In short, Paul does not counsel abstinence from these things, but the regulation of them in view of the fact that, firstly, "the time is straitened" (v.29, JND), secondly, that "the fashion (*'schema'*, the outward appearance of anything) of this world passeth away" (v.31). As W.E. Vine observes: "The transitory character of the world is sufficient to prevent our seeking to get all we can out of it". Matthew 6 verses 19-21 now become compulsory reading.

c) The advantages of single life in relation to service, vv.32-35

These verses must be understood in light of the overall teaching of the passage. That is, in the light of Christian service. These verses do not teach that there is any less holiness in marriage, but that, practically, the unmarried are in a position to devote themselves to the Lord and His work. Paul deals with the unmarried and married **man** (vv.32-33) and the unmarried and married **woman** (v.34), giving his reason in verses 32 and 35.

- **The married and unmarried man, vv.32-33.** "But I would have you without carefulness. He that is unmarried careth for the things that belong to the Lord, how he may please the Lord. But he that is married careth for the things that are of the world, how he may please his wife." This is perfectly clear. No comment is required.

- **The married and unmarried woman, v.34**. "There is a difference also between a wife and a virgin. The unmarried woman careth for the things of the Lord, that she may be holy both in body and in spirit (set apart to the service and interests of Christ): but she that is married careth for the things of the world, how she may please her husband." It is hardly necessary to say that a woman does not become 'unholy' when she marries.

155

- *The reason for this teaching*. "But I would have you without carefulness (that is, distracting care) … And this I speak for your own profit (*'sumphoros'*, 'in your best interests') not that I may cast a snare upon you (literally, 'throw a noose over you'), but for that which is comely (becoming), that ye may attend upon the Lord without distraction" (vv.31-35). The word "distraction" means to 'sit well beside … without being drawn away from the object in view' (W.E. Vine). We have an illustration of this in the case of Mary as opposed to Martha in Luke 10 verses 39-40.

5) STAYING UNMARRIED, vv.36-40

In the final verses of the chapter, Paul deals *(a)* with the marriage of single people (vv.36-38) and *(b)* the remarriage of widows (vv.39-40).

a) The marriage of single people, vv.36-38

"Now if any man think that he behaveth himself uncomely toward his virgin, if she pass the flower of her age, and ***need so require***, let him do what he will, he sinneth not: let them marry. Nevertheless he that standeth stedfast in his heart, ***having no necessity,*** but hath power over his own will, and hath so decreed in his heart that he will keep his virgin, doeth well. So then, he that giveth (*her*) in marriage doeth well; but he that giveth (*her*) not in marriage doeth better."

John Heading points out, forthrightly, that "regarding the man and 'his virgin', there has appeared much nonsense in translation and exposition", and notes that the AV reads as if it were a question of "a man and his fiancée" or "a man and his unmarried daughter". He continues: "Many commentators suggest that Paul had been asked about the duty of a father in connection with a daughter of age to marry. Such makes verse 37 ridiculous, since the verse obviously refers to the desire of the man to marry". With this in mind, John Heading recommends the following translation which, it has to be said, is most helpful:

"But if any one think that he behaves himself unseemly to his virginity, if he be beyond the flower of his age (perhaps, 'getting beyond his prime'), and so it must be, let him do what he will, he does not sin: let them marry. But he who stands firm in his heart, having no need, but has authority over his own will, and has judged this in his heart to keep his own virginity, he does well. So that he that marries, himself does well; and he that does not marry does better" (JND). In the first case we have a man who "cannot contain himself any longer ('need so require')", and in the second a man who has "all his impulses disciplined and under control ('having no necessity')" (Jack Hunter). In the first case, if the man feels that he must marry, he does well (compare v.9). In the second case, if the man decides he will not marry, he does better. He is then in a better position to care "for the things that belong to the Lord, how he may please the Lord" (v.32).

b) The remarriage of widows, vv.39-40

"The wife is bound by the law *as long as her husband liveth*; but if her husband be dead, she is at liberty to be married to whom she will; *only in the Lord.* But she is happier if she so abide, after my judgment: and I think also that I have the Spirit of God."

We should notice that for the woman, marriage is "as long as her husband *liveth*", not 'as long as he behaves himself', and that on his death, she is free to remarry but "only in the Lord". (Compare Romans 7: 2-3). This is important. Paul does not say: 'only in Christ', but: "only in the Lord", indicating that a new partner in life must not only be a Christian, he must be the *right* Christian. Everything must be subject to the Lord's will.

In saying: "she is happier if she so abide", Paul is not saying that the widow would not be happy in a second marriage but, bearing in mind the context, that she would be happier in the Lord's service since she would be able to care "for the things of the Lord" (v.34). In saying: "I think also that I have the Spirit of God", Paul is not expressing doubt in any way, but stating that what he says "is more than the opinion merely of a private individual" (Leon Morris).

1 CORINTHIANS

"Knowledge puffeth up, but love edifieth"

Read Chapter 8:1-13

This chapter continues the section of the epistle (Chapters 7-16) in which Paul deals with various questions which had been put to him by the assembly at Corinth. Paul evidently refers to their questions in Chapter 7 verse 1; 7 verse 25; 8 verse 1; 9 verse 3 and 16 verse 1.

As we noticed in introducing Chapter 7, Chapters 7-9 develop matters of personal liberty in relation to marriage (Chapter 7), eating food offered to idols (Chapter 8), and entitlement to financial support (Chapter 9). We observed that these chapters elaborate a common theme, namely that although there was liberty for all to marry, for all to eat food offered to idols, and for full-time workers to receive support, Paul himself did not exercise that liberty. In Chapter 7, he did not do so in order to secure greater freedom in service; in Chapter 8, he did not do so in order to secure the welfare of the 'weaker' brother (the brother with a "weak conscience" (v.12); in Chapter 9, he did not do so in order to secure his position against criticism.

It is quite possible that Chapters 7 and 8 deal with over-reaction to two matters raised in Chapter 6 where, having dealt with the believer and his brethren (vv.1-11), Paul then deals with the believer and his body (vv.12-20). In connection with the latter, reference is made to eating food offered to idols (vv.12-13a) and to involvement with the temple harlots (vv.13b-20).

- In connection with the command: "Flee fornication" (1 Corinthians 6:18), Paul warns the Corinthians in Chapter 7 against the danger of over-reaction to that injunction by maintaining celibacy: "Now concerning the things whereof ye wrote unto me: It is good for a man not to touch a woman.

Nevertheless to avoid fornication, let every man have his own wife, and let every woman have her own husband" (1 Corinthians 7:1).

- In connection with the statement: "All things are lawful unto me, but all things are not expedient…" (1 Corinthians 6:12), Paul warns them against the danger of acting upon his words: "all things are lawful unto me", whilst forgetting that he continued by saying that "all things are not expedient". Hence his warning: "But take heed, lest by any means this liberty of yours become a stumblingblock to them that are weak" (1 Corinthians 8:9).

The chapter addresses an everyday problem at Corinth: "Now as touching things offered unto idols" (v.1). We are told that the sacrifices were usually divided into three parts: one part was consumed on the altar, another was given to the priest, and the third part was retained by the offerer. If the priest did not require his portion, it was sent either to the temple dining room (yes, there really was such a place: see verse 10) or to the meat-market (the "shambles", 1 Corinthians 10:25) for sale. In consequence, anyone entertaining at home or in the idol's temple (v.10), would almost certainly have had to say, if asked, that 'the steak on the plate' had been previously "offered unto idols" (v.1).

We should remember that Paul deals here with the subject generally, whereas in Chapter 10 verses 19-33, he deals with specific aspects of the matter. As we shall see, Chapter 8 discloses that opinion amongst the believers at Corinth was divided over the issue:

- Some believers regarded idols as non-existent anyway, and, therefore, food offered to them was a meaningless ritual. It meant absolutely nothing. They, therefore, had *no* conscience whatever in the matter. Paul speaks for this group of people, which included himself, in saying: "we all have *knowledge*" (v.1), and goes on to define the "knowledge" in question: "we *know* that an idol is nothing in this world, and that there is none other God but one" (v.4). When Paul is dealing with a similar matter elsewhere, he puts it like this: "We then that are *strong* ought to bear the infirmities of the weak …" (Romans 15:1). The same 'strong' people are described in our current chapter as people with "liberty" (v.9).

- Some believers felt that to eat meat which had been offered to idols was really identification with idolatry, and, therefore, they had a bad conscience about the matter. In Paul's own words: "Howbeit there is not in every man that knowledge: for some with conscience of the idol unto this hour eat it as a thing offered unto an idol; and their conscience being weak is defiled" (v.7) or: "but some, being used until now to the idol, eat as of a thing sacrificed to an idol ..." (RV). This strongly suggests that the people concerned were not Jews, but Gentiles with a history of idol-worship. Paul describes them as believers with a weak conscience (vv.7, 10, 12). See also, again, Romans 15 verse 1.

It should be emphasised that the terms "strong" and "weak" are not used in connection with general spiritual health, but with reference to the consciences of those confronted with meat served at a meal in an idol's temple (v.10). As we shall see, Paul teaches very clearly, as he does in Romans 15 verse 1, that believers who, quite rightly, see no harm in eating food offered to idols, should nevertheless *not do so if it causes distress to believers without the same conviction*.

The Chapter may be divided as follows: *(1)* the contrast between knowledge and love, vv.1-3): "*knowledge* puffeth up, but charity edifieth" (v.1); *(2)* the conviction of the strong brother (vv.4-6): "we *know* that an idol is nothing in the world" (v.4); *(3)* the conscience of the weak brother (v.7): "there is not in every man that *knowledge*"; *(4)* the consideration for the weak brother (vv.8-13): "And through thy *knowledge* shall the weak brother perish?" (v.11).

1) THE CONTRAST BETWEEN KNOWLEDGE AND LOVE, vv.1-3

In these introductory verses, we should notice the following: *(a)* the principle on which the matter should be settled (v.1); *(b)* the pride associated with knowledge in itself (v.2); *(c)* the proof of true knowledge (v.3).

a) The principle on which the matter should be settled, v.1

Paul settles the principle on which the whole matter should be resolved: "Now as touching things offered unto idols, we know that we all have knowledge (that is, all knew that there was nothing in the idol itself). Knowledge puffeth up, but charity (love) edifieth" (v.1), meaning that knowledge in itself "puffeth up", that is, 'puffeth up' *myself,* whereas love, literally, 'buildeth up' ("edifieth", AV), that is, 'buildeth up' *others.* J. Hunter puts it as follows: "One inflates us with vanity, the other builds our strength of character, and fellowship with each other". If our knowledge outruns our humility, we will soon be in trouble!

We should notice that Paul is **not** saying that knowledge is wrong. We must not put a premium on ignorance! But neither is Paul saying that **all we need** is love! We must also remember that the passage does not refer to wrong doctrine or to immorality, but to the liberty to engage in something not in itself sinful, but which might become a stumbling-block to a fellow-believer.

To claim enlightenment on a matter and to have personal liberty in that matter, apart from any consideration of the effect that this may have on my brother, is nothing less than spiritual pride: it "puffeth up". The words "puffeth up" (*'phusioo'*) come from a noun meaning: 'a pair of bellows' (*'phusa'*). Knowledge of this sort is insubstantial. There is something vain and conceited about it. Brethren speak of 'their light' (!) and act arrogantly and discourteously, with an attitude of spiritual superiority towards fellow-believers. Their knowledge has simply made them 'puffed up'.

To claim enlightenment, and only exercise liberty, if at all, in the matter after due regard for a fellow-believer, is a policy of **love.** Paul makes the same point in Romans 14: "For if because of meat thy brother is grieved, thou walkest no longer in love" (v.15, RV); "So then let us follow after things which make for peace, and things whereby we may edify one another" (v.19, RV); "It is good not to eat flesh, nor to drink wine, nor do anything whereby thy brother stumbleth" (v.21, RV).

This can be applied in various ways. How about Sunday shopping? After all, "one man esteemeth one day above another: another esteemeth every day alike …" (Rom. 14: 5). What about recreation? Membership of tennis clubs, golf clubs, football teams etc. could be matters where personal liberty needs to be examined in view of the possible detriment to fellow-believers. But having said all this, the original problem at Corinth does have its modern counterpart. Listen to this: "Muslim influence is strong in the meat industry. Without realizing it you may soon be buying and consuming meat that conforms to Sharia law and has been blessed by an Imam. Will 'meats' again become a controversial issue among Christans?" (Colin F. Anderson, of Stratford, Ontario, writing in *Counsel,* Autumn 2014). The Bible is very up-to-date, isn't it!

b) The pride associated with knowledge in itself , v.2

"If any man **think** that he **knoweth** any thing, he **knoweth** nothing yet as he ought to **know**." The words: "If any man **think**", disclose a proud attitude.

There are two tenses involved here. In the first case ("If a man think that he **knoweth** any thing"), the tense indicates knowledge acquired. The man is saying: 'I know'. In the second and third cases ("he **knoweth** nothing yet as he ought to **know**"), the tense indicates 'the beginning of the practice of acquiring knowledge'.

W.E. Vine renders the verse as follows: "If any man imagine that he has fully acquired true knowledge, he has not even begun to know how it ought to be gained". This is the attitude that says: 'I have arrived spiritually', which is really an indication of ignorance. True knowledge in spiritual matters engenders humility and a deep sense of limited understanding.

c) The proof of true knowledge, v.3

"But if any man love God, the same is known of him." Notice, not now: "If any man **think**…" (v.2), but: "If any man **love God**". As J. Hunter points out: "knowledge acquires some **thing;** love's object is a **Person** - God Himself. It is one thing to know dogma and doctrine; another to know a person". Love for God manifests true knowledge. It is not a question of how much I know **about** God, but how much do I **love** God?

"But if any man love God, **the same is known of him**." W.E. Vine describes this as "God's approving knowledge … divine recognition and acknowledgement". This reinforces the principle on which the whole matter is resolved. "But if a person reached a decision as to meat offered to idols, on the ground of his genuine love for God, then he is owned of God, known of Him in the sense of being approved by Him" (J. Hunter).

2) THE CONVICTION OF THE STRONG BROTHER, vv.4-6

"As concerning therefore the eating of those things that are offered in sacrifice unto idols, we know that an idol is nothing in the world, and that there is none other God but one" (v.4). Here is the conviction of the strong brother. He can say: "**We know** that an idol is nothing in the world". He goes further in verse 6: "But **to us** there is but one God …" We must notice what Paul says about this brother's conviction, with which he agrees ("**we** know"; "to **us**").

In the first case ("there is none other God but one"), Paul emphasises that God is God **alone** (v.4). In the second case ("But to us there is but one God, the Father"), Paul emphasises the same fact, but goes on to point out what the one true God has **done** (vv.5-6). He is the God of creation and the God of redemption (v.6).

a) "There is none other God but one", v.4

"We know that an idol is nothing in this world (*'kosmos'*, the ordered universe), and that there is none other God but one." The two statements here are worthy of close consideration:

i) "An idol is nothing in this world." Paul elsewhere calls idols: "no gods". See Galatians 4 verse 8: "Howbeit then, when ye knew not God, ye did service unto them which by nature are no gods". Various Old Testament passages amplify this statement. "Thy children have forsaken me, and sworn by them that are no gods" (Jeremiah 5:7); "They have moved me to jealousy with that which is not god" (Deuteronomy 32:21); "Whosoever cometh to consecrate himself with a burnt offering … the same may be a priest of them that are no gods" (2 Chronicles 13:9). A galaxy of passages could be brought to bear upon the subject. See, for example, Psalm 115 verses 4-8; Jeremiah 10 verses 3-5. Elijah certainly proved that "an idol is nothing in this world!" See 1 Kings 18 verse 27.

Paul returns to the subject in 1 Corinthians 10:19-20 JND: "What then do I say? That what is sacrificed to idols is anything, or that an idol is anything? But what the nations sacrifice they sacrifice to **demons** and not to God". The subject here is idolatry and idolatrous practices (vv.14-22). He then goes on to deal, again, with eating meat offered to idols at social functions (vv.23-33).

ii) "There is none other God but one." Compare 1 Thessalonians 1 verse 9 ("the living and true God"); 1 Timothy 2 verse 5 ("For there is one God, and one mediator between God and men …"); 2 Kings 19 verse 15 ("thou art the God, even thou alone, of all the kingdoms of the earth").

These words also recall Deuteronomy 6 verse 4: "Hear, O Israel: The Lord our God is one Lord". This is cited in James 2 verse 19. Amongst other things, this reminds us of the doctrine of the Trinity. There are **not** three Gods, but **one** God. (The word "one" – *'echad'* - is used in the Old Testament to describe a plurality in unity: see, for example, Numbers 13: 23). The subject is too vast to pursue here.

b) "But to us there is but one God, the Father", vv5-6

"For though there be that are called gods, whether in heaven or in earth (as there be gods many, and lords many), but to us there is but one God, the Father, of whom are all things, and we in him; and one Lord, Jesus Christ (*notice the comma here*), by whom are all things, and we by him." Once again, the two statements here are worthy of close consideration:

i) "For though there be that are called gods, whether in heaven or in earth (as there be gods many, and lords many)" (v.5). The words: "For though there be that are called gods" could mean that 'such is the fact in the mythology of the heathen'. In other words, the heathen acknowledge a whole hierarchy of deities: some terrestrial, and some celestial. Others suggest that it means: 'though there are powers (compare 1 Corinthians 10:19-20) which are called gods': i.e. demons/evil spirits. The former seems much more likely. Notice the expressions "**called** gods" and "gods **many**, and lords **many**". Amongst the "lords many" must be the Baalim. The name Baal (and there were lots of them) means 'lord' or 'master'. This vividly contrasts with the second statement:

ii) "But to us there is but one God, the Father, of whom are all things, and we in him; and one Lord, Jesus Christ, by whom are all things, and we by him" (v.6). We must notice the double contrast in these verses:

- The heathen deities are **false**: they are "**called** gods". But the true God is not 'called God': He **is** God.

- The heathen deities are **plural**: "there be gods **many**, and lords **many**". But there is "**one** God, the Father" and "**one** Lord, Jesus Christ" (JND/ RV).

The words: **"One God, the Father"** emphasise that true religion is monotheistic, not polytheistic. The words: **"one Lord, Jesus Christ"** emphasise His authority.

But the statement: "to us there is but one God, the Father, of whom are all things, and we in him; and one Lord, Jesus Christ, by whom are all things, and we by him" contains more exquisite teaching.

- Concerning the Father. Notice, **not** 'our Father', **but** "the Father". The expression: "God, the Father" emphasises that in the Godhead, initiative, plan, purpose and design belong to Him. For example: "the **Father** sent the Son to be the Saviour of the world" (1 John 4: 14). Hence we read: "One God, the Father, of whom ('*ek*', meaning 'out of') are all things, and we in him ('for him', JND or 'unto him', RV)". That is, for His honour and glory. But how has this been accomplished? Read on!

- Concerning the Lord Jesus. "One Lord, Jesus Christ, by (through) whom are all things, and we by (through) him."

So the purposes and designs of **the Father** ("**of whom** are all things, and we **for** him", JND) are accomplished by **the Lord Jesus** ("**by whom** are all things, and we **by** him"). The "Father" is the source and goal of "all things, and we **for** him": the Lord Jesus is the executor of "all things, and we **by** him". He is "the agent through whom all things have come from God and will return to God" (Thomas Constable). The Lord Jesus Himself made this clear in John 14 verse 6.

But we should notice something more. In the **"all things"** we have God's work in relation to **creation**. In the **"we"**, we have God's purposes for **His people** (believers). In relation to creation ("all things"), it is from/out of the Father, and by the Lord Jesus. In relation to God's people ("we"), they are for the Father, and through the Son. In summary, if it is possible to summarise such profound things, God's purposes for creation and for His people are secured by His Son, the Lord Jesus Christ.

No small wonder, with such an appreciation of the glory and grace of God, that the 'strong' brother has no scruples about eating meat offered to idols. The meat had been offered to something that didn't even exist! But not everyone thought like that, which brings us to:

3) THE CONSCIENCE OF THE WEAK BROTHER, v.7

Paul now deals with those who **do** have a conscience in the matter. That is, the 'weak brother'. "Howbeit there is not in every man that knowledge: for some, with conscience of the idol unto this hour, eat it as a thing offered to an idol; and their conscience being weak is defiled." This does not contradict verse 1 ("Now as touching things offered unto idols, we know that we **all** have knowledge"): Paul refers here to the knowledge that believers are completely free "from old associations" (W.E. Vine).

Here, then, is a brother who is not altogether free from the influence of past idolatry. He feels that to eat meat which had been previously offered to idols implies continuing participation in idolatry. This is brought out in the latter part of verse 7: "But some, being used until now to the idol, eat as of a thing sacrificed to an idol" (RV).

Paul continues: "and their conscience being weak is defiled". That is, because of their sense of the reality of idols, they feel that they are involved in a sinful thing, and, therefore, have a bad conscience, and a bad conscience spoils communion with God.

4) THE CONSIDERATION FOR THE WEAK BROTHER, vv.8-13

Paul now deals with the way in which the brother with *no* conscience about eating meat offered to idols should act in view of the brother *with* a conscience in the matter. Or, the way in which the brother with the 'strong' conscience should act in view of the brother with the 'weak' conscience. Paul makes two points here: *(a)* liberty in the matter does not make us virtuous (v.8); *(b)* liberty in the matter must not stumble others (vv.9-13)

a) Liberty in the matter does not make us virtuous, v.8

"But meat commendeth us not to God: for neither, if we eat, are we the better; neither if we eat not, are we the worse." The food we eat has no effect on our morality or spirituality: it neither defiles us spiritually or enhances us spiritually. The "weak" brother has got it all wrong. He sees something evil in it which is not really there at all. What we eat does not influence God's approval of us: there is no advantage or disadvantage either way. Compare Mark 7 verses 18-19: "Whatsoever thing from without entereth into the man it cannot defile him: because it entereth not into his heart, but into the belly, and goeth out into the draught (drain or latrine), purging all meats". The sense of "purging all meats" is evidently, 'this he said, purging all meats', that is, making it clear that there is no moral significance in dietary matters. The Lord went on to show what does defile: "That which cometh out of the man, that defileth the man. For from within, out of the heart of men, proceed evil thoughts, adulteries, fornications …" (Mark 7:20-23). But, and here comes the all-important lesson:

b) Liberty in the matter must not stumble others, vv.9-13

While eating or not eating has no moral importance, something the brother with the "weak conscience" (v.12) had not appreciated, Paul now shows that another principle is involved: "But take heed lest by any means this liberty of yours become a **stumblingblock** to them that are weak" (v.9). How could that happen? We should notice the following:

i) The reason, vv.10-11. It could make the 'weak' brother do something which he actually feels is wrong. He will "be emboldened to eat those things which are offered to idols" (v.10). He will be emboldened to act against his own conscience. The scruples of his conscience will be violated with the result that "through *thy* knowledge" (i.e. that "an idol is nothing in the world", and therefore eating meat "meat in the idol's temple" has no moral or spiritual significance whatsoever), the "weak" brother is damaged. Hence the question: "And through thy knowledge shall the weak brother perish, for whom Christ died?"

In connection with this, we should notice that the word "perish" ('*apollumi*') does not mean "extinction, but ruin, not loss of being, but of well being" (W.E. Vine). As W.E. Vine points out in his *Expository Dictionary of New Testament Words*, this is clear from its use, for example, in connection with the marring of wine skins (Luke 5:37: 'the bottles shall perish'); the lost sheep (Luke 15:4, 6, where the word 'lost' is a form of '*apollumi*'); the lost son (Luke 15:24, as before). The wine-skins, the sheep and the son have not ceased to exist, but they have been badly damaged!

We should also note the words: *"for whom Christ died"*. That is, for his spiritual well-being. He died, not only to save him from perdition, but to bring him into happy communion with God. Oh, the love of Christ in doing this! Compare Romans 14 verse 15: "Destroy not him with thy meat, for whom Christ died".

The lesson is clear: we must do nothing - deliberately or thoughtlessly - which would deprive our brother of spiritual well-being. We can so easily trample on the sensitivities of our fellow-believers. In, admittedly, a rather different context, younger believers, including younger preachers, do well to bear this in mind. Consideration ought to be shown towards older believers in matters of dress and deportment, perhaps even in the way service is undertaken.

ii) The result, v.12. "But when ye sin so against the brethren, and wound ('*tupto*', to strike a blow, as in Luke 22:64) their weak conscience, ye sin against Christ." That is, to cause fellow-believers disquiet and loss of spiritual well-being is grievous to Him. We know that He feels deeply the hurt of His people when they are persecuted (see Acts 9:4-5). Here is another example in which He can be deeply grieved.

iii) The resolve, v.13. Paul states his own conviction. He will not cause his brethren to stumble ('offend', AV). "Wherefore, if meat make my brother to offend (the word is used in Matthew 17:27), I will eat no flesh while the world standeth, lest I make my brother to offend". The words: "while the world standeth" mean: 'for evermore'. It is not a case of being prepared to make an exception now and then: it is a permanent attitude. It is a case of "forbearing one another in love; endeavouring to keep the unity of the Spirit in the bond of peace" (Ephesians 4:2-3).

It must be emphasised that this is not compromise. Truth and morality are not involved. It is a question of restricting, not something sinful, but **something perfectly legitimate** in order not to stumble a fellow-believer. 'What my **conscience** may allow me to do, **love** for my brother may prohibit' (J. Hunter). Very well said!

1 CORINTHIANS

"Am I not an apostle?"

Read Chapter 9:1-14

As we noted in introducing Chapter 8, this chapter continues Paul's answers to questions raised by the assembly at Corinth. Chapters 7-9 develop matters of personal liberty in relation to marriage (Chapter 7), eating food offered to idols (Chapter 8), and entitlement to financial support (Chapter 9). We observed that these chapters elaborate a common theme, namely that although there was liberty for all to marry, for all to eat food offered to idols, and for full-time workers to receive support, Paul himself did not exercise that liberty. In Chapter 7, he did not do so in order to secure greater freedom in service; in Chapter 8, he did not do so in order to secure the welfare of the 'weaker' brother (the brother with a "weak conscience", v.12); in Chapter 9, he did not do so in order to secure his position against criticism. While Paul's refusal of support *did* earn him criticism (2 Corinthians 11:7), it effectively countered any suggestion that his ministry at Corinth was financially-motivated.

As Leon Morris points out, this chapter does not represent a change of subject: "Paul has been dealing with people who asserted their rights to the detriment of others. He has told them that this is wrong. He now proceeds to show that he himself had consistently applied this principle. He practises what he preaches".

1 Corinthians 9 comprises two main paragraphs: *(1)* Paul's authority (vv.1-14): he gives reasons for his entitlement to support; *(2)* Paul's service (vv.15-27): he gives reasons for his refusal of support.

Before we address the detail, however, it may be worth pointing out the structure of verses 9-12 and verses 13-15:

i) In verses 9-12, we have a *quotation*, from Deuteronomy 25 verse 4 (v.9), followed by an *explanation* (v.10), followed by an *application*: "Nevertheless we have not used this power; but suffer all things, lest we should hinder the gospel of Christ" (vv.11-12).

ii) In verses 13-14, we have *a quotation*, from Numbers 18 verses 1-15 (v.13), followed by an *explanation* (v.14), followed by an *application*: "But I have used none of these things … for it would be better for me to die, than that any man should make my glorying void" (v.15).

This illustrates the way in which we should read and study the word of God: *(i)* what does it say? *(ii)* what does it mean? *(iii)* how does it apply? Perhaps this will help us to become more like Ezra who "prepared his heart to seek the law of the LORD, and to do it, and to teach in Israel statutes and judgments" (Ezra 7:10). This brings us to:

1) PAUL'S AUTHORITY vv.1-14

In this section we should notice *(a)* Paul's credentials as an apostle (vv.1-2); *(b)* Paul's privileges as an apostle (vv.3-6); *(c)* Paul's precedents for support (vv.7-14).

a) Paul's credentials as an apostle, vv.1-2

"Am I not an apostle? am I not free? have I not seen Jesus Christ our Lord? Are not ye my work in the Lord? If I be not an apostle unto others, yet doubtless I am to you: for the seal of mine apostleship are ye in the Lord." Note: the first two questions are reversed in RV/JND: 'Am I not free? Am I not an apostle?'

The alternative translations do give immediate emphasis to the ensuing argument. So the opening words: "Am I not free?" bring us to the point of the chapter, that is: 'Am I not free to exercise liberty?' Just as in Chapter 8, the believer is not obliged to abstain from eating meats previously offered to idols, so here Paul is not obliged to support himself in his service. The four questions each demand a positive answer.

- "Am I not an apostle?" It has been pointed out that this was an obvious truth that should hardly need stating. Of course Paul was an apostle! As obvious as this was, it was doubted and denied by some at Corinth, making

it necessary for Paul to say: "Truly the signs of an apostle were wrought among you in all patience, in signs, and wonders, and mighty deeds" (2 Corinthians 12:12).

- *"Am I not free?"* If, as Paul has just pointed out (see 1 Corinthians 8:9-13), Christians in general may forego their rights in the interests of others, then he too is free to forego his special rights as an apostle. The "false apostles" (2 Corinthians 11:13) were 'on the take' (2 Corinthians 11:20), but Paul declined support at Corinth in order to preach there "the gospel of God freely" (2 Corinthians 11:7). "But what I do, that I will do, that I may *cut off occasion* ('the opportunity', JND) from them which desire occasion ('an opportunity', JND); that wherein they glory, they may be found even as we" (2 Corinthians 11:12). He was determined to act in this way to show that they had no superiority over him at all: they accepted support for their so-called ministry: he did not. They could not claim that he was seeking his own interests.

- *"Have I not seen Jesus Christ our Lord?"* This qualification for apostleship (Acts 1:21-22) was fulfilled on the road to Damascus. See Acts 9 verse 17. "Apostles were authoritative witnesses to the facts of the gospel, more especially to the resurrection (see, for example, Acts 1:21-22; 2: 32; 3: 15; 4: 33). Notice the significance of Ananias' words to Paul (Saul at the time): 'The God of our fathers hath chosen thee, that thou shouldest … see that Just One' (Acts 22:14). As Paul was not one of the original apostolic band, some have questioned his right to bear such witness, but on the Damascus road he was granted a special privilege – he saw the Lord" (Leon Morris).

- *"Are ye not my work in the Lord?"* This does not smack of pride. Paul was the instrument, but the power was the Lord's: "We are labourers together with God: ye are God's husbandry, ye are God's building. According to the grace of God which is given unto me, as a wise masterbuilder, I have laid the foundation …" (1 Corinthians 3:9-10). He did this in Acts 18. The very existence of the assembly at Corinth was evidence of his apostleship: "Do we begin again to commend ourselves? Or need we, as some others, epistles of commendation to you, or letters of commendation from you? Ye are our epistle written in our hearts, known and read of all men: forasmuch as ye are manifestly declared to be the epistle of Christ ministered by us, written not with ink, but with the Spirit of the living God; not in tables of stone, but in fleshy tables of the heart" (2 Corinthians 3:1-3) . See also 1 Corinthians 4 verses 14-15: "I write not these things to shame you, but as my beloved sons I warn you. For though ye have ten thousand instructors in Christ, yet have ye not many fathers: for in Christ Jesus I have begotten you through the gospel".

In Paul's words here: "the seal of mine apostleship are ye in the Lord". Leon Morris explains: "A *seal* was important in an age when many could not read. A mark stamped on clay, or wax, or some similar substance, was first of all a mark of ownership, and then a means of authentication. All could see the mark, and know what it signified. The Corinthians had been won for Christ by Paul, and they were thus the sign that attested his apostleship".

b) Paul's privileges as an apostle, vv.3-6

Having established his apostleship (vv.1-2), Paul now dwells on the rights associated with his apostleship. "Mine answer to them that do examine me is this …" (v.3). The word translated "answer" ('*apologia*') signifies properly a legal defence against a charge. The word "examine" ('*anakrinousin*'), another legal word, means a critical examination.

In answering their question(s), Paul in turn asks three questions (vv.4-7). In fact, as we shall see, he continues to ask questions (vv.8-13). The word "power" (vv.4, 5, 6, 12) means authority ('*exousia*'). See also verse 18.

Here are the questions: "Have we not power to eat and to drink? Have we not power to lead about a sister, a wife, as well as other apostles, and as the brethren of the Lord, and Cephas? Or I only and Barnabas, have not we power to forbear working?" or: "Have we not a right to eat and to drink? have we not a right to take round a sister [as] wife … Or I alone and Barnabas, have we not a right to work?" (JND/RV). Of each case, Paul says: "Nevertheless we have not used this power ('this right', JND); but suffer all things, lest we should hinder the gospel of Christ" (v.12). See also verse 15: "But I have used none of these things: neither have I written these things, that it should be done unto me". He had the right:

- **To eat and drink**, that is, at the expense of the assembly. "Have we not power to eat and to drink?" (v.4). This is a figurative reference to financial support. Although Paul had the legitimate right to financial support from the people to whom he ministered, he did not exercise that right (vv.12, 15).

- **To support for himself and for a wife**, that is, at the expense of the assembly. "Have we not power to lead about a sister, a wife, as well as other apostles, and as the brethren of the Lord, and Cephas?" (v.5). We should notice that the Lord's servants, and their wives, were to be maintained, and that unlike the other apostles, he was unmarried (although this is not specifically stated here). In passing, we should note that the wife must be a sister. As J. Hunter observes: "'The other apostles' are the twelve. He is not indicating their right to marry, but their right to be supported. Probably most were married. Next he mentions 'the brethren of the Lord'. This is a most illuminating reference, the only reference to some of the four brothers of the Lord (Mark 6:3) being engaged in an itinerant ministry propagating the gospel of Christ. Cephas (Peter) is mentioned as being most prominent among the apostles, and a notable example". Perhaps, however, the reference to Cephas "suggests that at least some of Paul's crtitics belonged to the Cephas party" (W.E. Vine). See Chapter 1 verse 12. (As Keith Krell points out, the case of Peter is "especially interesting" since he was "obviously married, yet still considered by the Roman Catholic church to be the first pope, in contradiction to the principle of mandatory celibacy").

- To refrain from secular employment. "Or I only and Barnabas, have not we power to forebear working?" (v.6). W.E. Vine points out that in mentioning Barnabas, he is referring to the first missionary journey, and perhaps to an agreement between them that they would earn their living where it was advisable to do so. Paul and Barnabas were not unique in that they did not have the same rights as the other apostles. They had the right to refrain from secular employment, but did not use that right. We know that Paul was a tent-maker (Acts 18:2-3). See also Acts 20 verses 33-34. But in this case, as in the two cases above, Paul did not exercise his legitimate rights (vv.12, 15).

In summary, Paul was **entitled** to support, but as we will see, he did not **demand** it. This brings us to:

c) Paul's precedents for support, vv.7-14

Paul's gives three precedents for his entitlement to support. He draws his first precedent from secular life (v.7); the second from agricultural life (vv.8-12) where he refers to Deuteronomy 25 verse 4; the third from religious life (vv.13-14) where he refers to Numbers 18 verses 1-15. In each case, he reaches a conclusion. In the first case, the conclusion is implicit in the questions. In the second and third cases, the conclusions are spelt out in detail.

i) The precedent from secular life, v.7

"Who goeth a warfare any time at his own charges? who planteth a vineyard, and eateth not of the fruit thereof? or who feedeth a flock, and eateth not of the milk of the flock?"

Having set out the three-fold precedent from normal life, Paul continues: "Say I these things as a man?", before passing to his second precedent: "or saith not the law the same also?" (v.8). In other words, having looked at the matter from a human standpoint ("Say I these things as a man?"), he proceeds to show that exactly the same principle was enshrined in the Mosaic law relating to animal husbandry (v.9).

The argument is clear. In the first case: "Who goeth a warfare any time at his own charges?", the meaning is: 'If someone serves as a soldier, it is at someone else's expense'. Paul refers here to fighting, farming, and feeding. He had done all three at Corinth:

- Fighting. There was certainly conflict at Corinth. Having testified to the Jews that Jesus was Christ, we are told that "they opposed themselves, and blasphemed" ('they opposed and spoke injuriously', JND), following which Paul "shook his raiment, and said unto them, Your blood be on your own heads; I am clean ..." (Acts 18:5-6). Paul was evidently alluding here to the responsibilities of a watchman: see Ezekiel 3 verses 17-21; 33 verses 1-9. Later at Corinth, "the Jews made insurrection with one accord against Paul, and brought him to the judgment seat ..." (Acts 18: 12).

While we are considering support for servants of God whose time is wholly spent in the Lord's service, it will not escape notice that we are all engaged in spiritual warfare. See, for example, Ephesians 6 verses 10-17.

- Farming. Paul was involved in this at Corinth. "I have planted, Apollos watered; but God gave the increase. So then neither is he that planted any thing, neither he that watereth; but God that giveth the increase ..." (1 Corinthians 3:6). Corinth was certainly one of the assemblies 'planted' by Paul.

It might be opportune to say that once a church had been established, Paul moved on, leaving the local believers to evangelise their own area. The assembly at Thessalonica is a case in point: "from you sounded out the word of the Lord not only in Macedonia and Achaia, but also in every place your faith to God-ward is spread abroad; so that we need not to speak any thing" (1 Thessalonians 1:8). Paul was a pioneer (Romans 15:20). We have become accustomed to having 'Gospel Campaigns' with an invited evangelist or evangelists. While this cannot be anything other than good, it does seem that in New Testament times, evangelists preached where there was no existing testimony or, to put in Paul's words, "not where Christ was named".

- Feeding. Paul was certainly involved in this at Corinth: "He continued there a year and six months, teaching the word of God among them" (Acts 18:11). He had certainly 'tended the flock' at Corinth.

But returning to the immediate context, Paul points out that "in an army, the soldiers are supported (Who ever goes to war at his own expense?). The farmer is fed by the field he works in (Who plants a vineyard and does not eat of its fruit?). The shepherd is supported by the sheep he cares for (Who tends a flock and does not drink of the milk of the flock?). Therefore, it should not seem strange to the Corinthian Christians that Paul has the right to be supported by the people he ministers to" (David Guzik: kindly supplied by Justin Waldron). This leads Paul to direct our attention to:

ii) The precedent from agricultural life, vv.8-12

"Do I speak these things after the manner of men?" (v.8, RV). That is, are these merely unrelated facts? Not so. There is Scripture to confirm: "saith not the law also the same" (v.8, RV). This is most important. Custom, however good, is not in itself sufficient. *"What saith the scripture?"*

Paul alludes to Deuteronomy 25 verse 4: "For it is written in the law of Moses, Thou shalt not muzzle the mouth of the ox when he treadeth out the corn". He quotes the same verse in a similar context when writing to Timothy: "For the scripture saith, Thou shalt not muzzle the ox that treadeth out the corn", adding: "And, The labourer is worthy of his reward" (1 Timothy 5:18). Here, Paul refers to both Old and New Testaments in making his point (Deuteronomy 25:4; 1 Timothy 5:18). It has been pointed out that the words: "Thou shalt not muzzle the ox that treadeth out the corn" refer to support while work is in progress, and: "The labourer is worthy of his reward" (citing Luke 10:7) refers to support when the work is done. In other words, servants of God should be supported while they are labouring, and when they have retired! Bear in mind the Retired Missionary Aid Fund!

In passing, we should notice that Paul confirms the inspiration of Scripture here: "For it is written in **the law of Moses**, Thou shalt not muzzle the mouth of the ox that treadeth out the corn, Doth **God** take care for oxen? Or saith **he** (that is God) it altogether for our sakes?" The "law of Moses" is nothing less than the Word of God.

Here we have a natural instruction which is designed to convey a spiritual lesson. The passage does **not** teach that God did **not** care for oxen (see Proverbs 12:10), but rather that He had man in mind. Let's read it again: "For it is written in the law of Moses, Thou shalt not muzzle the mouth of the ox that treadeth out the corn, Doth God take care for oxen? Or saith he it altogether **for our sakes?** For **our sakes, no doubt, this is written**: that he that ploweth should plow in hope; and he that thresheth in hope should be partaker of his hope". That is, hope of material support. (W.W. Wiersbe observes that "since oxen cannot read, this verse was not written for them".)

Notice that Paul reaches his conclusion by transferring from an ox to men, in this case, ploughmen and reapers. The principle is clear: those who procure food for others ought to share in it themselves. "If we have sown unto you spiritual things, is it a great thing if we shall reap your carnal things?" (v.11). This statement puts material and spiritual things in perspective. The material things are small in comparison with the spiritual. In a different connection, Paul argues similarly in writing to believers at Rome: "For if the Gentiles have been made partakers of their spiritual things, their duty is to minister unto them in carnal things" (Romans 15:27). We should note that the word "carnal" ('*sarkikos*' from '*sarx*', meaning 'flesh') is used in both passages in its literal sense: pertaining to the flesh, that is, to the body.

Others were making their claim for support, to which Paul says: "If others be partakers of this power over you (that is, the right to maintenance by the assembly), are not we rather?" (v.12) He has already given the reason: "Are ye not my work in the Lord? If I be not an apostle unto others, yet doubtless I am to you: for the seal of mine apostleship are ye in the Lord" (vv.1-2). See also Chapter 4 verses 14-15. Notice his reference to "others". Their identity is made clear in 2 Corinthians 11. Note, particularly, Paul's reference to them in verse 20: "For ye bear if any one bring you into bondage, if any one devour [you], if any one get [your money]" (JND).

Having established his right to support, Paul continues: "Nevertheless we have not used this power; but suffer all things, lest we should hinder the gospel of Christ" (v.12). He did not use his right in this way in order to silence any suspicion that he was serving God for what he could get out of it. The word "hinder" ('*enkope*') was used with reference to breaking up a road, or placing an obstacle in the path. Its verbal form ('*enkopto*') occurs in Galatians 5 verse 7: "Ye did run well, who did hinder you...?"

We must emphasise Paul's steadfast desire that nothing should impede the progress of the gospel. He was willing to face impoverishment ("suffer all things") rather than hindering the effectiveness of "the gospel of Christ". This is a timely reminder that we should countenance nothing in our lives, however legitimate, which could in any way impair our witness to others. Financial support in connection with the Lord's work is not an issue for most of us, but finance *per se* probably concerns us all in one way or another. Promotion in business life, with increased income, is certainly not wrong in itself, but it could erode spiritual life and lessen our involvement in the Lord's service.

iii) The precedent from religious life, vv.13-14

Paul's third precedent is taken from the support given to the Levites and priests in the Old Testament. "Do ye not know, that they which minister about holy things live of the things of the temple? And they which wait at the altar are partakers with the altar?" (v.13) Paul alludes here to Numbers 18 verses 1-15 which refers in the first place, to the Levites (vv.2-6), who were supported by the offerings of the people, and then to the priests (vv.7-18) who had an entitlement from the offerings on the altar. This was a particular feature in the peace offering. See Leviticus 7 verses 6, 8-10, 14, 28-36. See also Deuteronomy 18 verses 1-8. With this principle clearly established, Paul continues:

"Even so hath the Lord ordained ('even so did the Lord ordain', RV) that they which preach the gospel should live of the gospel" (v.14). Compare Matthew 10 verse 10: "the workman is worthy of his meat"; Luke 10 verse 7: "the labourer is worthy of his hire"; Galatians 6 verse 6: "Let him that is taught in the word communicate unto him that teacheth".

Thus far (vv.1-14) we have noticed Paul's reasons for his entitlement to support. In our next study, we will notice his reasons for refusing support.

1 CORINTHIANS

"I am made all things to all men"

Read Chapter 9:15-27

We have already noticed that Chapter 8 continues Paul's answers to questions raised by the assembly at Corinth. Chapters 7-9 develop matters of personal liberty in relation to marriage (Chapter 7), eating food offered to idols (Chapter 8), and entitlement to financial support (Chapter 9). We observed that these chapters elaborate a common theme, namely that although there was liberty for all to marry, for all to eat food offered to idols, and for full-time workers to receive support, Paul himself did not exercise that liberty. In Chapter 7, he did not do so in order to secure greater freedom in service; in Chapter 8, he did not do so in order to secure the welfare of the 'weaker' brother (the brother with a "weak conscience", v.12); in Chapter 9, he did not do so in order to secure his position against criticism. While Paul's refusal of support *did* earn him criticism (2 Corinthians 11:7), it effectively countered any suggestion that his ministry at Corinth was financially-motivated.

1 Corinthians 9 comprises two main paragraphs: *(1)* Paul's authority (vv.1-14): he gives reasons for his entitlement to support; *(2)* Paul's service (vv.15-27): he gives reasons for his refusal of support.

1) PAUL'S AUTHORITY, vv.1-14

In our previous study we divided these verses as follows: *(a)* Paul's credentials as an apostle (vv.1-2); *(b)* Paul's privileges as an apostle (vv.3-6); *(c)* Paul's precedents for support (vv.7-14). In connection with the third section (vv.7-14), we noted that Paul draws his first precedent from secular life (v.7), the second from agricultural life (vv.8-12), where he refers to Deuteronomy 25 verse 4, and the third from religious life (vv.13-14) where he refers to Numbers 18 verses 1-15. This brings us to:

2) PAUL'S SERVICE, vv15-27

In these verses we should notice the following: *(a)* what Paul did *not* do (vv.15-18); *(b)* what Paul *did* do (vv.19-27). In connection with the latter he says: "that I might by all means save some" (v.22), including both Jews and non-Jews (vv.19-23). He also tells us about his self-discipline in ensuring that his service was acceptable to the Lord (vv.24-27).

a) What Paul did not do, vv.15-18

i) He did not accept support. "But I have used none of these things: neither have I written these things, that it should be so done unto me: for it were better for me to die, than that any man should make my glorying void" (v.15). He had not exercised his right to support in the past, and was not suggesting that he should do so now. It might have been thought from what he had just said (see, for example, verse 7) that Paul was suggesting that he should have been supported, but he makes it crystal clear here that this was not the case. It should be noted that Paul evidently refers here to support at *Corinth* as opposed to support from elsewhere. See, for example, 2 Corinthians 11 verses 8-9 where, in his own words, he "robbed other churches, taking wages of them, to do you service", referring to support from the assemblies in Macedonia while he was at Corinth. Paul's glorying here was that he made known the gospel without charge.

ii) He did not glory in himself. "For though I preach the gospel, I have nothing to glory of: for necessity (*'ananke'*, 'what must needs be') is laid upon me; yea, woe is unto me, if I preach not the gospel" (v.16). We should note the emphasis here: "For though *I* preach, *I* have nothing to glory of ..." It has been pointed out (thanks to Justin Waldron) that "this does not mean that Paul was unwilling to obey, but that his will had no part in the call. It was God's choice and call". He was simply fulfilling the work entrusted to him. The words "laid upon" (*'epikeimai'*) mean: 'laid heavily'. They occur in Luke 5 verse 1: "And it came to pass, as the people **pressed upon him**". The words "necessity is laid upon me" remind us of the responsibility assigned to Paul: "But the Lord said unto him (Ananias), Go thy way: for he (Saul of Tarsus) is a chosen vessel unto me" (Acts 9:15); "The Holy Ghost said, Separate me Barnabas and Saul for the work whereunto I have called them" (Acts 13:2); "And he said unto me, Depart; for I will send thee far hence unto the Gentiles" (Acts 22:21). Jeremiah preached under divine compulsion: "I said, I will not make mention of him, nor speak any more in his name (the opposition was 'getting to him'). But his word was in mine heart as a burning fire shut up in my bones, and I was weary with forbearing, and I could not stay" (Jeremiah 20:9).

Paul took no credit for his gospel preaching. He did not glory in his enthusiasm or in his initiative. His service was initiated and empowered by God. Similarly, while Paul commended the stewardship of the "churches of Macedonia", he recognised that this flowed out of "the grace of God" bestowed upon them (2 Corinthians 8:1), reminding us that:

> *Every virtue we possess,*
> *And every victory won,*
> *And every thought of holiness,*
> *Are His alone.*

The words: "Woe is unto me, if I preach not the gospel" mean: 'Woe unto him' - and us - at the judgment seat of Christ, or in life now, before we "appear before the judgment seat of Christ" (2 Corinthians 5:10). He would be failing in his stewardship if he ceased to preach the gospel. Archippus was evidently in danger of reneging on his stewardship. See Colossians 4 verse 17. Compare the parable of the pounds: the man who did nothing is described as a "wicked servant" (Luke 19:22). This should make us examine our own service for the Lord. Perhaps at some point in the past, He said to us: "Son, go work to day in my vineyard", and we responded by saying: "I will not: but afterward … repented and went". Well and good! But how tragic if we responded by saying: "I go, sir: and went not" (Matthew 21:28-30).

He now expands his statement: "Necessity is laid upon me": "For if I do this thing willingly, I have a reward: but if against my will, a dispensation (omit '*of the gospel*') is committed unto me" (v.17). Paul is evidently saying that his service can be regarded in two ways:

- "If I do this thing willingly, I have a reward." (The word "reward" ('*misthos*') means "primarily wages, hire, and then, generally, reward", W.E. Vine). This could mean that "the man who preaches with a willing spirit merits a reward, whereas if he is unwilling he is not excused: he must still discharge his stewardship ('a dispensation is committed unto me')" (Leon Morris). Alternatively, but not vastly different, and fitting the context more comfortably, if Paul's service was engendered by his own enthusiasm, rather than by divine compulsion, then his labours were meritorious – they put him in a very good light. But Paul doesn't look at it in this way at all:

- ***"But if against my will, a dispensation is committed unto me."*** That is, if it is not my choice, but God's, then it is a case of acting as a steward. The word "dispensation" means 'stewardship'. It ***was a case of doing his duty.*** This explains: "for necessity is laid upon me". It was necessary for him to discharge the responsibility resting upon him. It was not a self-chosen vocation. He was called of the Lord. He had nothing to glory of as such: he could not claim a reward as of right in the circumstances. It was a case of: "We are unprofitable servants: we have done that which was our duty to do" (Luke 17:10).

In this case ("a dispensation is committed to me"), was any reward possible? After all, he was simply doing the job assigned to him, and there was little merit in that! The reward in this case was Paul's great satisfaction in preaching the gospel without expectation of financial support, particularly at Corinth: "What *is* my reward then? Verily that, when I preach the gospel (one word meaning 'preach good tidings', '*euangelizo*'), I may make the gospel of Christ without charge ('costless', JND), that I abuse not my power in the gospel" (v.18). "Paul's 'reward' is demonstrating love to people by freely preaching the gospel. His highest pay was the privilege of preaching without pay" (Leon Morris). The words: "that I abuse not my power in the gospel" mean 'not over-using' or 'using over much', his right in preaching the gospel. He had the right to support (his "power in the gospel", or "my right in [announcing] the glad tidings", JND), but he did not exercise that right (he did not "abuse" or 'over-use' that right). Paul uses the word "abuse" ('*katachraomai*') in 1 Corinthians 7 verse 31 with reference to the believer's use of the world. Paul delighted in not exercising his right ("power", AV) to the full (that is, his full right) by not accepting support.

Paul's satisfaction in this way derived from the fact that in declining support, he was free (with particular reference to Corinth, where some were saying: "I am of Paul") from "any one who would exercise compulsion over him, and from entangling dependence (see v.1)" (W.E. Vine). He was therefore able, as "free from all men", to make himself "servant unto all" (v.19). In saying: "though I be free from all men", Paul is not referring to his Roman citizenship (as some suggest), but to his freedom from human control (see W.E. Vine above). This certainly has the merit of a contextual explanation!

b) What Paul did do, vv.19-27

Paul now tells us what he did do in the circumstances: *(i)* in relation to others (vv.19-23); *(ii)* in relation to himself (vv.24-27).

i)   In relation to others, vv.19-23. "For though I be free from all men, yet have I made myself servant unto all, *that I might gain the more"* (v.19). Paul did not exercise his right to support so that he could be in a position, as "free from all men" (free from dependence on men and free from obligation to men), to serve all in order "to gain the more" or "to gain the most [possible]" (JND). As we noted in connection with verse 12, Paul was willing to forego anything that might in any way hinder "the gospel of Christ". In fact, he was willing to live in reduced circumstances with that in mind: "we ... suffer all things, lest we should hinder the gospel of Christ". The glory of Christ was everything to Paul.

This, surely, reminds us of the perfect Servant who "came not be ministered unto, but to minister, and to give his life a ransom for many" (Mark 10:45).

Paul now explains what he meant in saying: "For though I be free from all men, yet have I made myself servant unto all, *that I might gain the more"* (v.19). By refusing support, he was not under an obligation to any one group of people, and was, therefore, free to reach *all*, without offending any who might have thought that they had some claim on him by their financial or material support. So *who* could he gain? This follows: "the Jews ... them that are under the law ... them that are without law ... the weak" (vv.20-22). It is all summed up in the words: "that I might by all means save some" (v.22).

- "That I might ... gain the Jews", v.20. "And unto the Jews I became as a Jew, that I might gain the Jews." This was *national.* He resorted to the synagogues (Acts 13:1; 17:1; 18:4). He acknowledged his Jewish descent, saying: "Men and brethren" (see, for example, Acts 13:38).

- "That I might gain ... them that are under the law", v.20. "To them that are under the law, as under the law, that I might gain them that are under the law." This was *ceremonial.* He avoided those things which the Jew would find objectionable. He did not indulge in those things which would inflame the Jews. James acted similarly in recommending "that we write unto them (Gentile converts), that they abstain from pollutions of idols, and from fornication, and from things strangled, and from blood. For Moses of old

time hath in every city them that preach him, being read in the synagogues every sabbath day" (Acts 15:19-21). James and his colleagues made the same recommendation to Paul: "Thou seest, brother, how many thousands of Jews there are which believe, and they are all zealous of the law … that … all may know that thou thyself walkest orderly, and keepest the law …" (Acts 21:20-26).

It could certainly be said that the circumcision of Timothy took place in order to "gain … them that are under the law". In Luke's words, "Him (Timothy) would Paul have to go with him; and took and circumcised him, because of the Jews which were in those quarters: for they knew all that his father was a Greek" (Acts 16:3).

According to the Revised Version (with JND), verse 20 should read: "And to the Jews I became as a Jew, that I might gain the Jews; to them that are under the law, as under the law, *not being myself under the law*, that I might gain them that are under the law". As Leon Morris points out: "The Christian is 'not under the law, but under grace' (Romans 6: 14). Yet Paul conformed to practices which would enable him to approach them that are under the law with greater acceptability". In becoming "as a Jew", Paul is *not* making a doctrinal statement. He placed no value on Jewish ceremonies. (It should be said that there is no parallel with such practices as christening, which are downright erroneous.) Paul's motive in becoming "as a Jew" was to "gain them that are under the law".

- *"That I might gain … them that are without law", v.21.* "Them that are without law, as without law, (being not without law to God, but under the law to Christ), that I might gain them that are without law", that is: "those that were outside law, as in Romans 2 verse 14" (W.E. Vine). Do notice that when Paul says: "being not without law to God, but under the law to Christ", he is referring to himself, not to the Gentiles! "Them that are without law" are the Gentiles. So, in order to gain them, he associated with them, like Peter who incurred criticism in the process: "Thou wentest in to men uncircumcised, and didst eat with them …" (Acts 11:3).

Paul did not practice Jewish ordinances amongst Gentiles: that would have been a hindrance. "He met them on their own ground. When he says that he was *as without law* he does not wish to give the impression that he was under no restraint. So he adds that he is *not without law to God*, and that he is *under the law to Christ*. Both expressions indicate that he was no free agent, but the servant of God. But as far as his service would allow he conformed to Gentile practice, that he might *gain them that are without law*" (Leon Morris). Paul did not please himself. He was subject to the will of God. His liberty was not licence. He did not become self-indulgent, and cast off all restraint. A man "under the law to Christ" can answer the question: "And who is my neighbour?", by giving help to all in need, irrespective of their background, just like 'the good Samaritan' (Luke 10:25-37).

- "That I might gain ... them that are weak", v.22. "To the weak became I as weak, that I might gain the weak." For the expression "the weak", see Chapter 8 verses 10-13 and Romans 14 verse 1 – 15 verse 1. That is, "weak" in relation to the conscience. But here, Paul evidently refers here not to fellow-believers as in Chapter 8 ("the weak *brother*", v.8), but to unsaved people ("that I might ... save some"), people with various scruples, or as we would say today, 'hang-ups'.

Paul either engaged in legitimate things - or abstained - "that I might by all means save some". The words: "I am made all things to all men, that I might by all means save some", must not be misunderstood! Paul does not mean that his conduct was unprincipled, but "where no principle was at stake he was prepared to go to extreme lengths to meet people. Personal considerations are totally submerged in the great aim of by all means saving some" (Leon Morris).

Paul emphasises his motive in all this: "And this I do for the gospel's sake, that I might be partaker (meaning 'joint-partaker') thereof with you" (v.23) or: "that I might be partaker thereof (omitting 'with you')" (RV). That is, Paul would do nothing to hinder or obstruct the gospel. In the words of Jack Hunter: "He is not thinking of fellowship with the believers at Corinth, but all his labour expresses fellowship with the gospel, his share in making it known and seeing its results in others. What a joy it is for us to participate in such a work, to be allowed of God to have a part in it, to be able to spread the message with all its blessings. As others are helped and blessed, so our joy and blessing increases".

The overall point is clear: Paul did all this, not for personal or financial gain, but "for the gospel's sake". That is, what the gospel is in itself: "this ministry" (2 Corinthians 4:1). It is "the gospel of the glory of Christ" (2 Corinthians 4:4, JND): it is "the gospel of the glory of the blessed God" (1 Timothy 1:11, JND). The apostle was prompted by pure motives, unlike the "false apostles" (2 Corinthians 10:13), of whom he was obliged to say: "For we are not as many who corrupt ('make a trade of' by adulterating) the word of God; but as of sincerity, but as of God, in the sight of God, speak we in Christ" (2 Corinthians 2:17).

The rendering: "that I might be a partaker thereof" (RV) may well suggest, additionally, that Paul anticipated that he would share in the triumphs of the gospel, in the accomplishments of the gospel. This is borne out in verses 24-27: Paul wanted nothing to mar this prospect. He therefore tells us what he did:

ii) In relation to himself, vv.24-27

So what did Paul do in order to be a 'joint-partaker thereof?' He practised rigid self-discipline in two ways:

i)   As a runner, vv.24-26. The words: "Know ye not?" doubtless refer to the Isthmian Games which were held every three years at Corinth. They are said to have been second only to the Olympic Games. The object of every competitor was to gain the coveted garland and all that was associated with it. There was only **one** winner, but not so in the Christian race: "so run that **ye** may obtain". That is, be intent on the reward. In the Christian life, **all** "may obtain".

The words: "striveth for the mastery" (v.25) render a verb, *'agonizomai',* meaning: 'to compete in the games'. It gives us the word 'agony' from which we see that no half-hearted effort is meant. Every competitor had to undergo strict training for ten months. He was *"temperate in all things"* (v.25). Yet his reward, if successful, was *a corruptible crown* (in the Isthmian Games this was a pine wreath). The Christian has before him a much more worthwhile crown, namely an *incorruptible* one (cf. 2 Timothy 4:8). "The strenuous self-denial of the athlete in training for his fleeting reward is a rebuke to all half-hearted flabby Christian service. Notice that the athlete denies himself many lawful pleasures. The Christian must avoid not only definite sin, but anything that hinders his complete effectiveness" (Leon Morris).

For other occurrences of *'agon'*, see, for example, Colossians 4 verse 12; 2 Timothy 4 verse 7. The word "temperate" (*'enkrateuomai'*) means self-control. We should note that Paul says: "temperate in **all** things". The "incorruptible crown" is not liable to decay: it is an eternal reward. Like Paul, we must "press toward the mark for the prize of the high calling of God in Christ Jesus" (Philippians 3:13-14).

ii) As a boxer, vv. 26-27. The runner and the boxer are linked by the words: "I therefore so run, not as uncertainly (that is, not doubting the outcome); so fight I, not as one that beateth the air (that is, every blow counts and is effective)". In the first case ("I therefore so run, not as uncertainly"), he ran with an aim - to obtain the reward. In the second case ("So fight I, not as one that beateth the air"), he did not miss his aim. "Christian service is not just activity, it is activity focussed on a target, namely the building of the church and the defeat of the enemy who wants to destroy people" (supplied by Justin Waldron).

This is achieved, as already noticed, 'by rigid self-denial'. "But I buffet ('keep under') my body, and bring it into subjection." The word: "buffet" means, literally: to give myself a black eye! Not literally, of course! But Paul was master of his own body in sense of bodily appetites and desires. Compare Colossians 3 verse 5: "Mortify therefore your members which are upon the earth; fornication, uncleanness, inordinate affection, evil concupiscence, and covetousness, which is idolatry". Not to do so would mean loss of effectiveness in the conflict.

But there is more. "Lest that by any means, when I have preached to others, I myself should be a castaway (*'adokimos'*, meaning rejected or disapproved)." As Leon Morris points out, the word means: 'which has not stood the test', and in this context means disqualification. "Paul's fear was not that he might lose his salvation, but that he might lose his crown through failing to satisfy his Lord (cf. 1 Corinthians 3:15)." The chapter therefore concludes with a warning: what we **say** may be right, but are **we** right? What I have said is **one thing**, but what I am is **something else.**

The assessment here is made at the end of the race, and: "if a man also strive for masteries ('contend [in the games]', JND), yet is he not crowned, except he strive lawfully" (2 Timothy 2:5). We must 'keep the rules' ("strive lawfully") from the beginning to the end of life's journey ('the race').

1 CORINTHIANS

"Let him that thinketh he standeth take heed lest he fall"

Read Chapter 10:1-14

Having said: "I keep under my body, and bring it into subjection: lest that by any means, when I have preached to others, I myself should be a castaway" (1 Corinthians 9:27), Paul now "turns to the history of the people of God recorded in the Scriptures to show that the enjoyment of high privileges does not guarantee entry into final blessing" (Leon Morris). Chapter 10 commences with an example of people who became 'castaways'.

The connection between the two chapters is clear: "***For*** I would not have you ignorant, brethren ..." (v.1, JND). As noted in our previous study, the word "castaway" ('*adokimos*') carries the idea of disapproval - with consequent loss of reward. Very clearly, true believers may lose their reward through failure to exercise self-discipline. "Paul's fear was not that he might lose his salvation, but that he might lose his crown through failing to satisfy his Lord (cf. 1 Corinthians 3: 15)" (Leon Morris). The danger for servants highlighted at the end of Chapter 9 is now restated in connection with all believers.

We should notice that the words: "flee from idolatry" (v.14) lie at the heart of the chapter, which may be divided as follows. It has been said that the Corinthians were to "flee from idolatry" ***(1) on the ground of divine condemnation*** (v.1-14): "Neither be ye ***idolaters*** as were some of them" and there "fell in one day three and twenty thousand" (vv.7-8); ***(2) on the ground of communion*** (vv.15-22): "What say I then? That the idol is anything, or that which is offered in sacrifice to ***idols*** is anything? But I say, that the things which the Gentiles sacrifice, they sacrifice to devils (demons, JND), and not to God: and I would not that ye should have fellowship with devils (demons). Ye cannot drink the cup of the Lord, and the cup of devils (demons)" (vv.19-21); *(3) on the ground of conscience* (vv.23-33): "If any man say unto you, This is offered in sacrifice unto *idols*, eat not for his sake that shewed it, and for conscience sake … conscience, I say, not thine own, but of the other" (vv.28-29). God's people are, therefore, to "flee from idolatry":

1) ON THE GROUND OF DIVINE CONDEMNATION, vv.1-14

The 'key verse' to the passage (vv.1-14) is: "Wherefore let him that thinketh he standeth take heed lest he fall" (v.12). The words: "him that thinketh he standeth" are illustrated in verses 1-4, with their emphasis on the word: *"all"*. This occurs *five* times in connection with *five* examples: see verses 1 (where there are two examples), 2, 3, and 4. The words: "Take heed lest he fall" are illustrated in verses 5-10 with their emphasis on the word: *"some"*. This occurs *four* times in connection with *five* examples: see verses 6, 7, 8, 9 and 10. These verses may be divided as follows: *(a)* Israel's privileges (vv.1-4); *(b)* Israel's perversity (vv.5-10); *(c)* applying the lessons (vv.11-14). We should notice the importance of Old Testament history. It is not just 'history': it is the record of God's dealings and ways with men (vv.6, 11). The principles on which He did this are unchanged. In saying: "Moreover brethren, I would not that ye should be ignorant …" (v.1), Paul refers not so much to ignorance of the *facts* of Israel's history, but of the *lessons* of their history.

a) Israel's privileges, vv.1-4

As noted above, Israel were blessed in five ways, and this is emphasised by the use of "all" in each case:

i) They had the presence of God, v.1

"All our fathers were under the cloud." They were all delivered from Egypt. The cloud covered and protected them from their enemies.

We should notice that there is no reference here to the Passover and attendant events. We might have expected something like: 'All were delivered by blood' or: 'All were redeemed'. Perhaps this is explained by the fact that the passage deals with the wilderness journey and its discipline: the provision that God made for them *en route* to Canaan.

The words: "under the cloud" mean: 'under the protection of the cloud'. They enjoyed the presence of God. While the cloud is certainly associated with guidance ("And the LORD went before them by day in a pillar of a cloud, to lead them the way; and by night in a pillar of fire, to give them light", Exodus 13:21), here it is associated with protection from the re-imposition of bondage: "And the angel of God, which went before the camp of Israel, removed and went behind them; and the pillar of the cloud went from before their face, and stood behind them: and came between the camp of the Egyptians and the camp of Israel" (Exodus 14:19).

In the Millennium, "the LORD will create upon every dwelling place of mount Zion, and upon her assemblies, a cloud and smoke by day, and the shining of a flaming fire by night: for upon all the glory shall be a *defence*" (Isaiah 4:5). The Lord's people enjoy divine guidance and divine protection today: we are "kept by the power of God through faith unto salvation ready to be revealed in the last time" (1 Peter 1:5). Quite obviously, this does not mean that we are protected from all trouble. Just read what Peter says next! It means that we will be kept from the spiritual damage that Satan would inflict upon us through the trials and difficulties of life. Compare Isaiah 43 verses 1-2.

The assembly at Corinth enjoyed the presence of God. The believers there are described as: "the temple of God" and as such, "the Spirit of God dwelleth in you" (1 Corinthians 3:16).

ii) They had the power of God, v.1

"All passed through the sea." That is, they passed beyond the sphere of bondage. Egypt was stripped of its power to enslave. The passage at the Red Sea meant *deliverance* for Israel, and *defeat* for Egypt. So "under the cloud" meant that they were *protected* by His presence, and "through the sea" meant that they were *delivered* by His power.

The assembly at Corinth enjoyed the power of God. "But of him are ye in Christ Jesus, who of God is made unto us wisdom, and righteousness, and sanctification, and redemption" (1 Corinthians 1:30). They had the power of God in other ways too: see Chapter 1 verses 5, 7.

iii) They had the prophet of God, v.2

"All were all baptized unto Moses in the cloud and in the sea." That is, in their deliverance from Egypt they were baptised unto the **authority** of Moses, and were led and directed by him. They were no longer subject to Pharaoh. We should notice that in both Old and New Testaments, baptism associates men and women with a person. In the Old Testament, it is Moses: in the New Testament, it is the Lord Jesus. Like redeemed Israel, we are not to be an undisciplined rabble. The Lord Jesus said: "make *disciples* of all the nations" (Matthew 28:19, JND).

Moses was certainly a prophet (Deuteronomy 18:18), and while there can be no doubt that he refers in these verses (Deuteronomy 18:1-19) to the prophetic ministry generally, there can, equally, be no doubt that they find their ultimate fulfilment in the Lord Jesus (John 6:14, John 7:40, Acts 3:22-23). The words: "baptized unto Moses" imply, amongst other things, the following:

- **Recognition of his authority.** When this was challenged by Miriam and Aaron, the Lord said to them: "If there be a prophet among you, I the LORD will make myself known unto him in a vision and will speak unto him in a dream. My servant Moses is not so, who is faithful in all mine house. With him will I speak mouth to mouth, even apparently, and not in dark speeches; and the similitude of the LORD shall he behold: wherefore were ye not afraid to speak against my servant Moses?" (Numbers 12:6-8). This reminds us that the Lord Jesus said: "All power (*'exousia'*, meaning authority) is given unto me in heaven and in earth" (Matthew 28:18).

- **Recognition of his advocacy.** "And Moses cried unto the LORD, saying, Heal her (Miriam) now, O God, I beseech thee" (Numbers 12:13). This reminds us that "if any man sin, we have an advocate with the Father, Jesus Christ the righteous" (1 John 2:1).

- **Recognition of his apostleship**. He was the 'sent one' (the meaning of 'apostle'). Moses was certainly an apostle in this sense: "And God said unto Moses, I AM THAT I AM: and he said, Thus shalt thou say unto the children of Israel, I AM hath *sent me* unto you" (Exodus 3:14). This reminds us that the Lord Jesus is the "Apostle ... of our profession ('confession', JND)" (Hebrews 3:1).

As Leon Morris observes: "They were united to him (Moses), though we should not press this as though any other union can be anything like as close as the union between the Christian and the Christ".

The assembly at Corinth enjoyed relationship with the Lord Jesus. They were "sanctified in Christ Jesus, called (to be) saints" (1 Corinthians 1:2). God had called them "unto the fellowship of his Son Jesus Christ our Lord" (1 Corinthians 1:9). The Lord Jesus was in the fullest sense, the Prophet 'like unto' Moses' (John 6:14, John 7:40, Acts 3:22-23).

iv) They had the provision of God in food, v.3

"And did all eat the same spiritual meat" or: "and all ate the same spiritual food" (JND). The love that delivered them was the love that provided for them. The "manna" is called "spiritual meat" because of its origin. Paul is not "calling into question the physical reality of the manna" (Leon Morris). It is elsewhere called: "the corn of heaven … angels' food" (Psalm 78:24-25) or: "the bread of the mighty" (JND).

John 6 now becomes compulsory reading: "For the bread of God is he which cometh down from heaven, and giveth life unto the world" (v.33); "I am the bread of life, he that cometh to me shall never hunger; and he that believeth on me shall never thirst" (v.35); "I am the living bread which came down from heaven: if any man shall eat of this bread, he shall live for ever, and the bread that I will give him is my flesh, which I will give for the life of the world" (v.51); "He that eateth of this bread shall live for ever" (v.58).

If the children of Israel proved that God could "furnish a table in the wilderness" (Psalm 78:19), then the assembly at Corinth enjoyed the provision of the "Lord's table" (1 Corinthians 10:21) which refers, not to the Lord's supper (though this is included), but to all the benefits which we enjoy on the basis of the "blood of Christ" (1 Corinthians 10:16). We are always at "the Lord's table".

v) They had the provision of God in water, v.4

"All (did) drink the same spiritual drink." See, for example, Exodus 17 verses 5-6: "And the LORD said unto Moses, Go on before the people … Behold, I will stand before thee there upon the rock in Horeb; and thou shalt smite the rock, and there shall come water out of it, that the people may drink". The words: "spiritual drink" have the same meaning as: "spiritual meat" (v.3), that is, spiritual in the mode of provision and continuous flow.

The added words: "for they all drank of the spiritual Rock that followed them; and that Rock was Christ" imply that the water was provided by His personal presence. This is implicit in the words above: "Behold, I will stand before thee there upon the rock in Horeb …"

The Lord Jesus said: "Whosoever drinketh of the water that I shall give him shall never thirst; but the water that I shall give him shall be in him a well of water springing up into everlasting life" (John 4:14). He went on to say: "If any man thirst, let him come unto me and drink" with John's explanation: "But this spake he of the Spirit, which they that believe on him should receive" (John 7:37-39). The believers at Corinth, with all believers, had "*all* been baptised into one body" and had "*all* been given to drink of one Spirit (Chapter 12:13, JND).

These were the blessings of Israel in the wilderness, but the fact that they all enjoyed the marvellous goodness of God in this way did *not* mean that they could not incur divine displeasure and loss of blessing. Hence we now read: "But with many of them ('most of them', JND) God was not well pleased; for they were overthrown in the wilderness" (v.5), leading us to say that Israel's Messiah was quite unlike His people: He said: "And he that sent me is with me: the Father hath not left me alone; for *I do always those things that please him*" (John 8: 29). We therefore come to:

b) Israel's perversity, vv.5-10

The desert witnessed the shipwreck of God's people, and the relevant lesson is emphasised: "Now these things were our examples ('*tupos*': literally 'types of us', that is, examples of what will happen to us if we follow their example) to the intent that we should not lust after evil things, as they also lusted" (v.6). As a result of their sin, the children of Israel became subject to divine discipline, just as amongst the believers at Corinth there were some who were "weak and sickly … and many sleep" (1 Corinthians 11:30).

The five events mentioned are not in chronological order, but they are certainly in a significant order. We start with *lust* (v.6): that is, with lust after the old life: with wrong desires. This emphasises the need to "'keep thy heart with all diligence; for out of it are the issues of life" (Proverbs 4:23). We continue with *veneer* (v.7), referring to Exodus 32:5-6, and then with *blatant sin* (v.8), then with *total dissatisfaction* (v.9), then with *resentment of discipline* (v.10). The lesson follows: "Now all these things happened unto them for ensamples:

and they are written for our admonition, upon whom the ends of the world are come" (v.11). This is emphasised throughout the passage:

i) Iniquity, v.6

"Now these things were our examples, to the intent that *we* should not lust after evil things, as *they* also lusted". This evidently refers to Numbers 11 verses 4-6: "And the mixed multitude that was among them fell a lusting: And the children of Israel also wept again, and said, Who shall give us flesh to eat? We remember the fish, which we did eat in Egypt freely; the cucumbers, and the melons, and the leeks, and the onions, and the garlick: but now our soul is dried away: there is nothing at all, beside this manna, before our eyes". People with privileges can lose their desire for divine things. The people who sinned in this way were buried at Kibroth-hattavah, meaning 'graves of lust' (Numbers 11:34).

Do notice that there are *six* things mentioned here ("fish … cucumbers … melons … leeks … onions … garlick"): six is the number of man. It has also been said that the six things mentioned all grow (or swim) at ground level. Make of that what you want! It is worth noting too that they complained about lack of variety: "nothing at all, *beside* this manna" (Numbers 11:6). But it got worse. They said later: "our soul loatheth this light bread" (Numbers 21:5). So, in the first case, they did not want manna *by itself* (Numbers 11:6), and in the second, they did not want manna *in itself* (Numbers 21:5). All of which reminds us that if we get to the stage of wanting something to go with the Word of God, we will end up not wanting the Word of God at all. The words: "We *remember* the fish … cucumbers … melons … leeks … onions … garlick" (Numbers 11:5) remind us that "No man having put his hand to the plough, and looking back, is fit for the kingdom of God" (Luke 9:62).

Moses contrasted Egypt with Canaan: "For the Lord thy God bringeth thee into a good land, a land of brooks of water, of fountains and depths that spring out of valleys and hills; a land of wheat, and barley, and vines, and fig trees, and pomegranates; a land of oil olive, and honey" (Deuteronomy 8:7-8). Do notice that Moses lists seven things here - not six! God's blessings follow His character in all its perfection, not man in all his imperfection!

So, sadly, having saved Israel "from the hand of him that hated them" when "believed they his words" and "sang his praise", they then "soon forgot his works; they waited not for his counsel; but *lusted* exceedingly in the wilderness, and tempted God in the desert" (Psalm 106:10-14). They lusted after the old life with its pleasures and appetites. We should now read the following: Titus 3 verse 3: "We ourselves also were sometimes foolish, disobedient, deceived, serving divers **lusts** and pleasures ..."; 1 Peter 1 verse 14: "As obedient children, not fashioning yourselves according to the **former lusts** in your ignorance ..."

ii) Idolatry, v.7

"Neither be **ye** idolaters, as were **some of them**; as it is written, The people sat down to eat and drink, and rose up to play." Paul has already warned the Corinthian believers against the dangers of idolatry. See Chapters 5:10, 11 and 6:9.

Paul refers here to Exodus 32 verse 6. In what sense did they sit down "to eat and drink?" "And when Aaron saw it (the calf), he built an altar before it; and Aaron made a proclamation, and said, Tomorrow is a feast to the LORD. And they rose up early on the morrow, and offered burnt offerings, and brought peace offerings; and the people sat down to eat and drink, and rose up to play" (Exodus 32:5-6). They endeavoured to give their idolatry the veneer of respectability: Aaron said: "Tomorrow is a feast to the LORD". Having paid lip-service, the true state of their hearts became evident: "they rose up to play". Their lives betrayed their true affections. The veneer was evident. The word translated "play" here ('tsachaq') is elsewhere rendered 'mock'. Preachers have suggested that this was immoral play, in which case it could be said that they were turning "the grace of our God into lasciviousness" (Jude v.4). One thing is certain, they were dancing (Exodus 32:19).

iii) Immorality, v.8

"Neither let **us** commit fornication, as **some of them** committed, and fell in one day three and twenty thousand." Paul has already warned the Corinthian believers against fornication. See Chapter 6 verses 13-20. The apostle evidently refers here to Numbers 25 verse 9: "And those that died in the plague (as opposed to "one day") were twenty four thousand". The reference then is to Numbers 25 verses 1-9, which in turn refers to the "counsel of Balaam" (Numbers 31:16). In addressing the church at Pergamos, the Lord Jesus said: "Thou hast there them that hold the doctrine of Balaam, who taught Balak to cast a stumblingblock before the children of Israel, to eat things sacrificed unto idols, and to commit fornication" (Revelation 2:14).

iv) Ingratitude, v.9

"Neither let **us** tempt (*'ekpirazo'*) Christ, as **some of them** also tempted (*'pirazo'*), and were destroyed of serpents." While, according to J.N. Darby (see his marginal note), "Many read the Lord" (as opposed to "Christ"), and the RV margin reads similarly, it does seem that if "that Rock was **Christ**" (v.4) then: "Neither let us tempt **Christ**, as some of them also tempted" ought to be taken as it stands. After all, He was certainly there! See Isaiah 63 verse 9: "In all their affliction he was afflicted, and the **angel of his presence** saved them..."

Paul refers here to Numbers 21 verses 5-6: "And the people spake against God, and against Moses, Wherefore have ye brought us up out of Egypt, to die in the wilderness? For there is no bread, neither is there any water; and our soul loatheth this light bread, And the Lord sent fiery serpents among the people, and they bit the people; and much people of Israel died". They tried God with their dissatisfaction with His provision for them in redemption ("wherefore have ye brought us up out of Egypt?") and in the manna (our soul loatheth this light bread"). Similarly, all the provision that God had made for the assembly at Corinth did not prevent dissatisfaction there either. We meet this early in the epistle where they "were disgruntled with God's servants (Chapter 1:12)" (Keith Krell), and, therefore, exhibited their dissatisfaction with God's arrangements, all of which was part of 'defiling' (marring) "the temple of God" with exposure to divine judgment (1 Corinthians 3:17).

The reason for Israel's dissatisfaction is given: "And the soul of the people was much discouraged because the way" (Numbers 21:4). All of which reminds us to: "Do all things without murmurings and disputings" (Philippians 2:14). "Murmurings" follow:

v) Insurrection, v.10

"Neither murmur **ye**, as **some of them** also **murmured**, and were destroyed (*'apollumi'*) of the destroyer (*'olothrutees'*: 'to destroy especially in the sense of slaying', W.E. Vine)".

Paul refers here to Numbers 16 verses 14-41: "But on the morrow (that is, after the deaths of Korah, Dathan, and Abiram) all the congregation of Israel murmured against Moses and Aaron, saying, Ye have killed the people of the LORD" (v.41).

The murmuring here was discontent at divine discipline. Instead of humbling themselves, Israel murmured - and became subject to divine discipline yet again. See Numbers 16 verse 49: "Now they that died in the plague were fourteen thousand and seven hundred, beside them that died about the matter of Korah".

In summary, privileges are no guarantee against shipwreck and consequent discipline: with all their privileges "the Lord smote the people with a very great plague" (Numbers 11:33) ... "there fell of the people that day about three thousand men" (Exodus 32:28) ... "(there) fell in one day three and twenty thousand" (v.8) ... (they) "were destroyed of serpents" (v.9) ... (they) "were destroyed of the destroyer" (v.10). This brings us to:

c) Applying the lessons, vv.11-14

"Now all these things happened unto them for ensamples ('*tupos*', types): and they are written for our admonition ('*nouthesia*', 'a putting in mind', perhaps 'warning'), upon whom the ends of the world (ages) are come. Wherefore let him that thinketh he standeth take heed lest he fall" (vv11-12).

The words: "upon whom the ends of the world are come" (v.11) mean that we are at the end of the ages and have all the lessons of preceding ages available to us. Compare Romans 15 verse 4: "Whatsoever things were written aforetime were written for our learning, that we through patience and comfort of the scriptures might have hope".

The words: "Let him that thinketh he standeth" (v.12) point out the sure way to succumb to temptation, whereas to "take heed lest he fall" (that is, "fall" under divine judgment, see vv.8-10) is the sure way to overcome. Constant vigilance is necessary for spiritual well-being and avoidance of becoming "castaway" - rejected as to reward. What **we all have** does not infer that we are invulnerable. We must **"take heed"**.

Encouragement follows: "There hath no temptation taken you but such as is common to man ('as is according to man's nature', JND): but God is faithful, who will not suffer you to be tempted above that ye are able; but will with the temptation also make a way to escape, that ye may be able to bear it. Wherefore, my dearly beloved, flee from idolatry" (vv.13-14). Now read 1 John 5 verses 20-21. We should notice the following:

i) The nature of temptation. The things that the believers at Corinth were likely to encounter were not peculiar to themselves. It has been pointed out that "the three words translated into our English, 'common to man', are actually pressed into a single term. A more literal reading would be: 'No temptation has seized you that is not human' ('*anthropinos*', i.e. 'manlike'). No one can hide behind the argument that his sin is unique and so he can be excused" (Supplied by Justin Waldron).

ii) The limit to temptation. In saying: "God is faithful" (compare 1 Corinthians 1: 9), Paul is emphasising that He is aware of the limitations of His people. God allows only what He knows His people can overcome. He is thoroughly aware of our circumstances and capacity to endure temptation.

iii) The escape from temptation. Temptation carries the guarantee of victory over it! He will "make a way to escape". Closer examination will show that the use of the definite article ("the") with both "temptation" and "way of escape" (see RV: "*the* way of escape"), points to a particular way of escape that is available in each temptation. The expression: "way of escape" ('*ekbasis*') is, literally: 'a way out' or 'an exit'. In this case it is: "*flee* from idolatry". That's what Joseph did when tempted by Potiphar's wife. He "fled, and got him out" (Genesis 39:12).

It is worth noting that it is not a sin to be tempted: it is a sin to succumb to temptation. In the words of an oft-quoted proverb (people usually say, 'old Chinese proverb'): "You cannot stop a bird flying over your head, but you can stop it making a nest in your hair".

These notes contain valuable material extracted from notes taken of an address given by Mr. Richard Catchpole on 24th April 2004 at Bognor Regis. It pays to take notes!

1 CORINTHIANS

"The Lord's table"

Read Chapter 10:15-33

In our previous study, we noticed that the words: "Flee from idolatry" (v.14) lie at the heart of the chapter. The believers at Corinth were to "flee from idolatry" *(1) on the ground of divine condemnation* (vv.1-14): "Neither be ye *idolaters* as were some of them" and there "*fell* in one day three and twenty thousand" (vv.7-8); *(2) on the ground of communion* (vv.15-22): "What say I then? That the idol is anything, or that which is offered in sacrifice to *idols* is anything? But I say, that the things which the Gentiles sacrifice, they sacrifice to devils ('demons', JND), and not to God: and I would not that ye should have fellowship with devils (demons). Ye cannot drink the cup of the Lord, and the cup of devils (demons)" (vv.19-21); *(3) on the ground of conscience* (vv.23-33): "If any man say unto you, This is offered in sacrifice unto *idols*, eat not for his sake that shewed it, and for conscience sake … conscience, I say, not thine own, but of the other" (vv.28-29). God's people are, therefore, to: "Flee from idolatry" -

1) BEACAUSE IT INCURS CONDEMNATION BY GOD, vv.1-14

We suggested that the 'key verse' to this section of the chapter is: "Wherefore let him that thinketh he standeth take heed lest he fall (into judgment)" (v.12). The words: "him that thinketh he standeth" are illustrated in vv.1-4, with their emphasis on the word *"all"*. The words: "take heed lest he fall" are illustrated in vv.5-10, which commence with the words: "But with *many* ('most', RV) of them God was not well pleased" and continue with the word: *"some"* (vv.7, 8, 9, 10).

Having applied the lessons from the Old Testament (vv.11-14), Paul comes to the second of three reasons for fleeing idolatry (vv.15-22), but before considering this we should notice the way in which he concludes his first reason and commences the second: "Wherefore, my dearly beloved, flee from idolatry. I speak unto wise men; judge ye what I say" (vv.14-15).

- In the first case, he expresses his love for them: he calls them: "my dearly beloved" (v14). His warnings had been expressed out of love for them. Compare Philippians 4 verses 1-2. Euodias and Syntyche might have responded angrily if Paul had not twice addressed the believers at Philippi as: "my dearly beloved" (v.1). It is so important to say the right thing in the right way. Perhaps this is all part of Solomon's observation that "A word fitly spoken is like apples of gold in pictures of silver" (Proverbs 25:11).

- In the second case, he expresses his courtesy: "I speak as to wise men; judge ye what I say". He appeals to their spiritual discernment. There is no irony here, as there certainly was in 1 Corinthians 4 verse 10. Perhaps we should say that the word "courteous" (*'tapeinophron'*) in 1 Peter 3 verse 8 means to be "humble minded" (RV).

This brings us to the second reason why the believers at Corinth should "flee from idolatry" -

2) BECAUSE IT IMPAIRS COMMUNION WITH GOD, vv.15-22

With this in mind, Paul addresses *idolatry itself* (vv.15-22), and follows by addressing *idolatrous associations* (vv.23-33). (The passage actually concludes with Chapter 11:1.) In the second case, as already noted, Paul deals with the consumption of food offered to idols and the damage this may cause to other people's consciences.

The 'key' words in these verses are: "communion" (v.16), "partakers" (v.18), and "fellowship" (v.20). The three English words translate one original word which occurs in the passage either as a noun or an adjective. A different word is translated "partakers" in verses 17 and 21. Here is the passage:

"The cup of blessing which we bless, is it not the *communion* (*'koinonia'*: a noun meaning 'a having in common') of the blood of Christ? The bread which we break, is it not the *communion* (*'koinonia'*) of the body of Christ? For we being many are one bread, and one body: for we are all partakers (*'metecho'*) of that one bread. Behold Israel after the flesh: are not they which eat of the sacrifices *partakers* (*'koinonos'*, an adjective, 'having in common') of the altar? What say I then? That the idol is any thing, or that which is offered in sacrifice to idols is any thing? But I say, that the things which the Gentiles sacrifice, they sacrifice to devils (demons), and not to God: and I would not that ye should have **fellowship** ('*koinonos*', as above, an adjective) with devils (demons). Ye cannot drink the cup of the Lord, and cup of devils (demons): ye cannot be partakers ('*metecho*') of the Lord's table, and of the table of devils (demons)" (vv.16-21).

Bearing in mind the conclusion at the end of the passage: "Ye cannot drink the cup of the Lord, and cup of devils: ye cannot be partakers of the Lord's table, and of the table of devils" (v.21), we must notice what Paul says *(a)* about "the Lord's table" (vv.16-18); *(b)* about "the table of demons" (vv.19-20); *(c)* about the implications for the Lord's people (vv.21-22).

a) The Lord's table, vv.16-18

It should be carefully noted that Paul does not say "the Lord's supper" here (as in Chapter 11:20), but rather "the Lord's table" (v.21). There can be no doubt that he *is* referring to "the Lord's supper" here, not as a **commemoration** as in Chapter 11 verses 17-34, but rather as an expression of **communion.** This must be emphasised. In 1 Corinthians 11, the subject is **commemoration**, whereas in 1 Corinthians 10 the subject is **communion.** With this in mind, we must notice the following:

i) The meaning of "the Lord's table". In this connection, Paul uses two expressions: "partakers of **the altar**" (v.18) and partakers of **the Lord's table**" (v.21). The altar and the table are one and the same in the Old Testament. The first emphasises the place of **sacrifice** (it is an altar), and the second emphasises the place of **provision** (it is a table): "Ye offer polluted bread upon **mine altar:** and ye say, Wherein have we polluted thee? In that ye say, **The table of the LORD** is contemptible" (Malachi 1:7); "Ye say, **The table of the LORD** is polluted; and the fruit thereof, even his meat, is contemptible" (Malachi 1:12-13). Very clearly, the Lord's table is the altar. The sacrifices are called the "bread of God" (Leviticus 21:6, 17, 22).

While in the Old Testament, "the Lord's table" is actually an altar, it is called "the Lord's table" in view of **what it provides through death,** leading Paul to remind us here (vv.16-21) that we were brought into communion with God at the moment of salvation, and remain in communion with Him on the ground of sacrifice. We are *always* in the good of that table. Like Mephibosheth, we "eat continually at the king's table" (2 Samuel 9:13).

It, therefore, follows that in referring to "the Lord's table" (v.21) by using the symbols of the Lord's supper, Paul reverses the historical order, and refers to the "cup" before the "bread". This brings us to:

ii) The order, v.16. As noted above, Paul refers to the "cup" (the "communion of the blood of Christ") before the "bread" (the "communion of the body of Christ"). W.E. Vine deals with this with clarity: "The reference to the blood is put first because the death of Christ in the shedding of His blood, that is, the act of the giving up His life in vicarious sacrifice, is the very basis of all spiritual blessings ... The apostle's question ('The cup of blessing which we bless, is it not the communion of the blood of Christ?') therefore teaches us that believers have fellowship in all that is the outcome of the shedding of the blood of Christ". The "cup" is therefore placed first because it conveys the *basis* of fellowship: "the communion of *the blood of Christ*". This brings us to:

iii) The cup, v.16. We should notice that this is not followed by: "we being many are one cup". This emphasises that Christ was *alone in His death.* As noted above, the cup is placed first because it refers to the basis of communion, that is, our sharing in all that flows from the shedding of the blood of Christ. We should notice too that the emphasis is *quite different* in 1 Corinthians 11: "This cup is the new testament in my blood: this do ye, as oft as ye drink it, in remembrance of me. For as often as ye eat this bread and drink this cup, ye do shew the Lord's death till he come" (vv.25-26). Here, in 1 Corinthians 10, we should notice that it is "the cup of blessing which we bless".

- The "cup". Paul does not say 'the *wine* of blessing which we bless'. Whilst it is said that the cup stands, by metonymy, for its contents (i.e., wine), there is far more involved. The "cup" in Scripture is often the symbol of divine judgment: see Psalm 75 verse 8; Isaiah 51 verses 17, 22; Ezekiel 23 verses 32-33. The Lord Jesus Himself said: "O my Father, if it be possible, let this cup pass from me" (Matthew 26:39). See also Matthew 20 verse 22: "Are ye able to drink of the cup that I shall drink of?" The "cup" therefore reminds us that the blood of the Lord Jesus was shed under divine judgment.

(As a matter of interest, we are told that there are four cups present at the

Jewish Passover: *the cup of blessing* - all drink of it; *the cup of wrath* - none drink of it: it is poured out as they recount the ten plagues in Egypt; *the cup of salvation* - it is filled to overflowing and all drink; *the cup of the kingdom* - this looks to the future).

- *"The cup of blessing which we bless."* The word "blessing" (*'eulogia'*) means: literally, 'good speaking'. So "the cup" speaks well *to us.* The second reference to blessing ("which we *bless*") also translates *'eulogia'*, so *we speak well* of the cup! We should note that the Lord Jesus 'gave thanks' (1 Corinthians 11:24). Here the original word is *'eucharisteo'* meaning, as translated: 'giving of thanks, thankfulness' (W.E. Vine).

It must, therefore, be emphasised that there is no suggestion here of 'consecrating the emblems'. The Lord Jesus "took bread and blessed (*'eulogeo'*)..." (Matthew 26:26). He did not 'bless the cup': we should carefully note that the word *"it"* is italicised. Compare Mark 14 verse 22.

As already noted, the words "communion (or fellowship) of the blood of Christ" refer to the blessings which flow from the redemptive work of Christ.

iv) The bread, vv.16-18. Once again, we should notice that the emphasis is *quite different* in 1 Corinthians 11: "The Lord Jesus ... took bread: and when he had given thanks, he brake it, and said, Take, eat: this is my body, which is broken for you ('which is for you', margin): this do in remembrance of me" (v.23-24). But here, in 1 Corinthians 10, Paul does not refer to the body in which He "bare our sins" (1 Peter 3:24), but rather to "the communion of the body of Christ", that is, of His 'mystical body' (see Chapter 12:12): "for *we* being many are one bread (loaf), and one body".

The bread in 1 Corinthians 10 stands for our 'one-ness' in Christ, and for the fellowship which exists between all members of the body of Christ. The reading makes this clear: "The bread which we break, is it not the communion of the body of Christ? *For* we, being many, are one bread (loaf), and one body; for we are all partakers of that one bread" (v.17), or: "The bread which we break, is it not [the] communion of the body of Christ? *Because* we, [being] many, are one loaf, one body; for we all partake of that one loaf" (JND). The part that *each* believer takes indicates their individual fellowship with Christ on the ground of his death, and the fact that *all* partake is a token of the essential oneness of the members of the body of Christ.

This is illustrated from the Old Testament: "Behold Israel after the flesh: are not they which eat of the sacrifices partakers of the altar" (v.18), "that is to say, they are in fellowship with Him whose altar it is" (W.E. Vine). As already noted, the word "partakers" ('*koinonos*', as in v.16) means 'communion' or 'fellowship'. As W.E. Vine observes: "In certain offerings the offerers, after a part had been burnt on the altar, and a part had been given to the priest, ate the rest in the court of the tabernacle (Leviticus 7:15-21, Deuteronomy 12:5-7)". See also Deuteronomy 14 verses 22-27, where God's people, having come to Jerusalem ("the place which he shall choose to place his name there") with their "tithes" and "firstlings" were to "eat there before the LORD thy God". In this way, God's people indicated their national unity. Their 'one-ness' rested on the sacrifices upon the altar. This brought them into fellowship with the Lord, and with one another, which is exactly the teaching in 1 Corinthians 10.

In summary: "The communion of the blood of Christ" (v.16) emphasises the **basis** of communion or fellowship, whereas "the communion of the body of Christ" (v.16) emphasises the **sphere** of communion or fellowship. The words: "The cup of blessing which we bless, is it not the communion of the blood of Christ? The bread which we break, is it not the communion of the body of Christ?" display the doctrinal order: the fact that His blood is placed first reminds us that death must take place before His body (His church) could ever exist.

v) The participants at "the Lord's table". We should observe the use of "we" here: "The cup of blessing which *we* bless … The bread which *we* break" (v.16), as opposed to the use of "ye" in Chapter 11: "For as often as *ye* eat this bread, and drink this cup, *ye* do shew the Lord's death till he come" (v.26). In Chapter 10, Paul is discussing the basis and sphere of communion of all the Lord's people ("we"), but in Chapter 11 he is discussing the remembrance of the Lord Jesus in the local assembly ("ye"). In this connection, it is worth noting that it is "the bread which *we* break". The act of 'breaking bread' takes place when the individual believer takes their portion. The brother who actually 'breaks the bread' (as is our custom) does so as a matter of convenience for all present.

This brings us to:

b) The table of demons, vv.19-20

In these verses, Paul makes the point that while there was no reality in idols themselves, there was certainly reality in *idol-worship.*

i) So far as idols themselves were concerned (v.19), Paul emphasises that there was no life in the *images worshipped* (see for example, Psalm 115:4-7), and therefore offerings made to them carried no spiritual significance: "What say I then? That the idol is anything, or that which is offered in sacrifice to idols is any thing?" Compare Chapter 8 verses 4-6. Read Galatians 4 verse 8: "Ye did service unto them which by nature are no gods". The reality of idols only existed in the minds of the devotees.

ii) So far as idol-worship was concerned (v.20), Paul emphasises that there was a reality about *idol-worship*: "But I say, that the things which the Gentiles sacrifice, they sacrifice to devils (demons) …" Idol-worship was a Satanic device to enslave men and women. In Paul's later words: "Ye know that ye were Gentiles, *carried away* unto these dumb idols, even as ye were *led*" (1 Corinthians 12:2).

Involvement with idolatry must not, therefore, be regarded as a harmless practice which did not really matter since an idol did not exist anyway. Demon power was involved. So: "I would not that ye should have fellowship (*'koinonos'*) with devils (demons)" (v.20). As noted previously, the word *'koinonos'* is translated "partakers" in verse 18, and, in its noun form, "communion" in verse 16. We should now read 2 Corinthians 6 verses 14-18. This brings us to:

c) The implications for the Lord's people, vv.21-22

The conclusion is inescapable: the two communions are totally incompatible. Paul sums them up:

i) "The cup of the Lord, and the cup of devils", v.21: "Ye cannot drink the cup of the Lord, and the cup of devils (demons)." On the one hand we have sacred things: "the blood of Christ … the body of Christ" (v.16). On the other hand we have, not just profanity, but total evil. See, for example, Deuteronomy 32 verses 37-38: "Where are their gods … which did eat of the fat of their sacrifices, and drank the wine of their drink offerings?" The communion of the blood of Christ and communion with demons are totally incompatible.

ii) "The Lord's table, and … the table of devils", v.21. "Ye cannot be partakers (*'metochos'*) of the Lord's table, and of the table of devils (demons)." (The word *'metochos'* means: "sharing in, partaking of: translated 'partners' in Luke 5: 7", W.E. Vine). The same incompatibility (see above) is emphasised. The fact that it is called: "the Lord's table" suggests, additionally, His authority. It is, therefore, incompatible to think of being in communion with God through the death of His Son, and being involved in idolatry with its satanic associations.

This leads to two questions: "Do we provoke the Lord to jealousy?: are we stronger than he?" (v.22).

- In the first case ("Do we provoke the Lord to jealousy?"), Paul states that attempting to combine both must move Him to indignation. See Exodus 34 verse 14: "For thou shalt worship no other god: for the LORD, whose name is Jealous, is a jealous God"; Deuteronomy 32 verse 21: "They have moved me to jealousy with that which is not God". According to the RV ("Or do we provoke the Lord to jealousy?"), Paul is actually speaking in severer terms than suggested by the AV. Leon Morris explains: "The 'Or' at the beginning of the verse ... brings us to an alternative". Leon Morris continues by pointing out that Paul has been assuming that the Corinthians did not realise the implications of participating in idol feasts, and he has accordingly explained it. But suppose they did understand the significance of what they were doing? Then they were wilfully provoking the Lord

- In the second case ("Are we stronger than he?"), Paul sounds a warning: we cannot escape with impunity if we pursue such a course.

Paul now addresses the third reason why the Corinthians (and we) should "flee from idolatry". If we are to "flee from idolatry" on the ground of divine **condemnation** (vv.1-14), and on the ground of **communion** - with reference to idolatry itself (vv.15-22), then we are also to do so on the ground of **conscience** - with reference to food offered to idols. So believers should "flee from idolatry" -

3) BECAUSE IT INJURED CONSCIENCE, vv.23-33

Paul deals with this aspect of the subject as follows *(a)* the underlying principle in our relationship with others (vv.23-24); *(b)* our personal conscience in relation to food offered to idols (vv.25-27); *(c)* our attitude in relation to the consciences of others (vv.28-33, and 11:1).

a) The principle in our relationship with others, vv.23-24

"All things are lawful for me, but all things are not expedient: all things are lawful for me, but all things edify not. Let no man seek his own, but every man another's wealth" or "Let no man seek his own, but every man his neighbour's good" (RV). We should notice the emphasis here: "All things are lawful *for me,* but all things are not expedient" *for others.* "All things are lawful *for me*, but all things edify not." That is, 'they are lawful for me, but they do not always edify *other* people'.

This is perfectly clear: our conduct must always have others in mind. We must think positively, and bear in mind what is "expedient": that is, what is profitable or advantageous to others. We must also bear in mind what will "edify": that is, what will build up others. This is familiar territory! See 1 Corinthians 8 verses 9-13. The passage is relevant to this section of 1 Corinthians 10 in its entirety.

> *Others, Lord, yes, others,*
> *Let this my motto be,*
> *Help me to live for others,*
> *That I may live like Thee.*

b) Our personal conscience in relation to food offered to idols, vv.25-27

Having said (twice): "all things are lawful for me" (v.23), Paul envisages a believer in two situations: *(i)* choosing meat in the market (vv.25-26); *(ii)* attending a feast (v.27).

ii) Choosing meat in the market, vv.25-26. "Whatsoever is sold in the shambles (the meat market), that eat, asking no question for conscience sake: for the earth is the Lord's, and the fulness thereof." There was no need for a troubled conscience, and no need to create unnecessary difficulties. It was not necessary to ascertain if the meat had been offered to an idol before coming on sale, for the simple reason that "the earth is the Lord's, and the fulness thereof". This cites Psalm 24 verse 1. The expression: "and the fulness thereof" means: 'and all it contains'. He created it and, therefore, it is not evil in itself. Compare Romans 14 verse 14: "I know, and am persuaded by the Lord Jesus, that there is nothing unclean of itself". Note Paul's words here: "am persuaded by the Lord Jesus", which evidently refer to the Lord's teaching in Matthew 15 verses 11, 17-20. The fact that the meat may have been offered to an idol does not alter the case.

ii) Attending a feast, v.27. "If any of them that believe not bid you to a feast, and ye be disposed to go; whatsoever is set before you, eat, asking no question for conscience sake." Once again, in these circumstances, there was no need to raise unnecessary difficulties. Even if the restaurant is located within the precincts of an idol's temple (1 Corinthians 8:10). (McDonalds get everywhere, don't they!).

c) Our attitude in relation to the consciences of others, vv28-33

"But if any man say unto you, This is offered in sacrifice unto idols, eat not, for his sake that shewed it, and for conscience sake...conscience, I say, not thine own, but of the other: for why is my liberty judged of another man's conscience?" (vv.28-29). (Note: the repeated words "for the earth is the Lord's, and the fulness thereof" (v.29) are omitted by JND/RV).

The words: "if any man say unto you" refer to either a believer or an unbeliever. This is borne out by verses 32-33. The situation here illustrates the general principle in verse 24: "Let no man seek his own, but every man another's wealth" or: "Let no one seek his own [advantage], but that of the other" (JND). Believers are to respect - not injure - the consciences of others.

In the case of a fellow-believer here, we are not to offend a weaker brother's conscience by exercising our own liberty. This would impair fellowship: the strong brother exercising liberty in eating food offered to idols would be judged guilty of wrong-doing by the weaker brother, causing Paul to say: "Why is my liberty judged of another man's conscience?" (v.29).

Moreover: it would make for a misunderstanding of divine grace: "For if I by grace be a partaker, why am I evil spoken of for that for which I give thanks?" (v.30). That is, the grace of God enables the strong brother to eat food offered to idols, but if in so doing a weak brother is offended, we must not boast about our liberty in the matter. Far better not to exercise that liberty in the first place.

The passage concludes with two general principles: "Whether therefore ye eat or drink, or whatsoever ye do, do all for the glory of God. Give none offence, neither to the Jews, nor to the Gentiles, nor to the church of God" (vv.31-32).

- **"Do all for the glory of God" (v.31).** That is, act in a way which will bring glory to God in the happy undisturbed consciences of believers and, especially so far as Jews are concerned, in abstaining from "meats offered to idols" (Acts 15:29).

- "Give none offence" (v32). Provide 'no occasion for stumbling'. We must notice the three classes of people: "the Jews … the Gentiles … the church of God". As W.E. Vine points out, the phrase: "the church of God" is always used in the New Testament of a local assembly, not of the whole Church, the Body of Christ. All such assemblies are spoken of as: 'the churches of God'. See 1 Corinthians 11:16.

Paul exemplified this in his own life: "Even as I please all men in all things, not seeking mine own profit, but the profit of many, that they **may be saved**" (v.33). Compare Chapter 9 verses 19-23. He conducted himself, and regulated his life and activities, in order to help others: both saints and sinners!

This section of the epistle concludes with the words: "Be ye followers of me, even as I also am of Christ" (1 Corinthians 11:1) or: "Be ye imitators of me, even as I also am of Christ" (RV). Christians are to be like the Lord Jesus in seeking the blessing of others: "Look not every man on his own things (his own interests), but every man also on the things (interests) of others. Let this mind be in you, which was also in Christ Jesus …" (Philippians 2:4-5).

1 CORINTHIANS

"Is it comely that a woman pray unto God uncovered?"

Read Chapter 11:2-16

In these verses, Paul deals with the question of head-coverings in assembly gatherings. To many professing Christians, this is regarded as non-essential. We are told that 'as long as the heart is right, the question of a head-covering is really quite unimportant. A piece of material on a sister's head doesn't make any difference to her at all'. This teaching has been accepted wholesale in some places, and has almost inevitably led to further retrograde changes. Of course, it is important that the heart should be right, and when this is the case, biblical teaching on the subject will be gladly recognised and practised. After all, we should all count it a great privilege, whether brothers or sisters, to confess the headship of Christ. If there has been some kind of change, and the headship of Christ has been withdrawn or lost, we might have some reason for ignoring New Testament teaching on the subject. The very suggestion brings its own refutation!

1 Corinthians 11 clearly divides into two sections. In verses 2-16, Paul deals with the **Headship of Christ**, and the section commences: "Now I praise you" (v.2). The subject is developed with particular reference to public participation in assembly gatherings. In verses 17-34, Paul deals with the **Lordship of Christ**, and the section commences: "Now I praise you not" (v.17). The subject is developed with particular reference to the Lord's supper. In this study, we are particularly concerned with apostolic teaching in verses 2-16.

It is noteworthy that the passage commences with the words: "Now I praise you, brethren, that ye remember me in all things, and keep the ordinances ('traditions', RV; 'directions', JND: *'paradosis'*, something handed down: see 2 Thessalonians 2:15; 3:6), as I delivered them to you" (v.2). We should notice Paul's commendation before censure. That always makes censure more acceptable. In the words of W.E. Vine, "Where praise can be bestowed it is well to begin by giving it". See, for example, 1 Corinthians 1 verses 4-7; Revelation 2 verse 2.

Paul's teaching on the subject arose out of irregular practices in the assembly at Corinth. The words: "But I would have you know" (v.3), introduce a matter where deficiency existed. Paul refers to this in verses 4-5: "Every man praying or prophesying, having his head covered, dishonoureth his head. But every woman that prayeth or prophesieth with her head uncovered dishonoureth her head". We must notice that there were two irregularities. *(i)* Sisters were present in assembly gatherings with uncovered heads, and *(ii)* they were participating audibly. Paul deals with the first irregularity in this chapter, and the second irregularity in Chapter 14, which deals with the entire question of audible participation in assembly gatherings. We will see why Paul deals with the problems in this particular order later in our present study. However, it is possible that the second irregularity lies within the scope of verse 34: "And the rest will I set in order when I come".

Paul deals with the question of head-coverings in the assembly in four ways. He points out that the uncovered head of a sister, and for that matter, the covered head of a brother, is: *(1)* contrary to divine principle (vv.3-6); *(2)* contrary to creatorial precedent (vv.7-12); *(3)* contrary to spiritual propriety (vv.13-15); *(4)* contrary to apostolic practice (v.16). (Incidentally, there is no such word as 'creatorial', but it won't be long before it creeps into our dictionaries!)

1) IT IS CONTRARY TO DIVINE PRINCIPLE, vv.3-6

In the first place, Paul establishes the **principle** involved in headship (v.3), and then he refers to the **implications** in failing to display headship (vv.4-6). W.E. Vine helpfully points out that "the subject of the Headship of Christ here differs from that in Ephesians and Colossians, where not only is His relationship to the whole church in view but vital union with Him and His maintenance of its spiritual life. Here His Headship is confined to His authority and supremacy and direction over the individual".

a) The principle of headship, v.3

"But I would have you know, that the head of every man is Christ; and the head of the woman is the man; and the head of Christ is God." This verse describes a series of graded headships, culminating with the words: "the head of Christ is God". It might be helpful to deal with this first:

i) "The head of Christ is God." This emphasises two most important aspects of the subject. Firstly, that the principle of headship operates between divine Persons and, secondly, arising from this, that the principle of headship involves relationship, *not* inequality. The words: "the head of Christ is God" have particular reference to His manhood where, without for one moment resigning His absolute deity, the Lord Jesus was willingly subject to the will of God. Witness the following: "Then said he, Lo, I come to do thy will, O God" (Hebrews 10:9); "I seek not mine own will, but the will of the Father which hath sent me" (John 5:30); "O my Father, if it be possible, let this cup pass from me! nevertheless, not as I will, but as thou wilt" (Matthew 26:39) See also Philippians 2 verse 6-8. Turning to the future: "And when all things shall be subdued unto him, then shall the Son also himself be subject to him that put all things under him, that God may be all in all" (1 Corinthians 15:28). We should notice that Ephesians 5 verses 22-33 links headship with subjection.

ii) "The head of every man is Christ." This emphasises the authority of Christ in relation to the man (the male: 'aner'). When the Lord Jesus was here, He prayed: "I have glorified thee on the earth: I have finished the work which thou gavest me to do" (John 17:4). The Lord Jesus lived and died for the honour and glory of God. Every man in the assembly should bring honour and glory to Christ by subjection to Him. Men should, therefore, be marked by dignity and reverential awe. There should be nothing frivolous about their behaviour. They must act at all times with reference to His authority. They are responsible to Christ, and the relationship between Christ and God constitutes the pattern of this recognition. Headship involves devotion and love: it is not rigid tyranny.

iii) "The head of the woman is the man." This does not mean that the woman is not subject to Christ in the same degree as the man, but that she shows her subjection to Christ in her subjection to the man in the assembly. The woman does this by acknowledging that God has ordained that the man should be *directly* responsible to Christ in the assembly, whereas the woman is *indirectly* responsible to Him. We should remember that this passage does not infer either the superiority of the man, or the inferiority of the woman: it teaches that men and women, whilst equally important, have differing roles.

But where and how is this headship displayed? The answer is delightfully simple: both men and women display the headship of Christ in their heads! This brings us to:

b) The implications in failing to display headship

i) As to the man. "Every man praying (Godward) or prophesying (manward), having his head covered, dishonoureth (the word, '*kataischuno*', means 'to put to shame') his head" (v.4) or: "Every man praying or prophesying, having [anything] on his head, puts his head to shame" (JND). While it is true that a man praying whilst wearing a hat would bring shame on himself by acting inconsistently with his station, it is even more serious than that. He is dishonouring Christ. "In so doing, he dishonours Christ by taking from Him the honour due to Him as the head of the man" (J. Hunter, *What the Bible Teaches: 1 Corinthians*). The uncovered head symbolically displays the glory of Christ. The principle is expressed in verse 7: "For a man indeed ought not to cover his head, forasmuch as he is the image and glory of God". In the assembly, the man's head is a symbol of Christ: "the head of every man is Christ" (v.3). Therefore, if a man covers his head, he veils Christ's authority: and that is to bring shame on the glory of Christ.

ii) As to the woman. "But every woman that prayeth or prophesieth with her head uncovered dishonoureth ('*kataischuno*') her head" (v.5). This should be understood with reference to the statement that "the head of the woman is the man" (v.3). An uncovered woman praying or prophesying in the assembly at Corinth dishonoured the man by displaying *his* glory. After all, "the woman is the glory of the man" (v.7), and that glory must be covered. Christ's glory alone must be seen in the assembly. Rightly understood, verses 4-5 have nothing to do with local customs, or with 'brethren traditions', but everything to do with the glory of Christ.

At this point, we ought to address two conclusions which have been wrongly drawn from these verses:

i) That public participation by sisters in the assembly is permissible as long as they are covered. After all, Paul does say, "every woman praying or prophesying" (v.5, JND). While it could be argued that *silent* prayer is in view, that certainly could not be said of prophesying! The answer lies with the fact that Paul deals specifically with headship in 1 Corinthians 11, whereas he deals specifically with participation in assembly gatherings in 1 Corinthians

14. The apostle deals with the subject of headship *first,* because once this is rightly understood, there can be no question of sisters taking audible part. Recognition of the man's headship settles *both* questions. The woman is subject to the man. In any case, there can be no possible collision between 1 Corinthians 11 verses 4-5, and 1 Corinthians 14 verses 34-35, 1 Timothy 2 verse 8, and 1 Timothy 2 verses 11-12.

There is, however, another suggested explanation. We listen here to W.E. Vine: "However the words of this statement may be understood, no explanation can be admitted that violates the fundamental rule that 'a plain Scripture may not be set aside because of another not so easily understood'. The meaning of 1 Corinthians 14 verse 34 is quite unmistakable. Therefore this statement cannot refer to the gatherings of an assembly. There are other occasions than that of an assembly gathering when a woman can exercise the oral ministry of prayer or testimony". In this connection we may instance the prophecy of Philip's four daughters (Acts 21:8-9), but there is no suggestion that they exercised this ministry in assembly meetings.

ii) That the covering mentioned in this chapter is actually the woman's hair. Her hair, we are told, is a covering anyway, and therefore there is no need for anything further. Verse 15 is cited in support of this argument. A little thought will show that this conclusion must be wrong. If the covering in verse 15 and verse 6 are one and the same, we have some very strange teaching indeed. "If the woman be not covered (that is, has no hair), let her also be shorn: but if it be a shame for a woman to be shorn or shaven (having no hair in the first place), let her be covered (either grow her hair, or wear a hair-piece)." We don't even have to study the different Greek words here to see the inconsistency of the gainsayers! Paul's argument is very clear indeed: either a woman has her head covered in two ways, or not at all. Her *first* covering is her long hair: this is her natural glory, which was bestowed on womanhood at creation (v.15). The *second* covering, to be worn during assembly gatherings, is an artificial covering. In the western world, this usually takes the form of a hat, scarf or mantilla, but we must be careful not to lay down hard and fast rules about the precise nature of this head-covering. J. Heading *(The First Epistle to the Corinthians)* points out that "although such creation glory is for the pleasure of God in its rightful place (Rev. 4:11), yet in spiritual service even the best and most legitimate things of the flesh (and we do not use this term in any derogatory sense) are out of place. The hair, then, must either be covered or removed. Now God is not unreasonable in His holy demands, so He insists upon the covering of the hair and not its removal. This would avoid natural shame and embarrassment, and would of course permit the woman's glory to be manifested in its proper sphere". It is worth adding that throughout the passage, Paul refers to the covered or uncovered **head** of the woman, rather than to her covered or uncovered **hair.**

There are therefore two clear alternatives in verse 6: either: "Let her also be shorn" (in which case see Numbers 5:18: Deuteronomy 21:12) or: "Let her be covered". To preserve her glory as a woman, and at the same time to honour the man, she must cover her glory. We should also notice that it is not a question of husbands and wives here. The principle of headship does, of course, apply to marital relationships, see Ephesians 5 verses 22-25, but here it is not "head of the **wife**": it is **men** and **women.** The argument that if a woman wears a wedding ring, then she need not wear a hat, will not stand the light of holy Scripture. Neither, for that matter, will the argument based on Galatians 3 verse 28, where Paul states, amongst other things, that "there is neither male nor female". This passage refers to our standing in Christ, not to the local assembly. It is so important to interpret Scripture in context.

2) IT IS CONTRARY TO CREATORIAL PRECEDENT, vv.7-12

Paul now examines the subject in view of creation, and draws two important conclusions, each of which are introduced by the word "ought" (vv.7, 10), meaning: 'It is necessary' or: 'One must'. It has the idea of logical necessity.

a) That a man ought not to cover his head, vv.7-9

The couplet: "man ... woman" occurs three times in this paragraph, and on each occasion it has a different emphasis. Paul examines the relative position of man and woman, in order to emphasise why a man ought not to cover his head.

i) In creation glory, v.7. "*For a man* indeed ought not to cover his head, forasmuch as he is the image and glory of God: but the *woman* is the glory of the man." In the case of the man, he is "the *image* and *glory* of God". See Psalm 8: "Thou … hast crowned him with glory and honour" (v.5). Adam was the representative of God. The word: "image" (see Genesis 1:27) means the visible representation of God: in, for example, dominion and authority. The word: "glory" conveys the character of God. This description of the man, therefore, emphasises his dignity in the assembly. In the case of the woman, she is "the glory of the man". "She is not designed to reflect the glory of God as a ruler. She is the glory of the man … She always assumes his station; becomes a queen if he is a king, and manifests to others the wealth and honour which may belong to her husband" (C. Hodge, *A Commentary on 1 & 2 Corinthians*). See 1 Peter 3 verses 3-7.

ii) In creation order, v.8. "For the **man** is not of the woman; but the **woman** of the man." This emphasises the man's precedence in creation. See 1 Timothy 2 verse 13: "For Adam was first formed, then Eve".

iii) In creation purpose, v.9. "Neither was the **man** created for the woman; but the **woman** for the man." This emphasises the purpose of her creation: "And the LORD God said, It is not good that the man should be alone; I will make him an help meet for him (or, answering to him)" (Genesis 2:18). This is elsewhere rendered: "A helpmeet, his like" with a marginal note: "or counterpart" (JND). Eve was the complement or counterpart of Adam. As our contributor Justin Waldron points out, God "brought her to the man. Adam was not brought to Eve, but Eve was brought to Adam – her head".

b) That a woman ought to cover her head, vv.10-12

In this paragraph, Paul draws two important conclusions about the woman from the preceding verses:

i) Her subject position, v.10. "For this cause", that is, in view of God's purpose in creation, "ought the woman to have power (a sign of authority) on her head, because of the angels". That is, a sign that she is subject to authority. To which Paul adds: "because of the angels". We must think about this.

Since Paul has been appealing to precedent in creation, he is evidently now saying that the angels who saw divine authority flouted in Eden, expect to see it maintained in the church. Angels are interested spectators. They carefully observe the affairs and conduct of God's people: see Ephesians 3 verse 10; 1 Corinthians 4 verse 9; 1 Timothy 5 verse 21; 1 Peter 1 verse 12.

The angels who said at the Lord's birth: "Glory to God in the highest" (Luke 2:14) expect to see "glory to God" in the assembly. The Lord Jesus has been dishonoured by men, but angels expect Christ to be honoured in the assembly. We must remember too that there had been rebellion amongst the ranks of angels, but there was to be no rebellion in the assembled church.

ii) Her equal position, vv.11-12. "Nevertheless neither is the man without the woman, neither is the woman without the man, in the Lord. For as the woman is of the man, even so is the man also by the woman; but all things of God." These two verses have been properly termed 'safeguard verses'. They emphasise that what has been taught thus far, in no way infers an inferior place for the woman. A subject place is not an inferior place.

Man and woman are mutually dependent. In the assembly, both sexes are mutually dependent "in the Lord". It is beautiful to observe that in the assembly, the relative position of man and woman, as designed by God in creation, is to be exhibited. Paul has dealt with this in the preceding verses. Now he says that the mutual dependence of man and woman, as designed by God in creation, is also to be exhibited in the assembly. The assembly is the place where God's purposes for man and woman are fulfilled, and where the respective glories of man and woman are acknowledged.

When Paul says: "For the woman is of the man", he refers to creation. Adam exclaimed: "She shall be called, Woman, because she was taken out of the man" (Genesis 2:23). When he says: "even so is the man also by the woman", he refers to procreation. Eve exclaimed: "I have gotten a man from the LORD" (Genesis 4:1). (This could be rendered, 'I have gotten a man with the help of the Lord'.) Both quotations enable us to understand why Paul adds: "but all things are of God".

Paul deals with the mutual dependence of man and woman within marriage in 1 Corinthians 7 verses 3-4: "Let the husband render unto the wife due benevolence ('her due'): and likewise also the wife unto the husband. The wife hath not power of her own body, but the husband: and likewise also the husband hath not power of his own body, but the wife". Both passages emphasise, amongst other things, that God assigns equal importance to brothers and sisters in the assembly, and to man and wife in marriage. Referring to Aquila and Priscilla, Justin Waldron points out that "This godly couple complemented each other". Just read the references to them in the New Testament, noting the order of their names.

3) IT IS CONTRARY TO SPIRITUAL PROPRIETY, vv.13-15

Literally: "Is it becoming or fitting that a woman should pray to God uncovered?" That is, does a display of natural beauty and glory accord with ministry in the presence of God? In the assembly, no attention must be drawn to woman's beauty and glory. God's glory must have undivided attention.

Paul emphasises the unique position of the woman in this respect by contrasting the length of hair on men and women respectively.

i) There is no beauty and glory in a man with long hair! "Doth not even nature itself teach you, that if a man have long hair, it is a shame unto him?" (v.14). It is: "a shame unto him" because he has abandoned his own masculine dignity by looking like a woman. God expects men to look like men, and women to look like women. This applies to dress as well as hair. God has given to men and women distinctive glories, and these should be carefully maintained for His pleasure.

ii) There is beauty and glory in a woman with long hair. "But if a woman have long hair, it is a glory to her: for her hair is given her for a covering" (v.15). We should carefully note that the word "covering" here translates a different original word from that used in verses 5 and 13 (where 'uncovered' translates '*akatakaluptos*') and in verse 6 (where 'be not covered' translates '*katakaluptomai*'). Both words derive from '*kalupto*' meaning 'to cover'. Here (v.15) the word "covering" ('*peribolaion*') means: 'something thrown round': a mantle about her body. The same word is rendered "vesture" in Hebrews 1 verse 12. This emphasises the necessity for a second covering. As J. Heading observes: "even the natural senses of a believer would cause him or her to own that such natural glory has no place in spiritual service or in the presence of God".

4) IT IS CONTRARY TO APOSTOLIC PRACTICE, v.16

"But if any man seem to be contentious ('*philoneikos*', love of strife: eagerness to contend) we have no such custom, neither the churches of God." The words: "*we* have no such custom" refer to the apostles. Compare, for example: "For I think that God hath set forth us the apostles last ..." (1 Corinthians 4:9). Then there was assembly practice: "neither the churches of God". This suggests that this particular disorder was peculiar to Corinth. It is sobering to remember that while each assembly is responsible to the Lord alone, and that any idea of church federation is unknown in the New Testament, each local assembly is nevertheless *not* at liberty to introduce or allow whatever it thinks fit. In the days of the Judges: "every man did that which was right in his own eyes" (Judges 21:25), with dire consequences.

This attitude is ***still*** a recipe for disaster. We must recognise that apostolic teaching is binding on every assembly: Paul refers to his "ways which be in Christ, as I teach ***every where in every church***" (1 Corinthians 4:17).

Let every believer, whether brother or sister, esteem it a great honour and privilege to give glory to our beloved Lord by fully recognising His headship when we gather in assembly capacity. Perhaps we should add that a brother or sister's recognition of the Lord's headship involves more than not wearing or wearing a head-covering as the case may be. There are practical issues. On the one hand, men can fail to give an appropriate lead in assembly and domestic life: on the other, women can exercise excessive initiative and effectively take a leading part. It is not unknown for an assembly to have an 'oversight', and an 'undersight' as well! A 'word to the wise!'

1 CORINTHIANS

"The Lord's supper"

Read Chapter 11:17-34

Assembly fellowship is expressed in various ways, and in particular by participation in "the Lord's supper". Paul uses this term in 1 Corinthians 11 verse 20 to describe what we commonly call the 'breaking of bread', which is also a thoroughly Biblical expression: see Acts 20 verse 7. The Lord's supper is not optional: the Lord Jesus said: "***This do*** in remembrance of me" (Luke 22:19; 1 Corinthians 11:24). But, He expects more than reluctant compliance. If we love someone, it follows quite naturally that we will do all in our power to please them (see Genesis 29:20), and our love for Christ should not be an exception to this rule. The Lord Jesus said: "If ye love me, keep my commandments … he that hath my commandments, and keepeth them, he it is that loveth me" (John 14:15, 21).

Before considering various aspects of "the Lord's supper", we ought to examine the expressions: "the Lord's supper" and "the Lord's table".

a) "The Lord's supper"

i) It is "the **Lord's** supper". The Greek word (*'kuriakos'*) "signified pertaining to a lord or master" (W.E. Vine). "The word was used in the papyri in the sense of belonging to the Caesar, or Imperial" (*The Linguistic Key to the Greek New Testament*). Since it is **His** "supper", and He is the divine Host, we cannot do as we please or say what we like.

ii) It is "the Lord's **supper**". While, as we know, it was instituted "when even was come" (Matthew 26:20; Mark 14:17, JND), it is the type of meal rather than the time of day which is particularly important. See Revelation 3 verse 20: "I will come in to him, and **sup** with him, and he with me". Supper was a long meal, the main meal of the day, when members of the family and their guests spent time in conversation and reflection. It was unhurried, and more leisurely, than other meals. The "Lord's supper" is therefore an occasion when believers gather to spend time in praise and worship as they are 'occupied alone with Him'.

b) "The Lord's table"

Whilst our hymnology often uses this expression in relation to "the Lord's supper" or 'breaking of bread', it really means something quite different. In 1 Corinthians 10 verse 21, Paul uses the expression in connection with **fellowship with God.** In the Old Testament, the "Lord's table" was the altar (Malachi 1:7, 12), and the sacrifices on the altar are described as: "the bread of thy God" (Leviticus 21:8 etc). The altar was the place of fellowship with God, and this was expressed particularly in the peace offering, in which God, the priests, and the offerer and his family, all participated (see 1 Corinthians 10:18). We were brought into fellowship with God on faith in Christ. It was then that we took our place at "the Lord's table". Moreover, we are **always** there, and we will **never leave it**! While Paul certainly **alludes** to "the Lord's supper" in describing our place at "the Lord's table", he reverses the order of the emblems. The "cup of blessing" is placed first, because it is the **basis** of fellowship with God, and the bread second, where it is used as a symbol of fellowship between believers. Whilst "the Lord's supper" is essentially a time when we remember the Lord Jesus, it also expresses the principal benefits of "the Lord's table", namely, our fellowship with God, and with each other.

It might be helpful to notice that the Lord's teaching in John 6 verses 53-56 does not refer to "the Lord's supper". His words: "Whoso eateth my flesh, and drinketh my blood, hath eternal life" refer to salvation. The children of Israel had to appropriate the manna to stay alive in the wilderness, and men and women have to appropriate Christ in order to possess eternal life. See John 6 verses 47-51.

1 Corinthians 11 verses 17-34 may be divided as follows: **(1)** the abuse of the Lord's supper (vv.17-22): "**Now** in this that I declare unto you, I praise you not" (v.17); **(2)** the institution of the Lord's supper (vv.23-26): "**For** I have received of the Lord that which also I declared unto you" (v.23); **(3)** the examination in view of the Lord's supper (vv.27-34): "Wherefore, whosoever shall eat this bread, and drink this cup of the Lord, unworthily, shall be guilty of the body and blood of the Lord. But let a man examine himself …" (vv.27-28).

1) THE ABUSE OF THE LORD'S SUPPER, vv.17-22

The commencement of this section in the chapter should be compared with the commencement of the preceding section: *(i)* vv.2-16 are introduced with the words: "Now *I praise you*" (v.2); *(ii)* vv.17-34 are introduced with the words: "I *praise you not*" (v.17): this is repeated in v.22.

The passage commences with a note of authority: "Now in this that I *declare* (*'parangello'*) unto you, I praise you not" (v.17) or: "But in giving you this *charge*, I praise you not ..." (RV).

The threefold use of the phrase: "Ye come together" should be noted (vv.17, 18, 20). See also Chapter 14: 23. Two observations are necessary in this connection:

i) "When ye come together in the church", v.18, or: "when ye come together in assembly" (JND), or: "in congregation" (RV margin). It should be said that a local assembly is not the total of all believers in a given locality (!), but the total of believers *gathering together*.

ii) "When ye come together therefore into one place", v20. So the Lord's supper is observed by the whole assembly in one place. The New Testament does not envisage fragmentary meetings.

But although Paul uses the expression: "Ye come together", it becomes clear that in another sense they were *not* together. So:

i) "When ye come together in the church, I hear that there be *divisions* among you" (vv.18-19).

ii) "When ye come together ... *every one taketh before other* his own supper" (vv.20-22).

So the assembly was together physically, but not spiritually. The fellowship which should have been demonstrated by the supper was absent. We should therefore notice *(a)* the divisions (vv.18-19); *(b)* the description (vv.20-22).

a) The divisions, vv18-19

"For first of all, when ye come together in the church, I hear that there be divisions among you; and I partly believe it. For there must be also heresies among you, that they which are approved may be made manifest among you."

The word "divisions" ('*schisma*') means a schism or a rent. It occurs in Chapter 1 verse 10: "that ye all speak the same thing, and that there be no **divisions** among you"; Chapter 12 verse 25: "that there should be no **schism** in the body; but that the members should have the same care one for another". See also Matthew 9 verse 16: "the **rent** (caused by putting new cloth in an old garment) is made worse".

The context (see v.19) suggests that Paul is not referring here to the situation described in Chapter 1 verses 10-12, but to other divisions, viz. between the "haves" and the "have nots" (v.22). We should notice:

i) "I partly believe it" (v.18). Paul is indicating here that whilst he did not necessarily accept the suggested extent of the report, he did accept that there was basis for the report. He accepted that the position could be exaggerated. We are all prone to accept completely what we hear - and to add to it in our own minds!

ii) "For there must also be heresies, that they which are approved may be manifest among you" (v.19). The word "heresies" means, literally: "a choosing … then, that which is chosen, and hence, an opinion, especially a self-willed opinion, which is substituted for submission to the power of truth" (W.E. Vine). This lies behind a division, and leads us to say that it is so necessary to: "rightly divide the word of truth". This involves, for example, reference to the context in establishing the meaning of any one verse, together with comparison with other Scriptures dealing with the subject. Clear Bible teaching is a great bulwark against "heresies".

In what sense should we understand the statement: "For there must also be heresies among you?" It cannot be in the sense of God's will: "for God is not the author of confusion, but of peace, as in all the churches of the saints" (1 Corinthians 14:33). Compare Romans 6 verse 1: "Shall we continue in sin, that grace may abound?" The words must be understood in the sense that weakness in human nature makes it inevitable that heresies will come, with the result that "they which are approved of God may be made manifest among you". The maturity, or lack of it, of the Lord's people becomes particularly evident in times of crisis.

The word "approved" ('*dokimos*') means 'stand the test', as in James 1 verse 12: "Blessed is the man that endureth temptation: for when he is **tried,** he shall receive a crown of life". When the assembly encounters problems of this kind, it is soon evident who are "approved", that is, those who are not swayed by the divisive teaching and practice.

b) The description, vv.20-22

"When ye come together therefore into one place, this is not to eat the Lord's supper. For in eating, every one taketh before other his own supper: and one is hungry, and another is drunken. What! Have ye not houses to eat and drink in? or despise ye the church of God, and shame them that have not? What shall I say unto you? Shall I praise you in this? I praise you not."

It does seem from this that the believers at Corinth were treating the Lord's supper as a common meal, actually bringing food and drink for normal consumption, with the result "that some, who were poor, went hungry, and some, who were rich, drank too much" (Leon Morris). Hence verse 20: "it ('this', AV) is not to eat the Lord's supper" (JND). That is, their conduct effectively denied the truth of the Lord's supper. They were, in fact, eating their own supper. As W.E. Vine points out, since "there was no sharing … in reality it was not even a common meal, and to attach this to the Lord's supper was a gross abuse". The social divisions between the saints at Corinth were being emphasised by their conduct. Instead of endeavouring to close the disparity by sharing and fellowship, the gap was being enlarged. It was a negation of Chapter 12 verses 25-26: "That there should be no schism in the body; but that the members should have the same care one for another. And whether one member suffer, all the members suffer with it …" In so doing the Corinthians were 'despising the church of God' (v.22), that is, the local assembly. The word "despise" ('*kataphroneo*') means: 'to think slightly of' (W.E. Vine).

To summarise: we can effectively deny the value of the Lord's supper *(i)* by divisions over doctrine: these are caused by heresies; *(ii)* by failure to show true fellowship.

2) THE INSTITUTION OF THE LORD'S SUPPER, vv.23-26

"For I have received of the Lord that which also I delivered unto you…" Chronologically, this is the first account in the New Testament of the institution of the "Lord's supper". It was written before the Gospel records. It was a direct divine revelation to Paul: "For I have received of **the Lord**". He did not receive the information from the apostles present at the time in the upper room. In this connection, it should be noted that Paul uses some expressions not recorded in the Gospel records. We should notice the personal emphasis: "For **I** have received ..." Very clearly, it was one of the subjects dealt with when he was at Corinth in Acts 18: "For I have received of the Lord that which **also I delivered unto you** ..."

The connection is clear: to abuse the Lord's supper in the way described was to degrade something divinely instituted and divinely revealed. These verses may be divided as follows: **(a)** what the Lord did (vv.23-25); **(b)** what we do (v.26).

a) What the Lord did, vv.23-25

We must notice the following **(i)** the circumstances surrounding the institution of the supper (v.23); **(ii)** the way in which the Lord's supper was instituted (v.24); **(iii)** the reason for which the Lord's supper was instituted (vv.24-25); **(iv)** the symbols with which the Lord's supper was instituted (vv.23-25).

i) The circumstances surrounding the institution of the supper, v.23

"For I have received of the Lord that which also I delivered unto you, That the Lord Jesus, **the same night in which He was betrayed**, took bread."

- It was Passover night. "This is that night of the Lord" (Exodus 12:42). But no ordinary Passover night. The Lord Jesus said: "With desire I have desired to eat **this** passover with you before I suffer" (Luke 22.15). He was thoroughly aware of His coming suffering, witness His words: "before I suffer". See John 18 verse 4: "Jesus therefore, knowing all things that should come upon him, went forth ..." The Saviour's words: "**this** passover" indicate its importance. It marked the end of an era, and the commencement of something entirely new. Within a matter of hours, He was to die as "the Lamb of God". In Paul's words: "Christ our passover is sacrificed for us" (1 Corinthians 5:7). For centuries, Israel had kept the passover in remembrance of their deliverance from Egypt: now, another Lamb was to die, in order to deliver men and women from worse bondage.

- It was 'night' in another sense. "The night in which he was betrayed."

The imperfect tense suggests the rendering: 'the night in which He was being betrayed'. Judas was about his treachery, possibly at that very moment. The fact that the Lord Jesus instituted "the Lord's supper" at this time is, in itself, quite amazing. Human nature was at its worst in committing one of its foulest crimes, and it would have been perfectly reasonable for the Lord Jesus to have completely severed all connection with the human race. But in infinite grace He still valued the love and devotion of "His own" (John 13:1), and instituted the "supper" by which they could meet to remember Him.

At Corinth people were thinking of themselves: the Lord did not - even when He was being betrayed.

ii) The way in which the Lord's supper was instituted, v.24

"And when He had given thanks." See Matthew 26 verse 26: "And as they were eating (the passover), Jesus took bread, and blessed (it) …" The word "blessed" ('*eulogeo*') means: 'to speak well of'. This is far from a simple statement of fact. The Lord Jesus was about to suffer in a manner, and to a degree, that was totally unparalleled. In fact, it was in a manner and to a degree that no other person **could** ever suffer. He spoke about His body, and later about His blood, and He **gave thanks**! No Bible writer records the Saviour's words, for precisely the same reason that we do not know exactly what the Lord and His disciples sang before they "went out into the Mount of Olives". There is divine wisdom in this: if the Saviour's words had been recorded by the Gospel writers, they would have become a standard formula, and repeated on every occasion that believers meet for the Lord's supper! But we do know that earlier He said: "Now is my soul troubled; and what shall I say? Father save me from this hour: but for this cause came I unto this hour. Father **glorify thy name**" (John 12:27-28). We also know that in His 'high-priestly' prayer, He said: "I have glorified Thee on the earth: I have finished the work which thou gavest me to do" (John 17:4). Perhaps, therefore, the Lord Jesus 'gave thanks' because He knew that God would be glorified through His death, and that has certainly happened. Men and women, teenagers, boys and girls, saved because He suffered at Calvary, love to sing:

> *To God be the glory, great things He hath done;*
> *So loved He the world that He gave us His Son,*
> *Who yielded His life an atonement for sin*
> *And opened the life-gate that we may go in.*

iii) The reason for which the Lord's supper was instituted, vv.24-25

"This do in remembrance of *me* … in remembrance of *me*". See Luke 22 verse 19. The Passover was instituted "that thou mayest remember *the day* when thou camest forth out of the land of Egypt" (Deuteronomy 16:1-3). But here, it is: "in remembrance of *me*". Hence the emphasis in 1 Corinthians 11: "This is *my* body ... this cup is the new testament in *my* blood ... in remembrance of *me* (twice) ... the *Lord's* death ... this cup of the *Lord* ... the body and blood of the *Lord* ... the *Lord's* body". We ought to notice that the Lord Jesus did not say: 'This do *in memory* of me', but: "*in remembrance* of me". It is not a case of remembering someone that we had forgotten, but doing something quite deliberate. In the words of W.E. Vine: "The word 'remembrance' ('*anamnesis*') denotes a bringing to mind, and here an affectionate calling of the Person to mind". We should add that it is not so much our blessings and forgiveness that we are to remember at the Lord's supper, but rather the Saviour Himself.

The words: "this do" refer to our actual taking of the bread and cup, rather than to the actual breaking of the bread by the brother who does so "to enable the believers to break it decently and without difficulty" (W.E. Vine). He does not break the bread as their representative, but purely as their servant. We 'break bread' when we break off our individual piece. It is "the bread which *we* break", see 1 Corinthians 10 verse 16, where Paul refers to "the Lord's supper" in dealing with "the Lord's table".

People would have the greatest difficulty in complying, if any one of us was to make that request. Perhaps the first thing they would remember would be most uncomplimentary. Possibly they would have the greatest difficulty in remembering anything about us very clearly, and in any case, we might not really be worth a great deal of thought at all! **But this is the Lord Jesus**, and He will occupy the minds and hearts of His people for eternity! His command: "This do in remembrance of me" does not impose limitations: to the contrary, it opens vast horizons, and the well-known hymn describes the range:

> *Jesus! my Shepherd, Saviour, Friend,*
> *My Prophet, Priest, and King,*
> *My Lord, my Life, my Way, my End,*
> *Accept the praise I bring.*

iv) The symbols with which the Lord's supper was instituted, vv.23-25

"The Lord Jesus … took bread: and when he had given thanks, he brake it, and said, Take, eat; this is my body, which is broken for you: this do in remembrance of me. After the same manner also he took the cup, when he had supped, saying, This cup is the new testament in my blood: this do ye, as oft as ye drink it, in remembrance of me."

- The bread. "The Lord Jesus … took **bread:** and when he had given thanks, he brake it, and said, Take, eat; this is my body, which is broken for you" (vv.23-24), or: "This is my body, which [is] for you" (JND). The bread is a picture, or symbol, of His body. It could not possibly be His actual body, since He was bodily present at the time. The doctrines of transubstantiation and consubstantiation are blasphemous nonsense. The bread is a powerful reminder to believers that whilst the Lord Jesus was a perfect man, He was not a mere man. He is "Jesus the Son of God" (Hebrews 4:14), possessed of perfect humanity and perfect deity, not as a dual personality, but as "Emmanuel, which being interpreted is, God with us" (Matthew 1:23). "The Word became flesh and dwelt among us" (John 1:14, JND). Every time we 'break bread', we confess the doctrine of the Incarnation, and therefore the doctrines of Christ's stainless humanity and absolute deity. What a privilege!

But there is more. The bread tells us about the purpose of the Incarnation. The Lord Jesus said: "This is my body, **which [is] for you**" (JND). Peter refers to this: "Who his own self **bare our sins in his own body on the tree**" (1 Peter 2:24). We should notice the expressions: "His own self" and: "His own body". The first refers to His deity and the second to His humanity. See also Colossians 1 verses 21-22: "And you, that were sometime alienated and enemies in your mind by wicked works, yet now hath he reconciled in the body of his flesh through death …" The Son of God 'became flesh' in order to die for us at Calvary.

It is worth mentioning that the word "bread" here ('artos') signifies ordinary bread, rather than 'azumos' which denotes unleavened bread.

- The cup. "After the same manner also he took the **cup**, when he had supped (i.e. when the Passover had ended), saying, This cup is the new testament (or 'covenant') in my blood: this do ye, as oft as ye drink it, in remembrance of me" (v.25). The word "new" ('kainos') signifies: 'new as to form or quality' (W.E. Vine) as opposed to "new" in the sense of time. We know, of course, what was in the cup - "this fruit of the vine" (Matthew 26:29: see also Mark 14:24; Luke 22:18) - but the Saviour said: "this cup", rather than: 'this wine'. The word "cup" is often used in Scripture as a symbol of judgment and death, see Psalm 75 verse 8; Isaiah 51 verses 17, 22; Ezekiel 23 verses 32-33. The Lord Jesus Himself said: "O my Father, if it be possible, let this cup pass from me" (Matt. 26: 39). See also Matthew 20 verse 22: "Are ye able to drink of the cup that I shall drink of?" The cup reminds us, eloquently, that the blood of the Lord Jesus was shed under divine judgment.

But there is more. "This cup is the *new testament* (covenant) in my blood." The 'old covenant' was the law, under which God *demanded* righteousness, with the words: "*Thou* shalt ... *Thou* shalt not". Transgression carried a solemn penalty: "Cursed is every one that continueth not in all things which are written in the book of the law to do them" (Galatians 3:10). But under the 'new covenant', God *imparts* righteousness, with the words: "*I* will". See Hebrews 8 verses 8-12. When the 'old covenant' was instituted, animal blood was shed (Hebrews 9:19-20), but the 'new covenant' rests upon "the precious blood of Christ". When we take the cup, we are reminded of "Him that loved us, and washed us from our sins in His own blood" (Revelation 1:5). The cup reminds us that "without shedding of blood is no remission" (Hebrews 9:22).

b) What we do, v.26

"For as often as *ye* eat this bread, and drink this cup, *ye* do shew the Lord's death till he come." We should notice three things here: *(i)* the celebration of the Lord's supper; *(ii)* the proclamation at the Lord's supper; *(iii)* the duration of the Lord's supper.

i) The celebration of the Lord's supper

"For as *often* as ye eat this bread ..." While there is no specific command, it was evidently the practice in New Testament times to 'break bread' on "the first day of the week". W.E. Vine is worth quoting *in extenso*: "The narrative in Acts 20 is instructive and significant. Concerning the apostle's journey to Jerusalem via Troas, it is recorded that he 'was hastening, if it were possible for him, to be at Jerusalem the day of Pentecost' (v.16, RV). In spite of this, he 'tarried seven days' at Troas (v.6, RV), after arriving there on the second day of the week (our Monday). 'And upon the first day of the week (the seventh day of the stay), when we were gathered together to break bread,

Paul discoursed with them, intending to depart on the morrow' (v.7, RV). Clearly, he stayed all the week so as to be with them for the Lord's supper on the recognised day, trusting the Lord as to arriving at Jerusalem as he hoped. There is obviously a divine purpose in the mention of these details of time". "As often as", therefore, does not mean that it is left to the saints to choose any time they like - 'as and when they feel'. It simply means 'on every occasion that we do so'. For "first day of the week" see also 1 Corinthians 16 verse 2.

Two things emerge very clearly from the narrative in Acts 20: *firstly*, that the early believers 'broke bread' on the first day of the week and, *secondly*, that they broke bread in association with an established testimony. It was kept by the complete assembly. Hence, as already noted, the words "come together" in verses 17, 18, 20. See also verse 33. W.E. Vine continues: "Moreover, what is of paramount importance lies in the repeated 'in remembrance of me'. Where the hearts of the saints are thus attracted to Christ, the gathering to partake of the Lord's supper will have such *a soul-stirring effect, that such an arrangement as a fortnightly or monthly fulfillment will be out of the question*".

ii) The proclamation at the Lord's supper

"Ye do *shew* the Lord's death." The word *'katangello'* is used of preaching, see for example, Acts 4 verse 2 and Acts 13 verse 5. The act of 'breaking bread' is "a silent proclamation of the fact, significance and efficacy of the Lord's death" (W.E. Vine). So we sing,

> *No gospel like this feast,*
> *Spread for us, Lord, by Thee;*
> *No prophet nor evangelist*
> *Preach the glad news so free.*

But to whom do we make this proclamation? The answer is clearly, to visible and invisible observers. 1 Peter 1 verse 12 is an excellent commentary on the latter.

iv) The duration of the Lord's supper

Or, the anticipation at the Lord's supper. It is: "till he come". The Lord Jesus is coming back. He said so: "If I go and prepare a place for you, *I will come again*, and receive you unto myself; that where I am, there ye may be also" (John 14:3). The "Lord's supper" takes us back to His first coming with all its shame and suffering, and it takes us forward to His second coming with all its glory and victory. So we sing,

> *For that coming, here foreshown,*
> *For that day to man unknown,*
> *For the glory and the throne,*
> *We give Thee thanks, O Lord!*

One day, we will no longer keep "the Lord's supper": there will be no necessity to do so, for "we shall be like him; for we shall *see him* as he is" (1 John 3:2).

3) THE EXAMINATION IN VIEW OF THE LORD'S SUPPER, vv.27-34

We must now take careful note of the solemn warning. We should notice that the word "wherefore" occurs twice (vv.27, 33), and introduces the two parts to this section of the chapter *(a)* the consequences of improper behaviour (vv.27-32): *(b)* the exhortation to proper behaviour (vv.33-34).

a) The consequences of improper behaviour, vv.27-32

These verses deal with *(i)* guilt (v.27); *(ii)* self-examination (v.28); *(iii)* judgment (vv.29-32). The word *'krino'* (to judge) and its associates occurs five times in these verses.

i) Guilt, v.27

"Wherefore, whosoever shall eat this bread, and drink this cup of the Lord, unworthily (in an unworthy manner), shall be guilty of the body and blood of the Lord." We are all, of course, unworthy of the privilege of participating in the Lord's supper, but "unworthily" here refers to the current spiritual condition of the believer. To "eat" and "drink" in an unworthy manner implies behaviour that is unrighteous and evil, and, therefore, completely inconsistent with the death of the Lord Jesus as symbolised in the bread and cup. It implies that those concerned have failed to recognise the significance of His death. If we are "guilty of the body and blood of the Lord", we dishonour Him by treating His work at Calvary with indifference. We "eat of this bread, and drink this cup of the Lord, unworthily", when our lives are inconsistent with our profession at "the Lord's supper".

ii) Self-examination, v.28

"But let a man ('*anthropos*', man in general: not '*aner*', a male person) examine himself, and so let him eat of that bread (**not** refrain from eating the bread'), and drink of that cup." The word "examine" ('*dokimazo*') means: 'to test or prove'. We are, therefore, instructed to test or prove our fitness to participate in the Lord's supper. We must ensure that we are right in ourselves, right with our fellow-believers, and right with God. Otherwise we are "guilty". "**Let a man examine himself**."

iii) Judgment, vv.29-32

"For he that eateth and drinketh unworthily, eateth and drinketh damnation (judgment: '*krima*') to himself, not discerning ('*diakrino*') the Lord's body. For this cause many are weak and sickly among you, and many sleep. For if we would judge ('*diakrino*') ourselves, we should not be judged ('*krino*'). But when we are judged ('*krino*'), we are chastened of the Lord, that we should not be condemned with the world."

By saying: "not discerning the Lord's body", Paul is referring to the local assembly, and refers to the situation described in verses 20-22. It should be said that this is not the usual view! The words: "For this cause many are weak and sickly among you, and many sleep" must be understood with reference to 1 Corinthians 3 verse 17: "If any man defile (mar) the temple of God, him shall God destroy (mar); for the temple of God is holy, which temple ye are". The weakness, sickness and death here must be taken literally.

In saying: "But when we are judged, we are chastened of the Lord", Paul emphasises that His dealings with us are disciplinary, not condemnatory. He has in view spiritual betterment, as in Hebrews 12 verse 10: "for our profit, that we might be partakers of his holiness". See also Revelation 3 verse 19, "As many as I love, I rebuke and chasten: be zealous therefore, and repent".

The words: "that we might not be condemned with the world" mean that chastening has the effect of separating us from the worldly behaviour with its attendant condemnation. No believer will be condemned: but he will be chastened.

b) The exhortation to proper behaviour, vv.33-34

"Wherefore, my brethren, when ye come together to eat, tarry one for another (in the sense of wait until all the believers are present without the need to satisfy hunger and thirst, so that the Lord's supper can proceed without distraction). And if any man hunger, let him eat at home; that ye come not together unto condemnation. And the rest will I set in order when I come."

1 CORINTHIANS

"Diversities of gifts"

Read Chapter 12:1-12

1 Corinthians 12 is the first of a trilogy of chapters which examine the provision and exercise of gifts in the local church, and we ought to say immediately that the section has far greater value than historical interest. No part of the Word of God, Old or New Testaments, exists purely to inform our minds. New Testament teaching in connection with the local church is binding upon us at all times. Apostolic instruction in these chapters is as relevant to us today as it was for the church at Corinth at the time of writing.

Before studying 1 Corinthians 12, it will be helpful to notice the connection with Chapters 13-14. In general, Chapter 12 deals with the way in which gifts have been *provided*; Chapter 13 deals with the atmosphere by which they must be *permeated*; Chapter 14 deals with the principles on which they must be *practised*. 1 Corinthians 12 may be divided as follows:

1. The validity of the gifts (vv.1-3). They are validated by their emphasis on the Lordship of Christ.

2. The harmony in the gifts (vv.4-6). Many activities, but one God. "The same Spirit … the same Lord … the same God."

3. The profitability of the gifts, v.7. Many gifts, but one purpose. "The manifestation of the Spirit is given to every man to profit withal."

4. The variety in the gifts, vv.8-11. Many gifts, but one Spirit. "But all these worketh that one and the selfsame Spirit."

5. The necessity for the gifts, vv.12-26. Many members, but one body.

"Those members of the body, which seem to be more feeble, are necessary … there should be no schism in the body" (vv.22, 25). This section develops the analogy of the human body introduced in verse 12: "For as the body is one, and hath many members …" Paul deals first with the *"one body"* (vv.12-13), then with the *"many members"* (vv.14-26). He emphasises that no member should be *discouraged* (vv.15-20), *despised* (vv.21-22), *dishonoure*d (vv.23-25a), or *disinterested* (vv.25b-26).

6.   *The desirability of the gifts.* Many servants, but one way. "Desire earnestly the best gifts" (vv.27-31). That is, desirable for the assembly rather than for believers individually.

1) THE VALIDITY OF THE GIFTS, vv.1-3

The words: "Now concerning spiritual gifts" indicate that the Corinthians had raised the matter with Paul. Compare 1 Corinthians 7:1; 7:25; 8:1; 16:1. In this particular case, they had evidently asked him about speaking in tongues.

The first question that Paul settles is the way in which we can recognise true gifts from God. In this connection we should notice: *(a)* the difference in spiritual manifestations (v.1); *(b)* the source of spiritual manifestations (v.2); *(c)* the test of spiritual manifestations (v.3).

a) The difference in spiritual manifestations, v.1

Paul first investigates the entire question of spiritual manifestations. Do notice that he says: "I would not have you *ignorant*" (v.1) and then: "Wherefore I give you to *understand*" (v.3). While the opening words: "Now concerning spiritual gifts, brethren" (AV) appear to suggest that he has embarked immediately on the study of divine gifts, it must be born in mind that the word "gifts" has no counterpart in the original language, and that the words, literally translated, are: 'Now concerning spiritual things'. From what follows, it is clear that Paul includes both beneficial and harmful powers in the expression. Hence the use of 'pneumatikos' as opposed to 'charismata'. Verses 2-3 make it clear that Paul refers here to the whole realm of spiritual utterances. Since, therefore, the reference is to the entire unseen realm, whether good or evil, and not to the activities of the Holy Spirit alone, translators have supplied the word 'manifestations' in place of the AV's italicised "gifts". This conveys more accurately the original meaning, and maintains good English sense, leading to the rendering: "Now concerning spiritual [manifestations], brethren,

I do not wish you to be ignorant" (JND). According to W.E. Vine, as noted above, a more literal rendering would be: 'concerning spiritual things'. Even more literally: 'concerning spirituals', which does not read well in English! Compare 1 Corinthians 14 verse 1: "Follow after charity, and desire spiritual gifts ('spiritual [manifestations]'. JND), but *rather* that ye may prophesy". The two are compared and contrasted in 1 Corinthians 14.

Paul, therefore, commences with a warning. He demonstrates that there are two types of spiritual manifestations: those attributable to the Holy Spirit, and those attributable to satanic power. It was therefore a matter of great importance that the believers at Corinth should be in a position to discern (hence the need for the gift of "discerning of spirits", v.10) between divine spiritual manifestations, and others of a totally different source. The importance abides to the present day, but at Corinth there was added necessity to fully clarify the matter. Tongues were used - excessively so - as Chapter 14 makes clear - and in an atmosphere where so many were evidently participating, it would be easy for all to claim the direction of the Holy Spirit, when in point of fact, their contributions did not derive from Him at all.

b) The source of spiritual manifestations, v.2

In order to provide clear guidance in the matter, Paul compares the way in which the Corinthians had been spiritually influenced in the past, with the way in which they were now spiritually directed. In the past, prior to their conversion, the believers at Corinth had been given to idolatry. Paul uses significant language when describing their spiritual condition at this time: "Ye know that ye were Gentiles *carried away* unto these dumb idols, even as ye were *led*". The words: "carried away … as ye were led" refer back to Chapter 10: "What say I then? that the idol is anything, or that which is sacrificed to idols is anything? But I say, that the things which the Gentiles sacrifice, they sacrifice to devils, and not to God: and I would not that ye should have fellowship with devils" (vv.19-20).

But like the Thessalonians, the saints at Corinth had "turned to God from idols to serve the living and true God", and had, therefore, become subject to a vastly different spiritual authority. Christ, not idols, had become supreme. The Holy Spirit, not demons, now directed their lives. The new sphere into which the Corinthians had been brought is clearly inferred in the statements:

i) "Ye know that *ye were Gentiles"* or: "When ye were Gentiles" (JND). In Christ, such distinctions are done away.

ii) "Carried away unto these *dumb idols*." There was no communion between heathen gods and their devotees. But now men speak "by the Spirit of God!"

c) The test of spiritual manifestations, v.3

In view, therefore, of their transfer from idolatry to Christ, it was to be expected that His authority in the assembly would be recognised and acknowledged, leading Paul to say: "Wherefore I give you to understand, that no man speaking by the Spirit of God calleth Jesus accursed: and that no man can say that Jesus is the Lord ('Lord Jesus', JND), but by the Holy Ghost". Whereas once, when subject to demon power, they might have called "Jesus accursed", it could not be so now: demon power in their lives had been broken. For anyone to curse the name of the Lord Jesus Christ is clear evidence that they are subject to satanic power.

When the Spirit of God guides and directs His people, *the Lordship of Christ will be maintained.* It is important to notice the exact words of verse 3: "No man can say that Jesus is the Lord but by the Holy Ghost" or: "No man can say Lord Jesus, unless in the power of the Holy Spirit" (JND). It is significant that the unclean spirit cried: "Let us alone, what have we to do with thee, thou Jesus of Nazareth? art thou come to destroy us? I know thee who thou art, the Holy One of God" (Mark 1:24). Demons are, undoubtedly, most intelligent beings. They fully recognise and accept great fundamental facts which are largely rejected by men - professing Christians often included. In Mark 1, the deity of Christ is admitted by the demon, together with admission of His holiness. James states that demons fully accept the doctrine of the Godhead (James 2:19). But recognition of His Lordship, that is, willing submission to His authority, is another matter entirely. Demons do not own Him as Lord. It is, therefore, to be expected that in the assembly, there will not only be recognition of divine truth, but willing submission to Christ's authority. This involves, obviously, willing submission to "all the counsel of God" (Acts 20:27). True acceptance of His Lordship will obviate the sad censure: "Why call ye me, Lord, Lord, and do not the things that I say?" (Luke 6:46). Here is a warning for us all. We can say "Lord" superficially. In the words, again, of the Lord Jesus, quoting Isaiah 29 verse 13: "This people draweth nigh unto me with their mouth, and honoureth me with their lips; but their heart is far from me" (Matthew 15:8).

In short, the spiritual source of a man's ministry will be revealed by what he said about Christ. The criterion by which all ministry is to be judged, and all personal character is to be assessed, is not how attractive, charming or refined, the persons concerned happen to be, nor how professionally qualified they are to pass judgment, but rather, how faithfully they honour Christ. This is the test.

Paul has now prepared the way for examination of the provision and use of gifts in the assembly, by laying down the general principle that when the Holy Spirit is operative, the Lordship of Christ (notice that in fact it is the Lordship of "Jesus") will be maintained. This is fundamental, not only in the recognition of the genuine activity of the Holy Spirit and rejection of all counterfeit, but to the whole subject of gifts amongst the Lord's people. All divinely-given power and ability has one common end - to maintain Christ as Lord in the affections and lives of His people.

We must now notice what follows from this. When the Holy Spirit is at work in the assembly, we can expect:

2) HARMONY IN THE GIFTS, vv.4-6

In fact, the harmony in the exercise of gifts in the assembly will reflect **the harmony in the Godhead.** Hence we read: "There are diversities of gifts, but the same **Spirit.** And there are differences of administrations, but the same **Lord.** And there are diversities of operations, but it is the same **God** which worketh all in all". The words "diversities" and "differences" both translate the Greek word '*diairesis*'.

While Paul names the three Persons of the Godhead, he does not **expound** the subject here. He is concerned, rather, with its **application** to the local church. Divine provision has been made for the local assembly! This may be summed up in the words "harmony" and "diversity".

- Harmony. The perfect harmony and fellowship amongst divine Persons must reflect in the affairs of God's people. "There are diversities of gifts, but the **same Spirit.** And there are differences of administrations, but the **same Lord.** And there are diversities of operations, but it is the **same God** which worketh all in all." Each local church should bear the character of God in every way, and in this case, it should reflect the harmony of the Godhead.

- Diversity. The function of divine Persons differs: Scripture assigns to the *Father*, initiative and purpose, plan and design: to the *Son*, the execution and fulfilment of those plans and designs of which He is Himself the Centre: to the *Spirit*, the divine power and ability in which the Son accomplishes the Father's will. (A 'counterfeit trinity', functioning along the same lines, will appear at the end-time. See addendum.)

As already noted, divine provision has been made for the local assembly: Now there are "*diversities of gifts*, but the same Spirit"; "*differences of administrations*, but the same Lord"; "*diversities of operations*, but it is the same God which worketh all in all". "Gifts … administrations … operations" convey differing aspects of the subject:

- "Diversities of gifts." This conveys the idea of *ability.* The word "gifts" (*'charisma'*) means 'gifts of grace' (from *'charis',* meaning grace): "a gift involving grace (*'charis'*) on the part of God as the Donor" (W.E. Vine).

- "Differences of administrations." The Greek word here *('diakonia')* simply means 'service' and conveys the idea of *responsibility.*

- "Diversities of operations." The word means 'working' or 'works' (*'energema'*) and conveys the idea of *activity.* It refers to the power of God.

This is singularly interesting. We have been given *ability* to function in the assembly: with that ability has been given divinely-imparted *responsibility* to serve, and this should be discharged in *activity.* Personal responsibility is implicit on one hand, and on the other, perfect harmony with each other in exercising the gift imparted to us.

So, when the Holy Spirit is leading and directing the assembly, the Lordship of Christ will be maintained, and the assembly will be marked by a harmony which reflects the harmony of the Godhead. We must now notice what follows from this. When the Holy Spirit is at work in the assembly, we can expect:

3) PROFITABILITY THROUGH THE GIFTS, v.7

Here is the third feature of the Spirit's leading and direction in the assembly.

The various contributions will be to mutual profit. Hence we read: "But the manifestation of the Spirit is given to every man to **profit withal**". The purpose then of all gifts is, in the margin note of the Newberry's Bible, 'mutual profit'. Three important matters arise from this statement:

a) "The manifestation of the Spirit is GIVEN"

"The manifestation of the Spirit is **given**." So the exercise of the gift is not the exercise of natural ability: the two are not synonymous. We are in the spiritual realm here. Since, as noted above, the gifts "involve grace (*'charis'*) on the part of God as the Donor" (W.E. Vine), Paul describes the imparting of gifts as the "manifestation of the Spirit". The brother whose ministry has been used to such good effect has no reason to boast, for "What hast thou that thou didst not receive? Now if thou didst receive it, why dost thou glory, as if thou hadst not received it" (1 Corinthians 4:7). In the language of Romans 12 verse 3: "For I say, through the grace given unto me, to every man that is among you, not to think of himself more highly than he ought to think; but to think soberly, according as God hath dealt to every man the measure of faith". This is not to say that a man's gift should not be readily recognised and accepted by his brethren: rather, that the servant himself must recognise that all ability given is a divine bestowal. This is repeatedly stressed in the verses which follow in 1 Corinthians 12: "For to one is **given by the Spirit** the word of wisdom; to another the word of knowledge **by the same Spirit**". Moreover, the sovereignty of God in distributing the gifts is emphasised: "But all these worketh that one and the selfsame Spirit, dividing to every man severally as he will" (v.11). The clear lesson is that humility is essential in exercising gift.

b) "The manifestation of the Spirit is given to EVERY MAN"

"The manifestation of the Spirit is given to **every man**" (*'hekastos'*, meaning 'each', 'every' or 'everyone'). The apostle will shortly show, by the analogy of the human body, that each believer has due importance in the local assembly. It is unfortunate that the term 'gifted brother' is almost exclusively applied to men who excel in public preaching and teaching. We unwittingly convey the idea that such brethren are a class apart, and that their particular gift is the only one of any importance. On the contrary, every saint is gifted: "As every man (*'hekastos'*: everyone) hath received the gift ('a gift', JND), so minister the same one to another, as good stewards of the manifold grace of God" (1 Peter 4:10).

c) "The manifestation of the Spirit is given to every man to PROFIT WITHAL"

"The manifestation of the Spirit is given to every man to **profit withal**", from which we gather that the object of gifts bestowed is the edification and benefit of the assembly. Compare Proverbs 25 verses 11-14: "A word fitly spoken is like apples of gold in pictures of silver. As an earring of gold, and an ornament of fine gold, so is a wise reprover upon an obedient ear. As the cold of snow in the time of harvest, so is a faithful messenger to them that send him: for he refresheth the soul of his master. Whoso boasteth himself of a false gift is like clouds and wind without rain".

Ministry, in its widest sense, which does not accomplish spiritual profit, cannot, therefore, be directed by the Spirit of God. This, surely, is the criterion by which godly assembly elders should assess suggestions and ideas, particularly calls for change, put to them by assembly members. We could say that the words: "profit withal" may be amplified by reference to 1 Corinthians 14 verse 26: "Let all things be done unto edifying"; Chapter 14 verse 40: "Let all things be done decently and in order"; Chapter 16: 14: "Let all your things be done with charity".

While all men in the assembly should be encouraged to participate in prayer and thanksgiving (remember, this is not a gift), it does not follow that they are all preachers and teachers! While ability to preach and teach does not necessarily demand silver-tongued oratory, it does involve ability to communicate clearly and effectively, and even here things which are right and proper in themselves can be said at the most inappropriate times, and said at excessive length.

The expression in verse 7: "But the manifestation of the Spirit is given to every man to profit withal ('for profit', JND)", is expanded in verses 8-11, which brings us to:

4) THE VARIETY IN THE GIFTS, vv.8-11

"For to one is given ... to another ... to another." The picture is very clear: many gifts, but one Spirit. Unity, but diversity. We may notice *(i)* that each of these gifts derives from the same Source: "by the same **Spirit**" (vv.8-9); *(ii)* that each of these gifts operates in the same power: "All these worketh that one and the selfsame **Spirit**" (v.11); *(iii)* that each of these gifts is given with the same wisdom: "dividing to every man severally as *he* will" (v.11).

It is important to note that the gifts, though deriving from the same Spirit, are not given indiscriminately. There is divine wisdom underlying each bestowal. Hence, "dividing to every man severally as he will". This is exhibited in the expressions: "For to one is given … to another … to another". The word "another" is significant, and emphasises the divine wisdom of the Holy Spirit. The Greek word is not uniform throughout, and the variation indicates that different kinds of people receive different gifts. In the words of J.M.Davies (*The Epistles to the Corinthians*): "This suggests that the gifts are distributed according to the person's natural ability and temperamental difference. Doubtless God fits a man by nature for the gift He is to bestow upon him in grace at conversion".

a) "To one is given by the Spirit the word of wisdom"

"To one is given by the Spirit the word (*'logos'*) of wisdom; to another (*'allos'*, meaning a person of the **same kind**) the word (*'logos'*) of knowledge by the same Spirit" (v.8). There is no article before "word". It therefore refers to utterance, and the ability to communicate the Word of God to the Lord's people. Teaching is in view here. These gifts were necessary in view of the fact that the New Testament canon was not yet complete. It was not therefore a matter of study, but of **revelation.**

b) "To another faith by the same Spirit"

"To another (*'heteros'*, meaning a person of a **different kind**) faith by the same Spirit; to another (*'allos'*, a person of the **same kind**) the gifts of healing by the same Spirit; to another ('allos', person of the **same kind**) the working of miracles; to another (*'allos'*, person of the **same kind)** prophecy; to another (*'allos'*, person of the **same kind**) the discerning of spirits" (vv.9-10). These verses refer to the 'sign gifts' generally. (For 'sign gifts' see, for example, Hebrews 2:4). W.E. Vine makes the important point that "faith here is not that which is constantly exercised by every believer, but that special gift to which reference is made in Chapter 13 verse 2 ('though I have all faith, so that I could remove mountains')".

- As to **"miracles"**, see Acts 19 verse 11: "And God wrought special miracles by the hands of Paul". See also Acts 20 verses 9-12, with reference to Eutychus.

- As to the **"discerning of spirits"**, see Acts 13 verse 10 (with reference to Elymas: "O full of all subtilty and all mischief, thou child of the devil"); Acts 16 verse 18 (with reference to the "damsel possessed with a spirit of divination": "I command thee in the name of Jesus Christ to come out of her").

We should note the inclusion of "prophecy" in this category. We might have expected it in the first category (see v.8). However, its inclusion here, among the 'sign gifts', is explained by the fact that like the other gifts in the category, it would be withdrawn. Men speaking authoritatively in this way, as a result of direct revelation to them by God, were unnecessary with the completion of the Scriptures.

c) "To another divers kinds of tongues"

"To another (*'heteros'*, a person of a **different kind**) divers kinds of tongues; to another (*'allos'*, person of the **same kind**) the interpretation of tongues" (v.10). This verse refers to 'sign-gifts' specifically. As W.E. Vine points out: "Tongues were 'for a sign'. And especially to unbelieving Jews (see Chapter 14:21, 22, and the quotation from Isaiah 28:11, 13 relating to Israel) … The supernatural manifestations such as speaking with tongues and prophesying all took place within twelve years from Pentecost, as recorded in the Acts and on all occasions Jews were present". John Heading (*The First Epistle to the Corinthians*) points out "interpretation is an ability over and above the ability to speak".

We should make some general observations in connection with these interesting and significant verses:

i) It has been observed that in each group, the first gift mentioned is the basis of the gifts following. Hence:

- Knowledge must be expressed in wisdom: the brother with the word of knowledge must be a man of wisdom.

- The gifts of healing, working of miracles, prophecy, discerning of spirits, must be undertaken in faith: the brother with these gifts must be a man of faith.

- The gift of tongues is associated with the interpretation of tongues. Compare 1 Corinthians 14 verse 13.

ii) All the gifts mentioned were temporary in character. Scrutiny will show that they are all connected with the period of early church history. The gifts mentioned were essential to the maintenance of spiritual life amongst God's people until the final revelation of God in His completed Word. Hence, "the word of wisdom", and the "word of knowledge". That is, the ability to impart wisdom and knowledge. It is the idea of **direct** ability given. Time would be when knowledge "would vanish away" (1 Corinthians 13:8). The list here should be compared with those in Romans 12 verses 4-8 and Ephesians 4 verse 11.

These gifts "operated in the early days of the church to show forth the power of God in the new order He had established. New beginnings brought into evidence fresh manifestations of the power of God. None of these gifts operates today" (J. Hunter, *What the Bible Teaches – 1 Corinthians*).

iii) No reference is made to the evangelist. Paul is concerned here with ministry in the local assembly.

Divine attestation of the gospel, particularly in the context of testimony to the nation of Israel, the 'sign-people' (see Matthew 12:39; Luke 11:29; John 6:30: "What sign showest thou then, that we may see, and believe thee?"), underlies "the working of miracles ... divers kinds of tongues". It must be remembered that there was a synagogue at Corinth: in fact, "Crispus, the chief ruler of the synagogue, believed on the Lord with all his house" (Acts 18:8). The writer, however, is intent on establishing a very important fact: that however diverse the gifts of the Spirit may be, He imparts them all and operates in them all (v.11), in order that the entire assembly might profit from them all (v.7).

As we have already noted (see 'the necessity for the gifts') the following verses (vv.12-26), which refer to the functioning of the human body, beautifully illustrate the principle of diversity in harmony. Paul introduces this by saying: "For as the body is one, and hath many members, and all the members of that one body, being many, are one body: so also is Christ" (v.12).

Addendum

We should be aware that Satan will attempt to counterfeit the Godhead. See Revelation 13 which describes the aspirations of "the dragon ... the beast ... the false prophet". "And the dragon gave him (the beast) his power and his seat and great authority (v.2) … and he (the second beast, elsewhere called "the false prophet", Revelation 16:13) … causeth the earth and them, which dwell therein to worship the first beast, whose deadly wound was healed" (Revelation 13:12).

Initiative and purpose, plan and design will lie with Satan ("the dragon). The execution and fulfilment of those plans and designs will lie with "the beast". The power and ability in which "the beast" accomplishes Satan's designs will lie with "the false prophet".

1 CORINTHIANS

"Now ye are the body of Christ, and members in particular"

Read Chapter 12:12-31

As we have already noticed, 1 Corinthians 12 is the first of a trilogy of chapters which examine the provision and exercise of gifts in the local church. We also noted that the three chapters are connected in the following way: Chapter 12 deals with the way in which gifts have been ***provided***; Chapter 13 deals with the atmosphere by which they must be ***permeated*** and Chapter 14 deals with the principles on which they must be ***practised***.

We also suggested that 1 Corinthians 12 may be divided as follows: ***(1)*** the validity of the gifts (vv.1-3); ***(2)*** the harmony in the gifts (vv.4-6); ***(3)*** the profitability of the gifts (v.7); ***(4)*** the variety in the gifts (vv.8-11); ***(5)*** the necessity for the gifts (vv.12-26); ***(6)*** the desirability of the gifts (vv.27-31).

1) THE VALIDITY OF THE GIFTS, vv.1-3

In this connection we noted that the objective of the Holy Spirit's work and guidance in the assembly is to bring glory to the Lord Jesus. "Wherefore I give you to understand, that no man speaking by the Spirit of God calleth Jesus accursed: and that no man can say that Jesus is the Lord ('Lord Jesus', JND), but by the Holy Ghost." Any contribution to assembly life which in any way draws attention away from Christ or lessens His authority amongst the Lord's people is not directed by the Holy Spirit.

2) THE HARMONY IN THE GIFTS, v.4-6

We noted that the local assembly should function in a way which reflects the harmony between divine Persons in the Godhead. "Now there are diversities of gifts, but the same Spirit. And there are differences of administrations, but the same Lord. And there are diversities of operations, but it is the same God which worketh all in all."

3) THE PROFITABILITY OF THE GIFTS, v.7

We noted that "the manifestation of the Spirit is given to every man ('each', 'every' or 'everyone') to profit withal". Ministry, in its widest sense, which does not accomplish spiritual profit cannot, therefore, be directed by the Spirit of God. This should be a guiding principle for elders when assessing suggestions and ideas, particularly calls for change, put to them by assembly members.

4) THE VARIETY IN THE GIFTS, vv.8-11

These verses demonstrate that however diverse the gifts may be, the Holy Spirit both bestows them all, and operates in them all, to accomplish the desired profit mentioned in verse 7.

In this connection, we noticed that Paul refers to three groups of people each headed as follows: *(i)* those given "the word of wisdom" (v.8); *(ii)* those given "faith" (vv.9-10a); *(iii)* those given "divers kinds of tongues" (v.10b). These verses may be set out as follows: "For to one is given by the Spirit the word of wisdom; to another person of the same kind (*'allos'*) the word of knowledge by the same Spirit; to another person of a **different kind** (*'heteros'*) faith by the same Spirit; to another person of the same kind (*'allos'*) the gifts of healing by the same Spirit; to another person of the same kind (*'allos'*) the working of miracles; to another person of the same kind (*'allos'*) prophecy; to another person of the same kind (*'allos'*) the discerning of spirits; to another person of a **different kind** (*'heteros'*) divers kinds of tongues; to another person of the same kind (*'allos'*) the interpretation of tongues".

All this demonstrates the great principle of diversity in harmony: "But all these worketh that one and the selfsame Spirit, dividing to every man severally as he will" (v.11). The verses which follow (vv.12-26) state, and then illustrate, the principle of diversity in harmony by referring to the functions of the human body, to which each part contributes: "For as the body is one, and hath many members, and all the members of that one body, being many, are one body: so also is Christ" (v.12).   We therefore come now to:

5) THE NECESSITY FOR THE GIFTS, vv.12-26

In these verses, with all their doctrinal and practical teaching, Paul makes two important points:

- He addresses the statement: "***the body is one***", and reminds us that "by one Spirit are ('were', RV) we all baptized into one body" (v.13). Paul does this in verses 12-13.

- He addresses the statement: "***hath many members***", and describes their mutual dependence. Paul does this in verses 14-26, and reminds us that "the body is not one member, but many" (v.14). The fact that "the body is not one member, but many" is illustrated in verses 14-26, and applied in verses 27-31.

a) "The body is one", vv.12-13

Two connected statements call for attention: *(i)* "So also is Christ" and *(ii)* "For by one Spirit are ('were') we all baptized into one body".

i) "So also is Christ", v.12. "For as the body is one, and hath many members, and all the members of that one body, being many, are one body, ***so also is Christ***."

It will be readily noted that Paul is not teaching that Christ is Head of the body, the church, in this passage, something that he does elsewhere (see, for example, Ephesians 1:22-23; 5:23). While Paul is evidently referring here to: "the church, which is his body" (Ephesians 1:22-23), he later **applies** his teaching to the local church: see verse 27: "Now **ye** are (the) body of Christ, and members in particular" or, literally rendered (W.E. Vine): "Now ye are a body of Christ". In this connection, it is worthy of note that he does not suggest that particular gifts correspond to the various parts of the human body. He is stressing the unity of the body. The members of our bodies function in harmony, because they share in the common life of the body and therefore, ideally, the local church (see, again, v.27) should function harmoniously because its life is Christ. Each member expresses, in his or her appointed way, the very life of the body. Each functions differently, but all express the very life of Christ. The church is not an entity in itself. It is Christ dwelling in His people. We should notice that it is, literally: "so also is **the** Christ" (JND). That is, to use the theologians' term, the 'mystical Christ'. Christ and His people are one. The name of the church is Christ, in the same way that having created Adam and Eve, God "blessed them, and called **their** name Adam, in the day when they were created" (Genesis 5:2). We can go further and say that just as Eve was a "help meet" for Adam (his complement), so the church is the complement of Christ. The fact that Eve complemented a man made "in the image of God" reminds us that the church complements the Lord Jesus, who is the "brightness of his (God's) glory, and the express image of his person" (Hebrews 1:3).

ii) "For by one Spirit are we all baptized into one body", v.13. The words, better rendered: "For *in* (AV 'by') one Spirit were (AV 'are') we all baptized into one body" (RV), are an explanation of the preceding statement. The church is Christ dwelling in His people ***through the Holy Spirit.*** We should now notice the following:

- "For by one **Spirit**." While, as already noted Paul is stressing the unity of the body here, it will not go amiss to say that the Holy Spirit indwells each believer. Unlike Satan, the Spirit of God is omnipresent. He dwells in the entirety of His Person in each child of God. This is beyond human logic. We really cannot understand how a Person can be localised in an innumerable number of places. But what we cannot understand, we gladly accept by faith. Furthermore, contrary to common parlance in some circles, it is quite erroneous to say that we 'need more of the Spirit'. It would be more correct to say that the Spirit 'needs more of us'. Since the same Holy Spirit dwells in the totality of His Person in every believer, it is, therefore, quite obvious that there can be no confusion or collision in a local church when its members are functioning in their appointed place.

- "For by (in) one Spirit ***are (were) we all baptized into one body***." The key words are "one" and "all". The Lord Jesus is the Baptiser. The phrase is in the aorist tense. Paul is referring to something that has already taken place, and that took place once. The action or event is complete in itself. Acts 1 explains the event in question. The Lord Jesus is addressing the apostles: "For John truly baptized with water; but ye shall be baptized with the Holy Ghost ('in the Holy Ghost', margin) not many days hence" (Acts 1:5). Peter refers to this in Acts 11: "And as I began to speak, the Holy Ghost fell on them, as on us at the beginning. Then remembered I the word of the Lord, how that He said, John indeed baptized with water; but ye shall be baptized with ('in') the Holy Ghost" (Acts 11:15-16). Peter does not say or infer that

Pentecost was repeated, but that events in the household of Cornelius recalled the statement by the Lord Jesus that the baptism in the Holy Spirit was about to take place. Peter's words: "the Holy Ghost fell **on them,** as **on us** at the beginning" indicate something common to Jew and Gentile (they are actually mentioned in the reverse order: "them" and "us"). If the receipt of the Holy Spirit by Gentile believers in Acts 10 verses 44-45 was, in fact, a fresh outpouring of the Spirit, then it would follow that the receipt of the Spirit in all cases would constitute a fresh outpouring of the Spirit. It would also infer that the blessing of Gentile believers was a separate operation from the blessing of Jewish believers, so destroying the concept of one body taught in this very verse.

On the contrary, it is obvious that the Holy Spirit came once, on the day of Pentecost, and that all subsequent believers - Jews and Gentiles - participate and continue to participate, in the benefit of this one great event. It is to this one event that the Lord Jesus refers: "Ye shall be baptized in the Holy Ghost", and to which Paul refers in this verse: "For by one Spirit are ('were') we all baptized into one body". The word "baptize" is used in connection with the Holy Spirit's work on the day of Pentecost and conveys the complete change which took place in the experience of the disciples. On that day, they ceased to be individual disciples with only failing human resources, and became a living church with divine resources. On conversion, each child of God participates in this common baptism of the Spirit which took place once, and is made good in the experience of every believer on trusting Christ. Salvation brings into the good of the once-and-for-all work of the Lord Jesus at Calvary **and** into the good of the once-and-for-all coming of the Holy Spirit on the day of Pentecost.

It has been nicely said that in Genesis 2 the "Lord God … breathed into his (Adam's) nostrils the breath of life; and man became a living soul" (v.7), and that in Acts 2, in fulfilment of His words in John 20 verse 22, the Lord Jesus breathed on His disciples and they became a living church.

The baptism of the Spirit does not refer to the imparting of spiritual power, but to participation in the body. We should also say that it is quite erroneous to call "the baptism of ('in') the Spirit" a 'second blessing'. It refers, not to our daily lives, but to our spiritual position. The very word "baptized" signifies the end of something and the beginning of something new. This follows: "by one Spirit are (were) we all baptized into one body, whether we be Jews or Gentiles, whether we be bond or free …" (v.13). So, for believers, the "baptism of the Spirit" brought about the end of human divisions, whether racial ("Jews … Gentiles") or social ("bond … free").

- "Whether we be Jews or Gentiles." In the body, there are no *racial* divisions. National divisions are completely abolished. It is important to notice in this connection that Gentiles have not been included in Jewish blessings. Jew and Gentile have been made one on entirely new ground.

- "Whether bond or free." In the body, there are no *social* divisions. It therefore follows that in the local church, care should be taken to ensure that such divisions are studiously avoided. The assembly is not the place where we parade our business or educational qualifications (important though these are in other areas). The assembly is not a place to cultivate the friendship and fellowship of people belonging to our social class, to the exclusion of others. There should be no cliques amongst us! On the other hand, the assembly is not the place where we despise others with higher earthly callings than our own.

The reason follows: whatever our national and social status might be ("Jew … Gentile": "bond ... free"), we "have been *all* made to drink into one Spirit" (v.13). Although obviously connected with what we have said about being "baptized into one body", it is, nevertheless, rather different. In the first case, the 'baptism of (in) the Spirit' is corporate: in the second case, being made 'to drink into one Spirit' is individual. In both cases, Paul uses the aorist tense, that is, as previously noted, that the action or event is complete in itself: it has already taken place, and took place once. It has been said that to be 'baptized in the Spirit' means that the individual is in the element, but to "drink into one Spirit" means that the element is in us. J. Hunter (*What the Bible Teaches – 1 Corinthians*) puts it like this: the words "'and have been made all to drink into one Spirit' refer to the reception of the Spirit at conversion. Grammatically the presence in one verse of two aorist verbs, does not necessarily demand that they refer to the same event: the word 'and' introduces a new statement, and helps us to understand how we came into the good of the previous statements".

This can be illustrated from 1 Corinthians 10 where we read: "All were baptized unto Moses in the cloud and in the sea … and did all drink of the same spiritual drink" (vv.2, 4). J.M. Davies points out in this connection that "the baptism was a historical event, never repeated, whereas the drinking was both an initial and continuous experience"; that "the baptism unto

Moses was corporate and national, whereas the drinking was individual"; that "the baptism was positional: it brought them into a new and very definite relationship with Moses as their 'ruler and deliverer' whereas the drinking was experimental; it quenched their thirst"; that "in the baptism they were passive, but in the drinking they were active"; that "the baptism unto Moses was something which they were not actually conscious of, whereas the opposite is the case with the drinking". J.M. Davies puts the case brilliantly!

b) "Hath many members", vv.14-26

Paul now illustrates the principle of diversity in unity with reference to the human body. Four aspects are stressed: *(i)* no member is to be discouraged (vv.15-20); *(ii)* no member is to be despised (vv.15-22); *(iii)* no member is to be dishonoured (vv.23-25a); *(iv)* no member is to be disinterested (vv.25b-26).

i) No member is to be DISCOURAGED, vv.15-20. In a human body, all members are essential. In the assembly, therefore, none are to be discouraged. There should be no *inferiority complex*: none are *dispensable.* We should notice that Paul is not inferring that some saints have a ministry answering to feet, hands, ears, eyes, etc., but that although diverse, *each gift is essential.* We should notice the following:

- Feet and hands, and eyes and ears might well be suggestive. Feet are *lower* than hands. Ears are *further back* than eyes. Some saints might feel that they serve on a *lower level* than others - or that they are *less forward* than others. Not so, they are *equally part of the body* (vv.15-16).

- Not only are they equally part of the body - they are *essential to the whole body.* Because hands are not feet and *vice versa*, that does not mean that they stop functioning! Changing the figure, perhaps deliberately to emphasise that no particular gift is in view, Paul continues: "If the whole body were an eye, where were the hearing? If the whole were hearing, where were the smelling?" (v.17). Ability to *see*, but not *hear*, could be dangerous. For example, a bridge may look perfectly safe to us, but failure to hear a warning shout that its under-water foundations are giving way could land us in dire trouble. Similarly, ability to *hear*, but not *smell,* could be dangerous. (Supply your own illustration!).

Each of those parts of our body - feet, hands, ears, eyes, noses - are where **God put them.** "But now hath God set the members every one of them in the body **as it hath pleased him**" (v.18). So there should be no **dissatisfaction or discontent** with our place in the assembly: the important thing is to function **where we are.** We cannot govern **what** we are, and **where** we are, because that lies alone in the will of God. We cannot govern what gift we have. But we must **function, and exercise that God-given gift in the assembly.**

ii) No member is to be DESPISED, vv.21-22. In a human body, all members are indispensable. In the assembly, none are to be **despised.** There should be no **superiority complex:** all are **interdependent.** "And the eye cannot say unto the hand, I have no need of thee: nor again the head to the feet, I have no need of you. Nay, much more those members of the body, which seem to be feeble (like fingers and toes), are necessary" or "But much rather, the members of the body which seem to be weaker are necessary" (JND).

It is not, now, the lower members **looking up** and saying: 'Oh dear, I'm not on such a high spiritual level as that', or: 'Oh dear, I wish I was up there!', but a higher member **looking down,** and saying: 'You are of no importance compared with me. My gift … function is important and big enough for me not to need you!' The eye discerns: the hands move; the head directs: the feet move. The assembly needs people who can give guidance, and people who will follow guidance!

One member cannot dispense with another because **it seems called to higher service.** The **teacher** (some **wrongly think** that this is the best of all gifts) cannot dispense with **the evangelist.** Those who enjoy Bible study and give themselves wholly to it, are not to criticise those who seek to devote time and energy in 'hands on' service for God, and *vice versa.*

iii) No member is to be DISHONOURED, vv.23-25a. "And those members of the body, which we think to be less honourable, upon these we bestow more abundant honour; and our uncomely parts have more abundant comeliness." We should notice:

- What we do. "Upon these we bestow more abundant honour; and our uncomely parts have more abundant comeliness." The word "bestow" (*'peritithemi'*) means: 'to put around or on', and could refer to clothing. See Matthew 27 verse 28: "They ... put on him a scarlet robe".

- What God does. "For our comely parts have no need: but God hath tempered the body together, having given more abundant honour to that part which lacked." The words: "comeliness" and "comely" mean: 'elegance of figure'. Literally, 'well-formed'. The words: "honourable" and "honour" have the idea of value. In the words of Charles Hodge (*1 & 2 Corinthians*): "It is the *instinct of nature* to adorn the most the least comely parts of the body: and it is an *instinct of grace* to honour most those members of the church who least attract admiration". Or in the words of J.M. Davies: "The part that is less prominent is clothed, it is given more honour; and so the believer who may lack gift may be adorned with grace". This reminds us some believers in the assembly need particular encouragement, especially those who may not be quite so prominent as others. Hence we read: "in honour preferring one another" (Romans 12:10); "let each esteem other better than themselves" (Philippians 2:3).

"For our comely parts have no need." For example, the *face* is uncovered: other parts are *not.* Feet for example!! Paul observes that "God hath *tempered* the body together, having given more abundant honour to that part which lacked". The word "tempered" means: 'to mix or blend together', that is, in making the uncomely parts essential to the well-being of the whole or rest of the body. For this purpose: "that there should be no schism ('*schisma*') in the body" (v.25). This was particularly applicable to the situation at Corinth. See Chapter 1 verse 10: "Every one of you saith …" The word "schism" means a 'rent'. Compare Chapter 11 verse 18: "That there be no divisions ('*schisma*') among you". It seems unlikely that "our uncomely parts" are inward organs such as heart and lungs. It is more likely that they are "those members which should never be seen in public" (J. Hunter).

iv) No member is to be DISINTERESTED, vv.25b-26. In a human body, all members are blended together. In the assembly, none are to be disinterested. "That there should be no schism in the body; but that the members should have the same care one for another. And whether one member suffer, all the members suffer with it; or one member be honoured, all the members rejoice with it." We should notice the occurrence (twice) of "*one … all*" (v.26). Paul stresses three things:

- Mutual care. "The same *care* one for another." The early church certainly did this: see, for example, Acts 2 verses 44-45; 4 verses 34-35. Philippians 2 verse 20 is relevant here.

- *Mutual concern.* "And whether one member suffer, all the members suffer with it."

- *Mutual joy.* "Or one member be honoured, all the members rejoice with it." Acts 11 verses 22-23 is a case in point: Barnabas saw evidence of "the grace of God" at Antioch, and "was glad".

Pain or pleasure to one part is common to the whole. For example, grit in the eye is followed by the hand with handkerchief! The finger banged with a hammer finds solace in the mouth! Paul does not say that this ought to be the case, but that it *is* the case. If there is no mutual care, concern or joy, then there is no life at all! Incidentally, it does seem, sadly, that mutual concern can sometimes come more easily than mutual joy. It isn't always easy to rejoice with someone who is ahead of us in some way, whether in achievement, or promotion, or recognition, especially when they are 'just ahead'!

5) THE DESIRABILITY OF THE GIFTS, vv.27-31

With verse 27, Paul applies his illustrations: "Now ye are the body of Christ, and members in particular" or, bearing in mind the absence of the definite article ('the') before 'body': "ye are body of Christ ..." That is, not the complete body of Christ, but having its character. We should notice how he makes the application:

i) "Now ye are (the) body of Christ, and members in particular" (v.27). Paul is applying this particularly to the Corinthians. Hence the emphasis: "Now **ye** are the body of Christ, and members in particular". **This applies verse 14**: "For the body is not one member but many".

ii) "And God hath set some in the church ..." (v.28). **This applies verse 18**: "But now hath God set the members every one of them in the body as it hath pleased him".

iii) "First apostles (quite obviously, apostles were found in some local churches, Jerusalem in particular); secondarily, prophets; thirdly teachers, after that miracles, then gifts of healings, helps (those who give support and assistance, perhaps especially to the weak and needy: see 1 Thessalonians 5:14), governments (from '*kubernetes*', a pilot, referring to those who steer and guide assemblies: those who exercise 'oversight'), diversities of tongues" (v.28). **This applies verse 20:** "But now are they many members, yet but one body". It has been observed that Paul puts last what the Corinthians were evidently putting first (Chapter 14:12).

iv) "Are all apostles? are all prophets?, are all teachers?, are all workers of miracles? Have all the gifts of healing? Do all speak with tongues? do all interpret?" (vv.29-30). **This applies verse 19**: "And if they were all one member, where were the body?" The answer to the questions here is manifestly 'No!' This effectively deals with the suggestion that speaking with tongues is evidence of the possession of the Spirit. What arrant nonsense! All the believers at Corinth, and elsewhere, had been 'baptized in the Spirit' and had been "made to drink into one Spirit" (v.13), but not all spoke in tongues.

"But covet earnestly the best gifts." He tells us what "the best gifts" are in Chapter 14. They are the gifts which result in the edifying of the church: "Forasmuch as ye are zealous of spiritual gifts, seek that ye may excel to the edifying of the church" (Chapter 14:12). Do notice that the words: "Covet earnestly the best gifts" are addressed to the church at Corinth, not to individual believers in the church. As noted above, Paul develops this in Chapter 14. As we shall see, every local church should pray for those gifts - one in particular - that make for "edification, and exhortation, and comfort" (Chapter 14:3).

The "more excellent way" (v.31) is expounded in the next chapter. In the words of one of our current *clichés:*

Watch this space!

1 CORINTHIANS

"A more excellent way"

Read Chapter 13:1-13

Before studying 1 Corinthians 13, it will be helpful to notice again the connection between Chapters 12-14. In general, Chapter 12 deals with the way in which gifts have been **provided**; Chapter 13 deals with the atmosphere by which they must be **permeated**; Chapter 14 deals with the principles on which they must be **practised**.

The introduction to Chapter 13 lies at the end of Chapter 12: "But covet earnestly ('desire earnestly', RV) the best ('greater', RV) gifts: and yet shew I unto you a more excellent way" (Chapter 12:31). It is "a more excellent way" in that it reflects, not so much the *power* of God (as in the gifts), but the very *character* of God. "God is love" (1 John 4:8). If in Chapters 12 & 14, we have the gifts of the Spirit, then in Chapter 13, we have the fruit of the Spirit.

The AV translation: "charity" (Wycliffe's word) is most unhappy, but the translators did not use it without good reason. At the time, "love" tended to be associated with degrading sensuality. In fact, we are told that it is not used in classical Greek for the same reason.

The fact that '*agape*' is used of divine love is most significant. Only the love of God can enable us to cope with the demands of assembly life and service, not to mention service farther afield. (We should add that only the love of God can enable us to cope with the demands of life generally.) While the strength of '*phileo*' (also translated 'love' in the New Testament) cannot be doubted, it 'more nearly represents tender affection' (W.E. Vine, *Expository Dictionary of New Testament Words*). For examples of '*agape*' or '*agapao*', see John 3 verse 16: "For God so **loved** the world, that he gave his only begotten Son ..."; Galatians 2 verse 20: "The Son of God who **loved** me, and gave himself for me"; 1 John 3 verse 1: "Behold, what manner of **love** the Father hath bestowed upon us ..."

The chapter may be divided in the following way: *(1)* love's necessity (vv.1-3); *(2)* love's qualities (vv.4-7); *(3)* love's permanence (vv.8-13).

1) LOVE'S NECESSITY, vv.1-3

These verses emphasise love's necessity in three different ways. *(a)* "Though I speak", referring to the mouth, without love I convey nothing: love is to infuse our teaching (v.1); *(b)* "though I have", referring to the mind, without love "I am nothing" ('I am of no value', W.E. Vine): love is to infuse our intellect (v.2); *(c)* "though I give", referring to my means, without love I gain nothing, even though possessing, and giving, "all": love is to infuse our stewardship, whether it is stewardship of our substance or of ourselves (v.3).

a) My mouth, v.1

"Though I speak with the tongues of men and of angels, and have not charity, I am become as sounding brass, or a tinkling cymbal."

We should note that Paul puts "tongues" first here, whereas in Chapter 12 it is put last (vv.28, 30). The gift existed at Corinth, where there was a Jewish synagogue, and the Corinthian believers were zealous of this gift. See Chapter 14 verse 12. This stresses the danger of self-gratification: emphasising a desire to impress rather than acting in love. The gift of tongues, which existed at the time, was ineffective without love. The word "become" suggests degeneration.

However, the reference to: "the tongues of men and of angels" may well suggest the range of language, in particular, the range of people using it: men and angels. After all, angels always speak in the language of men! The expression: "tongues ... of angels" indicates authority, as in the giving of the law (Galatians 3:19). The verse can, therefore, be applied to our teaching and preaching, to our oral ministry in the assembly (and elsewhere). Paul calls it: "speaking the truth in love (*'agape'*)" (Ephesians 4:15). If love is absent, then preaching and teaching is wrongly motivated. In passing, we should remember that it is not a question of: 'Let go, and let God'. Effort is required on our part: so "**speaking** the truth in love"; "**take unto you** the whole armour of God" (Ephesians 6:13); "**walk** in the Spirit" (Galatians 5:16).

We should notice too that Paul does say: "Though *I* speak with the tongues of men and of angels …" There is an important lesson here: personal application is necessary before application to others. The apostle himself spoke with tongues. See Chapter 14 verse 18.

The words "sounding brass" probably refer to a gong. The "tinkling cymbal" (AV) is elsewhere rendered "clanging cymbal" (JND). The idea is that tongues, improperly used (the gift *did* have a proper use at the time) was a noise, but nothing more.

b) My mind, v.2

"And though I have (the gift of) all prophecy, and understand all mysteries, and all knowledge; and though I have all faith, so that I could remove mountains, and have not charity, I am nothing."

- As to "prophecy". See Chapter 14 verse 3: "He that prophesieth speaketh unto men to edification, and exhortation, and comfort". Prophecy, like apostleship, is a 'foundation gift': "built upon the foundation of the apostles and prophets (that is, the foundation laid by the apostles and prophets), Jesus Christ himself being the chief corner stone" (Ephesians 2:20). The gift would not be permanent: "whether there be prophecies, they shall fail" (v.8).

- As to "mysteries". See Romans 11 verse 25: "For I would not, brethren, that ye should be ignorant of this *mystery* … that blindness in part is happened to Israel"; 1 Corinthians 2 verse 7: "But we speak the wisdom of God in a *mystery* …"; 1 Corinthians 15 verse 51: "Behold, I shew you a *mystery* …"; Ephesians 3 verse 3: "How that by revelation he made known unto me the *mystery*"; 2 Thessalonians 2 verse 7: "For the *mystery* of iniquity doth already work"; Colossians 2 verse 2: "to the acknowledgement of the *mystery* of God"; 1 Timothy 3 verse 16: "Great is the *mystery* of godliness". W.E. Vine puts it like this: "In the New Testament it denotes, not the mysterious (as with the English word), but that which, being outside the range of unassisted natural apprehension, can be made known only by Divine revelation, and is made known in a manner and at a time appointed by God, and to those only who are illumined by His Spirit. In the ordinary sense a mystery implies knowledge withheld; its Scriptural significance is truth revealed".

- As to "knowledge". This is another 'foundation gift'. See 1 Corinthians

12 verse 8. Quite obviously, this does not refer to 'knowledge' in the general sense of the word, but to that particular need for knowledge before the completion of the Scriptures. Paul makes this clear later: "whether there be **knowledge**, it shall vanish away" (v.8), but we are to "grow in grace and in the **knowledge** of our Lord and Saviour Jesus Christ" (2 Peter 3:18).

Perhaps we should take the opportunity to say that, among other things, we may construe Paul's teaching here as a warning against intellectualism. While we certainly should not place a premium on ignorance, neither should we be proud of our knowledge or acquire it purely for our own mental satisfaction and the opportunity to impress other people. How do we view our understanding of God's Word, and how do we convey it to others? Paul prays that the Ephesians "being rooted and grounded **in love**, may be able to comprehend with all saints, what is the breadth, and length, and depth, and height; and to know the love of Christ, which passeth knowledge, that ye might be filled with all the fullness of God" (Ephesians 3:14-19). He goes on to say: "But speaking the truth in love, (ye) may grow up into him in all things, which is the head, even Christ: from whom the whole body fitly joined together, and compacted by that which every joint supplieth, according to the effectual working in the measure of every part, maketh increase of the body unto **the edifying of itself in love**" (Ephesians 4:15-16).

- As to "faith". This is yet another 'foundation gift'. See, again, 1 Corinthians 12 verses 8-9: "For to one is given by the Spirit the word of wisdom; to another the word of knowledge by the same Spirit; to another faith by the same Spirit ..." We note that W.E. Vine makes the important point that "faith here (1 Corinthians 12:9) is not that which is constantly exercised by every believer, but that special gift to which reference is made in Chapter 13 verse 2 ('though I have all faith, so that I could remove mountains')". The words: "so that I could remove mountains" means the removal of the biggest and highest obstacles.

While the context is entirely different, the words: "**faith which worketh by love**" (Galatians 5:6) are at least *applicable* here.

c) My means, v.3

i) As to my possessions. "And though I bestow all my goods to feed the poor ('If I shall dole out all my goods in food', JND) ... and have not charity, it profiteth **me** nothing." The "poor" might be 'profited', but **not** me!

Our sacrifices for the Lord (as we say) are of no value and will receive no reward if they are without love. Ananias and Sapphira are a case in point here. Read Acts 5 verses 1-11. It certainly was **not** a case of **"by love serve one another"** (Galatians 5:13) so far as they were concerned.

ii) As to my body. "And though I give my body to be burned … and have not charity, it profiteth me nothing." John refers to those who "loved not their lives unto death" (Revelation 12:11).

We should note, finally, 2 Peter 1 verses 5-7: "And beside this, giving all diligence, add to your faith virtue … and to brotherly kindness charity" (*'agape'*); Romans 13 verse 8: "Owe no man anything, but to love one another: for he that loveth (*'agapao'*) another hath fulfilled the law".

We must now reflect on what we have read, and ask why so many things, apparently so helpful in themselves, should nevertheless accomplish so little, if anything, in the sight of God. The answer lies in the words of John, already noted: "He that loveth (*'agapao'*) not knoweth not God; for God is love (*'agape'*)" (1 John 4:8). See also 1 John 4 verse 16: "He that dwelleth in love (*'agape'*) dwelleth in God, and God in him"; 1 John 4 verse 12; "If we love (*agapao*) one another, God dwelleth in us, and his love (*'agape'*) is perfected in us". Failure to speak, think and act in love means that we display nothing of God's nature. There is no family likeness, leading to the searching question: *'How much does God see of Himself in our lives?'*

Mouth, mind and means are all employed in the service of God because "the love (*'agape'*) of Christ constraineth us" (2 Corinthians 5:14) and because "the love (*'agape'*) of God is shed abroad in our hearts by the Holy Ghost which is given unto us" (Romans 5:5). If not, then there is nothing for God, and our service and ability is nothing more than self-indulgence.

2) LOVE'S QUALITIES, vv.4-7

Love is its own motive: it is developed in reference to others, but others are not the motive. The verbs here are 'doing words'. They are active, not abstract. It is not a question, for example, of 'feeling kind', but of 'being kind' (v.4) Paul himself exemplifies his teaching here. But do notice that **all these qualities are seen perfectly in the Lord Jesus. He displayed the love of God to utter perfection.** Why not read these verses like this: 'Christ suffereth long, and is kind … thinketh no evil; rejoiceth not in iniquity … never faileth …"

The section commences with a general statement: "Charity suffereth long, and is kind". We should notice:

i) "Love suffereth long" (RV). "Suffereth long" translates '*makrothumeo*', from '*macros*' meaning 'long' and '*thumos*' meaning 'temper'. "Love suffereth long", that is, towards other people. Love is *passive.*

ii) "And is kind." This translates '*chrestos*' meaning "good, gracious, kind" (W.E. Vine) It refers to benefit to others. It is serviceable or useful. Love is *active.* See Ephesians 4 verse 32.

The whole epistle demonstrates this. See 2 Corinthians 2 verse 4, where Paul tells the Corinthians how he wrote his first letter to them: "For out of much affliction and anguish of heart I wrote unto you with many tears ... that ye might know the *love* ('agape') which I have more abundantly unto you".

We must now notice *(a)* love's negative qualities (vv.4-6a); *(b)* love's positive qualities (vv.6b-7).

a) Love's negative qualities, vv.4-6a

In these verses, Paul refers to the things that love does *not* do. It must have been a salutary lesson to the believers at Corinth.

i) "Love envieth not." (RV). The word "envieth" translates '*zeeloo*'. Compare 1 Corinthians 3 verse 3: "For ye are yet carnal: for whereas there is among you *envying* ('*zeelos*') and strife ..." According to W.E. Vine: "envy desires to deprive another of what he has, jealousy desires to have the same sort of thing for itself".

ii) "Love vaunteth not itself." (RV). The word "vaunteth" translates '*perpereuomi*', from a root meaning 'vainglorious: braggart' (W.E. Vine). Compare 1 Corinthians 1 verse 29: "That no flesh should glory in his presence"; 1 Corinthians 9 verse 16: "For though I preach the gospel, I have nothing to glory of ..."

iii) "Love ... is not puffed up." (RV). The words "puffed up" translate '*phusioo*', from '*phusa*' meaning 'bellows'. A thing 'puffed up' is most unsubstantial! See 1 Corinthians 4 verse 6: "that no one of you be *puffed up* for one against another"; 1 Corinthians 4 verses 18-19: "Now some are *puffed up*, as though I would not come unto you ... I ... will know, not the speech of them which are *puffed up*"; 1 Corinthians 5 verse 2: "And ye are *puffed up*"; 1 Corinthians 8 verse 1: "Knowledge *puffeth up*, but love edifieth ..."

iv) "Love ... doth not behave itself unseemly." (RV). Reference might be made here to 1 Corinthians 7 in this connection, as also to the disorders in Chapter 11 verses 21-22. Love is not "unseemly" (*'aschemosune'*) which, according to W.E. Vine, "comprehends all kinds of bad manners". Love is therefore 'mannerly'.

v) "Love ... seeketh not her own." (RV), or: 'what is its own' (JND). See 1 Corinthians 10 verse 24: "Let no man seek *his own* (JND, 'his own advantage), but that of the other"; 1 Corinthians 10 verse 33: "Even as I please all men in all things, not seeking *mine own* profit". To which we may add the question of saints going to law (1 Corinthians 6) and the question of liberty in connection with meats (1 Corinthians 8).

vi) "Love ... is not provoked." (RV). We should note the omission of "easily" ("not easily provoked", AV). The word *'paroxuno'* means, primarily, to sharpen and means that "love is not roused to a spirit of anger or bitterness by injuries, actual or imagined" (W.E. Vine). The strife and divisions at Corinth (see 1 Corinthians 3:3) make this an appropriate observation.

vii) "Love ... taketh not account of evil." (RV) or: "thinketh no evil" (AV). Literally, reckoneth and imputeth no evil. See 1 Corinthians 4 verse 3; Chapter 9 verse 3, where Paul counters criticisms levelled at him. How prone we are to 'put it down' in our minds like an entry in a ledger. The word *'logizomai'* means 'to reckon'.

viii) "Love ... rejoiceth not in unrighteousness." ('iniquity', AV)" (RV). The word "unrighteousness" translates *'adikia'*, meaning that "love does not find joy in the wrong-doing of others" (W.E. Vine). See 1 Corinthians 5 where Paul had to say: "And ye are puffed up, and have not rather mourned, that he that hath done this deed might be taken away from among you ... Your glorying is not good. Know ye not that a little leaven leaveneth the whole lump" (vv.2, 6).

b) Love's positive qualities, vv.6b-7

i) "*Love ... rejoiceth with the truth.*" (RV). "Instead of feeling any satisfaction concerning evil-doing, love finds in truth ('*aleethia'*) a happy companion in its rejoicing" (W.E. Vine). Hence the necessity to "purge out therefore the old leaven" and "keep the feast ... with the unleavened bread of sincerity and **truth** ('*aleethia'*)" (1 Corinthians 5:7-8). Notice what John said about Gaius (3 John:3-4). Perhaps, on reflection, since the previous verses have spotlighted people's behaviour, we should look at these verses in the same way.

ii) "Beareth all things." The word '*stego*' means, primarily: 'to protect or preserve by covering, hence meaning to keep off something which threatens: to bear up against: to hold out against'. It occurs in 1 Corinthians 9 verse 12: "But we have not used this right, but we bear ('*stego*') all things ("suffer all things, AV), that we may put no hindrance in the way of the glad tidings of the Christ" (JND). The definition: 'to protect or preserve by covering' reminds us that the love that "rejoiceth in the truth" will be the love that "covers a multitude of sins" (1 Peter 4:8, JND). It does not parade other people's faults.

iii) "Believeth all things." Love is not gullible! But it is not suspicious either. It accepts at face value. In the words of Leon Morris: "It is not implied that love is deceived by the pretences of any rogue but that love is always ready to give the benefit of the doubt".

iv) "Hopeth all things." It looks for the best. See 2 Corinthians 7 verse 14: "For if I have boasted any thing to him of you, I am not ashamed; but as we spake all things to you in truth, even so our boasting, which I made before Titus, is found a truth". It has been said that love does not rejoice in pessimism.

v) "Endureth all things." Literally 'to abide under: to bear up courageously (under suffering)'. As, probably, in the case of the criticisms he faced.

3) LOVE'S PERMANENCE, vv.8-13

In this section, we should notice three temporary gifts (v.8) and three permanent graces (v.13). The key phrases are: "that which is perfect ... that which is in part" (v.10).

The passage makes a comparison between the failing of **certain** gifts and the permanence of love. **Love super-excels things temporary.** We must notice: *(a)* what is "in part" (vv.8-9); *(b)* what is "perfect" (v.10). But before that, do notice that love is never obsolete: "Charity never faileth". "The verb *'pipto'* usually denotes to fall. That which falls ceases its activity (that is sometimes the meaning) and that is what love never does" (W.E. Vine).

a) What is "in part", vv.8-9

"Whether there be prophecies, they shall fail; whether there be tongues, they shall cease; whether there be knowledge, it shall vanish away. For we know in **part**, and we prophesy in **part.**" The word "whether" is used in 1 Corinthians 3 verse 22; 8 verse 5; 10 verse 31 always with the idea that 'whether this or that', the compelling fact is "all are yours … there is but one God … do all to the glory of God", and here: "they shall fail".

i) "Whether there be prophecies, they shall fail ('done away', JND)." Literally: 'reduce to inactivity'. The passive voice is used here: made to cease … put out of commission beyond recall. Prophecy was a 'foundation gift'. It belongs to the second class of gifts listed in 1 Corinthians 12 verses 9-10a.

ii) "Whether there be tongues, they shall cease." Like the storm on Galilee! There is no ambiguity here! They belong to the third class of gifts listed in 1 Corinthians 12 verse 10b. The middle voice is used here. There is 'a built-in stop' (T. Ledger).

iii) "Whether there be knowledge, it shall vanish away (as with prophecies, 'done away', JND)." That is, knowledge without study, as in the case of prophesy. It belongs to the first class of gifts listed in 1 Corinthians 12 verse 8. This can hardly refer to 'knowledge' in the usually-accepted New Testament sense. See verse 12. Even heaven itself will not see the end of knowledge - how could it?! The reference is to 1 Corinthians 12 verse 8 (as noted above), where "knowledge" is a gift of the Spirit.

All three gifts cited above were transitional gifts, and were but 'part' and not the whole, that is, "that which is **perfect**". These gifts would discontinue when "in part" (meaning not all there, like a jig-saw puzzle with pieces missing) gives place to "that which is perfect". This brings us to -

b) What is "perfect", v.10

The expression "that which is perfect" must belong to the same realm referred to as "in part", that is, to the transmission of truth by revelation. The word "perfect" *('teleios')* signifies: "having reached its end (*'telos'*), finished, complete" (W.E. Vine). It does not refer to glory, but to the completion of the New Testament canon. (We ought to remember here that John wrote after Paul.) See Colossians 1 verses 24-26. For the word "perfect", see, for example 1 Corinthians 2 verse 6: "We speak wisdom among them that are perfect"; 1 Corinthians 14 verse 20: "In understanding be men (margin 'perfect') ("grown men")" (JND).

The three gifts mentioned above were connected with the church in its infancy. Thus: "When I was a child, I spake as a child, I understood as a child, I thought as a child; but when I became a man, I put away childish things" (v.11). The change from infancy to maturity is gradual and progressive. Compare 1 Corinthians 14 verse 20: "Brethren, be not children in understanding … but in understanding be men".

As noted above, Paul points out that prophecy, tongues and knowledge belong to the infancy of the church. Hence the reference to childhood: "I spake as a *child* (compare, "tongues ... shall cease"), I understood as a child (compare, "knowledge ... shall vanish away"), I thought ('reasoned', JND) as a *child* (compare, "prophecies ... shall fail") …" (v.11), but, continuing the analogy of childhood and manhood, Paul emphasises that the time would come when these things would no longer be necessary. Thus: "when I became a *man*…"

The contrast between childhood (with its immaturity - but not its imperfection - or to use Paul's expression, "in part") and manhood (with its completeness, or to use Paul's expression, "perfect") continues in verse 12: "For *now* (at the time of writing, *not* now in this life) we see through a glass darkly ('in a mirror darkly', RV, where "darkly" is literally 'in an enigma', *'en ainigmati'*); but then face to face: now I know (*'ginosko'*: in the process of knowing*)* in part; but *then* shall I know (*'epiginosko'*: know in full) as also I am known (*'epiginosko')*". Partial vision or understanding would give place to clarity. This is *not* a contrast between things now, and things in heaven, *but* a contrast between what is fragmentary and what is complete. Bearing in mind that the passage deals with the communication of God's word, the words "face to face" (evidently referring to Numbers 12:8, where "dark speeches" is, literally, 'enigmas') refer to "clear vision through possession of the complete Word of God" (W.E. Vine).

It is suggested that in this context, the words: "but then shall I know as also I am known" indicate that Paul then expected to understand up to the measure of his God-given capacity to do so. God knew his capacity, and would impart His word to him accordingly. He says in effect: 'I shall know to the extent that God measures my capacity to know'. After all, bearing in mind Numbers 12 verse 8 and that "there arose not a prophet since in Israel like unto Moses, whom the LORD knew face to face" (Deuteronomy 34:10), it may well be that Paul is alluding here (v.12) to the Lord's perfect knowledge of Moses, and implying that He knew his (Paul's) own capacity too.

"And now abideth (singular: with a plural subject: it should, by the rules of strict grammar, read 'abide': but singular indicates that all three are mutually complementary) faith, hope, charity, these three; but the greatest of these is charity" (v.13). Love not only **excels things which are impermanent** (prophecy, tongues, knowledge), it also excels things **which are permanent** - "faith, hope".

"Now" (so you see) why love is the greatest - because love "believeth all things and hopeth all things". It has been said that faith will give place to sight, and hope will be realised, but love will remain for ever! How fitting that the last word in the chapter is *agape*!

1 CORINTHIANS

"Seek that ye may excel to the edifying of the church"

Read Chapter 14:1-19

INTRODUCTION

As we have noted, 1 Corinthians 12-14 are a trilogy of chapters which examine the provision and exercise of gifts in the local church. **Chapter 12** describes the provision of gifts in the local assembly; **Chapter 13** describes the atmosphere in which they are to be exercised, and **Chapter 14** describes the principles which are to govern their use.

We have also noted that Chapter 12 commences: "Now concerning spiritual gifts brethren" or: "Now concerning spiritual **manifestations** brethren, I do not wish you to be ignorant" (JND). The word "gifts" (AV) or "manifestations" (JND), is literally, 'spirituals' ('*pneumatikos*'), which does not read well in English. The following verses make it clear that Paul comprehends both beneficial and harmful powers in the expression: those attributable to the Spirit of God, and those attributable to satanic power: hence the necessity for the believers at Corinth to carefully distinguish between them.

1 Corinthians 14 commences with the same expression: "Follow after charity, and desire spiritual gifts ('spirituals'), but rather that ye may prophesy" (v.1). In both cases (Chapter 12 verse 1; Chapter 14 verse 1), the word is used in the context of oral contributions at assembly gatherings. This strongly suggests that the expression refers to spiritual 'utterances', and particularly, bearing in mind the comparison with prophecy in Chapter 14 verse 1 to the use of tongues. Speaking in tongues in the assembly was evidently one of the matters raised with Paul by the Corinthians themselves. Paul, therefore, refers to this in Chapter 12 verse 1, but before dealing with the subject specifically in Chapter 14, he deals in Chapter 12 with gifts in general. The use of tongues had got out of hand at Corinth, and was not being used for its original purpose.

Paul makes a very important statement in Chapter 13: "Whether there be prophecies, they shall fail; whether there be tongues, they shall cease; whether there be knowledge, it shall vanish away" (v.8), and continues: "For we know in part, and we prophesy in part. But when that which is perfect is come, then that which is in part shall be done away" (vv.9-10). In the analogy that follows, Paul points out that "prophecies" and "tongues" belong to the infancy of the church: "When I was a child I spake as a child ('tongues … shall cease'), I understood as a child ('knowledge … shall vanish away'), I thought ('reasoned', JND) as a child ('prophecies … shall fail'): but when I became a man, I put away childish things" (v.11). The word "perfect" ('*telios*') means: 'having reached its end, finished, complete'. What had previously been "in part" would become "perfect". Paul refers here to the completion of the New Testament canon.

This leads us to observe that it is in Chapter 13 that we are clearly told that tongues, with other gifts necessary for the well-being of the early church, would cease. Chapter 14 does not deal with their **cessation**, but with **their regulation**. This explains such statements as: "Desire earnestly spiritual gifts, **but rather that ye may prophesy**" (v.1, RV); "Now I would have you all speak with tongues, **but rather that ye should prophesy**" (v.5, RV); "Wherefore, my brethren, **desire earnestly to prophesy,** and forbid not to speak in tongues" (v.39, RV). These passages therefore teach us that the gift of tongues, and for that matter, the gift of prophecy too, was to be regulated **while it existed.** While both gifts were temporary, they were quite different. The first involved speaking in a language **foreign** to the local church. The second involved speaking **in** the language of the local church.

PRELIMINARY OBSERVATIONS

1) All gifts are charismatic. The word "gift" comes from a Greek word ('*charisma*') meaning 'freely given', or 'gift of grace'. For example: "Having then **gifts** differing according to the grace that is given to us …" (Romans 12:6); "Ye come behind in no **gift**, waiting for the coming of our Lord Jesus Christ" (1 Corinthians 1:7); "Stir up the **gift** of God, which is in thee" (2 Timothy 1:6).

2) The gift of tongues was not given to every believer. Hence the questions: "Are all apostles? are all prophets? are all teachers? are all workers of miracles? have all the gifts of healing? do all speak with tongues? do all interpret?" (1 Corinthians 12:29-30). The answer is manifestly *'No!'*.

3) Tongues are temporary in character. As we have seen, they are mentioned in 1 Corinthians, an early epistle, but not in Romans and Ephesians, later epistles. This shows that the gift was declining even in New Testament times. In the words of Harry Bell (late of Jarrow on Tyne): "The gift of tongues ceased after the kingdom ceased to be offered to Israel".

4) The Corinthians were putting first what God put last. "God hath set some in the church; first, apostles; secondarily, prophets; thirdly, teachers; after that, miracles; then gifts of healing, helps, governments, *diversities of tongues*" (1 Corinthians 12:28). See also 1 Corinthians 12 verse 10. But the Corinthians were "zealous of spiritual gifts" (Chapter 14:12). It has been pointed out that they were people of extremes: once they "were carried away unto these *dumb* idols" (Chapter 12:2): now they were zealous in their desire to speak in *tongues*!

5) The gift of tongues was a known language. "And they were all filled with the Holy Ghost, and began to speak with other *tongues* ('*glossa*'), as the Spirit gave them utterance" (Acts 2:4). With this result: "the multitudes came together and were confounded, because that every man heard them speak in his *own language* ('*dialektos*')" (Acts 2:6). Luke continues: "And they were all amazed and marvelled, saying one to another, Behold, are not all these that speak Galileans? And how hear we every man in our *own tongue* ('*dialektos*'), wherein we were born?" (Acts 2:7-8) Luke continues further: "Cretes and Arabians, we do hear them speak in our *tongues* ('*glossa*') the wonderful works of God" (Acts 2:11). Quite evidently there is no difference in meaning, anymore than when we speak today of our 'mother *tongue*' as opposed to 'another *language*'. The use of '*glossa*' in 1 Corinthians must therefore refer to a known language, not to some ecstatic utterance. Hence, "with men of other tongues ('*glossa*') and other lips will I speak unto this people" (1 Corinthians 14:21). The words used in this chapter: "*unknown* tongue" (AV) must be amended to simply: "tongue". The word "unknown" is in italics: it does not exist in the original text. It is clear from Acts 10 verse 46 ("they heard them speak with tongues") that the word '*glossa*' is used of the same thing as '*dialektos*' in Acts 2.

It is worth noticing that in Acts 2, Peter did not preach (i.e. afterwards) in tongues. Their use arrested the attention of the crowds, and gained attention for the preaching of the gospel. While the early history of the church was attended with 'sign-gifts' (tongues, healing etc.), the power of the Holy Spirit was demonstrated in bold and faithful gospel preaching. His great work is to glorify the Lord Jesus (see John 16:14). Preaching and teaching which does not give pre-eminence to Christ is powerless.

6) The gift of tongues was a sign. It, therefore, follows that it *must* be a known language. As we shall see, it was a sign to unbelievers. 1 Corinthians 14 verse 22 refers to Isaiah 28 verses 11-12, and J.H. Large is worth quoting at length here: "Owing to the people's unbelief and disobedience, God was going to punish them by bringing in the invader. They would not heed God's plain messages delivered in their own tongue so they would have the unusual experience of hearing God speaking providentially to them by the fact of foreign conquerors coming into their midst speaking other tongues, namely not unintelligible sounds but meaningful language - very meaningful! When this came to pass they would very forcibly be reminded of God's warnings, yet even so they would not, as a people, turn to the Lord. The 'tongues' at Pentecost were a sign to the Christ-rejecting nation of Israel that God was fulfilling His word; see e.g. Acts 2 verse 36".

We should note the Lord's words in Mark 16 verses 17-20: "These *signs* shall follow them that believe. In my name they shall cast out demons, they shall speak with new tongues, they shall take up serpents, and if they drink any deadly thing, it shall not hurt them; they shall lay hands on the sick and they shall recover … and they went forth, and preached everywhere, the Lord working with them, and confirming the word with *signs* following". The fact that the use of tongues was a sign is confirmed by its effect on the three occasions in Acts on which it was used:

- Acts 2:4. "And they were all filled with the Holy Ghost, and began to speak with other tongues, as the Spirit gave them utterance", with the result that "the multitudes came together and were confounded, because that every man heard them speak in his own language. And they were all *amazed and marvelled* ". Acts 2:4-6. *We should note the Jewish setting.*

- Acts 10:45-46. "And they of the circumcision which believed were *astonished,* as many as came with Peter, because that on the Gentiles was poured out the gift of the Holy Ghost. For they heard them speak with tongues (*'glossa'*) and glorify God". *We should note the Jewish observers*. The gift of tongues on this occasion was a sign to prejudiced men of the circumcision party that the gospel embraced Gentiles as well as Jews, and on the same terms.

- Acts 19:6. "And when Paul laid his hands upon them, the Holy Spirit came

upon them; and they spake with tongues (*'glossa'*) and prophesied." In this case the use of tongues was a sign of something new: John's baptism (the baptism of repentance) had been superseded by baptism in the name of the Lord Jesus (vv.4-5). **We should notice the Jewish setting**: "And he went into the **synagogue**" (v.8).

7) The gift of tongues was no evidence of spirituality. Corinth was evidently the most carnal of the assemblies!

8) The gift was to be exercised with care. It was not a 'free for all'. "If any man speak in an (*unknown*) tongue, let it be by two, or at the most by three, and that by course: and let one interpret" (1 Cor. 14:27).

The Epistle to the Hebrews provides us with a good summary: "How shall we escape, if we neglect so great salvation; which at the first began to be spoken by the Lord, and was confirmed unto us by them that heard him; God also bearing them witness, both with **signs and wonders and with divers miracles, and gifts of the Holy Ghost,** according to his own will" (Hebrews 2:3-4). The passage sets out the parameters for the gift's use very clearly: "Wherefore tongues are for a **sign**, not to them that believe, but to **them that believe not**" (1 Corinthians 14:22).

CHAPTER ANALYSIS

1 Corinthians 14 may be divided as follows. In this study, we will address the first of the four suggested sections (vv.1-19)

1) The relative **profit** of tongues and prophecy (vv.1-19). Paul determines here the value of tongues and prophecy in edifying the church: the gift must be regulated by the test of edification.

2) The relative **purpose** of tongues and prophecy (vv.20-25). Having demonstrated that tongues do not edify the church, Paul determines the reason for their existence at all. His conclusion is clear: the gift of tongues was a sign to unbelievers.

3) The **participation** in tongues and prophecy (vv.26-35). In this section Paul sets out the principles which were to govern their use in the local church.

4) The conclusion (vv.36-40). "Wherefore, brethren, covet to prophesy, and forbid not to speak with tongues. Let all things be done decently and in order" (vv.39-40).

1) THE RELATIVE PROFIT OF TONGUES AND PROPHECY, vv.1-19

This section may be divided into three paragraphs, each of which constitutes a test: *(a)* which of the two edifies - tongues or prophecy? (vv.1-5); *(b)* which of the two makes for clarity of utterance - tongues or prophecy? (vv.6-11); *(c)* which of the two makes for intelligent understanding - tongues or prophecy? (vv.12-19).

a) Which edifies - tongues or prophecy?, vv.1-5

Attention is drawn to three couplets: *(i)* "he that speaketh in an (*unknown*) tongue … he that prophesieth" (vv.2-3); *(ii)* "He that speaketh in an (*unknown*) tongue … he that prophesieth" (v.4); *(iii)* in summary, "he that prophesieth … he that speaketh with tongues" (v.5). As already noted the word "unknown" is italicised in the AV text, emphasising its absence in the original text, and pointing to the fact that when the gift was used it was in a known language.

We should carefully note that the apostle is *not* stating that the gift did not exist, but that it was not to be used by itself in the assembly. The possession of the gift was no reason for its indiscriminate use. Gifts are not bestowed for self-promotion, but for the edification of the whole assembly. Neither are gifts to be used as frequently as possible, whether it is appropriate or not. This is now emphasised.

- "He that speaketh in an (*unknown*) tongue, speaketh not unto men, but *unto God*: for no *man* understandeth him" (v.2). That is, the gift was being used in the wrong place. Since the gift was a sign to unbelievers (v.22) - not the Lord's people - none would hear or understand. Only God could understand the substance of the utterances.

- "But he that prophesieth speaketh unto men to *edification* (to build up), and *exhortation* (to stir up) and *comfort* (to cheer up)" (v.3). The order is important: "*edification*", that is, doctrine; "*exhortation*", that is, the practice of the doctrine; "*comfort*", that is, the strength that doctrine imparts. We should remember that while the teacher has superseded the prophet, this verse is equally applicable to both!

- "He that speaketh in an (*unknown*) tongue **edifieth himself**; but he that prophesieth edifieth the church" (v.4). The phrase "edifieth himself" must mean that he understood what he said, since what cannot be understood cannot edify. This is confirmed later in the chapter: "But if there be no interpreter, let him keep silence in the church; and let him speak **to himself**, and to God" (v.28).

- "I would that ye all spake with tongues, but rather that ye prophesied: for greater is he that prophesieth than he that speaketh with tongues, except he interpret, that the church may receive edifying" (v.5). Paul desired the best for the saints, hence: "But covet earnestly the best gifts" (Chapter 12:31). That is, those gifts which would edify the church, particularly prophecy, see verse 3.

The words: "except he interpret" show us that the ability to interpret makes the gift of tongues edifying in the same way as prophecy. If tongues can be interpreted, the church can then be edified. If any man can interpret tongues as well as speak in them, then there was no need to speak in them in the first place. See verse 13. Compare verses 27-28. We should add, of course, that servants of God preaching in foreign countries usually need interpreters in their ministry. But, the fact that the visiting brother speaks in a different language to his audience does not constitute a sign! If anything, it is an acknowledgment of the confusion following the erection of the tower of Babel (Genesis 11:1-9).

But how is this edification to be achieved? This brings us to the second and third points in connection with the relative profit of tongues and prophecy. It will be achieved *(ii)* by clarity of utterance, and *(iii)* by clarity of understanding. So:

b) Which makes for clarity of utterance- tongues or prophecy?, vv.6-11

Paul deals with this by referring *(i)* to himself (v.6); *(ii)* to musical instruments (vv.7-8); *(iii)* to the Corinthians themselves (vv.9-11).

i) **Reference to himself, v.6.** "Now, brethren, if I come unto you speaking with tongues, what shall I profit you, except I shall speak to you either by revelation, or by knowledge, or by prophesying, or by doctrine?" There would be no profit if he spoke to them in tongues. Notice that he refers to the means of **acquiring** truth: "by revelation … knowledge", and then to the means of *imparting* truth: "by prophesying … doctrine". The New Testament *prophet* was involved with "revelation" and "prophecy": the Bible *teacher* is involved with "knowledge" and "doctrine" (teaching). This suggests a transition from temporary gifts to permanent gifts.

ii) Reference to musical instruments, vv.7-8. "And even things without life giving sound, whether pipe or harp, except they give a distinction in the sounds, how shall it be known what is piped or harped? For if the trumpet give an uncertain sound, who shall prepare himself to the battle?"

The instruments can be subdivided. The pipe and harp bring *joy and pleasure.* The trumpet brings *warning and direction.* But all are valueless unless played clearly. If the Lord's people are to be helped in either way, they must be placed in a position to understand what is said.

iii) Reference to the Corinthians themselves, vv.9-11. "So likewise ye, except *ye* utter by the tongue words easy to be understood, how shall it be known what is spoken? For ye shall speak into the air. There are, it may be, so many kinds of voices in the world, and none of them is without signification. Therefore if I know not the meaning (*'dunamis'*) of the voice, I shall be unto him that speaketh a barbarian; and he that speaketh shall be a barbarian unto me."

While Paul is referring, in context, to tongues, we ought to make an application here. We do need to appreciate the value of using "words easy to be understood" (v.9). Gospel preaching must be simple, even though the subject matter is profound. We need to bear in mind the ability and capacity of our hearers. The word "meaning" ("if I know not the meaning of the voice", v.11) signifies the force or power of what is spoken.

By referring to "so many kinds of voices" (v.10), Paul is evidently referring to human languages and this is confirmed in verse 11. A "barbarian" was any non Greek-speaking person (that is, in the view of Greek speakers!), the equivalent of the 'Berber' of Egyptian terminology.

In summary, Paul, musical instruments, and the Corinthians themselves, could accomplish nothing at all, without *clear expression.* This brings us to:

c) What makes for clarity of understanding - tongues or prophecy?, vv.12-19

There is need for *(i)* clarity of understanding on the part of the speaker (vv.12-15), and *(ii)* clarity of understanding on the part of the hearer (vv.16-19).

i) Clarity on the part of the speaker, vv.12-15. "Even so ye, forasmuch as ye are zealous of spiritual gifts, seek that ye may excel to the edifying of the church. Wherefore let him that speaketh in an (*unknown*) tongue, pray that he may interpret. For if I pray in an (*unknown*) tongue, my spirit prayeth, but my understanding is unfruitful. What is it then? I will pray with the spirit, and I will pray with the understanding also: I will sing with the spirit, and I will sing with the understanding also." Attention is drawn to the following:

- "Forasmuch as ye are zealous of spiritual gifts" (v.12), literally, 'zealous of spirits' ('*pneumaton*')' (RV margin). This is not easily explained. The word used (the plural of '*pneuma*') is slightly different to that employed in Chapter 12 verse 1 and Chapter 14 verse 1. Charles Hodge suggests that "the most probable explanation … is to be sought from Chapter 12 verse 7, where it is said that 'to every one is given a manifestation of the Spirit'".

- "Excel." The word ('*perisseuo*') means to 'abound' (RV), 'to be over and above'. It is used in Luke 15 verse 17: "have bread **enough and to spare**".

- "Pray that he may interpret" (v.13). Why? The answer follows: "For if I pray in an (*unknown*) tongue, my spirit prayeth, but my understanding is unfruitful (not, 'I have no understanding')" (v.14). That is, by praying in a foreign language, his personal understanding of what he was saying would be unfruitful **for others**: they would not understand what he was saying. The verse does **not** mean that the man himself didn't know what he was saying. That would reduce him to a robot, and completely negate the emphasis on the word "understanding". The word "understanding" occurs seven times in verses 14-20. It is so important to understand what we are saying, especially if we are quoting somebody else!

We must remember that when the gift was used in its proper sphere, that is, to the unbeliever, the hearer would fully understand that his own language was being spoken. This was the proper use of the gift. Its use in the assembly, while permitted, was not its intended purpose.

- Contributions to the assembly must be twofold. Firstly, "with the spirit", that is, with spiritual intelligence. The speaker must understand what he himself is saying. At the same time, secondly, "with the understanding", that is, the speaker must be intelligible to others (v.15), otherwise no one will understand. See verse 16: "Else when thou shalt bless with the spirit, how shall he that occupieth the room of the unlearned say Amen at thy giving of thanks, seeing he understandeth not what thou sayest?" For "pray" and "sing" see Romans 15 verse 9; Ephesians 5 verse 19, James 5 verse 13 where "psalms" (*'psallo'*) means, literally 'to play a stringed instrument with the fingers' (W.E. Vine). The RV reads: "let him sing praise".

ii) Clarity on the part of the hearer, vv.16-19. This is stressed by the words already partly quoted above: "Else, when thou shalt bless with the spirit, how shall he that occupieth the room of the unlearned ('fills the place of the simple [Christian]' (JND), say Amen at thy giving of thanks, seeing he understandeth not what the sayest? For thou verily givest thanks well, but the other is not edified. I thank my God, I speak with tongues more than ye all: yet in the church I had rather speak five words with my understanding, that by my voice I might teach others also, than ten thousand words in an (*unknown*) tongue". We should note the following:

- That Paul refers to the "unlearned" (v.16). This translates *'idiotes'* (see also Acts 4 verse 13 - "ignorant" and 2 Corinthians 11 verse 6 - "rude") and evidently refers, according to W.E. Vine, to "those who have no knowledge of the facts relating to the testimony borne in and by a local church". See also verses 23-24, where it does seem that Paul is referring to believers.

- That it is Scriptural to say "Amen" (v.16). This implies acquiescence and unity. It reminds us that those who pray publicly should remember that they do so representatively.

- That "giving of thanks" edifies (v.17). This does not mean that our public prayers should be sermons, but that the Lord's people should be refreshed and helped by our thanksgiving.

- That Paul was an example of his own ministry (vv.18-19). He spoke with tongues. The New Translation reads: "I thank God I speak in a tongue (singular) more than all of you". The manuscripts here evidently vary. See JND margin. According to John Heading, Paul refers here to "his constant use of Greek on his missionary journeys rather than his mother tongue Hebrew".

This is supported by the fact that Paul continues: "yet *in the church* I had rather speak five words with my understanding, that by my voice I might teach others also, than ten thousand words in an (*unknown*) tongue".

In summary, all must be undertaken lovingly, helpfully, intelligently and considerately. Having considered *(1)* the relative *profit* of tongues and prophecy, vv.1-19 we must next consider *(2)* the relative *purpose* of tongues and prophecy (vv.20-25), and *(3) participation* in tongues and prophecy (vv.26-35), before noting *(4)* the conclusion (vv.36-40).

1 CORINTHIANS

"Let all things be done unto edifying"

Read Chapter 14:20-40

We have already noted that 1 Corinthians 14 may be divided as follows: *(1)* The relative *profit* of tongues and prophecy (vv.1-19). In these verses Paul determines their value in edifying the church. The use of these gifts in the local church must be regulated by the measure in which they help the Lord's people. *(2)* The relative *purpose* of tongues and prophecy (vv.20-25). Having demonstrated that tongues do not edify the church, Paul determines the reason for their existence at all. His conclusion is clear: the gift of tongues was a sign to unbelievers. *(3)* The *participation* in tongues and prophecy (vv.26-35). In this section Paul sets out the principles which were to govern their use in the local church. *(4)* The conclusion (vv.36-40).

1) THE RELATIVE PROFIT OF TONGUES AND PROPHECY, vv.1-19

This section comprises three paragraphs, each of which constitutes a test: *(a)* which edifies - tongues or prophecy? (vv.1-5); *(b)* which makes for clarity of utterance - tongues or prophecy? (vv.6-11); *(c)* which makes for intelligent understanding - tongues or prophecy? (vv.12-19).

2) THE RELATIVE PURPOSE OF TONGUES AND PROPHECY, vv.20-25

Paul begins this section of the chapter with an exhortation to maturity. The believers at Corinth should have known better than to conduct themselves as they did: "Brethren, be not children in understanding: howbeit in malice be ye children, but in understanding be men" (v.20). Paul uses two different words in saying "children".

- In the first place, he says: "Be not *children* in understanding" where the word "children" (*'paidon'*) "signifies a little or young child" and is

278

used here "metaphorically of believers who are deficient in spiritual understanding" (W.E. Vine). It is used of the disciples in John 21 verse 5 ("Children, have ye any meat?") where, according to W.E. Vine, it is an "affectionate and familiar address by the Lord to His disciples, almost like the English 'lads'".

- In the second place, he says: "Howbeit in malice be ye **children** (*'nepos'*)", meaning 'a babe'. That is, someone unable to think or speak maliciously. He continues: "but in understanding be **men** '(*teleios'*)", meaning 'of full age' (RV margin), or 'perfect' or 'full grown'. The word "understanding" here (*'phren',* meaning 'the mind') differs from the word "understanding" (*'nous'*) in verses 14, 15, 19. Differentiating between the two words is not an easy task for the layman! One thing is abundantly clear: assembly fellowship demands spiritual maturity and responsibility. For "understanding", see Psalm 119 verse 130.

Having said this, Paul continues by telling them **what** they should have understood ("in understanding be men"), and does this by referring to Isaiah 28 verses 11-12 which reads: "For with stammering lips and **another tongue** will he speak to **this people** (that is to the Jewish people) … Yet they would not hear". Here is Paul's quotation: "In the law it is written, With men of other tongues and other lips will I speak unto **this people**; and yet for all that will they not hear me, saith the Lord" (v.21).

The way in which Paul works on his text is well worth noting, not only in the way that he uses it to develop his argument, but in the way that it illustrates a very sound approach to Bible study, namely *(i)* what does the passage **say** (v.21); *(ii)* what does the passage **mean** (v.22); *(iii)* how does the passage **apply** (vv.23-25). We will follow Paul's method here in our own study at this point in the chapter:

i) What the passage says, v.21. "In the law it is written, With men of other tongues and other lips will I speak unto **this people**; and yet for all that will they not hear me, saith the Lord." In this case "the law" evidently refers to the Old Testament in general. See, for example, John 10 verse 34: "Is it not written in your **law**, I said, ye are gods", referring to Psalm 82 verse 6; John 12 verse 34: "We have heard out of the **law** that Christ abideth forever", referring to Psalm 72 verse 17; John 15 verse 25: "that the word might be fulfilled that is written in their **law**, They hated me without a cause", referring to Psalm 69 verse 4.

ii) What the passage means, v.22. "Wherefore tongues are for a sign not to them that believe, but to them that believe not: but prophesying serveth not for them that believe not, but for them which believe." In the Old Testament, the uninterpreted tongue was a judicial sign. In Isaiah 28, God stated His intention to speak to His people through a foreign power, Assyria, thus pronouncing judgment on them, for the following reasons:

- Because they had rejected God's word. They had heard the message: "This is the rest wherewith ye may cause the weary to rest; and this is the refreshing", but they did not respond: "yet they would not hear" (Isaiah 28:12). While the "rest" and the "refreshing" are not defined here, there can be no doubt that they are explained by Isaiah 8 verses 13-14 which refers to similar circumstances: "Sanctify the LORD of hosts himself; and let him be your fear, and let him be your dread. And he shall be for a sanctuary". The Lord Himself would be their "rest" and their "refreshing" in the same way that seven hundred years later the Lord Jesus said: "Come unto me, all ye that labour and are heavy laden, and I will give you rest ... and ye shall find rest unto your souls" (Matthew 11:18-29).

- Because of the way in which they regarded God's word. It was nothing more to them than childish and annoying repetition: "But the word of the LORD was *unto them* precept upon precept, precept upon precept; line upon line, line upon line; here a little, and there a little" (Isaiah 28:13).

In view of the fact that Isaiah 28 refers to the unbelieving Jew, Paul concludes: "Wherefore tongues are a sign (i.e. of judgment consequent upon unbelief), not to them believe, but to *them that believe no*t". The purpose of prophecy is quite different: "But prophesying serveth not for them that believe not, but for *them which believe*" (1 Corinthians 14:22).

iii) How the passage applies, vv.23-25. In these verses, Paul visualises "the whole church ... come together into one place", as he does in verse 26. We must notice the words "*whole* church" and "*together into one place*". There were evidently no 'house-meetings' (in the modern sense of the expression) at Corinth: there were no fragmentary groups. Compare 1 Corinthians 11 verse 18: "When ye come together in assembly" (JND); 1 Corinthians 11 verse 20: "When ye come together therefore into one place". Paul describes here an assembly meeting where "all speak with tongues" (v.23), and another assembly meeting where "all prophesy" (vv.24-25):

- "All speak with tongues", v.23. "If therefore the whole church be come together into one place, and all speak with tongues, and there come in those that are unlearned (*'idiotes'*, evidently referring to believers unaccustomed to the use of tongues), or unbelievers, will they not say that **ye are mad**?" While it could be argued that the "unbeliever" would not be a Jew, since the use of tongues was a sign to the Jews, it seems more likely that Paul is describing the effect upon any "unbeliever" if "**all** speak with tongues". The confusion would be indescribable. Hence the need for the gift to be properly regulated: see verses 27-28.

- "All prophesy", vv.24-25. "But if all prophesy, and there come in one that believeth not, or one unlearned, he is convinced of all, he is judged of all: and thus are the secrets of his heart made manifest; and so falling down on his face, he will worship God, and report that God is in you of a truth." These verses emphasise the power of God's Word. It will have a fourfold effect on the visitor.

- "He is convinced of all" or: "he is convicted by all" (JND): his conscience is touched. We should notice that the 'corporate' behaviour of the assembly has a profound effect upon him: "He is convinced of **all**". This emphasises the value of godly behaviour and practice in a local assembly.

- "He is judged by all" or: "he is judged of all" (JND): the word "judged" (*'anakrino'*) is rendered "examined" in 1 Corinthians 9 verse 3, that is, the teaching searches and sifts him. Once again, Paul emphasises the value of seemly 'corporate' practice.

- "And thus are the secrets of his heart made manifest." This does not infer public exposure, but rather that his very life and character is brought before him.

- "And so, falling down on his face, he will worship God, and report that God is in you of a truth." W.E. Vine suggests that this indicates conversion, and this may well be the case. At the very least, he will acknowledge that he is in the presence of God, not amongst a bunch of lunatics.

3) PARTICIPATION IN TONGUES AND PROPHECY, vv.26-35

What kind of meeting will make for the result above? The answer is clear from these verses: it will be an **orderly** meeting. We should notice the following in this section: *(a)* the regulating *principle* (v.26); *(b)* participation in *tongues* (vv.27-28); *(c)* participation in *prophecy* (vv.29-33); *(d)* participation by *sisters* (vv.34-35).

a) The regulating principle, v.26

"Let all things be done unto edifying." This principle is to govern both the contributions, and the contributors. Paul looks at assembly meetings in Corinth, asking the question: "How is it then brethren?", and then proceeds to answer for them: "when ye come together, every one of you hath a *psalm*, hath a *doctrine*, hath a *tongue*, hath a *revelation*, hath an *interpretation*". W.E. Vine suggests that this indicates that believers were coming together having predetermined what they would say and how they would contribute, and that this made for confusion. It was, therefore, of utmost importance that all brethren should regulate their contributions with reference to the overall welfare and well-being of the assembly. The principle remains. Favourite hymns and favourite passages are not necessarily edifying and helpful or appropriate at all times in assembly gatherings. It is also far from helpful to arrive at the meeting fully determined to address the assembly on a particular subject whether or not it is suitable for the occasion. Such so-called 'ministry' is often unsuitable for *any* occasion! The principle on which participation should be made is expressed here, and in 1 Corinthians 12 verse 7: "But the manifestation of the Spirit is given to every man to *profit withal*". This is followed by specific instructions:

b) Participation in tongues, v.v27-28

It might be helpful at this juncture to briefly restate the summary given in our previous study, namely:

- That *all* gifts are charismatic. The word "gift" comes from a Greek word *('charisma')* meaning 'freely given' or 'gift of grace'. See, for example, Romans 12 verse 6; 1 Corinthians 1 verse 7; 1 Timothy 1 verse 6.

- That the gift of tongues was not given to *every* believer. "Are all apostles? are all prophets? are all teachers? are all workers of miracles? have all the gifts of healing? do all speak with tongues? do all interpret?" (1 Corinthians 12:29-30). The answer is manifestly: *'No!"*

- That tongues are *temporary* in character. They are mentioned in 1

Corinthians: an early epistle. See 1 Corinthians 13 verse 8. But they are not mentioned in Romans and Ephesians, later epistles, where further reference is made to gifts. This demonstrates that the gift was declining even in New Testament times as explained by Harry Bell: "The gift of tongues ceased after the kingdom ceased to be offered to Israel".

- That the Corinthians were putting **first** what God put last. "God hath set some in the church; first, apostles; secondarily, prophets; thirdly, teachers; after that, miracles; then gifts of healing, helps, governments, **diversities of tongues**" (1 Cor. 12:28. See also Chapter 12: 10).

- The gift of tongues was a known language. See, for example, Acts 2 verse 4: "And they were all filled with the Holy Ghost, and began to speak with other **tongues** (*'glossa'*), as the Spirit gave them utterance". With this result: "the multitudes came together and were confounded, because that every man heard them speak in his **own language** (*'dialektos'*)" (Acts 2: 6). Continue to read Acts 2, noting verses 8 and 11. The use of *'glossa'* in 1 Corinthians must therefore refer to a known language, not to some ecstatic utterance. Hence, "with men of other tongues (*'glossa'*) and other lips will I speak unto this people" (1 Cor. 14:21). The words used in this chapter "*unknown* tongue" (AV) must be amended to simply "tongue".

- That the gift of tongues was a sign. It, therefore, follows that it **must** be a known language. As we shall see, it was a sign to unbelievers. 1 Corinthians 14 verse 22 refers to Isaiah 28 verses 11-12 which makes clear that "foreign conquerors … speaking other tongues, namely not unintelligible sounds but meaningful language" was a sign of divine judgment on the nation (J.H. Large). In this connection, we should note the Lord's words in Mark 16 verses 17-20: "These **signs** shall follow them that believe. In my name they shall cast out demons, shall they speak with **new tongues** … and they went forth, and preached everywhere, the Lord working with them, and confirming the word with **signs** following".

- That the gift of tongues was no evidence of **spirituality**. Corinth was the most carnal of the assemblies!

- That the gift of tongues, was to be exercised with care: "If any man speak in an (*unknown*) tongue, let it be by two, or at the most by three, and that by course: and let one interpret" (1 Corinthians 14:27).

The last of these brings us back to our current passage, and stresses some important principles:

i) The use of tongues was not to be excessive: "If any man speak in an (*unknown*) tongue, let it be by two, or at the most by three".

ii) Brethren were to take part one at a time: "and that by course", or "and separately" (JND). Participation was to be orderly.

iii) There was to be one interpreter: "and let one interpret". This could mean that one was to interpret for them all, or that only one was to interpret at any given time: interpretations were not to be given simultaneously. As J. Hunter observes: "If this (the first case) were so it would fully ensure that only one could take part at a time, the next speaker having to wait until the interpretation was finished". "But if there be no interpreter, let him keep silence in the church; and let him speak to himself, and to God." Compare verse 4: "He that speaketh in an (unknown) tongue edifieth himself".

c) Participation in prophecy, vv.29-33

"Let the prophets speak two or three, and let the other judge. If anything be revealed to another that sitteth by, let the first hold his peace. For ye may all prophesy one by one, that all may learn, and that all may be comforted. And the spirits of the prophets are subject to the prophets. For God is not the author of confusion, but of peace, as in all churches of the saints." We should notice the following:

i) As with tongues, participation in prophecy was not be excessive. "Let the prophets speak **two or three**" (v.29). We also notice that there was no question of one man in control.

ii) The prophets were to be listened to with discernment: "and let the other (Greek '*allos*', meaning 'of the same kind', that is, another prophet) *judge*" (v.29).

iii) The prophets were to participate with mutual consideration. "If any thing be revealed to another that sitteth by, let the first hold his peace" (v.30). "No one was to prolong his speaking so as to occupy the whole time, or even extend his speaking to an undue length. Each was to recognise that others possessed the gift besides himself" (W.E. Vine). In other words: 'Don't 'hog' the meeting!' Attention is drawn to the expression: "If any thing be **revealed** to him that sitteth by". The gift of prophecy involved direct revelation.

iv) The prophets were to be orderly in participation. "For ye may all prophesy **one by one**" (v.31). Such orderliness would promote the benefit of the company: "that all may learn, and that all may be comforted (exhorted)". It does not take too much imagination to visualise a meeting in which several people are all trying to speak at once!

v) The prophets were to exercise self-control: "and the spirits of the prophets are subject to the prophets" (v.32). They were to take part with intelligence and understanding. They were not to be excitable, and certainly not to lapse into an ecstatic condition. Their business was to communicate the Word of God clearly and intelligently.

These important principles reflect the harmonious way in which God Himself acts: "For God is not the author of confusion, but of peace, as in all churches of the saints" (v.33). Hence: "Let all things be done decently and in order" (v.40). In summary, a local assembly should be characterised by divine order, reverence, harmony and mutual consideration. It is clear that no assembly is free to 'do its own thing': "For God is not the author of confusion, but of peace, **as in all churches of the saints"**. See also Chapter 11 verse 16.

d) Participation by sisters, vv.34-35

"Let your women keep silent in the churches: for it is not permitted unto them to speak: but they are commanded to be under obedience, as also saith the law. And if they will learn anything, let them ask their husbands at home: for it is a shame for women to speak in the church." This is the third of three prohibitions so far as participation in the assembly gatherings is concerned. So far as tongues are concerned: "But if there be no interpreter, let him keep silence in the church" (v.28); so far as the prophets are concerned: "If any thing be revealed to another that sitteth by, let the first hold his peace" (v.30); now: "Let your women keep silence in the churches" (v.34). Only the men are to participate: the sisters have no part in the **oral** ministry of the assembly. To quote David Newell's footnote (*1 Corinthians 12-14: An Outline*): "This is not to demean the sisters but simply to follow the divine order for the gatherings of saints". He then quotes J.N. Darby: "You will find all honour done to women in the Gospels; but the Lord Jesus never sent out a woman to preach, **neither** did a man ever go and anoint Christ for His burial".

We should notice:

i) "Let your women keep **silence** (*'sigao'*) in the churches: for it is not permitted unto them to **speak**" (v.34). The "silence" here must be the same as in verse 28: "Let him keep silence in the church". See also verse 30. The word "speak" (*'laleo'*) here must have the same meaning as throughout the passage. It cannot mean 'chatter', as some suggest, otherwise verses 28-29 would become a nonsense: 'But if there be no interpreter, let him keep silence (*'sigao'*) in the church; and let him chatter to himself, and to God. Let the prophets chatter two or three, and let the other judge'. There is no need to say more about this ridiculous suggestion.

ii) "Let your women keep silence in the **churches**." Notice the **plural** here, following the plural in verse 33, as opposed to verse 28 where it is in the **singular**, referring particularly to Corinth where the gift of tongues existed. Compare 1 Corinthians 11 verse 16 which shows that "Corinth was alone in allowing women to be uncovered" (J. Hunter). Evidently Corinth was also alone in the matter of sisters' participation.

iii) "They are commanded to be under obedience (JND, 'but to be in subjection'), as also saith **the law**" (v.34). This is the second reference to "the law" in this chapter (see verse 21) and again indicates the Old Testament generally, with particular reference to Genesis 3 verse 16: "Thy desire shall be to thy husband, and he shall rule over thee". The reasons are given in 1 Timothy 2 verses 11-15: "Let the woman learn in silence with all subjection. But I suffer not a woman to teach, nor to usurp authority over the man, but to be in silence. For Adam was first formed, then Eve. And Adam was not deceived, but the woman, being deceived, was in the transgression". Teaching in connection with participation in the Assembly prayer meeting is given in the same passage: "I will therefore that **the** men (*'aner'*: male persons) pray in every place" (1 Timothy 2:8, JND).

iv) "And if they will learn any thing, let them ask their husbands at home (JND, "ask their own husbands at home"): for it is a shame for a woman to speak (*laleo*) in the church" (v.35). J. Hunter is worth quoting in full here: "Leadership is vested in the man. Both the man and the woman occupy a place of honour bestowed upon them by God, and all godly persons will acknowledge this to be so, and submit to the ordering of the wisdom of God. The women, if not clear in their minds concerning any matter, must not ask questions publicly, but seek help of the men-folk at home. The word rendered 'husbands' ('*aner*') while used in certain contexts in that way, is really men as distinct from women. The matter is concluded by the strong statement: "it is a shame for a woman to speak in the church". The word translated 'shame' ('*aischros*') means 'disgraceful, unbecoming, indecorous, indecent'".

The following was written by Andrew Borland in a booklet entitled: 'Women's Place in the Assemblies':

> "An argument frequently encountered from those who are advocating the more public participation by women in Assembly gatherings is that there are numerous instances in the Old Testament records of the prominence of women in the affairs of the nation of Israel. That goes without gain-saying; but the argument is invalid, because it assumes that what was permissible then is permissible now in a New Testament local church. It is contended that in Old Testament times there were prophetesses who communicated messages to the people. 'Miriam the prophetess, the sister of Aaron, took a timbrel in her hand; and all the women went out after her with timbrels and with dances. And Miriam answered them (the women,) Sing ye to the Lord, for he hath triumphed gloriously; the horse and his rider hath he thrown into the sea' (Exodus 15:20-21).
>
> Deborah was not only a judge among the people, to the shame of the men of Israel, none of whom was fit to act in that capacity, she was also a prophetess (Judges 4:4), and composed the song of victory preserved in Judges 5. (When it came to public leadership, a man was nominated: see Judges 4:6. In this respect there is no record that Deborah ever left her location 'under the palm tree', Judges 4:5). When the Temple in Jerusalem was being renovated in the reign of good king Josiah, the long lost Book of the Law was discovered, and the king and his courtiers were disturbed when they read its contents (2 Chronicles 34:8-19). While it was to Huldah, the prophetess, Josiah went and made enquiry for guidance, it was the king himself who read 'the words of the book' in the temple (2 Chronicles 34:30). So far as her 'prophesying' was concerned, there is no suggestion that Huldah ever left 'the college', referring to the second quarter of Jerusalem.
>
> It is strange that some have taken these examples as justification

for advocating public participation by women in the preaching of the gospel. 'Yet not so strange', writes C. F. Hogg, 'in view of the growing ignorance of the Scriptures and lack of intelligence in their interpretation'.

Anna, the daughter of Phanuel, probably the oldest woman in Jerusalem, is called a prophetess, perhaps the last of the line of such women in pre-Christian times. What an example she has set for all women who profess the Christian faith; for it is recorded of her that she spoke of the infant Messiah whom she had seen to all them who looked for redemption in Israel! (Luke 2:38). Evidently she had a circle of friends who frequented the Temple, and it was they (perhaps men like Joseph of Arimathea) to whom she witnessed, not publicly, but privately, as she met them during their visits to the Temple. She does not serve as a precedent for those who advocate the public oral ministry of women in a local church.

Argument for such ministry is sometimes founded on the fact that 'Philip the evangelist' had 'four daughters, virgins, who did prophesy' (Acts 21:9). It is, however, very precarious to build an argument on such a statement, for no indication whatsoever is given that those women exercised their gift in any place other than their own home. The context mentions the house of Philip of Caesarea where Paul found hospitality. Strange, too, isn't it, that while the apostle stayed there for many days, a prophet named Agabus had to come from Jerusalem to inform him that he would suffer at the hands of the Gentiles if he proceeded to that city. Why were the prophetesses superseded, if their ministry was of great importance? No others are mentioned in The Acts of the Apostles, and that fact in itself may be of disconcerting significance to those who press for the introduction of the public ministry of women into the Assemblies."

To this we should add that the fact that 1 Corinthians, not to mention 1 Timothy, forbids public participation by sisters in assembly gatherings, cannot be attributed to local culture or local customs, as some suggest.

4) CONCLUSION, vv.36-40

The assembly at Corinth was not to regard itself as a law unto itself. Paul advances two reasons:

a) The Word of God did not originate in them

They were not the source of the Word of God. "What! came the word of God out from you?" (v.36). Since they did not originate the Word of God, they could not set their own precedents in the matters discussed. If the Word of God had found its source in them, then they might well have the right to interpret it. But this was not the case. They were not free to do as they pleased. W.E. Vine has some telling comments here: "Being the first of the churches to depart from the word of God, especially in relation to women taking part (the immediate context), they were setting themselves up as a superior authority, so the apostle censures them".

b) The Word of God did not come to them alone

They were not the sole recipients of the Word of God. "Or came it unto you only?" (v.36). It was not a special revelation to them, making them different to everyone else. They were given no 'special treatment'. W.E. Vine again: "Were they the sole recipients and repositories of such a revelation that they could introduce such practices? Could they act on their own and ignore other churches? This was arrogance indeed. Independent authority was not invested in them". W.E. Vine continues: "Yet, today, we have the same attitude, and the same claim to be progressive and liberated. But it is **progressing away from the Word of God; liberation from obedience to it**".

Paul's teaching in respect of the local church is as mandatory as his teaching elsewhere: "If any man think himself to be a prophet, or spiritual, let him acknowledge that the things that I write unto you are the commandments of the Lord" (v.37). As J. Hunter rightly observes: "The unmistakable claim of Paul, that he is writing the word of God, cannot be ignored, and everyone must submit himself to the teaching marked by apostolic authority, no matter what experience he may claim". But there is a warning: "if any man be ignorant, let him be ignorant ('*agnoeo*' in both cases)" (v.38). In the words of W.E. Vine: "Persistent ignorance is culpable ignorance ... Unwillingness to submit prevents the possibility of being instructed".

Paul concludes: "Wherefore, brethren, **covet to prophes**y, and forbid not to speak with tongues" (v.39). The chapter, therefore, ends as it begins: "Follow after charity, and desire spiritual gifts, but **rather that ye may prophesy**" (v.1). In this way, the two gifts were to be valued and regulated, whilst they existed. The overall principle was: "Let all things be done decently and in order ('*taxis*', 'an arranging or arrangement')", that is, "in a seemly manner, and according to divine arrangement" (W.E. Vine). Compare 1 Chronicles 15 verse 13.

Happy is the assembly whose gatherings are governed by the principles taught in this passage of Holy Scripture.

1 CORINTHIANS

"He rose again the third day according to the scriptures"

Read Chapter 15:1-11

Broadly speaking, the epistle deals *(i)* with things that Paul had heard about the assembly at Corinth (Chapters 1-6): see 1 Corinthians 1 verse 11 and Chapter 5 verse 1; *(ii)* with things Paul had been asked by the assembly at Corinth (Chapters 7-16): see Chapter 7 verse 1 ("Now concerning the things whereof ye wrote unto me") and the expressions "now concerning" or "now as touching" (Chapters 7:25; 8:1; 12:1; 16:1).

Paul makes two references to his first visit to Corinth in the epistle: *(i)* in Chapter 2, where emphasis is placed on the ***manner of his preaching***: "And I, brethren, when I came to you, came not with excellency of speech or of wisdom, declaring unto you the testimony of God … And I was with you in weakness, and in fear, and in much trembling …" (vv.1, 3); *(ii)* in Chapter 15, where emphasis is placed on the ***matter of his preaching***: "For I delivered unto you first of all that which I also received, how that Christ died for our sins according to the scriptures …" (v.3).

1 Corinthians 15 may be simply divided into two major sections, each dealing with a question: *(1) the fact of resurrection* (vv.1-34): "How say some among you that there is no resurrection of the dead?" (v.12); *(2) the form of resurrection* (vv.35-58): "How are the dead raised up? and with what body do they come?" (v.35).

Alternatively, the first major section (vv.1-34) could be rightly entitled: *'The resurrection of the Saviour'*, and the second (vv.35-58) *'The resurrection of the saints'*.

It has been suggested that the doctrine of the Sadducees had infected the assembly at Corinth. "How say *some* among you …" See Matthew 22 verse

23: "The same day came unto him the Sadducees, which say that there is no resurrection"; Acts 23 verse 8: "For the Sadducees say that there is no resurrection, neither angel, nor spirit".

1) THE FACT OF RESURRECTION, vv.1-34

This section of the chapter can be analysed as follows: *(A)* the facts established (vv.1-11); *(B)* the facts expounded (vv.12-34).

A) The facts established, vv.1-11

In these verses we have a threefold witness: *(a)* the witness of Paul's preaching (vv.1-3a); *(b)* the witness of the prophetic scriptures (vv.3b-4); *(c)* the witness of people at the time (vv.5-11).

a) The witness of Paul's preaching, vv.1-3a

We should note the following: *(i)* the consistency of Paul's preaching (v.1); *(ii)* the results of Paul's preaching (vv.1-2); *(iii)* the priority in Paul's preaching (v.3); *(iv)* the authority of Paul's preaching (vv.3-4).

i) The consistency of Paul's preaching, v.1. "Moreover, brethren, I declare unto you the gospel which I preached unto you" or: "But I make known unto you, brethren, the glad tidings which I announced to you" (JND).

- The word rendered "*declare*" or 'make known' (*'gnorizo'*) is used particularly in relation to *the Lord's people*. See, for example, John 17 verse 26: "And I have declared unto them thy name"; Colossians 4 verse 7: "All my state shall Tychicus declare unto you". Hence, here, Paul says: "Moreover, brethren …" (The word "brethren" includes both brothers and sisters.)

- The word rendered "*preached*" (*'euangelizo'*) is used particularly in relation to *sinners.* (The words: "the gospel which I preached unto you" are, literally: 'the evangel which I evangelised'.) It may be worth noting that in Acts 20 verses 7 and 9, the word "preach" (AV) means: 'discoursed or dialogued' (*'dialegomai'*). In 1 Corinthians 15 verses 11-12, a different word (*'kerusso'*) is used, meaning 'herald'.

So Paul is restating here what he preached: "declare" (present tense), referring to what he was saying at the *time of writing*; "preached" (past tense), referring to what he said at the **time of his visit.** There was no divergence from his original preaching. Paul had not changed his mind! The gospel does not change! Compare Galatians 1 verses 8-9.

ii) The results of Paul's preaching, vv1-2. "Moreover, brethren, I declare unto you the gospel which I preached (*'euangelizo'*) unto you, which also ye have received, and wherein ye stand; by which also ye are saved, if ye keep in memory ('hold fast', JND) what I preached unto you, unless ye have believed in vain." Paul, therefore, refers to three results of his ministry: "which ye have also **received,** and wherein ye **stand** (*'histemi'*); by which also ye are **saved**".

- As to: "**which ye have also received**", see Acts 18 verse 8: "and many of the Corinthians hearing, believed, and were baptized".

- As to: "**wherein ye stand**" (*'histemi'*), see Romans 5 verse 2: "by whom (the Lord Jesus) also we have access by faith into this grace wherein we stand (*'histemi'*)". We stand - not fall - before God. It is a righteous standing. It is a permanent standing.

- As to: "**by which also ye are saved, if ye keep in memory what I preached unto you, unless ye have believed in vain**", we must note that the present tense is used here leading to the rendering "by which also ye are **being saved**". Salvation in that sense is dependent on "if ye hold fast ('keep in memory', AV) the word which I announced unto you" (JND). Compare Colossians 1 verses 21-23 where the words: "**if ye continue in the faith** grounded and settled ..." warn against departure from "**the** faith". Departure from the faith is apostasy. Continuity proves the reality of salvation.

It may be worth noting that the word translated "vain" here (*'eike'*), means: 'to no purpose' (v.2). As Paul goes on to point out, this would have been the case if Christ had not been raised from the dead. A different word (*'kenos'*), meaning 'empty', is used in verses 10 and 14, and in verse 17 the word rendered "vain" (*'mataios'*) means 'void of result'.

iii) The priority in Paul's preaching, v.3. "For I delivered unto you **first of all** that which I also received ..." That is, "first of all" in relation to **importance.** Thus, the first subject in Paul's preaching, in order of importance, was "Christ died for our sins ..." Notice the Lord's priority in dealing with the paralytic: see Matthew 9 verse 2.

iv) The authority of Paul's preaching, v.3. "For I delivered unto you first of all that which I also received …" Paul did not communicate his own ideas: "I **delivered** unto you … that which I also **received**". Compare Chapter 11 verse 23: "For I received of the Lord that which also I delivered unto you …" Compare Galatians 1 verses 11-12. Moreover, Paul did not alter the truth imparted to him. He communicated what he had received – no more, no less. Paul preached with conviction, arising from the divine revelation given to him. This leads to:

b) The witness of the prophetic scriptures, vv.3b-4

We must notice that this is placed before the witness of men. Experience in itself is a dangerous thing: our experiences must always be understood in the light of the Word of God.

The unity and consistency of the Scriptures is emphasised: "For I delivered unto you first of all that which I also received (**the New Testament**), how that Christ died for our sins (because of our sins) according to the scriptures; and that he was buried, and that he rose again the third day according to the scriptures (**the Old Testament**)".

In each case, whether the death, burial, or resurrection of the Lord Jesus, everything took place "according to the scriptures". We must never forget that God's Word is "for ever … settled in heaven" (Psalm 119:89), and "the scripture cannot be broken" (John 10:35).

i) His death was "according to the scriptures"

There were occasions when His life was threatened by the Jews. See, for example, Luke 4 verses 28-30; John 8 verses 58-59; John 10 verses 30-31. Had the Lord Jesus died on any of these occasions, it would not have been "according to the scriptures". The Lord himself made this clear: "Thinkest thou that I cannot now pray to my Father, and he shall presently give me more than twelve legions of angels? But how then shall the **scriptures be fulfilled**, that thus it must be?" (Matthew 26:53-54).

ii) His burial was "according to the scriptures"

Had the Lord Jesus been buried in a common grave, that too would **not** have been "according to the scriptures". But Isaiah 53 verse 9 must be fulfilled:

"And (men) appointed his grave with the wicked (plural: 'wicked people'), but he was with the rich (singular: 'rich man') in his death" (JND).

In connection with the Lord's burial, it is most significant that Mark uses two different words in connection with the Lord's body: "Joseph of Arimathaea … went in boldly unto Pilate, and craved the **body** of Jesus" (Mark 15:43). The Greek word is *'soma'* and means: "properly, a human body, a living thing, a Person, a temple in which the Holy Ghost could dwell" (H. St.John citing Abbott-Smith's *Lexicon*). The Lord's body could never see corruption (Psalm 16:10). But a different word is used in Mark 15 verse 45: "And when he (Pilate) knew it of the centurion, he gave the **body** to Joseph". The Greek word here is *'ptoma',* meaning 'a corpse' (RV: see JND margin), literally, 'a fallen thing'. It is used in Matthew 24 verse 28: "For wheresoever the carcase (*'ptoma'*) is, there will the eagles be gathered together". Norman Crawford (*What the Bible Teaches – Luke*) sets out the difference between the two words as follows: "To Joseph, the body of the Lord Jesus was precious, and not a mere corpse as it was to Pilate".

In passing, we must carefully note the words: "Christ died **for our sins** according to the scriptures". It is important that we do not create the wrong impression in the minds of unregenerate men and women. All too often we hear gospel preachers tell unconverted people that Christ bore their sins on the cross, and then go on to tell them that if they do not repent and believe, their sins will take them to hell! The Lord Jesus died on behalf of all men – it is quite correct to tell men and women that Christ died for them – the Bible does not teach 'limited atonement' – but only believers can say: 'Christ bore my sins on the cross'. Peter is writing to believers in saying: "Who his own self bare our sins in his own body on the tree" (1 Peter 2:24), and, for that matter, it will be the regenerate remnant in Israel who will say: "He was wounded for our transgressions, he was bruised for our iniquities: the chastisement of our peace was upon him; and with his stripes we are healed. All we, like sheep, have gone astray … and the Lord hath laid on him the iniquity of us all" (Isaiah 53: 5-6).

iii) His resurrection was "according to the scriptures"

Similarly, the Lord's resurrection was "according to the scriptures", in at least three ways:

- It was "according to the scriptures" because it was foreshadowed in

the ceremonial law. His resurrection was anticipated in the Old Testament "feasts of the LORD" (Leviticus 23:2). Paul refers to the 'feast of firstfruits' (Leviticus 23:9-14) in 1 Corinthians 15 verse 20: "But now is Christ risen from the dead, and become the firstfruits of them that slept". It is noteworthy that the 'sheaf of the firstfruits' was to be presented to God on "the morrow after the sabbath" (Leviticus 23:11) or, as Luke puts it, "upon the first day of the week" (Luke 24:1). His resurrection was, therefore, "according to the scriptures". It fulfilled the 'typical teaching' of the Old Testament. As "the firstfruits of them that slept", the risen Lord Jesus is the guarantee of a harvest to follow (1 Corinthians 15:22-24).

A further example is found in the ceremonial law relating to the cleansing of the leper, where two birds prefigure the death, resurrection and ascension of the Lord Jesus (Leviticus 14:1-7),

- *It was "according to the scriptures" because it was the subject of prophecy.* See, for example, Psalm 16 verses 10-11: "Thou wilt not leave my soul in hell; neither wilt thou suffer thine Holy One to see corruption. Thou wilt shew me the path of life ..." Having referred to this passage on the day of Pentecost, Peter explained to the crowds that it could not possibly refer to David since he was "both dead and buried", but "being a prophet", David "spake of the resurrection of Christ" (Acts 2:25-32). See also Isaiah 53 verse 10: "He shall see his seed, he shall prolong his days, and the pleasure of the Lord shall prosper in his hands".

- *It was "according to the scriptures" because it was typified in some Old Testament biographies.* See, for example the experiences of Isaac and Jonah.

The words: "rose again the third day according to the scriptures" ("hath been raised on the third day according to the scriptures", RV) are in the Greek perfect tense, and stress the continuous results and efficacy of His resurrection. For "the third day", see the *Addendum* ("Three days and three nights").

The reasons for the Lord's resurrection include the fact that the Scriptures said He would rise from the dead; that He said He would rise from the dead; that He was the Son of God (Romans 1:4); that evidence must be furnished that God accepted His work at Calvary as the basis of our salvation (Romans 4:25); that evidence must be furnished of His complete victory over sin and death; that it was impossible for Him to be held by death (Acts 2:24, 27).

c) The witness of people at the time, vv.5-11

We must notice that in referring to the resurrection appearances, Paul draws attention to occasions when the Lord revealed Himself to both individuals and to groups of people. (It is noticeable that no direct references are made to the women to whom He revealed Himself. It is generally said that this was because, at the time, the evidence of women was inadmissible in law.) The following should be read in this connection: Acts 1 verse 3: "To whom (the apostles) also he shewed himself alive after his passion by many (infallible) proofs" and Acts 10: 40-41: "Him God raised up the third day, and shewed him openly, not to all the people, but unto witnesses, chosen before of God, even to us who did eat and drink with him after he rose from the dead".

We should notice that Paul refers here to two categories of witness: those to whom the Lord revealed himself whilst on earth (vv.5-7), and Paul himself, to whom the Lord revealed himself from heaven (vv.8-10). The appearances listed by Paul are:

i) "And that he was seen of Cephas" (v.5). The RV has, better, "He **appeared** to Cephas". The words: "seen of Cephas" do not convey the right idea at all! See Luke 24 verse 34: "The Lord is risen indeed, and hath appeared to Simon".   Note: while Simon saw the empty tomb (Luke 24:12), the words: 'appeared to Cephas' refer to an event not recorded in detail in the Gospels. See Luke 24 verse 34. (It was evidently before, or at the time of, the encounter on the road to Emmaus.) It was a strictly private revelation. Whilst we may speculate, we do not know what took place between the Lord and Peter.

ii) "Then of ('to', RV) the twelve" (v.5). The word "then" (*'eita'*) means: 'after an interval'. So verses 7 and 24. Paul refers here to John 20 verse 19. The expression: "the twelve" (not 'the eleven') is evidently a technical term for the apostolic band. See John 20 verse 24: "But Thomas, one of the twelve…"

iii) "Then ('After that', AV) he appeared to above five hundred brethren at once, of whom the most remain until now, but some also have fallen asleep" (v.6, JND). Evidently more than the one hundred and twenty of Acts 1 verse 15! We should notice that the expression "fallen asleep" is never used of the Lord Jesus.

iv) "Then ('After that', AV) he appeared to James" (v.7, JND). This could be James son of Alphaeus. Mary, wife of Cleophas (Alphaeus and Cleophas are evidently one and the same) was the sister of Mary, the mother of the Lord Jesus (John 19:25). ('Alphaeus' is a Greek name which expresses a Hebrew name. The same Hebrew name can also be expressed in Greek as 'Cleophas' or 'Clopas'). The James mentioned here (v.7) is probably the same as "James, the Lord's brother" (Galatians 1:19). The word "brother" can be translated 'kinsman'. Another possibility is that it was James the brother of John (Acts 12:2). This incident is unrecorded elsewhere.

v) "Then (see note at v.5) to all the apostles" (v.7). See, for example, Matthew 28 verse 16: "Then the eleven disciples went away into Galilee, into a mountain were Jesus had appointed them. And when they saw, they worshipped him" and Acts 1 verse 4: "And being assembled together with them (the apostles, Acts 1: 2), commanded them that they should not depart from Jerusalem".

Thus far, men saw the Lord Jesus on earth. But now we have something significantly different. Paul saw the Lord Jesus in the sphere of His ascended glory.

vi) "And last of all he was seen of me also, as one born out of due time" (v.8): or: "And last of all, as one born out of due time, he appeared to me also" (RV): or "and last of all, as to an abortion, he appeared to me also" (JND). J.N. Darby's translation here is most unattractive. We should note the following:

- His inferiority. That is, only, in terms of time. The words "born out of due time" translate one word (*'ektroma'*) from a verb meaning: 'to miscarry'. In the words of W.E. Vine: "He thus self-depreciatingly speaks of himself in view of his pre-conversion life, in contrast to the circumstances of 'the Twelve'. They were disciples before they became apostles, and theirs was a gradual training. His was a sudden change from antagonism to apostleship. His use of the term expresses his strong feeling regarding himself as a bitter opponent of Christ before his sudden change. That he puts 'to me also' (v.8, RV) at the end of his statement is expressive of his humbleness of mind, and this is continued in verse 9". This leads to:

- His ineligibility. The word "For" (*"For* I am the least of all the apostles, that am not meet to be called an apostle, because I persecuted the church

of God") links verses 8-9. We should notice that he calls himself here "the least of all the apostles"; "less than the least of all saints" (Ephesians 3:8); and the "chief of sinners" (1 Timothy 1:15). While the expression: "the church of God" may refer to the local church (its general meaning: in this case, possibly, "the church which was at Jerusalem", Acts 8:1), these words may have a wider meaning here. The word "persecuted" means 'to pursue'.

- His indebtedness. Paul's testimony: "But by the grace of God I am what I am" (v.10) emphasises that the risen Christ had changed his life, so while once he "persecuted the church of God", now he says: "but I laboured more abundantly than they all". So:

- His industry. "I laboured (*'kopiao'*, rendered "toiled" in Luke 5 verse 5, and "wearied" in John 4 verse 6) more abundantly than they all: yet not I, but the grace of God which was with me." The same word is used of a sister, Persis: see Romans 16 verse 12. Men are not the only people who 'toil!' The words "not in vain" or 'not found in vain' (RV) mean 'not found empty'. After all, our "labour (*'kopiao'*) is not in vain in the Lord" (1 Corinthians 15:58).

We, therefore, have, firstly, the grace of God in *salvation*: "But by the grace of God I am what I am", and, secondly, the grace of God in *service*: "But I laboured more abundantly than they all: yet not I, but the grace of God which was with me".

Looking back over the six resurrection appearances (vv.5-10), Paul concludes: "Therefore whether it were I or they, so we preach (present continuous tense), and so ye believed" (v.11). Whether Paul himself ("I") or the other apostles ("they"), there was unity of testimony. They preached a gospel which included Christ's resurrection. The word "preach" (*'kerusso'*) means, as noted above, 'to herald' or 'proclaim'. This section of the chapter, therefore, concludes as it commenced, with reference to *preaching* and *believing.* The message proclaimed to them, and believed by them, was attested both by the witness of the Scriptures and by the witness of men. The passage ends with on-going preaching: "Therefore whether it were I or they, *so we preach* ..." The apostles were "stedfast, unmoveable, always abounding in the work of the Lord ..." (v.58).

ADDENDUM

"Three days and three nights"

According to Norman Crawford (*What the Bible Teaches - Luke*) there are fourteen references in the New Testament to "the third day". However, the Lord Jesus stated quite categorically that "as Jonas was three days and three nights in the whale's belly; so shall the Son of man be three days and three nights in the heart of the earth" (Matthew 12:40). The expression: "the third day" is usually explained with reference to the Hebrew custom of treating part days as full days. If the Lord had said: "three days" without reference to nights, there would be no dispute. In that way, you can make 'Good Friday' fit with 'Easter Sunday'! A Friday crucifixion would give three days: one full day and part of two others. But the Lord Jesus was very specific – "three days *and three nights*". Is it, therefore, correct to say that the Lord was crucified on 'Good Friday'?

It is important to notice that the trial of the Lord Jesus took place, not 'on the preparation of the sabbath', but "on the preparation of the Passover" (John 19:14), and that the first day of the seven-day feast of unleavened bread, "when they killed the Passover" (Mark 14:12) was to be observed as a sabbath (Exodus 12:16; Leviticus 23:7). It was with this in mind that John observed: "for that sabbath day was an high day" (John 19:31), distinguishing this particular sabbath from the regular weekly sabbaths. We are told that the "high" sabbath coincided with the regular Saturday sabbath once in every seven years and that the Jews adjusted their calendar to ensure that the 14th Nisan (Exodus 12:6) never fell on the regular sabbath. So the days commencing at 18.00 on Thursday and on Friday were both regarded as sabbath days. On this reckoning, the Lord Jesus was crucified on a Thursday, not on a Friday.

a) He was crucified at 09.00 on Thursday, and died at 15.00.
b) He was placed in Joseph's tomb by the commencement of the "high" sabbath, i.e. prior to 18.00 on Thursday: *one day.*
c) He was in the tomb from 18.00 on Thursday to 0600 on Friday: *one night*.
d) He was in the tomb from 06.00 on Friday to 18.00 on Friday: *one day*.
e) He was in the tomb from 18.00 on Friday to 0600 on Saturday: *one night*.
f) He was in the tomb from 06.00 on Saturday to 18.00 on Saturday: *one day*.

g) He was in the tomb from 18.00 on Saturday to, say, 0600 on Sunday: **one night**.

This *may* help us to understand the relationship between "the third day" and "three days and three nights". The Lord rose from the dead on the third of the "three days" **commencing** at 18.00 on Thursday, Friday and Saturday.

Additionally, we have the words "**after** three days" (Mark 8:31). On the basis that the Lord was crucified on the Thursday, and bearing in mind the Hebrew custom of treating part days as full days, this *could* mean 'after the three days **ending** at 18.00 on Thursday, Friday and Saturday'.

1 CORINTHIANS

"But now is Christ risen from the dead"

Read Chapter 15:12-34

We have already noticed that this marvellous chapter may be divided into two major sections, each dealing with a question: *(1) the fact of resurrection* (vv.1-34): "How say some among you that there is no resurrection of the dead?" (v.12); *(2) the form of resurrection* (vv.35-58): "How are the dead raised up? and with what body do they come?" (v.35). Alternatively, the first section (vv.1-34) could be entitled: 'The resurrection of *the Saviour*', and the second (vv.35-58): 'The resurrection of *the saints*'.

1) THE FACT OF RESURRECTION, vv.1-34

As we have already noticed, this part of the chapter falls into two sections: *(A)* the facts established (vv.1-11); *(B)* the facts expounded (vv.12-34).

A) The facts established, vv.1-11

We considered these verses in our previous study, and noticed that they relate the facts of the Lord's resurrection in three ways: *(i)* the witness of Paul's preaching (vv.1-3a); *(ii)* the witness of the prophetic Scriptures (vv.3b-4); *(iii)* the witness of people at the time (vv.5-11). This brings us to:

B) The facts expounded, vv.12-34

In these verses, the resurrection of the Lord Jesus is discussed in three ways: *(a)* the resurrection and gospel preaching (vv.12-19): Paul discusses the implications for the gospel if there is no resurrection; *(b)* the resurrection and God's programme (vv.20-28): Paul discusses the indispensability of resurrection in future events; *(c)* the resurrection and Christian practice (vv.29-34): Paul discusses the impact of resurrection on Christian living.

a) The resurrection and gospel preaching, vv.12-19

Paul discusses here the consequences if "Christ be not risen". He lays before us the woeful implications if there is no resurrection.

Having stressed that the Lord's resurrection was an essential part of apostolic preaching, the apostle asks the question: "Now if Christ be preached ('*kerusso*', a verb, to preach as a herald: see also Luke 24 verse 47; Acts 8 verse 5) that he rose from the dead ('hath been raised from the dead', RV: 'is raised from among [the] dead', JND), how say some among you that there is no resurrection of the dead?" (v.12). (For the technically minded Paul uses the Greek preposition '*ek*' here, meaning 'out of' the dead'.) As noted in our previous study, it has been suggested that the doctrine of the Sadducees had in some way infected the assembly at Corinth. "How say **some** among you ..." See Matthew 22 verse 23 and Acts 23 verse 8. Alternatively, Paul may be referring here to the influence of Greek philosophy. See Acts 17 verses 18 and 32.

Very clearly, Christ's resurrection is evidence and confirmation that there **is** such a thing as resurrection. The implications if this is not the case follow: *(i)* the implications for Christ (vv.12-13); *(ii)* the implications for the preachers (vv.14-16); *(iii)* the implications for the believer (vv.17-19). These verses emphasise the necessity to 'think through' Bible doctrine: to weigh its meaning, and, therefore, be in a position to assess the implications of false teaching. The passage demonstrates the horrifying consequences if there is no resurrection.

i) The implications for Christ, vv.12-13. "Now if Christ be preached that he rose from the dead, how say some among you that there is no resurrection of the dead? But if there be no resurrection of the dead ('if there is not a resurrection of [those that are dead]', JND), then is Christ not risen." To deny the fact of resurrection is to deny Christ's resurrection: "neither hath Christ been raised" (v.13, RV).

John Heading points out that "the Corinthians did not dispute the fact of faith that Christ had been raised - they merely reasoned about the resurrection of the bodies of the saints ... But Paul carried their argument to its conclusion. The saints are so blessed by being one with Christ, that if they are not raised, then neither is He! ... Hence in the light of the previous paragraph, namely the testimony of the Scriptures and of all the eye-witnesses, the Corinthians were on illogical ground".

ii) The implications for the preachers, vv.14-16. "And if Christ be not risen ('if Christ hath not been raised', RV), then is our preaching ('*kerugma*', a noun, preaching as a herald: see also Chapter 2:4) vain, and your faith is also vain. Yea, and we are found (meaning 'discovered' or 'detected') false witnesses ('*pseudomartus*': see also Matthew 26:60) of God; because we have testified ('*martureo*': see also, for example John 4:39) of God that he raised up Christ: whom he raised not up, if so be that the dead rise not. For if the dead rise not, then is not Christ raised." Compare verse 13: "But if there be no resurrection of the dead, then is not Christ risen". The preachers had emphasised the Lord's resurrection: it was the hallmark of their preaching: "so we preach ('*kerusso*', to preach as a herald) and so ye believed" (v.11). But "if Christ is not raised" (v.14, JND) that preaching was "vain". The underlying Greek word ('*kenos*') means 'empty of quality': 'worthless': it secures nothing: it is devoid of all truth, reality and power. The same word ('*kenos*') occurs in Luke 1 verse 53: "the rich hath he sent *empty* away". See also Ephesians 5 verse 6.

In this case, both the "preaching" and their "faith" were vain. The latter reflects the character of the former! Moreover, the preachers had misrepresented God Himself: they were "false witnesses of God". To summarise: there was nothing in the preaching (it was "vain"), but even more seriously, it was downright falsehood.

iii) The implications for the believer, vv.17-19. "And if Christ be not raised, your faith is vain; ye are yet in your sins. Then they also which are fallen asleep in Christ are perished. If in this life only we have hope in Christ, we are of all men most miserable." In these circumstances, "your faith is vain". The word '*mataios*' means 'fruitless' or 'void of result' (W.E. Vine). See also 1 Corinthians 3 verse 20. The reasons follow:

- There is no deliverance from sin. "Ye are yet in your sins" (v.17). Compare Romans 4 verse 25: "Who was delivered for our offences, and was raised again for our justification ..." If there is no resurrection, then there is no pardon. The sin question has not been settled after all. If the Lord Jesus has not been raised, then He could not have been delivered up for our offences. He Himself would have been claimed by death as one who was sinful.

- There is no hope for the dead. "Then they also which are fallen asleep in Christ have perished" (v.18). The word "perished" translates '*apollumai*', meaning, not loss of being, but loss of well-being.

- There is no joy in life. "If in this life only we have hope in Christ, we are of all men most miserable" (v.19). The words "most miserable" (*'eleeinteros'*) mean: 'most pitiable'. The word *'eleeinos'* is only found in Revelation 3 verse 17. In the words of Charles Hodge: "And we, if all our hopes in Christ are confined to this life, are the most miserable of men". We are in a worse position than the unsaved. They can at least say: "Take thine ease, eat, drink, and be merry" (Luke 12:19), and: "Let us eat, drink, for tomorrow we die" (1 Corinthians 15:32). In these circumstances, believers have nothing at all. There could be no fulfilment and satisfaction, however transient, in life.

But now the theme changes to a positive argument. Paul now discusses the results attaching to Christ's resurrection. So:

b) The resurrection and God's programme, vv.20-28

"But now is Christ risen from (*'ek'*) the dead, and become the firstfruits of them that slept." The word "risen" is in the perfect tense, that is, a past action with present consequences. In this section we must notice the words "firstfruits … afterwards … then", which suggest the following *(i)* resurrection and Christ personally (vv.20-23a); *(ii)* resurrection and Christ's people (v.23b); *(iii)* resurrection and Christ's reign (vv.24-28).

i) Resurrection and Christ personally, vv.20-23a. "But now is Christ risen from the dead, and become the firstfruits of them that slept. For since by man came death, by man came also the resurrection of the dead. For as in Adam all die, even so in Christ shall all be made alive. But every man in his own order; Christ the firstfruits …" 'But now is Christ risen from *among* the dead.' Not part of general resurrection, but a selective resurrection. We must notice three things about the Lord Jesus here:

- He is "the firstfruits of them that slept", v.20. His resurrection is viewed here in its representative character. "And become the firstfruits of them that slept ('of those fallen asleep', JND: 'of them that have fallen asleep' W.E. Vine)." The word "firstfruits" indicates, as already noted, the representative character of the Lord's resurrection, just as the first sheaf of harvest was presented to God as a thank-offering, and was a pledge and the assurance of the ingathering of the whole harvest. It was the promise and pledge of more to come. His resurrection lays the basis for others to follow. Compare Romans 8 verse 23: "We have (that is, we have now) the firstfruits of the Spirit", that is, the pledge of the coming completion of all that God has in

mind for His people. Note references in the epistle to the 'feasts' of passover (1 Corinthians 5:7), unleavened bread (1 Corinthians 5:8), and firstfruits (1 Corinthians 15:20). Significantly, the priest was to "wave the sheaf before the LORD, to be accepted for you: on the morrow after the sabbath the priest shall wave it" (Leviticus 23:11), that is, "the first day of the week" (Luke 24:1).

In resurrection, the Lord Jesus is "the firstfruits" (here), and "the firstborn" (Colossians 1:18). The expression "firstborn" (see also Colossians 1:15) is not time-related, but refers to priority and pre-eminence. For "firstborn" see also Romans 8 verse 29. The Lord Jesus is the divine prototype: we shall be like Him!

For "them that slept", see Daniel 12 verse 2: "And many of them that sleep in the dust of the earth shall awake, some to everlasting life, and some to shame and everlasting contempt"; Matthew 27 verse 52: "And many bodies of the saints which slept, arose …"; John 11 verse 11: "Our friend Lazarus sleepeth"; Acts 13 verse 36: "For David, after he had served his own generation by the will of God, fell on sleep".

- He is the Head of a new race of men, vv.21-22. We should notice that verses 21-28 survey the history of man, and show that resurrection is essential to the fulfilment of God's prophetic programme. Thus: "For since by man came death, by man also came the resurrection of the dead". The Lord Jesus is "the last Adam" (v.45). There are only two federal headships: those of Adam and Christ. There will not be another. Resurrection came by a perfect Man. "If we believe that **Jesus** died and rose again, even so them also which sleep in **Jesus** will God bring with him" (1 Thessalonians 4:14).

The two consequences of the two headships follow: "For as in Adam all die, so also in Christ all shall be made alive …" or: "For as in *the* Adam all die, thus also in *the* Christ (RV concurs) shall all be made alive" (JND). Adam stands at the head of the natural race: Christ stands at the head of the spiritual race. We should notice that the words: "in Christ shall all be made alive" do not refer to all men, but only to those: "in Christ". Compare 2 Corinthians 5 verse 17: "If any man be in Christ, he is a new creature …"

- He is first in rank, v.23. "But every man in his own order; Christ the firstfruits; afterward they that are Christ's at his coming." The word "order" (*'tagma'*) was: "especially a military term, denoting a company" (W.E. Vine). So we have the idea of military order: each in his own rank. Two of these

'ranks' occur here: "Christ the firstfruits" and "they that are Christ's at his coming". This brings us to:

ii) Resurrection and Christ's people, v.23b. "But every man in his own order; Christ the firstfruits; *afterward they that are Christ's at his coming.*" The word "coming" translates *'parousia'* meaning 'presence'. Paul, therefore, refers here to the Lord's presence with His saints. What will happen after that? This follows:

iii) Resurrection and Christ's reign, vv.24-28. Resurrection is essential to the fulfilment of God's prophetic programme. Note: It does seem that verses 24-28 are a parenthesis, and that the mainstream of Paul's argument runs as follows: "But every man in his own order; Christ the firstfruits; afterward they that are Christ's at his coming (v.23) … Else what shall they do that are baptized for the dead, if the dead rise not at all?" (v.29).

The parenthesis begins: "Then cometh the end …" (v.24). That is, the end of time. The word "then" (*'eita'*) indicates an interval (this is explained in verse 25), as in verse 5 ('then to the twelve') and verse 7 ('then to all the apostles'). We should notice, however, that the word "then" in verse 28 means: 'immediately'. The word "end" here (*'telos'*) means: 'the final issue', which is explained by the words: "when he shall have delivered up the kingdom to God, even the Father" (v.24). We must, therefore, notice:

- The course of the programme, v.24. "Then cometh the end (as already noticed, the end of time), when (whensoever) he shall have delivered up the kingdom to God, even the Father", which will be "when he shall have put down (*'katargeo'*, meaning 'abolished': rendered inactive) all rule (*'arche'*) and all authority (*'exousia'*) and power (*'dunamis'*)." That is the authority and power with which the rule is exercised.

- The certainty of the programme, vv.25-26. "For he must reign, till he hath put all enemies under his feet" (v.25). This will be after the final rebellion at the end of the Millennium. See Revelation 20 verses 9-10. The words: "For **he** must reign" remind us that it will not be the dragon, or beast, or the false prophet, or prime ministers or presidents who will reign, but Christ!

"The last enemy that shall be destroyed (as above, *'katergeo'*, meaning 'abolished' or 'reduced to inactivity': 'non effect') is death" (v.26). Death, which claims the bodies of men, is classed as an active foe. This is the main point of the passage here: it stresses, not only the fact of resurrection, but that death itself will be abolished.

- *The consummation of the programme, vv.27-28.* "For he hath put all things under his feet. But when he saith, All things are put under him, it is manifest that he is excepted, which did put all things under him. And when (whensoever) all things shall be subdued unto him, then (thereupon) shall the Son himself be subject unto him that put all things under him, that God may be all in all."

Paul cites Psalm 8 verse 6 here, referring to Adam: "For thou hast put all things under his feet". But while Adam lost that dominion, Christ will hold it in glory, and when the time comes for Him to say "that all things are put in subjection" (v.27, JND), that is, when Psalm 8 has been fulfilled, then the obvious exception is God Himself: "It is manifest ('evident', JND) that he is excepted, which did put all things under him" (v.27). The Lord Jesus will be the perfect steward. ***He will rule for God.*** He will bring eternal glory to God. In Paul's words: "And when all things shall be subdued unto him, then shall the Son also himself be subject unto him that put all things under him, that God may be all in all" (v.28). No wonder God says: "Behold my servant, whom I uphold, mine elect, in whom my soul delighteth ..." (Isaiah 42:1). He cried: "It is finished" at Calvary (John 19:30). He will say: "It is done", having executed judgment on earth prior to His public return as "KING OF KINGS, AND LORD OF LORDS" (Revelation 16:17; 19:16). And then, with "all things under him", He will say again, in effect: "I have glorified thee on the earth: I have finished the work which thou gavest me to do" (John 17:4).

This completes the parenthesis. It ends (v.28) as it begins (v.24): verse 28 defines the "end" (v.24), and the intervening statements lead to this goal. Having completed the parenthesis, Paul now turns to:

c) The resurrection and Christian practice, vv.29-34

Paul now deals with the subject experimentally. He points out the implications for service and conduct if there is no resurrection: *(i)* baptism is pointless (v.29); *(ii)* faithfulness is pointless (vv.30-32); *(iii)* evil conduct is promoted (vv.33-34).

i) Baptism is pointless, v.29. "Else what shall they do which are baptized for the dead, if the dead rise not at all? Why are they then baptized for the dead?" This has been explained in various ways, including being baptised on behalf of unbaptised people and, being baptized as filling the ranks of believers who have died in conflict (it is said that a military term is employed here). Both explanations are unacceptable, particularly the first!

The general meaning is clear: if there is no resurrection, baptism loses its overall significance. If there is no resurrection, baptism can only be in view of death, and those who are baptized are testifying (in emerging from the water) to something that does not exist! Baptism, therefore, is in view of death only. What is the point of that: "if the dead rise not at all?"

But what is the precise significance of the twice-repeated expression: "for the dead?" The explanation lies in the preposition *'huper'* rendered "for" ("for the dead") which carries the meaning 'in view of'. W.E. Vine points out the absence of punctuation in the original text, and renders the verse as follows: "Else what shall they do which are baptized? It is for (i.e. in the interests of) the dead, if the dead are not raised at all. Why then are they baptized for them?" W.E. Vine continues: "If there is no resurrection of the dead, the ordinance, instead of setting forth the identification of believers with the risen Christ had no meaning at all either for Him or for them; for all perish at death: see verse 18".

Some long years ago, further help was given by W.B.C. Beggs in the *Believer's Magazine.* This is reproduced in the Addendum.

ii) Faithfulness is pointless, vv.30-32. "And why stand we in jeopardy every hour?" (v.30). The word "jeopardy" means: 'at risk' or 'facing danger'. Compare Luke 8 verse 23. After all, Paul said: "But none of these things ("bonds and afflictions") move me, neither count I my life dear unto myself" (Acts 20:23-24). Paul continues: "I protest by your rejoicing which I have in Christ Jesus, I die daily" (v.31) or: "I protest by that glorying in you, brethren, which I have in Christ Jesus our Lord, I die daily" (RV), meaning: 'As surely as I boast of you - rejoice over you - which boasting is in Christ Jesus, I die daily'. The words "I protest" are a strong affirmation (*'nee'*): an adverb of affirmation used in oaths. Paul, therefore, assures them of two things of equal certainty: firstly, he rejoiced over them and, secondly, he died daily. Weymouth renders this: "I protest (swear), brethren, as surely as I glory over you, which I may justly do in Christ Jesus our Lord, that I die day by day". The connection between Paul glorying in them and Paul dying daily may be that he is emphasising the danger and risk incurred in his service for God, which resulted in the salvation of souls over whom he could rejoice. For "I die daily" see 2 Corinthians 1 verses 8-9; and Chapter 4: 11: "We ... are always delivered unto death ..."

Paul continues further: "If after the manner of men (i.e. to speak after the manner of men) I have fought with wild beasts at Ephesus, what advantageth it me, if the dead rise not? Let us eat and drink, for tomorrow we die" (v.32). W.E. Vine points out that as a Roman citizen Paul "could not be compelled to fight with actual beasts in an arena; nor could he be flung to the lions", and concludes that the words: "I have fought with wild beasts at Ephesus" refer: "to his experiences at the hands of an infuriated mob". He continues: "His stay there was long, and what he here mentions was no doubt previous to the occurrence recorded in Acts 19". There is certainly no reference to this in Acts 19. Notice his later reference to the lion: "I was delivered out of the mouth of the lion ..." (2 Timothy 4:17).

What purpose all this risk, danger and exposure to death if there is no resurrection? "What advantageth it me (profiteth me), if the dead rise not?" Compare Chapter 13 verse 3 and Chapter 14 verse 6. In the current passage, Paul refers to future reward. His adversity is all completely pointless if "the dead rise not", and if this is the case, then: "Let us eat and drink, for tomorrow we die", that is, live 'as if there is no tomorrow'.

The reverse must be stressed. The doctrine of resurrection should promote continuing faithfulness and loyalty in service and testimony.

iii) Righteous living is endangered, vv.33-34. "Be not deceived: evil communications corrupt good manners. Awake to righteousness, and sin not; for some have not the knowledge of God: I speak this to your shame" or "evil company doth corrupt good manners" (RV). We should notice *firstly*, the danger which threatened them, and *secondly*, the deliverance from that danger.

- The danger which threatened them, v.33. The words: "Be not deceived" explain the connection. Paul sounds a warning. If they allow themselves to be deceived by false teaching, in this case, false teaching about resurrection (v.12), they lay themselves open to evil conduct. They must, therefore, steer clear of those who propagate this error (the people to whom he refers in verse 12). The word "communications" ('*homilia*') is plural ('evil companies' or 'associations') and refers to "an association of people, those who are

of the same company" (W.E. Vine). In this case, "bad companionships ... the wrong kind of company" (Leon Morris). The word "manners" (*'ethe'*) means "a habit" or "custom" (W.E. Vine) and refers to behaviour or conduct. The words: "Evil communications corrupt good manners" are said to be a quotation from the Greek poet Menander. The word "corrupt" (*'phtheiro'*) means 'to destroy by corruption'.

- The deliverance from danger, v.34. "Awake to righteousness, and sin not; for some have not the knowledge of God: I speak this to your shame", or: "Awake up righteously, and sin not: for some have no knowledge of God: I speak this to move you to shame" (RV/JND). They are to have done with the deception of false teaching with its moral danger (v.33). The RV ("Awake up righteously") emphasises the need to return to soberness of mind after being under the influence of evil doctrine. The words: "for some (evidently the "some" of v.12) have no knowledge of God" refer, not just to lack of knowledge, but to culpable ignorance. W.E. Vine points out that Paul uses the word *'agnosia'*, meaning reprehensible ignorance, as opposed to *'agnoia'*, meaning: 'no knowledge'. The word *'agnosia'* is used in 1 Peter 2 verse 15: "the *ignorance* of foolish men". Paul adds: "I speak this to move you to shame" (RV). Compare Chapter 4 verse 14. The believers at Corinth prided themselves on their wisdom and intelligence, and yet they evidently allowed false teaching to go unchecked! It is almost a re-run of Chapter 5 verses 1-2.

Addendum

'BAPTISED FOR THE DEAD'

by W.B.C.Beggs

With reference to the question in the September issue of 'The Believer's Magazine' in connection with the expression 'Baptised for the dead' (1 Corinthians 15:29), we agree that this expression has been subjected to many various interpretations, but not one has gained for itself universal acceptance. Several of those explanations were indicated in the answer to the question, and accordingly it is unnecessary to repeat them here.

In his suggested interpretation S.H.R. simply states what most Bible students already recognise, viz 'The verse in question ... is introduced because of its significance, as being an ordinance setting forth death and resurrection,' and he is correct when he says, 'Why be baptised at all if there is no resurrection?' While what S.H.R. says is true, yet he has not given any clue to the real meaning of the expression **'Baptised for the dead'.**

A great deal has been written about the significance of the preposition 'for' (Greek *huper*). We are given to understand that this Greek preposition may be translated in a variety of ways, such as 'above', 'over', 'on behalf of', 'for the realisation of', 'about', 'concerning', etc., but its precise meaning depends greatly on the context in which it is found. This is particularly so in the verse before us, and we judge that here the preposition must bear the meaning 'as', or 'as being', so that the verse would read: 'What shall they do which are baptised as **being dead**?' If the dead rise not at all, why are they then baptised **as being dead?'**

This simply means that there can be no reason whatever to take the position of being dead people (in figure in baptism) unless resurrection follows (as indicated by the emergence from the baptismal waters).

In acknowledging that we have died with Christ we are baptised **as dead people**, and emerge as those who are **alive from the dead** This is true morally meantime, but it presents in figure the Christian teaching that just as we may die physically, so surely will there be a glorious resurrection.

1 CORINTHIANS

"It is sown...it is raised"

Read Chapter 15:35-49

As we have already noticed, this chapter may be divided into two major sections, each dealing with a question: *(1) the fact of resurrection* (vv.1-34): "How say some among you that there is no resurrection of the dead?" (v.12); *(2) the form of resurrection* (vv.35-58): "How are the dead raised up? and with what body do they come?" (v.35). Alternatively, the first section (vv.1-34) could be entitled 'The resurrection of *the Saviour*', and the second (vv.35-58) 'The resurrection of *the saints*'.

1) THE FACT OF RESURRECTION, vv.1-34

This part of the chapter, dealing with the first question above, falls into two sections as follows: *(A)* the facts established (vv.1-11); *(B)* the facts expounded (vv.12-34).

A) The facts established, vv.1-11

The facts of the Lord's resurrection are attested in three ways: by *(a)* the witness of Paul's preaching (vv.1-3a); *(b)* the witness of the prophetic Scriptures (vv.3b-4); *(c)* the witness of people at the time (vv.5-11).

B) The facts expounded, vv.12-34

In these verses, the resurrection of the Lord Jesus is discussed in three ways: *(a)* the resurrection and gospel preaching (vv.12-19): Paul discusses the implications for the gospel if there is no resurrection; *(b)* the resurrection and God's programme (vv.20-28): Paul discusses the indispensability of resurrection in future events; *(c)* the resurrection and Christian practice (vv.29-34): Paul discusses the impact of resurrection on Christian living.

This brings us to:

2) THE FORM OF RESURRECTION, vv.35-58

We may divide the second major section of the chapter as follows: *(A)* the manner of resurrection (vv.35-49); *(B)* the moment of resurrection (vv.50-58).

A) The manner of resurrection, vv.35-49

In these verses, Paul deals with the following: *(a)* objections to resurrection (v.35); *(b)* illustrations of resurrection (vv.36-41); *(c)* the superiority of the resurrection body (vv.42-44); *(d)* the permanence of the resurrection body (vv.45-49).

a) Objections to resurrection, v.35

" 'But' some man ('some one', JND) will say, How are the dead raised up? and with what body do they come?" Leon Morris puts it like this: "*But*" is the strong adversative *'alla'*. Far from conforming to the kind of conduct Paul has just outlined, someone (the word is indefinite) will offer an objection. Paul gives the objection either in quotation, or in the sort of words he would imagine the objector to use. *How are the dead raised up?* queries the mechanics of the process. *With what body do the come?* inquires as to the form they will have ... It was obvious to these Greek sceptics that a body quickly decomposes, and they thought to laugh the whole idea of resurrection out of court with their query as to the body. What kind of body would arise from a heap of decomposed rubbish?"

These objections arise from thoughtlessness. Hence, in replying, Paul says, "Thou fool! That which thou sowest is not quickened except it die" (v.36). It is foolishness to think that a body cannot live again because it dies. After all, a seed cannot live unless it dies! It should be said that in the New Testament, four different words are rendered "fool". In this case, the word is *'aphron'* meaning, amongst other definitions: "the lack of commonsense perception of the reality of things natural and spiritual" (*Hasting's Bible Dictionary*, quoted by W.E. Vine). "It is foolish, he says, because everywhere around you are examples of what is happening in resurrection" (Ray Stedman, supplied by Justin Waldron).

i) The first question: "*How* are the dead raised up?", is answered in vv.37-41:

they are raised by the power of God: as in nature so in resurrection: "God giveth it a body ... So also is the resurrection of the dead" (v.42).

ii) The second question: "And with *what* body do they come?" is answered in vv.42-49: the body is raised "in incorruption ... in glory ... in power". It is raised "a spiritual body". Believers will "bear the image of the heavenly". They will be like "the Lord from heaven!" (v.47, AV).

b) Illustrations of resurrection, vv.36-41

In this connection, Paul employs *(i)* botanical similitudes (vv.36-38); *(ii)* zoological similitudes (v.39); *(iii)* celestial and terrestrial similitudes (v.40); *(iv)* astronomical similitudes (v.41).

i) Botanical similitudes, vv.36-38

"Thou fool! That which thou sowest is not quickened, except it die" (v.36). In the realm of agriculture and horticulture, death is necessary and change is necessary. The Lord Jesus cited this principle: "Verily, verily, I say unto you, Except a corn of wheat fall into the ground and die, it abideth alone: but if it die, it bringeth forth much fruit" (John 12:24).

In these verses, Paul emphasises the *form* of resurrection. He emphasises the identity between the present condition of the body and its future state. "And that which thou sowest, thou sowest not the body that shall be, but bare grain, it may chance of wheat, or of some other grain" (v.37). In what way is a field of waving corn the same as the seed sown by the farmer? Certainly not in appearance! But each plant and the seed from which it sprang is the same organism! To change the metaphor dramatically: in what way is a mighty oak linked with an acorn? Certainly not in appearance! But it is the same individual organism!

It is significant that Paul does not say: 'God giveth it a *new* body', but: "God giveth it a body" (v.38). Believers often speak, gladly, of their 'new body'. Strictly speaking, believers will not have a 'new body': if this were the case, then the very word 'resurrection' would be inapplicable! The body that went into the tomb at Bethany was the body in which Lazarus emerged from the tomb. The body that went into Joseph's tomb was the body in which the Lord Jesus rose from the dead. In resurrection, the Lord's people will have the same bodies, but they will be changed bodies: new in form. See Philippians

3 verse 21: The Lord Jesus will "**change** our vile body ('body of humiliation', JND), that it may be fashioned like unto his glorious body". See also verse 51: "We shall all be **changed**".

The seed is not the final plant. The final plant bears no resemblance to the seed, but they are indissolubly linked! We do not sow a plant (!) but "bare grain" (v.37). What is deposited in the earth is very different from what springs from it. At the moment, we are "bare grain", and just as it is impossible to infer from looking at a seed what the ultimate plant will be like, so we cannot really begin to imagine what **we** will be like in resurrection! Nature teaches us that the final state of the body will not be like the first! **THE GRAVES OF CHRISTIANS ARE THE SEED BEDS OF RESURRECTION!**

Nature is rich in variety, not every plant looks the same, and resurrection will be rich in variety as well! "But God giveth it a body as it hath pleased him, and to every seed his own body" (v.38). There will be no uniformity in resurrection, other than that our bodies will be "fashioned like unto his glorious body".

The processes in nature operate because of divine power –"God giveth it a body as it hath pleased him" - and what happens in that sphere will happen in resurrection. God will exert His mighty power! This is the answer to the first question: "How are the dead raised up?" In a different connection, the Lord Jesus drew attention to the power of God in nature in Mark 4 verses 26-29: "So is the kingdom of God, as if a man should cast seed into the ground, and should sleep and rise, night and day, and the seed should spring and grow up, he knoweth not how. For the earth bringeth forth fruit of herself; first the blade, then the ear; after that, the full corn in the ear".

Paul now diverts from the figures of 'sowing' and "bare grain" (he returns to it in vv.42-44: "sown … sown … sown") in order to develop the words "to every seed his own body". So:

ii) Zoological similitudes, v.39

"All flesh is not the same flesh: but there is one kind of flesh of men, another flesh of beasts ('*ktenos*', referring to beasts of burden), and another of fishes, and another of birds." This emphasises God's ability to suit different forms of life to their environment.

Hence:

>*"Men" and "beasts"* are suited by God to the land: Genesis 1:24-25.

>*"Fishes"* are suited by God to the seas: Genesis 1:20-21.

>*"Birds"* are suited by God to the skies: Genesis 1:21.

The words: "All flesh is not the same flesh" deny the theory of evolution. "There is such a difference that a trained scientist can tell whether a single cell comes from a human, an animal, a bird, or a fish" (Ray Stedman, supplied by Justin Waldron). The lesson of this verse is that if God can suit different forms of life to their environment on earth, then He is perfectly able to suit resurrected believers for heaven!

iii) Celestial and terrestrial similitudes, v.40

Paul refers here to the distinctive glories of celestial and terrestrial bodies. "There are also celestial bodies, and bodies terrestrial: but the glory of the celestial is one, and the glory of the terrestrial is another." The "celestial bodies" could possibly refer to the planets: they are solid bodies: stars, we are told, are actually gas.

We have to ask: 'What, exactly, is Paul saying here?' He is not saying, evidently, that the "glory of the celestial" is superior to the "glory of the terrestrial". He is not making a comparison at all. He is saying, surely, that there is a variety in imparted glory.

Heavenly bodies differ from earthly bodies in glory, emphasising again that both have a glory suited to the realm in which they are located. The "glory of the terrestrial" evidently refers to the glories of our earthly *creation*, with its coming glory in the Millennium, of which it is said: "the whole earth is full of his glory" (Isaiah 6:3) and which in the Millennium will "be filled with the knowledge of the glory of the LORD, as the waters cover the sea" (Habakkuk 2:14). The "glory of the celestial" evidently refers to the radiant glory of *the heavens*, of which David said: "The heavens declare the glory of God: and the firmament sheweth his handiwork" (Psalm 19:1). It is a different kind of glory from the beauties of earth. In the next verse (v.41) he concentrates on the "glory of the terrestrial" in making the same point, namely, that it is not a question of degree, but of type.

It has been suggested that "celestial bodies" refers to **angels**, and "bodies terrestrial" refers to **men.** We do know, of course, that Adam was the crowning glory of God's creation. God made man "a little lower than the angels, and hast crowned him with glory and honour" (Psalm 8:5).

iv) Astronomical similitudes, v41

"There is one glory of the sun, and another glory of the moon, and another glory of the stars: for one star differeth from another star in glory." "Arcturus, Orion, and Pleiades" (Job 9:9) all differ. This emphasises the distinctive glories of the sun, moon and stars, but the stars each have their distinctive glories. As J.M. Davies observes: "The difference between the glory of the one and the glory of the other is not one of degree, but of kind".

Both verses emphasise that just as every plant does not look the same ("to every seed his own body", v.38), and the heavens and the earth do not look the same (v.40), and the heavenly bodies do not look the same (v.41), so in resurrection believers will all have glorified bodies, but retain individuality.

The question is sometimes asked: 'Will we recognise each other in heaven?' Undoubtedly! Isaiah exhorts us: "Lift up your eyes on high, and behold who hath created these things, that bringeth out their host by number: **he calleth them all by names** by the greatness of his might, for that he is strong in power; not one faileth" (Isaiah 40:25-26). See also Psalm 147 verse 4. The God who knows and names each star will maintain the individuality of each believer! Paul certainly expected to recognise the Thessalonian believers in heaven: "For what is our hope, or joy, or crown of rejoicing? Are not even ye in the presence of our Lord Jesus Christ at his coming? For ye are our glory and joy" (1 Thessalonians 2:19-20). God delights in variety. Changing the metaphor (considerably!) we are told that no two snowflakes are alike! This brings us to:

c) The superiority of the resurrection body, vv.42-44

As the heavenly bodies differ from the earthly bodies, and as each star differs from another star, so the resurrection body will differ from the present body. Paul now deals with the ways in which it will differ, and refers again to his first illustration: hence "sown … sown … sown". In each case, we must remember, Paul is referring to the believer's body - **not** to the Lord's body. His body was **not** "sown in corruption".

i) "It is sown in corruption; it is raised in incorruption", v.42

"It is sown in corruption." At present, the body tends to decay. It is subject to disease, death and entire dissolution. "Dust thou art, and unto dust thou shalt return" (Genesis 3:19). Of Lazarus it was said: "Lord, by this time he stinketh" (John 11:39). The Lord's body, for obvious reasons, did not "see corruption" (Acts 2:27, 31).

"It is raised in incorruption." There will be no decomposition with the resurrection body! It will be indestructible and imperishable. It will be free from all impurity, and incapable of decay. It is "raised in incorruptibility" (JND). The words: "raised in incorruption" imply that whilst it is perfect at the moment of resurrection, there is the possibility of future corruption, whereas "raised in incorruptibility" implies that it will never corrupt!

ii) "It is sown in dishonour; it is raised in glory", v.43

"It is sown in dishonour." This does not mean a dishonourable death! It means "shorn of its glory: despoiled of its short-lived attractiveness which it had in life". It is sown a marred body, having been exposed to sickness and disease. Paul describes the present state of our body as "the body of our humiliation" (Philippians 3:21, JND), not because, in itself, it is worthless and to be despised (*contra* 1 Thessalonians 5:23), but because it is subject to "sufferings and indignities and all the effects of sin" (W.E. Vine).

"It is raised in glory." This describes the new state of the body. It will not be subject to shame, sickness and suffering. It will be a "body of glory" (Philippians 3:21, JND). In the words of C.H.Spurgeon: "The righteous are put into their graves all weary and worn; but as such they will not rise. They go there with the furrowed brow, the hollowed cheek, the wrinkled skin; they shall wake up in beauty and glory". In the words of Leon Morris: "The resurrection body in Paul's view is a glorious body, just as far surpassing the present body as does the beautiful plant the seed from which it has sprung".

iii) "It is sown in weakness; it is raised in power", v.43

"It is sown in weakness." The noun form of the word "weakness" ('*astheneia*') is often rendered "infirmity" See, for example, Romans 8 verse 26. The body is "sown" weary, tired, and careworn. There is nothing more absolutely powerless than a corpse. The weakness which belonged to it in life is perfected in death.

"It is raised in power." It will be instinct with energy. Our resurrection body will be based on the prototype – the Lord's resurrection body. The word rendered "power" (*'dunamis'*) is elsewhere rendered "strength" or "might".

iv) "It is sown a natural body; it is raised a spiritual body", v.44

"It is sown a natural body." "The word *'psuchikos'*, 'natural', more literally signifies belonging to the soul (*'psuche'*) … In the present verse it might be translated 'soul-governed'" (W.E. Vine). In the words of Charles Hodge, it is: "a body adapted to our lower nature", or, turning now to Leon Morris, a body which "has to do with the present life in all its aspects. The natural body is the vehicle through which we express ourselves". It is "an organism by which, through the soul, the self, is expressed and developed, and enters into relation with others" (W.E. Vine).

"It is raised a spiritual body." While the "natural body" is "ill-adapted for life in the world to come" (Leon Morris), the "spiritual body" is "attuned to the spirit" (Leon Morris), that is, it will be adapted to "our higher nature" (Charles Hodge). It will be "the perfect vessel, not for physical, biological life, but for spiritual life … It does not mean a body composed of spirit, but a body which expresses spirit. Just as the present body expresses the life of the soul, so that body will express the life of the spirit" (J. Hunter, *What the Bible Teaches – 1 Corinthians*). At the moment, spiritually-minded believers, enjoying the blessings of salvation to the full, could well, at the same time, be weak, ill and incapacitated. Their bodies have not kept pace with their spiritual development. But in resurrection those same believers will have bodies adapted to existence in heaven, through which they will reflect spiritual life to the full. There will be no hindrance from our current limitations then! We should stress that the "spiritual body" will not be ethereal – devoid of substance. The Lord's resurrection body was certainly not ethereal!

The words: "There is a natural body, and there is a spiritual body" are better rendered: "If there is a natural body, there is also a spiritual [one]" (JND). See RV. Paul alludes here to his previous teaching that just as is in nature there is both a distinction and a connection between a seed and the resultant plant, so there is a connection between the natural body and the spiritual body.

If the present body is wonderful - what of the spiritual body? If the present life is wonderful - what about resurrection life? It is well worth pointing out that the believer's body is "sown" after, generally, a period of deterioration, but it will be raised, not by a gradual process, but instantaneously – "in a moment, in the twinkling of an eye, at the last trump" (v.52).

d) The permanence of the resurrection body, vv.45-49

In these verses we must notice *(i)* that the natural gives place to the spiritual (vv.45-46): in this connection, the Lord Jesus is described as "the last Adam"; *(ii)* that the earthly gives place to the heavenly (vv47-49): in this connection, the Lord Jesus is described as "the second man".

i) The natural give place to the spiritual, vv.45-46

"And so it is written (in Genesis 2:7), the first man Adam (once again, Paul did not believe in evolution: "the *first man* Adam") was made a living soul; the last Adam *was made* (omit *was made*: hence the italics) a quickening spirit. Howbeit that was not first which is spiritual, but that which is natural; and afterward that which is spiritual." As Leon Morris points out: "Characteristically, Paul appeals to Scripture to clinch his argument. This is not something he has thought up for himself". But if "Adam was the progenitor of the race, and his characteristics are stamped on the race" then "Christ is the last Adam, the progenitor of the race of spiritual men" (Leon Morris). There is no further order: only "the first man Adam" and the "last Adam".

"The first man Adam." He is the head of a fallen race. Since he is described as "the first man", there was no pre-Adamic race. He was "*made* a living soul". Life was communicated to him. He was "made a *living soul*". God breathed into Adam's body "the breath of life (lives)" and he became "a living soul". As W.E. Vine points out: "here the soul stands for the person, the entire man, the animate creature himself. He was formed for existence on earth with a body adapted for the present state of being".

"The last Adam." He is called "the last Adam", not 'the second Adam', because there will not be another after Him. As "the last Adam", He is final and conclusive. He is the head of a new race. There will be no further headship. "That the last Adam became 'a life-giving spirit' does not convey the least suggestion that He merely became a spirit. The word ('life-giving') is here mentioned as additional to what is conveyed in the description of

Him as the last Adam; it emphasises that He is a Being above the natural, Who being Himself 'the Life', has the power of imparting it, a power lacking in the first Adam" (W.E. Vine).

The words: "Howbeit that was not first which is spiritual, but that which is natural; and afterward that which is spiritual" refer to: "a principle relating to the development of human life; it begins with the merely natural and subsequently receives the spiritual. The principle is not to be illustrated, save in a secondary way, by the order of Cain and Abel, Ishmael and Isaac, Esau and Jacob; for the first in each case was more evil than what the word 'natural' signifies" (W.E. Vine). These words, rather, reflect the principle that "he taketh away the first, that he may establish the second" (Hebrews 10: 9).

ii) The earthly gives place to the heavenly, vv.47-49

"The first man is of the earth, earthy: the second man is the Lord from heaven. As is the earthy such are they also that are earthy: and as is the heavenly, such are they also that are heavenly. And as we have borne the image of the earthy we shall also bear the image of the heavenly." It has been suggested that in speaking of the Lord Jesus as "the last Adam", emphasis is placed on His ability to **give** of life ("the first man Adam was made a living soul; the last Adam … a quickening spirit"), whereas "the second man" emphasis is placed on the **source** of that life ("the second man is of heaven").

"The first man." There is no need to repeat "the first man **Adam"** (v.45). Paul refers to Adam, "the first man" to emphasise his origin. He was "of the earth, earthy" (v.47) or "out of [the] earth, made of dust" (JND). The expression: "of the earth, earthy" certainly refers to the fact that Adam was formed from the dust of the ground, but it means more than that: he was "earthy" in character as well as in origin. This, according to W.E. Vine, is the reason why the article before "earth" and "heaven" is omitted. This lays emphasis "on the nature and condition of the two who are mentioned".

"The second man." This emphasises the origin of the "last Adam". He is "out of heaven" (JND). In the words of W.E. Vine: "He is essentially, characteristically and perpetually heavenly". He is the head of a new order - the heavenly order. The expression: "the second man", together with the expression: "the first man", emphasises that there are only 'two men'. It seems more appropriate to read: "the second man", rather than: 'the last man'. As John Heading points out: "There are … thus only two types of life;

one, now fallen", originating in a man on earth, "and the other", originating in a man from heaven, "eternal in Christ".

It should be noted that the name "the Lord" ("the second man is the Lord from heaven") is omitted in the RV ("the second man is of heaven") and by JND ("the second man, out of heaven).

At present, as descended from Adam, we bear (from '*phoreo*', to bear continually) "the image of the earthy" (v.49). But just as the Lord Jesus "dieth no more; death hath no more dominion over him" (Romans 6:9), so we also will, in resurrection, "bear (continually) the image of the heavenly" (v.49). Once we were in "the first man Adam" who was "of the earth", but now we are in "the last Adam" who is "from heaven". John puts it like this: "It doth not yet appear what we shall be (as things are at present, it is impossible to conceive what God has in mind for His people): but we know that, when he shall appear, we **shall be like him**; for we shall see him as he is" (1 John 3:2).

1 CORINTHIANS

"In a moment, in the twinkling of an eye"

Read Chapter 15:50-58

As we have already noticed in past studies, this chapter may be divided into two major sections, each dealing with a question: *(1) the fact of resurrection* (vv.1-34): "How say some among you that there is no resurrection of the dead?" (v.12); *(2) the form of resurrection* (vv.35-58): "How are the dead raised up? And with what body do they come?" (v.35). Alternatively, the first section (vv.1-34) could be entitled 'The resurrection of *the Saviour*', and the second (vv.35-58) 'The resurrection of *the saints*'.

1) THE FACT OF RESURRECTION, vv.1-34

This section of the chapter, dealing with the first question above, may be divided as follows: *(A)* the facts established (vv.1-11); *(B)* the facts expounded (vv.12-34).

2) THE FORM OF RESURRECTION, vv.35-58

We may divide this part of the chapter as follows: *(A)* the manner of resurrection (vv.35-49); *(B)* the moment of resurrection (vv.50-58).

A) The manner of resurrection, vv.35-49

In this section, Paul deals with the following: *(a)* objections to resurrection (v.35); *(b)* illustrations of resurrection (vv.36-41); *(c)* the superiority of the resurrection body (vv.42-44); *(d)* the permanence of the resurrection body (vv.45-49). This brings us to:

B) The moment of resurrection, vv.50-58

In these verses, Paul deals with the resurrection of believers, rather than with the rapture of believers. He emphasises the change in the bodies of the saints, rather than the change in their location. In 1 Thessalonians 4 verses 13-18, by contrast, he deals with the rapture of believers, rather than their resurrection, and emphasises the change in location rather than the change in their bodies. We should note that Paul deals here with *two* simultaneous events: the *resurrection of sleeping saints*, and the *change in living saints*. However, for ease of expression, we will use the word "change" in our headings to cover both events.

With this in mind, these verses may be divided as follows: *(a)* disqualification (v.50); *(b)* transformation (vv.51-53); *(c)* exultation (vv.54-57); *(d)* exhortation (v.58).

a) Disqualification, v.50

"Now this I say, brethren, that flesh and blood *cannot inherit* the kingdom of God; neither doth corruption inherit incorruption." Something has got to happen. We cannot go to heaven in our bodies in their present form! As Leon Morris points out: "'Flesh and blood' is a not uncommon way of referring to life here and now (for example, Galatians 1:16; Hebrews 2:14)". Bodies suited to this world can never, in their present form, pass into the realm of heaven. In the words of W.E. Vine: "Flesh and blood together constitute a perishable nature, and nothing perishable can enter into possession of an imperishable Kingdom (see 1 Peter 1:4)". Paul refers to two classes of believer:

i) The living. "Flesh and blood cannot inherit the kingdom of God." He refers here to those that are "alive, and remain unto the coming of the Lord" (1 Thessalonians 4: 15, 17). These are the believers to whom the Lord Jesus referred in saying: "whosoever *liveth* and believeth in me shall never die" (John 11: 26).

ii) The sleeping. "Neither doth corruption inherit incorruption ('*aphtharsia*')." He refers here to believers "which sleep in Jesus" (1 Thessalonians 4:14). The Lord Jesus referred to them in saying: 'he that believes in me, *though he have died*, shall live' (John 11:25, JND).

325

Paul makes the same distinction in verses 52-54: "the **dead** shall be raised incorruptible, and **we** shall be changed". He continues, "for this **corruptible** (sleeping saints) must put on incorruption, and this **mortal** (living saints) must put on immortality".

The expression: "kingdom of God" is a vast term. Here it evidently refers to the heavenly sphere. This is clear from the context: "And as we have borne the image of the earthy, we shall also bear the image of the **heavenly.** Now this I say, brethren, that flesh and blood cannot inherit the **kingdom of God**" (vv.49-50). See 2 Timothy 4 verse 18: "And the Lord shall deliver me from every evil work, and will preserve me unto his **heavenly kingdom** ..." That is, a kingdom administered from heaven. We must distinguish between the kingdom of God in its heavenly aspect ("flesh and blood cannot inherit the kingdom of God") and the kingdom of God in its earthly aspect. Men of "flesh and blood" will inherit the Millennial kingdom. J.M. Davies states: "Here, the 'kingdom of God' is to be interpreted as referring to the final state of glory mentioned in verses 24 and 28".

The 'heavenly inheritance' and "incorruption" are linked in 1 Peter 1 verses 3-4: we have been "begotten ... again unto a lively hope by the resurrection of Jesus Christ from the dead, to an inheritance incorruptible ('*aphthartos*'), and undefiled, and that fadeth not away, reserved **in heaven** for you".

b) Transformation, vv.51-53

"Behold, I shew you a mystery; We shall not all sleep, but we shall all be **changed**, in a moment, in the twinkling of an eye, at the last trump: for the trumpet shall sound, and the dead shall be raised incorruptible, and we shall be changed. For this corruptible must put on incorruption, and this mortal must put on immortality."

These verses are introduced with the words: "Behold, I shew you a mystery ..." As to the word "mystery" generally, explanations are given, for example, in Ephesians 3 verses 3-5: "the mystery ... which in other ages was **not made known** unto the sons of men, as it is **now** revealed unto his holy apostles and prophets by the Spirit ..."; Matthew 13 verse 35: "I will open my mouth in parables; I will utter things which have been kept secret from the foundation of the world". How thankful we are to God for divine revelation! In the Scriptures, a "mystery" is not something that cannot be understood, but something revealed that was previously unrevealed! "Men could never have worked out for themselves what will happen at the second coming, but God has revealed it" (Leon Morris).

The words here: "Behold, I shew you a mystery" do not imply that *resurrection* was something previously unrevealed – the Old Testament speaks about the subject – but that resurrection with a changed and glorified body was unrevealed.

We must now notice *(i)* the certainty of the change (v.51); *(ii)* the suddenness of the change (v.52); *(iii)* the signal for the change (v.52); *(iv)* the nature of the change (vv.52-53).

i) The certainty of the change, v.51. "We shall not all sleep, but we **shall** all be changed." Notice that Paul does not say: 'We shall not all die', but: "We shall not all **sleep**". The very word "sleep" stresses that in death, people do not cease to exist. See, for example, the position of the rich man and Lazarus after their death (Luke 16:19-31); the position of the thief on the cross after death ("Today shalt thou be with me in paradise", Luke 23:43); the souls under the altar (Revelation 6:9-11). The word "sleep" occurs eighteen times in the New Testament, with four references to ordinary sleep and fourteen to physical death. Sleep implies a future awakening, but it must be stressed that in this case it is **physical** awakening. See Daniel 12 verse 2.

We must also notice that death ("sleep") is not inevitable". "We shall **not all sleep**, but we shall **all be changed**." See, again, 1 Thessalonians 4 verse 15: "We which are alive and remain unto the coming of the Lord". There will be no omissions: there is no thought of partial rapture: "We shall **all** be changed". In 1 Thessalonians 4, Paul addresses particularly the position of those who die before the Lord's coming. Here he addresses the position of those who are alive at the Lord's coming. Having said that "flesh and blood cannot inherit the kingdom of God", how then can the living enter that kingdom? The answer is that "we shall all be changed!"

Men "changed the glory of the uncorruptible God into an image made like to corruptible man" (Romans 1:23), but God is going to change us into likeness to Christ!

ii) The suddenness of the change, v.52. It will not be a long drawn-out affair (Leon Morris). It will be "in a moment, in the twinkling of an eye". There will be no interval once the "last trump" is sounded: the change will be instantaneous. It will be "in a moment". The Greek word is *'atomos'* meaning, literally: 'not cut' or 'that which cannot be cut, or divided'. It signifies the shortest possible moment of time. It will be "in the twinkling (*'rhipe'*) of an eye". In the Classics, the word is used (we are told) in connection with 'the rush of a storm; the flapping of wings; the buzz of a gnat; the quivering of harp strings; the twinkling of the stars'. The idea is rapidity of movement. Leon Morris tells us that it is: "the time it takes to cast a glance, or perhaps to flutter an eyelid".

iii) The signal for the change, v.52. "In a moment, in the twinkling of an eye, at **the last trump**: for the **trumpet shall sound**." See also 1 Thessalonians 4 verse 16: "For the Lord himself shall descend from heaven with a shout, with the voice of the archangel, and with the **trump** of God ..." This is the last sound that believers who are "alive and remain" will hear on earth!

This should not be confused with Revelation 11 verse 15 where the "seventh angel sounded; and there were great voices in heaven, saying, The kingdoms of this world are become the kingdoms of our Lord, and of his Christ; and he shall reign for ever and ever". This particular trumpet is the last in a series, and is followed by divine judgment. See Revelation 11 verses 17-19.

In the Old Testament, silver trumpets (Numbers 10) were blown for four reasons, and while they have no immediate connection with "the last trump", their use certainly reminds us of four things that will happen when the Lord comes. They were blown to gather the people (vv.3-4); they were blown to initiate movement (vv.5-6); they were blown to signal victory (v.9); they were blown at times of rejoicing (v.10). Now apply all that to "the last trump!"

iv) The nature of the change, vv.52-53. "The dead shall be raised incorruptible, and we shall be changed. For this corruptible must put on incorruption, and this mortal must put on immortality." We must notice, again, the two classes of believer here:

- *"The dead."* "The dead shall be raised incorruptible." As we know, the word "incorruptible" (*'aphthartos'*) means 'not liable to decay'.

- *"We."* "We shall be changed" (*'allasso'*, meaning: 'to make other than it is', or 'to transform'). Compare Philippians 3 verses 20-21: "For our conversation is in heaven; from whence also we look for the Saviour, the Lord Jesus Christ; who shall change (*'metaschematizo'* meaning 'to fashion anew' - stressing the change outwardly) our vile body ('body of humiliation') that it may be fashioned (*'summorphos'*, perhaps stressing the change inwardly, in nature, in essence) like unto his glorious body, according to the working of his mighty power whereby he is able even to subdue all things unto himself".

Paul continues: "For this corruptible *must* put on incorruption (*'aphtharsia'*), and this mortal *must* put on immortality (*'athanasia'*)" (v.53). We must notice, yet again, the two classes of believer here:

- *Those who have died*: "this corruptible must put on incorruption (as above)". This refers, as noted, to believers who have died over the hundreds of years, whose bodies have crumbled to dust. They will be raised with 'incorruptibility' (JND), not ever liable to corruption.

- *Those who are alive*: "this mortal must put on immortality (as above)". This refers to believers alive at the moment of the Lord's return. Instead of mortality (meaning 'liable to death'), they will put on immortality (meaning 'deathlessness'). W.E. Vine points out that *'athanasia'* ("immortality") actually means more than 'deathlessness': it suggests the quality of life enjoyed: see 2 Corinthians. 5 verse 4 where we are told that for the believer, what is mortal will be "swallowed up of life".

The word "must" "predicates the necessity of the change for conditions essential to the Kingdom of God. The verb rendered 'put on' (metaphorical of the putting on of a garment) is in the aorist tense, signifying the momentary character of the event" (W.E. Vine).

It is helpful to link the above with John 11 verses 25-26 thus: "I am the resurrection, and the life: he that believeth in me, though he were dead ('though he have died', JND), yet shall he live (*'this corruption must put on incorruptibility'*): and whosoever liveth and believeth in me shall never die (*'this mortal must put on immortality'*)".

The words: "this mortal must put on immortality" point us to other relevant passages. See, for example, Romans 8 verse 11: "He that raised up Christ from the dead shall also quicken your *mortal* bodies by his Spirit that dwelleth in you"; 2 Corinthians 5 verse 4: "For we that are in this tabernacle do groan, being burdened: not for that we would be unclothed, but clothed upon, that *mortality* might be swallowed up of life". John expresses the object of it all in saying: "It doth not yet appear what we shall be, but we know that, when he shall appear, we shall be *like him* ..." (1 John 3:2). We should note that in 2 Timothy 1 verse 10, the word *'apharsia'* is translated 'immortality' (AV): it should read 'incorruptibility').

c) The exultation, vv.54-57

"Victory!" We should notice the three occurrences of the word here: "Death is swallowed up in victory" (v.54); "O grave, where is thy victory?" (v.55); "But thanks be to God, which giveth us the victory" (v.57). We must notice *(i)* the time of the victory (v.54); *(ii)* the finality of victory (vv.55); *(iii)* the thanksgiving for the victory (vv.56-7).

i) The time of the victory, v.54. "So *when* this corruptible shall have put on incorruption, and this mortal shall have put on immortality, *then* shall be brought to pass the saying that is written, Death is swallowed up in victory." This cites Isaiah 25 verse 8: "He will swallow up death in victory; and the Lord God will wipe away tears from off all faces ..." The victory here is the complete removal of the physical effects of sin. The word "then" (*'tote'*) signifies 'immediately'. It is not *'eita',* meaning: 'after an interval'.

ii) The finality of the victory, v.55. "O death, where is thy sting? O grave (most manuscripts have 'death' here: the *texus receptus* has *'hades'*: see JND margin), where is thy victory?" or: "O death, where is thy sting? O death, where is thy victory?" (RV/JND).

While Paul is speaking about the abolition of death at the end of time, it could be said that for the believer: "The last enemy that shall be destroyed is death". This cites Hosea 13 verse 14: "I will ransom them from the power of the grave; I will redeem them from death. O death, I will be thy plagues; O grave, I will be thy destruction. Repentance shall be hid from mine eyes". J.M. Davies suggests that the words: "O death, where is thy sting" may be the triumphant shout of those who will be living, whereas: "O grave (following the AV), where is thy victory?" may refer to sleeping saints, and that both would join in the shout: "Death is swallowed up in victory".

iii) The thanksgiving for the victory, vv.56-57. "The sting of death is sin; and the strength of sin is the law. But thanks be unto God, which giveth us the victory through our Lord Jesus Christ."

The words: "The sting of death is sin; and the strength of sin is the law" remind us, firstly:

- that sin has given death its terror. Were it not for sin, death would hold no terror. The word translated "sting" (*'kentron'*) is said to refer primarily to "the sting of bees, serpents, and the like". Death is a "malignant adversary" (Leon Morris). Where sin has been pardoned, there is no sting. Then it reminds us, secondly:

- that the law has given sin its power. As Leon Morris helpfully observes: "The law, though it is divine in origin, and Paul can speak of the commandment as 'holy, and just, and good' (Romans 7:12), is quite unable to bring men to a state of salvation. Indeed, by setting before men the standard that they ought to reach and never do, it becomes sin's stronghold. It makes sinners of us all. It condemns us all".

For the believer: "the sting (sin) has been removed, and that which gives it strength, the law, has been fully satisfied in the death of Christ. In His death its penalty has been exacted (Romans 10:4) and its curse removed (Galatians 3:13)" (J.M. Davies). For the believer, death is simply passing out of this life into the immediate presence of the Lord ((Philippians 1:21, 23). No wonder Paul says: "But thanks be unto God, which giveth us the victory through our Lord Jesus Christ". VE Day was a great occasion, and so was VJ Day, but the final victory over sin and death will be unparalleled!

While verses 55-57 will be completely fulfilled in the future, the present tense – "*giveth* us the victory" - suggests present triumph. In view of the coming triumph over sin and death, we may stand around a believer's grave and say *now*: "O death, where is thy sting? O grave, where is thy victory?" because, for the believer, death has no sting. Christ has borne our sin. He has met the claims of the law of which it is said: "Cursed is every one that continueth not in all things which are written in the book of the law to do them" (Galatians 3:10). The victory is secured "through our Lord Jesus Christ" because He "died for our sins ... and that he was buried, and that he rose again the third day ..." (vv.3-4).

d) Exhortation, v.58

"Therefore, my beloved brethren, be ye stedfast, unmoveable, always abounding in the work of the Lord, forasmuch as ye know that your labour is not in vain in the Lord." The word "therefore" introduces the practical consequences of all that Paul has taught in connection with resurrection. Why such confidence here? The chapter's teaching gives the complete answer! We must notice, in the words of Justin Waldron, *(i)* what we should be; *(ii)* what we should do; *(iii)* what we should know.

i) What we should be

"Therefore, my beloved brethren, be ye *stedfast, unmoveable* …" Compare Haggai 2 verse 4: "Yet (in spite of their current difficulties) now be strong, O Zerubbabel, saith the LORD, and be strong, O Joshua son of Jehozadak, the high priest; and be strong all ye people of the land, saith the LORD, and work: for I am with you saith the LORD of hosts".

The word "stedfast" (*'hedraios'*) is used in Colossians 1 verses 23: "continue in the faith grounded and settled (*'hedraios'*) …" The word "unmoveable" (*'ametakinetos'*) is matched in Colossians 1 verse 23 by the words: "be not moved away (*'metakineo'*)". It means: 'not turning aside'. Do notice that Paul says: "my *beloved* brethren". His ministry, even though it involved some corrective teaching (see, for example, vv.35-36), flowed out of his love for the believers at Corinth. This always gives power and appeal to teaching.

ii) What we should do

We must be "always abounding in the work of the Lord". They (and us) were to be "stedfast … unmoveable" in doctrine, and "always abounding in the work of the Lord" evangelically. A good balance! Rather like the good balance in the make-up of Deborah and Lapidoth (Judges 4:4), if their names are anything to go by! Deborah (meaning 'like a bee') was married to Lapidoth (meaning 'torch'): so activity was married to light. It must have been a well-balanced marriage! We all need that kind of *spiritual* balance. Some of us, and some assemblies, have plenty of activity, but not much light. And some of us, and some assemblies, have plenty of light, but not much activity! Think about it!

iii) What we should know

"Forasmuch as ye know (*'oida'*: 'ye are fully assured', W.E. Vine) that your labour (*'kopos'*: 'toil': 'working to the point of exhaustion) is not in vain in the

Lord." Do **we** have the same assurance? "The word 'vain' (*'kenos'*) means 'empty', and has special reference to quality (see vv.10, 14)" (W.E. Vine).

"In the Lord" denotes: "in the sphere and under the direction of His authority and control. Only thus can any service be of true quality and fruitfulness" (W.E. Vine). We do need to take care in ensuring that our labour is "in the Lord".

It is not without significance that Chapter 16 commences with reference to: "the first day of the week" (v.2). The "first day of the week" is resurrection day! All four Gospel writers refer to: "the first day of the week!" It was a marvellous day: "Then the same day at evening, being the first day of the week ... came Jesus and stood in the midst, and saith unto them, Peace be unto you ... Then were the disciples glad when they saw the Lord" (John 20:19-20).

1 CORINTHIANS

"Maran-atha"

Read Chapter 16:1-24

The final chapter of this epistle may be divided as follows. *(1) Collection for the saints* (vv.1-4): "Now concerning the *collection* for the saints, as I have given order to the churches of Galatia, even so do ye" (v.1); *(2) Coming to the saints* (vv.5-12): "Now I will *come* unto you" (v.5); "Now if Timotheus *come*" (v.10); "touching our brother Apollos, I greatly desired him to *come* unto you" (v.12); *(3) Commands to the saints* (vv.13-14): "Watch ye, stand fast in the faith, quit you like men, be strong. Let all your things be done with charity"; *(4) Concern for the saints* (vv.15-18): "they have addicted themselves to the *ministry of the saints*" (v.15): "that which was lacking on your part *they have supplied*. For they have *refreshed my spirit and yours*" (vv.17-18); *(5) Compliments to the saints* (vv.19-24): "The churches of Asia *salute* you. Aquila and Priscilla *salute* you much in the Lord ... All the brethren *greet* you. *Greet* one another with an holy kiss. The *salutation* of me Paul with mine own hand" (vv.19, 20, 21).

1) COLLECTION FOR THE SAINTS, vv.1-4

This section of the chapter commences with the words: "Now *concerning* the collection for the saints", and it is generally thought that this indicates a subject about which the assembly at Corinth had sought Paul's advice. See also previous references: "Now *concerning* the things whereof ye wrote unto me: It is good for a man not to touch a woman" (Chapter 7:1); "Now *concerning* virgins" (Chapter 7:25); "Now as *touching* (JND *'concerning')* things offered unto idols" (Chapter 8:1); "Now *concerning* spiritual gifts" (Chapter 12:1). We now learn that a *gifted church* should be a *giving church.*

We should notice that the words "collection" and "gatherings" (vv.1, 2) translate the same Greek word *('logia')*. In the words of J. Hunter: "Here Paul brings before the Corinthians the example of the churches of Galatia, and in 2 Corinthians 8 verses 1-4 the example of the Macedonians: in 2 Corinthians 9 verse 2 he sets before the Macedonians the example of the Corinthians". There is evidently no other reference in the New Testament to Paul's "order *('diatasso')* to the churches of Galatia". The word *'diatasso'* is elsewhere translated 'command' or 'appoint'.

Paul refers to this particular collection in Romans 15 verses 25-26: "But now I go unto Jerusalem to minister unto the saints. For it hath pleased them of Macedonia and Achaia to make a certain contribution for the poor saints which are at Jerusalem." See also 2 Corinthians 8-9. Paul's guidance in connection with help for "the poor saints … at Jerusalem reflects his earlier teaching: "If we have sown unto you spiritual things, is it a great thing if we shall reap your carnal things?" (1 Corinthians 9:11).

It is well-worth noting that while Paul and the other apostles made known the needs of distressed saints, they did not advertise their personal needs. We should also notice that in 1 Corinthians 11 verse 22, Paul refers to "them that have not", emphasising the importance of attending to the needs of local believers. It has been said, in a different connection, that "the light that shines the furthest shines the brightest nearer home".

While this was evidently a special collection, we must notice certain abiding principles.

i) It was to be **regular:** "upon the first day of the week" (v.2). That is the day on which we remember the giving God. God gave His Son. The Lord Jesus gave Himself. The Holy Spirit gives gifts.

ii) It was to be **personal**. There was to be a sense of personal responsibility. It was to be shared by all: "**every one** of you" (v.2).

iii) It was to be **prepared:** "let every one of you **lay by him in store**" (v.2), or: "let each one of you put by at home" (JND). Compare 2 Corinthians 9 verse 7: "every man according as he purposeth in his heart". The expression: "lay by him" *('thesaurizo')* occurs in Matthew 6 verses 19-20 ("Lay not up for yourselves treasures upon earth … but lay up for yourselves treasures in heaven"); James 5 verse 3 ("Ye have heaped treasure together for the last days").

iv) It was to be **proportionate**: "As God hath prospered him" (v.2) or: "As he may prosper" (RV). The "poor widow" exceeded this: she "cast in **all** that she had" (Mark 12:41-44). See also Luke 21 verses 1-4.

The reason follows: "that there be no gatherings when I come" (v.2). In the words of A.G. Clarke: "It is from such a store that gifts are made to various objects as exercised by the Spirit of God, and thus the embarrassment of a sudden call is avoided, 2 Corinthians 9 verse 5". Or: "The systematic laying up in store would ensure that the assembly was not suddenly faced with an appeal for help when the apostle arrived" (J. Hunter). In addition to the above, we should notice:

v) It was to be **properly supervised**: "And when I come, whomsoever ye shall approve by your letters, them will I send to bring your liberality ('bounty', JND) unto Jerusalem. And if it be meet that I go also, they shall go with me." It is important to notice that the assembly which provided the funds was to select its representatives. Not one representative either, but a plurality. We must listen again to A.G. Clarke: "This wise arrangement (he refers to Acts 6:3-6; 1 Corinthians 16:1-4; 2 Corinthians 8:18-21; and 9:3-5) leaves no room for unkind suspicions, increases the confidence of the saints, and spreads the burden of responsibility". Hence the necessity, in Paul's own words, to provide "honest things, not only in the sight of the Lord, but also in the sight of men" (2 Corinthians 8:21). It would be disastrous if the assembly treasurer turned out to be someone like Judas who was "a thief, and had the bag, and bare what was put therein" (John 12:6). Sadly, this is not unknown.

2) COMING TO THE SAINTS, vv.5-12

This section of the chapter refers *(a)* to the coming of **Paul** to Corinth (vv.5-9); *(b)* to the possibility of **Timothy** coming to Corinth (vv.10-11); *(c)* to the desire of Paul for **Apollos** to come to Corinth (v.12).

a) Paul's coming to Corinth, vv.5-9

Paul now discusses his visit to Corinth in general terms. We should notice the following:

i) The direction from which he would come to Corinth, v.5. "Now I will come unto you, when I shall pass through Macedonia: for I do pass through Macedonia" or: "But I will come to you **when I shall have gone through**

Macedonia; for I do go through Macedonia" (JND). Paul's detractors gladly seized on this statement as evidence of his capricious mind. You can almost hear them talking: 'He can't be trusted: one moment he says that he's coming directly from Ephesus to Corinth, thence to Macedonia and return before setting out for Judaea (see 2 Corinthians 1:15-16), now he tells us that he's coming via Macedonia. You just don't know where you are with him". 2 Corinthians 1 verse 15 - 2: 1 is now compulsory reading.

ii) The desire to come to Corinth, vv.6-7. "And it may be that I will abide, yea, and winter *with you*, that ye may bring me on my journey whithersoever I go. For I will not see you now by the way; but I trust to tarry a while *with you*, if the Lord permit." So Paul visualised the possibility of '*abiding*' with them (v.6). He did not wish to see them "*by the way*", that is, while on a journey, but to "*tarry a while*" (v.7). The expression (twice), "with you" (vv.6, 7) conveys rather more than simply presence. W.E. Vine points out that the preposition '*pros*' ("with"), expresses more than just presence with them (which would be expressed by '*sun*' or '*meta*'): it implies, rather, special interest in them, and intimate intercourse (compare '*pros*' in John 1 verse 1: "*with* God", and 1 John 1 verse 2: "that eternal life, which was *with* the Father"). W.E. Vine continues: "In verses 6 & 7 there is emphasis on 'you', expressing his affectionate interest in them". So while Paul intended to do at least two things when visiting Corinth - "the rest will I set in order *when I come*" (Chapter 11:34), and "*when I come*, whomsoever ye shall approve" (Chapter 16:3) - his visit was motivated by far more than a sense of duty. He loved the saints at Corinth. The Second Epistle lays bare his heart. See Chapters 2:3; 2:4; 2:9; 7:12. All this reminds us that *the Lord's people should always come together out of mutual love and affection.*

The expression: "bring me on my journey", together with other similar expressions in the New Testament, indicates the fellowship and support given to servants of God engaged in itinerant ministry. We should also notice such expressions as: "and it may be ... whithersoever I go ... if the Lord permit". Paul was conscious that his movements were in the Lord's hands.

iii) The delay in coming to Corinth, vv.8-9. "But I will tarry at Ephesus until Pentecost. For a great door and effectual is opened unto me, and there are many adversaries." As J. Hunter observes: "The word "*door*" indicates opportunities to enter with the gospel; "*great*" signifies that they were quite exceptional and extensive opportunities; "*effectual*" indicates that Paul was using them to the full and was achieving results". It is not therefore surprising to read: "and there are many adversaries". The New Translation suggests that this was quite normal: "For a great door is opened unto me and an effectual [one], and [the] adversaries many" (JND). Paul is here referring to his visit to Ephesus in Acts 19.

The reference here to "Pentecost" is to the feast taking place **before** he visited Corinth, and should not be confused with the reference in Acts 20 verse 16, which was **after** visiting Corinth.

Current blessing and encouragement did not make him unmindful of the assembly at Corinth, which, to us, may be rather surprising in view of its condition!

b) Timothy's coming to Corinth, vv.10-11

"Now if Timotheus **come**, see that he may be with you without fear: for he worketh the work of the Lord, as I do. Let no man therefore despise him: but conduct him forth ('set him forward on his journey') in peace, that he may come unto me: for I look for him with the brethren." Compare Chapter 4 verse 17: "For this cause have I **sent unto you Timotheus**, who is my beloved son, and faithful in the Lord, who shall bring you into remembrance of my ways which be in Christ, as I teach every where in every church". (Acts 19 verse 22 *could* refer to this journey, although only Macedonia is mentioned.) The words: "my ways which be in Christ" refer, not so much to Paul's personal life, but to his teaching. The following verse (1 Corinthians 4:18) explains Paul's cautionary remarks in our current passage: "Now some are *puffed up*, as though I would not come to you".

J. Hunter summarises this nicely: "He is concerned about the manner of Timothy's reception, for there were those in Corinth who were proud and arrogant (Chapter 4:18) and would probably make it difficult for him. Paul wants his visit to be peaceful, and assures them that Timothy is doing the work of the Lord as himself, and on that ground should command respect". Compare Philippians 2 verses 19-22: "I have no man likeminded, who will naturally care for your state ..."

It has been suggested that Paul had in mind Timothy's comparative youth (see 1 Timothy 4:12) in saying: "Let no man therefore despise him". Although the words are different, this may well be the case. Here, the word 'exoutheneo' ("depise". AV) means: "to make of no account, to regard as nothing, to despise utterly, to treat with contempt" (W.E. Vine). In 1 Timothy 4 verse 12, the word is *'kataphroneo'* ("despise", AV), meaning: 'to think slightly of, to despise': literally: "to think down upon or against anyone" (W.E. Vine). Timothy evidently arrived safely, see 2 Corinthians 1 verse 1.

If the visit of Paul emphasises that the Lord's people should come together out of mutual love and affection, then the visit of Timothy indicates that they should also come together **with mutual regard and esteem.** They should value each other. Compare Numbers 11 verses 26-30. 1 Corinthians 12 verse 25 was to be practised: "the members should have the same care one for another".

c) Apollos' coming to Corinth, v.12

"As touching our brother Apollos, I greatly desired him to **come** unto you with the brethren: but his will was not at all to **come** at this time; but he will **come** when he shall have convenient time." Apollos' reason for not visiting Corinth is clear: not: 'he would like to come, but ...", rather: "his **will** was not at all to come" at that time. Notice, in passing, that Paul did not *command* Apollos to "come unto you". He did not control the movements of other servants of the Lord.

We should also notice that there was no rivalry amongst the Lord's servants. Although "his will was not at all to come at this time" (possibly because of the party spirit in the assembly, see Chapter 1 verse 12), the fact that Paul "greatly desired him to come" demonstrates that there was no rivalry amongst these servants of God. Compare 1 Corinthians 3 verse 8: "Now he that planteth (Paul) and he that watereth (Apollos) are one": that is, one in aim and objective. There was evidently no thought in Paul's mind that Apollos should not go, lest he should steal a march on him! This verse would have been a blow to those who cried: "I am of Paul". Their champion is urging his rival to come to Corinth! Paul and Apollos would have both endorsed Psalm 133 verse 1: "Behold, how good and how pleasant it is for brethren to dwell together in unity".

The word "convenient" ("he will come when he shall have *convenient* time") means: 'a favourable and fitting time' or: "when he shall have opportunity" (RV). We should notice that when Apollos made an earlier visit to Corinth, his attitude was quite different: "And when he (Apollos) was *disposed* to pass into Achaia, the brethren wrote ..." (Acts 18:27). The word "disposed" means: "to wish, to purpose, to will deliberately" (W.E. Vine).

So if the visit of Paul reminds us that when saints come together, they do so out of mutual love and affection, and the visit of Timothy reminds us that when saints come together, they do so with mutual respect and esteem, then the visit of Apollos reminds us that when saints come together, they do so, **not as rivals, but in happy fellowship with each other.** We should notice that the chapter describes two further 'comings': *(i)* the coming of Stephanas, Fortunatus and Achaicus (vv.17-18) and *(ii)* the coming of the Lord, "Maran-atha" (v.22).

3) COMMANDS TO THE SAINTS, vv.13-14

"Watch ye, stand fast in the faith, quit you like men, be strong. Let all your things be done with charity." The first four of these are rather like sharp military commands. They are in the present continuous tense.

a) "Watch ye"

This emphasises the need for vigilance: **don't sleep!** The Greek word *('gregoreo')* is used in connection with the detection of danger. See Acts 20 verse 31: "Therefore **watch** *('gregoreo')*, and remember that by the space of three years, I ceased not to warn every one night and day with tears". That is, in view of Acts 20 verses 28-30. See also Colossians 4 verse 2: "Continue in prayer, and **watch** *('gregoreo')* in the same"; 1 Thessalonians 5 verse 6: "Therefore let us not sleep as do others; but let us **watch** *('gregoreo')* and be sober"; 1 Peter 5 verse 8: "Be sober, be **vigilant** *('gregoreo')*; because your adversary the devil, as a roaring lion, walketh about ..."; Revelation 3 verse 2: "Be **watchful** *('gregoreo')*, and strengthen the things that remain, that are ready to die".

At Corinth, there was need for vigilance in connection with "all the evils that he had exposed amongst them, the evils of dissension, fornication, litigation, fellowship with demons, abuses at the Supper etc." (J. Hunter).

b) "Stand fast in the faith"

This emphasises the need for stability: **don't desert!** J. Hunter takes "this to mean that we must take a definite stand, a firm stand, to maintain the truth at all cost". The Greek word *('steko')*, translated "stand fast", has the sense of adhering to the faith (W.E. Vine). It is associated with the word "stand" *('histemi')*: "Moreover brethren, I declare unto you the gospel which

I preached unto you, which also you have received, and wherein ye **stand**". (The passage continues: "By which also ye are saved (being saved) if ye keep in memory what I have preached unto you".) The need to "stand fast" is emphasised in Ephesians 4 verse 14: "That we henceforth be no more children, **tossed to and fro**, and carried about with every wind of doctrine". The word *'steko'* ("stand fast") is used in Galatians 5 verse 1: "**Stand fast** therefore in the liberty wherewith Christ hath made us free"; in Philippians 1 verse 27: "**Stand fast** in one spirit, with one mind ..."; in Philippians 4 verse 1: "**Stand fast** in the Lord"; in 1 Thessalonians 3 verse 8: "For now we live if ye **stand fast** in the Lord"; in 2 Thessalonians 2 verse 15: "**Stand fast,** and hold the traditions which ye have been taught whether by word, or by our epistle".

The saints at Corinth were to be "stedfast (*'hedraios'*), unmoveable, always abounding in the work of the Lord" (Chapter 15:58). They were to be steadfast in doctrine. The doctrine of resurrection had been denied. But steadfastness in doctrine was to be matched by zeal in evangelism.

c) "Quit you like men"

This emphasises the need for maturity: **don't be childish!** Literally: 'play the man'. Paul is possibly referring here to 1 Kings 2 verses 2-3: "I (David) go the way of all the earth: be thou (Solomon) strong therefore, and shew thyself a man". On the other hand, Paul may have been referring to the rallying call of the Philistines. See 1 Samuel 4 verse 9. How about that!

It could be said that maturity was needed at Corinth. See Chapter 3 verses 1-3: "And I, brethren, could not speak unto you as unto spiritual, but as unto carnal, even as unto **babes** (*'nepios',* literally, 'not speaking') in Christ. I have fed you with milk, not with meat: for hitherto ye were not able to bear it, neither yet now are ye able. For ye are yet carnal ... for while one saith, I am of Paul; and another, I am of Apollos; are ye not carnal, and walk as men?" See also Chapter 13 verse 11: "When I was a **child** (*'nepios'*), I spake as a **child** (*'nepios'*), I understood as a **child** (*'nepios'*); but when I became a man, I put away **childish** (*'nepios'*) things". See still further - Chapter 14 verse 20: "Brethren, be not **children** (*'paidion'* - young or little children) in understanding: howbeit in malice be ye **children** (*'nepios'*), but in understanding be **men**".

d) "Be strong"

This emhasises, obviously, the need for strength: **don't be weak!** Literally, in the passive voice, 'be strengthened' ('*krataioo*', from '*kratos*', strength). The word is used in Ephesians 3 verse 16: "That he would grant you, according to the riches of his glory, to be **strengthened** with all might by his spirit in the inner man". See also Ephesians 6 verse 10: "The power of His **might** ('*kratos*')"; Colossians 1 verse 11: "His glorious **power** ('*kratos*')".

The instructions given to Joshua illustrate what it means to "be strong". See Joshua 1 verses 6-9. That is, **strong for the task**: "Be **strong** and of a good courage; for unto this people shalt thou divide for an inheritance the land, which I sware unto their fathers to give them" (v.6). Further, **strong for the teaching**: "Be thou **strong** and very courageous, that thou mayest observe to do according to all the law which Moses my servant commanded thee: turn not from it to the right hand or the left, that thou mayest prosper" (v.7). Further still, **strong for the trials**: "Be **strong** and of a good courage: be not afraid, neither be thou dismayed for the LORD thy God is with thee whithersoever thou goest" (v.9).

e) "Let all your things be done with love"

"Let all things ye do be done in (Greek '*en*') love" (JND) or: "Let all that ye do be done in love'" (R.V.), that is, in the very atmosphere of love. Perhaps this refers particularly to the four things mentioned above ("Watch ye, stand fast in the faith, quit you like men, be strong"), but, in all probability, Paul refers here to conduct in general. Compare 1 Corinthians 13.

Paul was himself an example of his own ministry. See Chapter 16 verse 24: "My **love** be with you all in Christ Jesus. Amen". He had the moral right to say: "Let all your things be done with love". See 2 Corinthians 2 verse 4: "For out of much affliction and anguish of heart I wrote unto you with many tears, not that ye should be grieved, but that ye might know the **love** which I have more abundantly unto you". See also Chapter 4 verse 14: "I write not these things to shame you, but as my **beloved** sons ('*teknon*' - children) I warn (admonish) you"; Chapter 10 verse 14: "Wherefore, my dearly **beloved,** flee from idolatry"; Chapter 15 verse 58: "Therefore my **beloved** brethren".

4) CONCERN FOR THE SAINTS, vv.15-18

In this paragraph, Paul refers to concern for the Lord's people on the part of the house of Stephanas (vv.15-16) and on the part of Stephanas, Fortunatus and Achaicus personally (vv.17-18).

a) On the part of the house of Stephanas, vv.15-16

"I beseech you, brethren, (ye know the house of Stephanas, that it is the firstfruits of Achaia, and that they have addicted themselves to the ministry of the saints) that ye submit yourselves unto such, and to every one that helpeth with us and laboureth." Perhaps these believers are mentioned here as examples of the exhortations in verses 13-14. We should notice:

i) Salvation. "Firstfruits of **Achaia**." See Chapter 1 verse 16: "And I baptised also the household of Stephanas: besides, I know not whether I baptised any other". Note that in Romans 16 verse 5, Epaenetus is called the 'firstfruits of **Asia** for Christ' (JND). The AV has "firstfruits of Achaia". The word "firstfruits" stresses the Godward aspect of salvation: it is of great joy to Him.

ii) Service. "Have addicted (*'tasso'*) themselves to the ministry (*'diakonia'*) of the saints." The word is used in Luke 7 verse 8: "For I also am a man **set** ('placed', JND) under authority". It means 'set' or 'appointed'. So they 'have set or appointed themselves to the ministry of the saints'. This was something quite deliberate, not obedience to a command, or a sudden whim, but pursuit of a set policy. "This was their business in life, their service for Christ, rendered of their own accord, willingly and voluntarily, with the sole aim of benefiting others" (J. Hunter). It was to the "**service of the saints**". There is no suggestion here that the "house of Stephanas" were great preachers: rather, "whosoever of you will be the chiefest, shall be the servant of all" (Mark 10:44).

iii) Submission. "That ye submit yourselves unto such, and to every one that helpeth with us and laboureth" or: 'That ye also be in subjection to such, and to every one that helpeth in the work, and laboureth' (RV). The expression: 'be in subjection to such' (RV) indicates that those who serve are to be served. If the house of Stephanas had 'set (*'tasso'*) themselves', now the saints at Corinth are to set themselves (*'hupotasso'*) to acknowledge and respect all such. That is, they were to acknowledge and respect "every one that helpeth (Greek *'sunergeo'*: to be a co-worker) with us and laboureth

(Greek 'kopiao', meaning hard work with attendant weariness)" or: "And to every one joined in the work and labouring" (JND).

b) On the part of Stephanas, Fortunatus and Achaicus, vv.17-18

"I am glad of the coming of Stephanas and Fortunatus and Achaicus: for that which was lacking on your part they have supplied. For they have refreshed my spirit and yours: therefore acknowledge ye them that are such." These brethren had come from Corinth to Paul at Ephesus.

The words: "that which was lacking on your part they have supplied" could mean either that these three brethren had provided what the assembly at Corinth had no opportunity to give, or that they had provided what the assembly had failed to give. Compare Philippians 2 verse 30: "for the work of Christ he (Epaphroditus) was nigh unto death, not regarding his life, to supply your lack of service toward me".

The word translated "coming" ('parousia') means 'presence'. The words could read: 'I am rejoicing in the presence of Stephanas ...' The word "refreshed" ('anapauo') is used in connection with Titus in 2 Corinthians 7 verse 13: "His spirit was **refreshed** by you all". It means: 'to give rest from labour' and is translated "rest" in Matthew 11 verse 28: "I will give you **rest**". Such servants of God, having such a valuable ministry, are to be recognised and acknowledged.

It could be that it was from these three brethren that Paul heard such things as those mentioned in Chapter 5 verse 1. Perhaps they brought the questions to which he evidently refers in this epistle (see, for example, Chapter 7:1).

5) COMPLIMENTS TO THE SAINTS, vv.19-24

The closing verses of the epistle include salutations from Asia (vv.19-20); salutations among themselves (v.20); salutations from Paul (vv.21-24)

a) Salutations from Asia, vv.19-20

"The churches of Asia salute you. Aquila and Priscilla salute you **much in the Lord**, with the church that is in their house (compare Romans 16:5). All the brethren salute you." Note that Aquila is put first here, perhaps in view of teaching in 1 Corinthians 11. The order of their names varies.

b) Salutations amongst themselves, v.20

"Greet (salute, JND) ye one another with an holy kiss." See 2 Corinthians 13 verse 12; Romans 16 verse 16; 1 Thessalonians 5 verse 26. It is "an *holy* kiss".

c) Salutations from Paul, vv.21-24

"The salutation of (me) Paul with mine own hand." See 2 Thessalonians 3 verse 17; Colossians 4 verse 18. We should carefully notice the words: "If any man love (*'phileo'*: it is used in John 5 verse 20 of the love of the Father for the Son) not the Lord Jesus Christ, let him be Anathema, Maranatha". As W.E. Vine points out: "Maranatha" is best rendered: 'The Lord cometh'. The coming of the Lord Jesus is the occasion of a solemn warning. Paul's use of "Anathema" here hardly refers to the disinterested world at large. Its use in Galatians 1 verses 8-9 supports the suggestion that Paul has false teachers particularly in view here: "But though we, or an angel from heaven, preach any other gospel unto you than that which we have preached unto you, let him be **accursed** (*'anathema'*). As we said before, so say I now again, If any man preach any other gospel unto you than that ye received, let him be **accursed**". In his Second Epistle to the Corinthians, Paul refers to "false apostles, deceitful workers, transforming themselves into the apostles of Christ … whose end shall be according to their works" (2 Corinthians 11:13-15).

"The grace of our Lord Jesus Christ be with you. My love be with you all in Christ Jesus, Amen." As J. Hunter observes: "'My love' shows that despite all his warnings, rebukes and threats, he still loves them dearly. Their defections never reduced his love for them, for his love was centred 'in Christ Jesus'". It has been pointed out that out of Paul's thirteen letters in the New Testament, this is the only one in which he concludes by affirming his love for his readers, and this was the very church which resisted him most!

1 Corinthians

1 Corinthians

1 Corinthians

1 Corinthians